GW01606243

A CENTURY NOT OUT

One Hundred Years of the I'Anson Cup

INCORPORATING A CUP FOR CRICKET BY L.T. POPE

A CENTURY NOT OUT

One Hundred Years of the I'Anson Cup

By Graham Collyer

INCORPORATING A CUP FOR CRICKET BY L.T. POPE

Cricket on the Green
A player's soliloquy

(From a player who has often appeared in first-class cricket)

As one beneath the Great Game's spell,
(Who played himself, though seldom well)
All the great players at their best
I've watched through many a tedious test.
In such displays, plain truth to tell,
I've little interest.

Where turnstiles groan against the strain
From sweltering crowds from bus or train,
Where pressmen hang around the bar
Hoping for 'incidents' or war;
Where managers tot up their gain
I almost pray for rain.

Far finer cricket's to be seen,
Down where I live on Tilford Green.
There we can play for cricket's sake,
Not with a livelihood at stake.
Nobody yet was known to poke,
The whole day through at Tilford Oak.

Nor do they stop for trivial hurt
When Thursley's grappling with Churt.
And pulses quicken, hearts are still
When Grayshott goes to Shottermill.
No stopping for a spot of rain,
No scampering, a roof to gain.

The lads down here surpass their form
When fielding in a thunderstorm.
No wasting time to move a screen,
Such pansy things we've never seen.
No prodding turf or patting pitch,
We're not quite certain which is which.

And if our umpires give them out
On hearing long leg's hopeful shout
While staunch amid the foeman's bray,
Contemptuously he turns away;
What matter? They can take the lot,
Fortune, they know, blows cold or hot.

Drink it in, all else to shame,
And revel in our Glorious Game.
Thirsty? Your throat is dry you say?
The local's just across the way.
Let's wander in the evening glow
And try the self-same Barley Mow.

Farnham Herald, 5 October 1951

Tilford Green and the Barley Mow.

First published in Great Britain in 2002 by
The Breedon Books Publishing Company Limited
Breedon House, 3 The Parker Centre,
Derby, DE21 4SZ.

ISBN 1 85983 327 6

Printed and bound by Butler & Tanner, Frome, Somerset, England.

Jacket printing by Lawrence Allen.

Contents

Dedication

This history of the oldest village cricket league in the country is dedicated to all those players, past and present, who have continued to cherish the great heritage left us by those founding fathers who came together in the Fox and Pelican in Grayshott on 23 January 1901.

Edward Blakeway I'Anson is framed by the two trophies bearing his name. The original cup, won outright by Tilford in 1910, is on the right.

The Fox and Pelican public house in Headley Road in Grayshott c.1910. In the early days there was always free bread and cheese on the counter for patrons.

Grayshott before World War One. The Fox and Pelican is just out of shot on the far left.

Introduction

SOON after the death of L.T. Pope in 1979, I received a telephone call from his widow Joan with the offer of her late husband's cricket scrapbooks and memorabilia. It was to be the start of a journey that has led to the publication of this book, and with it the reprinting of Theo Pope's classic history of the first half-century of the I'Anson Cup Competition, entitled *A Cup for Cricket.*

The scrapbooks contained cuttings of reports of I'Anson and Miller Cup matches taken from the *Herald* for much of the period that Theo Pope was news editor of the local newspaper. They gave me a wonderful start in my quest to bring the history of the oldest village cricket league in the country up to date.

Theo Pope was more than just a name to me. He was my journalistic mentor, for it was as a 16-year-old that I came under his wing in the *Herald* offices in West Street, Farnham, and learnt the art of newspaper reporting. He was a firm but fair boss, whose insistence on fact before fiction and 100 per cent accuracy was paramount.

For a sport-mad teenager brought up in a family steeped in I'Anson Cup cricket, I could not have wished for a better 'editor'. (The quote marks are deliberate because that is what I thought he was when I started at the *Herald* in 1960. In fact, the managing director, Oliver Meddows Taylor, the son-in-law of E.W. Langham, the founder and proprietor of the newspaper, was the editor. It was not until after the death of Mr Langham and the purchase of the company by Ray [now Sir Ray] Tindle in the late 1960s that Theo Pope became the editor.) He taught me so much about my chosen profession, but, more than that, he made sure that I also shared his passion for the I'Anson Cup.

This history has been made possible by people such as Theo Pope and 'Harry' Knight, the secretary of the competitions from 1935 to 1958, with whom he collaborated in the production of *A Cup for Cricket.* They left a rich seam of material from which I have drawn much of the content. I must also thank the secretaries who followed, 'Mickey' Bicknell, Peter Warman, Jim Cornwell, Alan Staves and Cliff Jarrett, for leaving comprehensive minutes of meetings. My gratitude also to Peter Thompson, the editorial manager of the *Herald*, who is a cricket buff, for allowing me unfettered access to the bound volumes of a century of back issues of the newspaper, and to my good friend Carl Obert, the long-time sports editor, who played I'Anson Cup cricket for many years, for his encouragement and assistance in this project.

Finally, my thanks to all my management colleagues for many years of good company and camaraderie, and to my wife Ann for her forbearance and understanding during my secretaryship, a period of my life that was in no small way predetermined by the day I walked into Theo Pope's office as a callow youth 41 years ago.

Graham Collyer
Hindhead
November 2001

The first 50 years

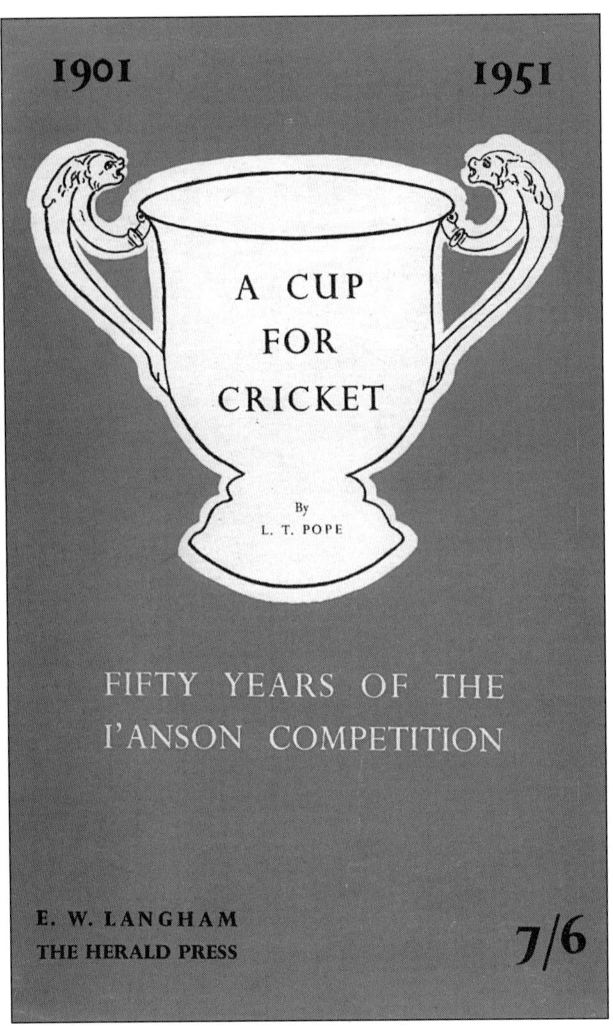

The cover of A Cup for Cricket, *published in 1951.*

THE golden jubilee of the I'Anson Cup Competitions in 1951 was marked by two significant events: the launch of L.T. Pope's book, *A Cup for Cricket*, and an anniversary dinner.

Theo Pope was aided and abetted in the production of the book by H.J. ('Harry') Knight, the secretary/treasurer of the competitions who, said the author, 'worked very hard over a period of months collecting and supplying information and assisting in other ways'. Both men had the right credentials for the job. Theo Pope, a resolute opening batsman for Headley before World War Two, was the news editor on the *Herald*, the local newspaper whose faithful reporting of the competitions had been a feature over the previous 50 years. 'Harry' Knight had first played in the competitions for Frensham in 1929 and had been the wicketkeeper in 1932 when the club first won the I'Anson Cup. Moreover, he had been the secretary of the competitions since 1935.

The author also mentioned W.W. (Bill) Stratford, 'whose wonderful character first prompted the thought of recording the history', and A.J. Stevens, the president, 'who contributes such a delightful foreword'.

Discreet items on both the news and sports pages of the *Herald* preceded the launch of the book, published by E.W. Langham, the founder and proprietor of the newspaper, with a cover price of 7s 6d (37.5p), on Saturday, 4 August 1951. The notices announced: 'Ready shortly... the book that everyone interested in local village cricket has been waiting for.' There was a warning that the edition would be limited, and confirmation that the proceeds would benefit the funds of the competitions.

The *Herald* was, as always, subdued when, in its issue of 10 August, it reported the appearance of the book. The three-line heading read:

'A CUP FOR CRICKET'
ENTHUSIASTIC RECEPTION
COPY IN MCC LIBRARY

The article said: 'It would have been surprising if the publication of a book of such outstanding local interest as *A Cup for Cricket* – Fifty Years of the I'Anson Competition had not been given a "rousing reception". Yet the enthusiasm which greeted its appearance on Saturday must have been very gratifying both to the I'Anson Competition secretaries and to the author. Dozens of copies were sold immediately, through the competition secretary and the various clubs, and orders are being received from far and wide.

'As the title makes clear, the book deals with the half-century during which the I'Anson Cup has been competed for by local cricket clubs. This year is its golden jubilee.

'As we have been promised a review of the book from the pen of one whose name is a "household word" throughout the land, in cricketing circles, we do not now give more than some factual information concerning it.

'Full bound in green cloth, *A Cup for Cricket* comprises 128 pages of text and 17 pages of illustrations. The text deals first with the start of the competition and then chapter by chapter with the fortunes of the various clubs which have competed, mentioning by name literally hundreds upon hundreds of men who in their day were regular players for their respective clubs. The reproductions of the group photographs enable the reader, in many cases where names gently stir a memory, to look upon the old familiar faces.

'We are pleased to be able to print a letter addressed personally to the author by the secretary of the MCC, Col. R.S. Rait Kerr, who writes as follows: "It is a notable achievement that this competition amongst the villages of Grayshott area should have reached its golden jubilee, and, moreover, that your very excellent book should record the event. I hope that during the next 50 years the competition may prove as successful as it has to date in stimulating the standard of cricket in the clubs taking part. When I have read the book it will be placed in the permanent reference library of the MCC, where it will be a useful addition to the records of club cricket".'

L.T. Pope, author of A Cup for Cricket, *presents on this occasion the Miller Cup in 1969 to Whitehill II's Ray Jones, who was standing in for honeymooning skipper Harry Hawkins.*

The *Herald* continued: 'Letters of appreciation have also been received from Sir Home Gordon, Bt, a distinguished writer on cricket, Mr H.D.G. Leveson Gower, former president of Surrey County Cricket Club, who has often visited this district and takes a lively interest in the competition, and Mr R.C. Robertson-Glasgow, an outstanding player for Oxford University and Somerset in former days, whose fame as a cricket writer extends far beyond these islands. Some 25 years ago Mr Robertson-Glasgow played for Grayshott in the I'Anson Cup Competition. Another letter is from Mr M.W. Payne, former Cambridge University captain and Middlesex player, who assisted Tilford for some years between the wars. He now lives in London. His brilliant batting in Tilford matches is well remembered by older players.'

Many other letters were received from people prominently associated with local clubs, as well as from much further afield, and there was even a request to send a copy to Siam.

The *Herald* reported that a review in *The Cricketer* said: 'Whatever one may feel about competitive cricket, *A Cup for Cricket* is so charmingly written by L.T. Pope that one is tempted to look up the first train to Farnham and immediately join one of the 11 neighbouring village clubs who take part in the I'Anson competition.'

Henry G. Tickner, who lived in Rosyth, Scotland, told the newspaper he was one of the youngest members of the Shottermill side that won the cup just prior to World War One. 'It is now 37 years since I left those happy and contented days of village life and cricket to go overseas in World War One... and although now separated by a lifetime as a civil servant in a nationalised industry, I can still recall with pride those eventful, enterprising and certainly most interesting days, and still enjoy very much following the progress of the competition,' he said.

John Arlott sent a congratulatory letter, and A.E. Kent, then aged 80, the first secretary of the competitions, was one of many former players who sent good wishes and commended the book.

Toward the end of year, the *Herald* carried an advertisement for books at Christmas that stated that 'only a few more dozen copies [were] left of this unique work'. A year later, at a dinner to celebrate the first and only time Elstead have won the I'Anson Cup, E.A.M. (Arnold) Gee, a vice-president of the competitions, said the book was the 'competitions' bible' and he thought everyone should have a copy.

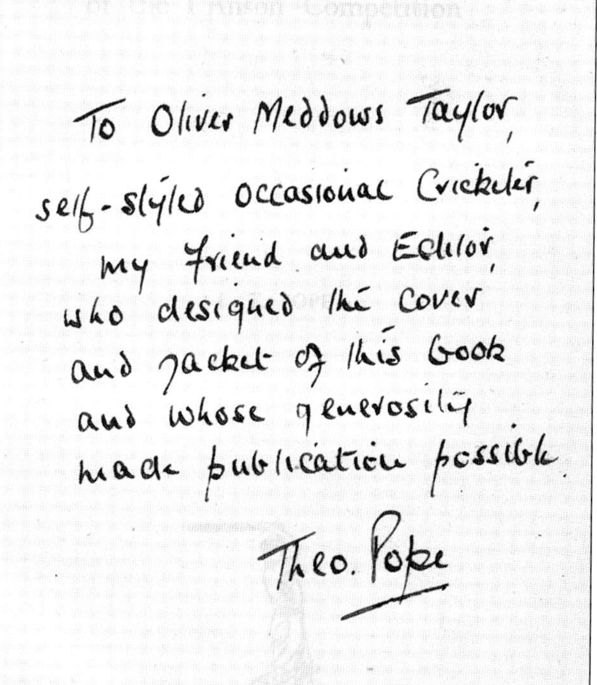

The copy of A Cup for Cricket *with this dedication was discovered in a specialist bookshop in Gloucestershire.*

Nowhere was it recorded how many copies of the book were produced, but within a year it had become a collector's item. Many copies have been lost in the intervening half-century, but those that remain are treasured possessions. Occasionally, one will turn up in a second-hand bookshop, and this writer has seen prices ranging from £3 to £30 being asked. Last year he discovered in a bookshop in Gloucestershire a very special edition, possibly the first off the press, with a signed message by the author, that read: 'To Oliver Meddows Taylor, self-styled occasional cricketer, my friend and editor, who designed the cover and jacket of this book and whose generosity made publication possible. Theo Pope.'

Fifty years on, and more than 20 years after the death of L.T. Pope, it is time to re-issue his acclaimed book, which was dedicated to 'all who have played for the cup' and then bring the story of the oldest continuous village cricket league in the country up to date.

Foreword

By The President

MANY are the books on cricket, biographical, autobiographical, statistical, fictional; most of them lay stress on village cricket, the fount and origin, and still the basis of our national game.

But I wonder how many enthusiasts have before this undertaken the arduous task of compiling a record of a village competition covering a period of 50 years, interspersed with numerous personal anecdotes, rummaged out of shattered old score books and picked up from some of the old players themselves as well as from other readily, and at times discursively, reminiscent old gentlemen.

I gather Mr Pope, ably seconded by Mr H.J. Knight, has spent a hectic six months or more of weekends searching out and visiting his material, with the results so ably and humorously set out in this book. Most certainly the whole local cricketing fraternity, and I hope many an outsider, too, will find much of interest and many a happy recollection in its perusal.

How worth while it has all been! What Englishman is there whose heart does not leap in springtime at the first note of the cuckoo, and then it leaps again at that soft, unmistakable tap of ball on bat nearby and he knows the zenith of the year is at hand.

Cricket has been described as leisurely warfare with all its schemes and counter-schemes; so, in a way it is, but it is also a vital picture of life itself with its preparations, its anxious hopes and fears, its set determination, its successes, its failures, the screwing up of every nerve, every sense and muscle guided warily by a brain keyed to its highest pitch of activity till the battle has been fought out. The spectators, often strongly partisan, always full of criticism, both of the

A.J. Stevens makes the first presentation of the Stevens Cup in 1953. The Thursley captain is Albert Rapley.

kindly and political variety, shout their advice, applause and cutting sarcasms and enjoy the reactions of the players as incident follows incident. What other game brings out so clearly cut the characters of its participants for all to see?

One hundred and 50 years ago the village players were described as an 'open, spirited, good humoured race' always ready for a game of cricket, 'batting, bowling and fielding as if for life' at the end of 12 or 14 hours of field labour. At the beginning of this century the village population and habits had largely changed, while in the last 50 years the change has been hastened and emphasised by the coming of motor power, whereby instead of long walks to the field of play, one is carried there restfully, if expensively. This makes it easier to commence play punctually and generally to introduce more regularity into the framework of the game, though its spirit continues unchanged.

And this spirit is what Mr I'Anson recognised and loved and so successfully perpetuated. Who, with the love of the game, that is of his fellow men in their finest expression of active enjoyment, at heart can fail to hope that it may continue to be perpetuated in the form in which he has himself seen and enjoyed it, or can fail to try to do his best to that end?

This gracious portion of Old England covered by the I'Anson Competition is still threaded with unspoilt old time lanes and footpaths, dotted with aged homesteads and little churches, blessed with pretty valley vistas or purple panoramas, gemmed with flowers, gay with the song of birds and flicker of butterflies and, with its expanse of fir and heather, warmly clad winter and summer alike. From the distant past it has been the home of tillers of the soil with the numerous highly skilled country craftsmen, who kept the rustic economy self-sufficient. Hard and long were the hours they worked then; their work done, what greater delight had they than assembling for the matches, the rigour of the game, the subsequent, or intermediate, flow of beer, the heated post-mortems and so back to the weekly round.

Surely this cricket business represents a very vital bit of English life and character, but the separate actors who make up the whole, slide in a generation or two into oblivion with but here and there an outstanding exception. Mr Pope thinks these bucolic famous men, and in their way and time they were famous, are worthy of praise and a secure place in village history, so, in this record he sets out a certain number of statistics with many a peep into the past, giving lively pictures of characters who might else be lost to memory, unsung, as those other nameless toilers told of by Gray:–

Beneath those rugged elms, that yew tree's shade
Where heaves the turf in many a mouldering heap.
Each in his narrow cell for ever laid,
The rude forefathers of the hamlet sleep.

Today, may it re-echo thro' Valhalla. The sound of the willow is heard again, the sun shines, the descendants of those forefathers gird on their panoply for the fight, they scan the field, note the slight spot in the short-mown sward, their leaders ponder whose bowling wiles to pit against which well known opponent, and where to place the field to block his favourite shots. The umpires are out, the game is on. Come, raise a glass to glorious VILLAGE CRICKET, its players, supporters and recorders!

A.J. Stevens.

The Golden Age

THERE was a period in cricket history men called the Golden Age. Exactly when it began is a matter of opinion, but all agree that it ended with World War One. That end was not yet in sight at the turn of the century, with Queen Victoria on the throne, Dr W.G. Grace delighting the crowds at Lord's, and country house cricket in full flower.

Among the pines and heather where the borders of Hampshire, Surrey and Sussex meet, village clubs were springing up, often under the benevolent patronage of the local squires, many of whom were themselves keen players. The national game had a universal appeal at a time when there were few distractions. Each village was a self-contained community. Men made their own amusements, and cricket was chief among them. A match with a neighbouring club was more than a game; it was a social event. The horses were harnessed to the brake, the team assembled, and off they went along the dusty roads and sunken lanes, with a 'four-and-a-half' – a cask of beer or cider to the uninitiated – and a thick rug to spread across the players' knees for a hand of cards on the way. Someone would produce a concertina, and song and laughter rose above the clopping of the horses' hooves. Often grounds verged on the primitive, but everyone enjoyed the match. When it was over, a visit to the 'local' usually preceded the slow journey home in the gathering dusk. Happy days, indeed.

A glance at some of the old photographs shows what stalwarts the players were. Moustaches were the rule rather than the exception, often giving the wearer an appearance of maturity beyond his years. Play in ties, braces, fancy belts, workaday trousers, and even bowler hats, was not uncommon. A man could keep wicket in a bowler without exciting undue comment. The Bourne had a celebrated long-stop who favoured that type of headgear, and always halted the ball's progress with his knees. It was said of Charles Courtnage, who played half-a-century for Headley, that he had the hardest knees in Hampshire, and this must have been his Surrey counterpart! Some pavilions were open sheds, but with a locked cupboard for two important items, the tackle and the beer cask. There was a source of strong refreshment at most matches, the object of pious pilgrimage at stated intervals, and the astonishing sight of one prominent captain leading his men in single file to their well-earned reward is still recalled with delighted chortles. Since there were no boundaries, and every run was a run, thirst must have been considerable. Pads and batting gloves were not found indispensable by everyone. Nowadays, batsmen who wear only one pad are a dwindling race. Then, those who wore none formed quite a strong minority; but they all took their cricket seriously, and the records show that there were players equal to, if not better than, the best of the moderns.

'ALL OUT IN ONE OVER'

The season began later and finished earlier than now, for the harvest had to be taken into account. Men worked hard and played hard. William Barber, a Selborne local preacher, could walk 13 miles to a match at Haslemere and back again in the evening, and think little of it. At Blackmoor, young players rose at 6am in the summer to practise in a glade behind the church before going off to the day's work. The merry men of Shottermill could laugh when a wheel came off the brake on the homeward journey, pitching them out into the ditch, 'all out in one over,' as a veteran recalls. Fixtures were sometimes a problem. Clubs had difficulty in finding enough opponents within reasonable distance; so

St Edmund's School at Hindhead in the early years of the 20th century. R.C. Robertson-Glasgow played for Grayshott while a teacher there, and wrote amusingly of his colleagues in his autobiography.

there were makeshift games, like married versus single, choir v congregation, and gardeners v coachmen. Good players were always in demand for country house matches. A note from the squire by the morning post, and they would be off in a brake, they knew not where, save that it was to cricket.

R.C. Robertson-Glasgow, celebrated Oxford University and Somerset googly bowler who became a journalist and author. He appeared for Grayshott in the 1920s.

Slowly time was bringing changes on the borders. Haslemere was expanding with faint rumblings of urban status, contractors were putting up the first huts at Bordon Camp, and new communities were rising in their wake. The effect was felt at Headley, one of the largest rural parishes in England, and the growing hamlet of Grayshott achieved ecclesiastical independence and sought the civil equivalent. George Bernard Shaw left 'Blen-Cathra' – soon to become St Edmund's School and in due time have as a master R.C. Robertson-Glasgow – but not before he had had a hand in a new venture, the launching of the Fox and Pelican Inn, a public-house with a difference, independent of the brewers, controlled by a local organisation, and started with a Bishop's blessing. Dr Arthur Conan Doyle, living and writing at 'Undershaw', hard by Hindhead cross-roads, saw his adopted village rapidly growing in favour as a health resort and welcoming, in 1898, a new manager to the Hindhead Stores, A.E. Kent, soon to become secretary of the Grayshott Cricket Club and organise its first annual dinner.

This dinner, which was to see the birth of the I'Anson Cup Competition, took place at the Fox and Pelican in November 1900, with Edward Blakeway I'Anson, a vice-president of the club and member of a family long associated with Grayshott, in the chair. During the speeches, A.E. Kent suggested that if someone would be good enough to offer a cup for competition among the surrounding villages, it would encourage local men to practise. There was a shrewd idea as to whom that 'someone' would be, and when, towards the end of the

Sir Frederick Pollock, who built Hindhead Copse beside the Portsmouth Road at Hindhead in 1884, was a leading light in the founding of the Grayshott and District Refreshment Association that built the Fox and Pelican.

evening, the chairman offered to give a cup there was prolonged applause.

DONOR OF THE CUP

Edward Blakeway I'Anson, elder son of Edward I'Anson, JP, was born in London and educated at Cheltenham College and Cambridge University, where he gained his BA and MA degrees. Following his father's profession, he was architect and surveyor to St Bartholomew's Hospital, was responsible for much notable work in London, and was architect for hospitals and convalescent homes in various parts of the country, becoming a Fellow of the Royal Institute of British Architects. His family's connection with Grayshott began in 1861, when his father bought an estate there and the son conceived a love for that village which has been described as almost a passion. For cricket he had to go farther afield and was a member of the Headley club, which had been formed well back in the 19th century. When he gave the cup his playing days were over, but his devotion to the game remained. He resided in London, where his sister kept house for him – he was unmarried – and spent his week-ends in Grayshott. Among his local memorials is Grayshott Parish Church, built not far from the present cricket ground to his design – he was honorary architect and a generous subscriber – but his memory is perhaps most strikingly perpetuated in the competition to which he gave his name. Half-a-century has gone by since the first cup was offered and the donor died nearly 40 years ago, but there are still former players who recall his special gift for making friendships and his fine character, reflecting so much that is best in English country life.

St Luke's Church at Grayshott was designed by E.B. I'Anson as a gift to the village.

There were those who said the competition would lead to free fights, and it is on record that the donor of the cup was not without misgivings. In the event the prophets of gloom were all proved wrong, and the competition served to raise the standard of play in the villages and became a triumphant success. Among the firmest advocates of the idea was W.W. Stratford, headmaster of Blackmoor School, a man of remarkable character, whose wise counsel was invaluable in the early years and who was to become known as the 'Father of the Competition.' His club was one of the six originally invited to join. Liphook alone declined. The decision to start the competition was made at a meeting at the Fox and Pelican on 23 January 1901, when the clubs represented were Blackmoor (W.W. Stratford), Churt (F.C. Wattridge), Grayshott (A.E. Kent), Headley (W.G. Sweetman) and Lynchmere (Walter Harding). Thus there were three Hampshire clubs, one from Surrey and one from Sussex. The Sussex link ended in 1910, but Hampshire and Surrey have been fairly equally represented throughout the 50 years. A.E. Kent was appointed secretary, an office he held continuously until 1924, and rules were drawn up based on those of the West Surrey Village Cup Competition. They provided for four matches, two home and two away, for each club.

The early years

THE competition started in the following May, and in August Lynchmere and Grayshott, both unbeaten, met in the deciding match, Lynchmere, under the captaincy of Walter Harding, winning by an innings to become the first holders. The cup was presented to Walter Harding by E.B. I'Anson at the Grayshott annual dinner, held at the Fox and Pelican in October. W.W. Stratford declared that the three reasons for Lynchmere's success were good generalship, good fellowship, and good fielding. The custom of presenting the cup at the Grayshott dinner continued up to the date of the donor's death, and he made a point of being there to hand over the trophy.

Lynchmere, winners of the I'Anson Cup in the first two years. Standing, from left: J. Adams, P. Pheasant, G. Madgwick, D. Payne, C. Madgwick, A.W. Smith, W. Merridan. Seated: William Harding, A. Harding, Walter Harding, E. Moorey, P. Madgwick. On ground: G. Puttick, A. West.

The first suggestion about home and away matches was made at the competition annual meeting in January 1902, and it was brought up again in the next few years, but the clubs continued to meet each other only once up to 1907. Frensham were newcomers in 1902, and they played at Lynchmere on the day of King Edward VII's coronation. Lynchmere again won the cup, going through the season without defeat, and Hesketh Prichard, the Hampshire fast bowler, was so struck by their prowess that he wrote an article in a London sporting magazine describing the village cricket played at Lynchmere as quite amazing. Once more the issue depended on the final match with Grayshott, also unbeaten, and again Lynchmere won by an innings, G. ('Ranjhi') Madgwick carrying his bat for 76 in a total of 202 for 9 declared. In 1903 the same two unbeaten teams met in their third encounter. The match, staged at Lynchmere, aroused tremendous interest, as victory for the home side would have meant permanent possession of the cup. Morning rain cleared off in time for the game, and Grayshott, under the captaincy of their president, A. Ingham Whitaker, JP, who had played for Harrow in earlier years, put Lynchmere out for 76 and won easily, Sir Arthur Conan Doyle – he had been knighted in 1902 – a powerfully-built forcing bat, making top score.

A Winners v The Rest match was played at Grayshott Hall on a Wednesday in August, W.W. Stratford appropriately captaining the Rest. Grayshott won, and the president and his wife entertained the teams to supper after the game. Grayshott Hall, scene of every Winners and Rest match up to World War One, was originally known as Grayshott Farm, and Tennyson lived there for a time. When the property came into A. Ingham Whitaker's hands in 1886 he erected the present mansion, which displays the motto 'Pax Intrantibus' – 'Peace to those entering' – a fitting sentiment for one who was the soul of hospitality. In a large field opposite the rear entrance, and on the north side of the Grayshott-Headley Road, he laid down a cricket pitch, carefully tended by the Hall staff. Visiting teams were entertained to tea and supper by the squire and his lady, and, in the occasional event of an all-day match, lunch as well. After 1914 the ground was ploughed up for agricultural use and never reverted to cricket, but the pavilion was removed to the new recreation ground nearer the village, and there, at the close of the half-century, it still stands.

Frensham first joined the I'Anson Cup Competition in 1902. The 1905 team was, standing, from the left: W.S. Harding, T.C. Brown, J. Aslett, W.H. Gower, F. Hiscock, J. Darlow, H. Newman. Seated: H.F. Harben, W. Burrage, T.H. Chuter, H.F. Capper. On ground: E. Fullbrook, W.E. Chuter, H. Chuter.

MATCH TO REMEMBER

The year 1903 was notable for a match which produced the highest total ever made by a team in the I'Anson Cup. Playing on C.E.N. Charrington's ground at Frensham Hill (now Frensham Heights School), Blackmoor declared at 300 for 5, W. Read scoring 117, the competition's first century. C. Knight made 53. Frensham responded with 147 for 4, F.C. Capper, Charrington's secretary, getting 80 not out. H.D. Harben, a fine bat who afterwards became MP for Worcester, was with him in a big opening stand. The ground at Frensham Hill, not the one now in use, was a beautiful stretch of turf near the front of the house, looking out towards Hindhead. Frensham's ground was at Pierrepont, but they played all their cup games at Frensham Hill owing to Charrington's interest in the competition. A great patron of the game, he ran his own team, for which most of the leading players in the district, including Conan Doyle, appeared from time to time. Among their opponents were MCC, Free Foresters and I Zingari. Charrington employed a professional, T.G. Brown, formerly of Sussex, about whose prowess many stories are told. There was cricket somewhere in the district on most days of the week, and some famous people played. In 1904, for instance, J.M. Barrie's Authors' XI, meeting the Artists in Farnham Park, included E.V. Lucas, A.E.W. Mason and Maurice Hewlett. Barrie lived at Black Lake in those days. In the same year Hampshire played the South Africans at Alton, the first match of that class ever held in the town. The county captain was E.M. Sprot, who played a few times for Grayshott, and was afterwards for many years president of The Bourne Cricket Club. In such an atmosphere the standard of village cricket could hardly fail to be high. At that time, of course, the cup matches formed only a small proportion of the clubs' fixture lists, and they also met each other in non-competitive games.

Blackmoor were the winners in 1906. Standing, from the left: J. Mitchell, A. Everett, J. Broadwood, A. Dawson, A. Hoar, P.S. Grieg. Seated: G. King, J.M. Dickinson, W.W. Stratford (captain), G. Oliver, W. Read. On ground: G. Cozens, G. Chiverton.

Tilford and Shottermill came into the competition in 1904 and the latter lifted the trophy at their first attempt. The feat was the more notable because the condition of their ground at Lion Green was such that all their matches had to be played away. They were captained by William Balchin, who was in the winning Lynchmere team of previous years. At the Grayshott dinner that winter Colonel W.G. Nicholson, MP for Petersfield, president of the Hampshire County Cricket Club and a former Hampshire player, proposed the toast of the competition. Shottermill again won in 1905, playing one or two matches on Haslemere recreation ground. Newcomers were The Bourne. Blackmoor's turn came in 1906. They went through the season undefeated, and when he received the cup, W.W. Stratford was able to say that the competition had done much to foster village cricket and had brought about a great spread of good sportsmanship and good feeling. The following season a new star appeared on the horizon, A.H. Hartwright, Camelsdale's schoolmaster, whose superb all-round form won the cup again for Lynchmere. He scored three centuries in the competition that year and finished with a batting average of 73, never since approached. That was also the year in which home and away matches were first introduced.

A.H. Hartwright helped Lynchmere win the cup for the third time in 1907, and scored three successive centuries.

Tilford in 1908, the start of a run that led to them claiming the original cup outright. Standing: W. Annells (scorer), P. Lonsdale, Revd C.A. Hamilton, A. Poulter, Charles Fry, H. Sanders (umpire). Seated: W. Willmore, G.E. Chambers, J.G. Poulter (captain), G. Lonsdale, B.W. Bentinck. On ground: Colin Fry, W. Warner.

WON THE CUP OUTRIGHT

In 1908 the team honours went to Tilford, who lost only to Lynchmere, and their captain, J.G. Poulter, attributed their success almost entirely to excellent fielding. Next year Tilford were beaten by Lynchmere alone, and their good all-round play enabled them to retain the trophy, and win it outright in 1910, still under Poulter's captaincy. This was a

The first I'Anson Cup, won outright by Tilford in 1910 and housed in the Barley Mow.

The medal presented to Bill Merrett when Tilford did the hat-trick in 1910. The reverse depicts the Tilford Oak.

great feat, and when Tilford held a dinner at the Barley Mow, A.W. Rowden, KC, JP, recited a poem of his own composition, *The Men of Tilford*, introducing the names of all the players. Now that the cup had gone, the future of the competition, which had given new life to village cricket in the neighbourhood, was uncertain, but F.B. I'Anson rose to the occasion and gave another trophy, with the proviso that it could never be won outright. The Bourne dropped out at the end of the season to play in the Farnham and District League, and Lynchmere also withdrew to enter a higher class of cricket, in which they met with great success.

The only one of the original teams still in the competition who had not won the cup, Churt, became first holders of the new trophy, defeating Shottermill in an all-day play-off at Grayshott. They were captained by H.A. Baker, who, standing for Petersfield as a Liberal, had been beaten by Colonel Nicholson in the first of the two general elections of 1910. He was a good batsman and skipper, and made some notable scores, one of them being 92 in Churt's 185 for 1 declared at Grayshott. In the play-off that year Shottermill, who had several young players, were said to have suffered from a new disease, not unknown in later years, 'cupitis'! Incidentally, Tilford did not win a match throughout the season.

Haslemere Working Men, the first and only non-village club ever admitted to the competition, appeared in 1912, when Blackmoor, still under W.W. Stratford's leadership, won the cup for the second time. Edward Blakeway I'Anson died in London in November at the age of 69. On the suggestion of W.W. Stratford, it was decided that in future the cup should be presented at the Winners and Rest match, a practice still followed. New arrivals in 1913 were Hindhead. They lost their first match to Shottermill, who went on to win the cup with some excellent batting and bowling feats, and they did it again in 1914, with Charles Pescod as their star performer. When A. Ingham Whitaker handed the cup to G. Knottley in August he spoke in sombre terms of the war just starting, foreseeing a long and bitter struggle, with the world never quite the same again. Recalling the occasion not long since, one former player who was there that day observed: 'We took his words lightly then, but he was right.' It was the end of an age.

Between the wars

NOT until 1920 was the competition resumed. Some clubs, like the Haslemere Working Men, had gone out of existence. The Working Men's successors, the Haslemere Comrades, were proposed for admission, but were not elected, and the season started with half-a-dozen teams, among them Whitehill, a club which had been running a Wednesday team for some years before the war. Their captain was W.W. Stratford, for Blackmoor had been disbanded and all the players had joined Whitehill. The fact that the competition annual meeting was held at the Royal Huts Hotel, Hindhead – the landlord, Ben Chandler, was a noted 'character' and good cricketer – instead of at Grayshott was another indication of change. Scores generally were low, as was to be expected. Grayshott had a new sports ground of ten acres given by A. Ingham Whitaker, who continued to take a keen interest in the game, and it was fitting that the first post-war winners of the trophy should be the village where the competition was born. E. Johnson was captain of Grayshott, and it was like old times when they celebrated their success with a dinner at the Fox and Pelican, with the president in the chair he had occupied so often in the past.

If pre-war days were the Golden Age, the period now starting was the Age of the Motor Car. The usual mode of conveyance was now a lorry, sometimes covered and sometimes not, used for other purposes during the week and turned into a coach by the addition of a few wooden forms. A rough and ready method, but it had the advantage of cheapness. Often the owner or driver was a member of the team, or umpire or scorer, and had more than a business interest in the fortunes of the club. W. Martin, of Churt, for instance, son of F.C. Martin, drove the team for a number of years between the wars, always playing in away matches, whether first or second XI fixtures, and as he was more than useful with the bat, his presence in the side was greatly valued. In most villages the team lorry ran round picking up players at strategic points and waiting for the latecomers, if necessary. Song and laughter still floated up from the sunken lanes along the county borders, and successful sides bedecked their lorries with laurels for the homeward journey. There was always a stop at a hostelry in the evening, and it was not uncommon to see three or four conveyances outside the Crossways Inn at Churt, the halfway stage on several different routes. The laurels, or lack of them, told the whole story, and on passing another lorry there was little need for the thumbs up or down gesture of a later period.

BUSH TELEGRAPH

It was the heyday, too, of the bush telegraph system. Small boys on bicycles would arrive with the tea score of a distant match, scraps of information passed from player to player, and clubs seldom left a ground without knowledge of how their nearest rivals had fared. Even carrier pigeons were pressed into service. Exactly how all the up-to-the-minute reports arrived none could tell, but arrive they did. Wider use of the telephone and motor transport later made such news a commonplace, and nowadays a motorist or motor-cyclist will arrive at tea-time with tidings of several other games. The old magic has gone.

Shottermill won the cup for the fifth time in 1921, and it

The Royal Huts Hotel at Hindhead crossroads in 1909. The landlord, Ben Chandler, was a good cricketer, and in 1920 he hosted the first annual meeting to be held after World War One.

was William Balchin who received the trophy from Miss I'Anson, sister of the donor. The following year saw the advent of the Miller Cup, given for competition among the Second XIs and junior clubs, and henceforth the two competitions ran side by side. Churt were the I'Anson winners that year, captained by the village schoolmaster, A.R.T. Baker, brother of two men who had been professionals for Surrey. W.W. Stratford crowned a wonderful career by leading Whitehill to victory in 1923, when the former Blackmoor players took chief honours, and the next winners were Thursley. Admitted in 1921, Thursley were captained by M.L. Rapley, whose brother, V.C. Rapley, displayed the form which made him one of the best all-rounders the competition has known. The year marked the end of A.E. Kent's association with the competition. He resigned the secretaryship at the annual meeting of delegates at Grayshott, and at the next annual meeting W.W. Stratford, on behalf of the clubs, presented him with a silver cup in recognition of his splendid record of service. The new secretary was R.L. Robinson, of Grayshott.

SIGNIFICANT EVENT

There was another significant event in 1925. The Bourne returned to the competition after a long run of success in the Farnham and District League – with which the competition held a series of annual Bank Holiday matches in the first half of the decade. With the then record number of ten clubs competing, The Bourne, skippered by G. Arnold, won the cup and also carried it off for the next three years under the same skipper, attaining a high standard. Outstanding in a fine team was Lewis Goodchild, whose all-round record for those four years is not likely ever to be surpassed. In 1927 H.M. Edmead, of Hindhead, succeeded R.L. Robinson as secretary. All this time the centre of gravity, as it were, was moving northwards away from Grayshott, and there was a break with long-established tradition in 1928, when the Winners and Rest fixture was held at The Bourne. Since that date it has always taken place on the winners' ground. In February of that year A. Ingham Whitaker left Grayshott, heavy taxation after the war having caused him to sell Grayshott Hall. It was the end of another chapter, and never again was he able to present the trophy in the time-honoured way. He died while on holiday at Bruges in 1933, leaving the memory of a generous spirit.

The Bourne withdrew their strongest team from the I'Anson Cup in 1929 and promoted the Miller Cup side, who had secured that trophy for two years running. They were not quite good enough to win the I'Anson, and the honour fell once more to Grayshott. Miss I'Anson had the pleasure of handing the cup to F. Puttick. In 1930 G.M. Hubbuck, of Headley, became secretary, H.M. Edmead having moved to Guildford. The Bourne's erstwhile Miller Cup side achieved their ambition in 1930 by winning the cup after a play-off with Grayshott at Churt, and thereafter The Bourne reverted to the practice of running teams in both competitions. Grayswood, once joint runners-up, dropped out at the end of the season. Whitehill had been building up a strong side for several years, with W.W.'s son, W.A. Stratford, holding the captaincy, and success once more crowned their efforts in 1931. Next season Frensham reappeared and Rowledge were also admitted, and the former went on to lift the trophy with bowling and fielding unrivalled between the wars. The captain was Guy Alder. Hindhead left the fold in 1932, after playing a few matches, owing to team-raising difficulties. Kingsley were new entrants in 1933 and they finished runners-up to Tilford, who were led to victory by J. Eddey, a most consistent and successful bowler over a long period of years.

RULES REVISED

The secretary, with characteristic energy, undertook in 1933 the revision of the rules, which had remained practically unaltered since the beginning. This was not an easy task, but in due course the revision was completed and approved. One clause was that competing clubs must be within a radius of eight miles of Grayshott. On the other hand, the fact that Grayshott was no longer the centre of the competition area was acknowledged by the transfer of the annual meeting to Churt in the same year, and in that village it is still held. The following year was the start of another triumphant period for The Bourne. S. Briggs led them to victory after a play-off with Rowledge, notable for low scoring – there was only one double-figure contribution in four innings. A. Arnold was skipper for their 1935 win, and L. Goodchild was captain in 1936, when, with 12 teams taking part, The Bourne were undefeated, the only game they failed to win being that at Tilford, part of which was broadcast by the BBC. The holders won for the fourth time running in 1937, again with L. Goodchild as captain. Instead of Winners v The Rest, there was a match between The Bourne First and Second XIs, the 'seconds' having won the Miller Cup, but this departure from custom was not a success.

Meanwhile, there had been another change in the secretaryship, G.M. Hubbuck resigned in 1935 and H.J. Knight, of Frensham, took over the duties. Two popular innovations introduced that year were a match between teams representing the Hampshire and Surrey clubs in the competition, and the first annual dinner, attended by some famous cricketers. At the dinner the retiring secretary received a silver-plated inkstand and silver pen from the clubs, the gift being handed to him by Lawrence Bell, of

Frensham. In 1936, A.J. Stevens, former captain and later president of The Bourne, was appointed first president of the competitions, and there could not have been a happier choice. Binsted were newcomers that year. Most grounds were in fine condition, and during the middle and late thirties there was an unusual number of high totals and individual scores. The competition flourished as never before.

In 1938 the cup at long last went to Headley, due in large measure to the all-round brilliance of Frank Kenward and the astute captaincy of E. Nash. A year later war broke out again, but not before The Bourne had made sure of the cup. There was one more season, with familiar figures missing from some of the teams, and The Bourne, captained by L. Goodchild, beat Headley in a play-off at Frensham. The cup was presented by H. Sanders, JP, who was umpire at Tilford when they won the first trophy outright. After 1940 the competition closed down for 'the duration'.

New horizons

PEACE and the post-war world brought fresh problems for cricket, the old village communal life had largely disappeared. People no longer as a matter of course found their amusements in the place where they lived. There was an acute housing shortage and 'evacuees' gave place to 'squatters' as a strange new word in the rural vocabulary. At least one ground taken over by the military during the war now bore a rash of huts occupied by folk whose interest in cricket could not be expected to extend to the removal of their only place of abode. Most of the younger men were still in the Forces – some had lost their lives – and the cricketers who remained were ten years older. The competition secretary was not yet back in the district and the outlook was rather bleak.

However, there were bright spots. A yearning for the pursuits of peace, with cricket foremost among them, turned men's minds to bygone summer days, and there were volunteers willing to get things started again. J.G. Caesar, a member of the Frensham team in pre-war days, contacted the secretary and a meeting of club representatives was called. The competitions were fortunate in having in L.M. Mileham, the Whitehill captain, a player with untiring energy and organising ability, to take over the difficult job of assistant secretary. He drew up a fixture list for nine I'Anson teams to begin the 1946 season. His own club had no ground. The Canadian troops stationed at Bordon Camp had levelled it, but the end of hostilities arrived before the work had been completed and Whitehill saw no immediate prospect of play there. Headley was similarly affected. The Rectory Field, where there had been cricket for generations, was in a sad state. The two clubs had to play all their matches away, and when they met each other The Bourne ground was generously placed at their disposal. Several clubs were unable to compete at all. The Bourne scored 250 against Whitehill, still the highest post-war total, in their very first match, and they went on to win the cup by a comfortable margin, losing only once. Their captain was W. Poulter.

FOR THE FIRST TIME

The 1947 season found L.M. Mileham still acting as secretary, and he succeeded in getting the Miller Cup Competition restarted. Ten clubs entered for the I'Anson Cup, and Headley and Whitehill were once more playing on their own grounds, though conditions were far from perfect. There was a close struggle all through the summer between Rowledge and The Bourne, culminating in a play-off at Grayshott, which enabled Rowledge, led by J. Peach, to lift the trophy for the first time. J. Voller, of The Bourne, made 141 not out at Shottermill, the highest individual score ever put together in the competition. H.J. Knight returned to take over the secretaryship in 1948, and at the annual meeting L.M. Mileham was thanked for his fine work in the interim period. The Bourne and Headley finished the season on level terms, a play-off at Rowledge enabling J.G. Caesar, who had been playing for The Bourne since the war, to lead the Surrey club to yet another victory. The Bourne gained an early advantage in 1949, but

J.G. Caesar (seated centre) captained The Bourne to the I'Anson Cup in 1948, following a play-off against Headley. Standing, from the left: F. Clarke (scorer), F. Cordier, K. Bicknell, J. Stonard, J. Seddon, H.J. Knight (umpire), H.C. Bicknell. Seated: J. Tanner, J. Voller, W. Poulter, J.G. Caesar, S. Briggs, H.G. Arnold.

Rowledge beat them after being behind on the first innings, completing the 'double' against the holders in the return game when needing 140 to win. Rowledge eventually won the trophy by a good margin, and R. Crumplin received the cup. The Rowledge batting was particularly powerful and they made 230 against The Rest. The admission of Elstead that year brought a welcome accession of strength to the competition. In 1950 Headley went into the lead in June and held it until dismissed for eight by Grayshott in the final match. The Bourne, under W. Poulter, drew level and easily won the play-off at Tilford. Two players, F. Kenward, captain of Headley, and J. Warner, captain of Tilford, each made 1,000 runs during the season, though not all in cup games, and the former had the distinction of recording the first century in the Hants v Surrey series, revived in 1948.

The early post-war seasons revealed one acute problem – transport. In the last few years before the war lorries had been giving place to coaches, and cars owned by playing members were also widely used. Now petrol restrictions had reduced the number of privately-owned vehicles, and coach-hiring was a more expensive business than ever before. Few firms were willing to undertake the work, and most of those which did so, mindful of rising costs, insisted on a booking for every Saturday at a standard charge, irrespective of distance. There was no question of exclusive use. Several teams were conveyed in one coach on the same afternoon, with the result that one team would arrive much too early and another late. No one liked the system, but nothing could be done about it. Clubs' transport costs rose steeply, with players' travelling fees covering only a small proportion of the outlay. That particular difficulty remains unsolved, but clubs can take comfort from the fact that it is new only in form. At one annual meeting in 1905 it was recorded that 'brake fees were nearly four times as much as in the previous year'. The club survived, and no doubt those of today will also continue to flourish.

GROUND IMPROVEMENTS

Towards the close of the half-century there were signs of a return to the playing conditions of the thirties. Grounds were much improved. Frensham had moved from Pierrepont to the Hollowdene recreation ground, and a big scheme for levelling the outfield there was launched. Whitehill had a level playing area for the first time in their history, Churt made strenuous efforts to improve their table, an extension scheme for Rowledge recreation ground was under way, and Headley had a fine new playing field. Other clubs were not behindhand in the good work. Spectators were as numerous as ever, and the standard of play advanced considerably. This was particularly encouraging because clubs now have to fend more and more for themselves. No longer does an impressive list of vice-presidents, good for a guinea or half-a-guinea each, adorn the front of every fixture card, guaranteeing solvency. People no longer have the money. Their interest in the game has not waned, but there are so many calls upon their purses. Some, of course, gallantly continue their support, but in the main those who play now have to devise means of meeting their own expenses and probably cricket is none the worse for that. Competitions and ground collections are very important matters and not a few highly-ingenious moneymaking efforts have been thought out.

Another encouraging portent was the increase in the number of teams seeking admission to the Miller Cup. The 1950 total of 15 was the highest ever, and for the first time it was necessary to run the competition in two sections. Among those teams there was a fair proportion of young players. The calls of National Service robbed many clubs of their colts at the most vital stage of development, and in the first few years after the war those who had been called up tended to drift out of the game on their return. The foremost performers in the competitions were the men who had led the field before the war, and the average age of some teams was depressingly high. Gradually there was a change for the better. The young players started to come back and, despite the increase in other amusements, the boys leaving school were turning once more to the game. This was just another instance of cricket's adjustment to the needs of the times. If, in the Jubilee year, clubs do not command all the youthful talent they desire, it can at least be said that once more the sons are coming forward to follow in their fathers' footsteps.

The increasing popularity of the competitions, and the record number of clubs wishing to enter for the Miller Cup during the past two seasons, led to a need for careful consideration of future policy. At the annual meeting in December 1950, a strong committee was appointed to go into the whole question, bearing in mind the possibility of starting a third competition. Experience has shown that 12 is the maximum entry if undue overlapping with football is to be avoided, and ten is the ideal number. The experiment of running the Miller Cup in two sections, with a play-off between the winners of each, did not meet with general favour, and the 1951 plan is only one section with 15 teams playing a limited number of games. A far from perfect compromise, obviously, and with 12 teams competing for the I'Anson Cup and many clubs running sides in both competitions, the problem of arranging fixtures is enormous. Any promotion and relegation system on soccer lines seems impracticable because inevitably the stronger clubs would soon have two teams in the premier section. On the other hand, there is reluctance to discourage clubs who wish to join the competitions. So the committee's task is far from easy, but they have the guidance of the words engraved on the I'Anson Cup, 'to encourage village cricket'.

Servants of the game

THE I'Anson Cup Competition has been particularly fortunate in its officials, and the five honorary secretaries who held office during the 50 years were all men who were heart and soul in the game. Prominent cricketers themselves, they had first-hand experience of the views and outlook of the ordinary player and, while they were keenly interested in their own clubs, there was nothing partisan or petty in their handling of the competition's affairs. No one ever questioned their integrity; their conduct inspired general respect and esteem and they put in many hours of hard work behind the scenes.

A.E. Kent, the founding secretary of the I'Anson Cup Competition, was the manager of the Hindhead Grocery and Supply Store in London Road, close to the crossroads (telephone Hindhead 2). He is believed to have lived above the business. Albert Kent is pictured in the Grayshott team of 1920.

A.E. Kent, the first secretary and the man who occupied the position longest, had in many ways a harder task than his successors. It fell to him to build up the organisation from scratch. A strong character, infinite tact and unbounded enthusiasm and energy were essential. He had all those qualities and more. A native of the county which bears his name, he learned his cricket on Sevenoaks Vine. In his own club, Grayshott, he held practically every office in the years before World War One and had to his credit many fine batting and bowling feats. Convinced from the start of the need for the competition, he raised it from small beginning to something approaching the present-day set-up. It was a steady evolution and nothing was lost in the process. When he attended the first annual dinner of the competitions in 1935 he told the company that during the many years he was I'Anson secretary he did not have two protests, adding: 'If there was any dispute I used to see the fellows concerned and the whole thing was settled in a very amicable manner.' His annual re-election during the first 14 seasons was automatic, 'it being generally thought that he was the right man for the place', in the words of a 1902 report. When the competition was resumed after the war he still enjoyed the confidence of the clubs and was able to get things restarted on a sound footing. The claims of business gradually became more pressing and, after safely launching the Miller Cup Competition in 1922, he expressed a wish, at the annual meeting in the following January, to resign, but at the urgent request of the club delegates he agreed to carry on for one more year. In 1924 his resignation took effect and warm tributes were paid to his services. He left the village to join his son in business at Egham in 1930 and is now living in retirement at Seaford, Sussex.

SPEECHES WITH PADS ON

The new secretary, R.L. Robinson, was also a Grayshott man. Like his predecessor, he played for the club for many years, afterwards acting as scorer. His quiet, sterling character was reflected in his work. Extremely thorough in everything he undertook, he filled the office most successfully in a rather difficult interim period. He resigned in 1927 and H.M. Edmead, of the Hindhead club, took over the reins. Keen and active, he was captain of Hindhead for a number of seasons, and was a good wicketkeeper. The link with Grayshott was not broken, for he also played for that club for some years. Harry Edmead's cheery speeches at the annual presentation of the two trophies are well remembered. On more than one occasion he played in the Winners v Rest match and had to come straight off the field with his pads on for the ceremony. In the course of time his business necessitated residence at Guildford and for one season he ran the two competitions from that town. It was not practicable for this to continue, and in 1930 he resigned. He still lives at Guildford and has always kept up his interest in the game.

H.M. Edmead, secretary from 1927-30, who played for Hindhead and Grayshott.

The next secretary, G.M. Hubbuck, of Headley, was a great worker. A member of a family with long local associations, he was steeped in the lore of village cricket and all his work for the I'Anson Cup was governed by the thought of what Edward I'Anson would have wished. For years he was a tower of strength in the Headley team, holding a number of offices, including those of captain and secretary. Older players will have a mental picture of Geoffrey Hubbuck thundering up to deliver those fast, rising balls, which often spelt a batsman's undoing and he was usually good for runs in a crisis. His rather battered trilby graced many a stricken field, and there was a shrewd tactician's brain beneath it. He took office at a time when the competitions were growing and the focus shifting towards Farnham. Under his wise guidance the transition was safely carried through without any sacrifice of the essential spirit. Possibly his greatest achievement was the long-overdue revision of the rules with the introduction of the radius clause which prevented any radical departure from tradition. He was intimately acquainted with all the clubs and players, often travelling from ground to ground on his bicycle on a Saturday afternoon and his periodical notes on the season's progress, sometimes written in amusing racing metaphors, were widely read. One year he even compiled a list of the leading batting and bowling averages for the whole competition halfway through the season, and anyone who knows the difficulty of collecting such information will appreciate the effort entailed. Although he held office for only five years, he made a lasting mark on both competitions. He also did outstanding work in organising school sport and many of the prominent cricketers of a later generation received their first coaching from him. He left the district in 1935 and now resides at Petersfield.

'ALL FOR THE GOOD OF THE GAME'

H.J. Knight, of Frensham, had youth, infectious enthusiasm and a special flair for organisation among his assets when he took over the secretaryship in 1935. A member of the 1932 Frensham cup-winning side, he was – and is – an able batsman and wicketkeeper, equally capable of snapping up a catch behind the stumps or grabbing a subscription from an Aberdonian. He will to this day cheerfully rattle a collecting box under the nose of a defeated opponent, and, moreover, get a contribution. 'It's all for the good of the game', is his motto, and he makes a habit of accomplishing tasks that would daunt most people. Invariably knowing the right person to approach for anything he wanted, he launched a number of successful innovations, including an annual dinner and various representative matches. From time to time during his secretaryship the rules have been amended and the competitions improved in various ways. The peak of success was reached in the late thirties, when the clubs flourished as never before. In 1936 part of a match was broadcast and the I'Anson Cup became known to an ever-widening circle. The war caused a temporary setback, but there are now signs of a return to former glories. Throughout the years Harry Knight's keenness has never wavered, and his knowledge, experience and shrewd business sense are always at the disposal of the competitions. He has had some tricky problems to face and many administrative difficulties, but, being in constant touch with the clubs and players, he has overcome most of them by personal contact. Any reverse merely spurs him to greater effort, and only those most closely associated with him realise the hours he puts into his voluntary task. In post-war years he has played for The Bourne. There were some half-hearted attempts at umpiring before he began the 1950 season in the Second XI and finished up as a wicketkeeper for the first team, again being in a cup-winning side after a lapse of 18 years – all for the good of the game! After 16 years as competition secretary he sometimes talks of resigning, but no one takes that too seriously. What they said in 1902 still holds good.

THE PRESIDENT

A. Julius Stevens, first president of the competitions, is a member of an old Farnham family. Educated at

Marlborough and Oriel College, Oxford, he made the law his profession, and in his early years lived at the house now known as Ipsley Lodge, where the Hog's Back rises up from Runfold, and played cricket for Tongham. He moved to The Bourne after his marriage in 1905 and was captain of the club when they entered the competition. A steady batsman with a good defence, he made a lot of runs for The Bourne both in the competition and the Farnham League of which he afterwards became president. His playing days extended into the years after World War One, and many will recall his opening partnerships with H. Hack. Their running between the wickets was an object lesson in that difficult art. Having been president of both the league and the competitions, as well as a very able performer on the field, A.J. Stevens has a wide knowledge of the game and a deep affection for it, and his kindly philosophy is reflected in his speeches on important occasions. Whenever he presents the cup, as he has done many times, everyone on the ground has the feeling that he regards it as a real pleasure and not as a duty, and he enters thoroughly into the spirit of any cricket function. The competitions have been extremely fortunate to have the benefit of his generous support and helpful advice for so many years. Incidentally, his brother, the Vicar of Wrecclesham (the Revd J.R. Stevens) is another cricket enthusiast, and the acceptance, in the autumn of 1950, of Wrecclesham's application for admission to the Miller Cup Competition provided a further link with the family, for the vicar is president of that club.

The chairmen of the annual meeting of delegates have played an important part in shaping the destinies of the I'Anson Cup Competition, particularly in the early days. Doyen of them all was, of course, W.W. Stratford, who first occupied the chair in 1902, and did so in all on 17 different occasions, the last in 1931. G. Arnold has been chairman eight times.

The standing sub-committee, first formed in 1921 and afterwards from 1932 onwards, known as the stewards, have also done much to ensure smooth working on the administrative side. Two to start with and later increased to three, the number was stabilised at five in 1934 and some distinguished players have been included among the 24 men who have served in that capacity. Outstanding among them in point of service is E. Johnson. First elected in 1924, he has been a steward without a break since 1935. He has been elected 21 times altogether, E.W. Newman coming next with nine. The secretaries and other officials of the village clubs have also contributed their quota of willing service.

MEN IN WHITE COATS

Lastly, the umpires, whose knowledge and skill – or lack of it – can make or mar the game. Generally speaking, the competitions have been well served by the men in white coats. There have been some very good umpires, mostly old players, and others less good, with the former predominating. Gay or gloomy, taciturn or garrulous, their dispositions are as varied as those of the players. Some cry 'Chuck 'er up!' – a dying race, these – and others use the forefinger. Some give correct signals, others no signals at all, and still others indicate the nature of runs with a general sweep of the arm. A few will declare: 'I umpire for such-and-such a village'; others admit only to umpiring. One and all, they do their best in a thankless job. Officially neutral umpires for every match remains a Utopian dream, because (a) there would not be enough volunteers, and (b) their expenses would be too high for the clubs to meet. Most umpires act as such on account of an interest in their village team. They enjoy the social side of a match and, being human, could not be expected to take the same interest among strangers. In recent years there has been a general improvement in the standard of umpiring and an increasing desire on the part of those officials to do their job well. Even Test Match umpires make mistakes; the important thing is that the mistakes should not be one-sided. There is an authentic story of one celebrated 'character' many years ago who thus addressed a member of the fielding side: 'You know I'm fair, Master X?' On receiving a tactful reply in the affirmative, he remarked, 'Yes, I'm fair, but when this little ***** gets down to the other end I'm going to give him out!' That was in the distant past, and times have changed. Today the competitions have every reason to be satisfied with their umpires, who all too seldom receive the praise they deserve. People often say 'Well played'. How many, at the end of a good game, ever think of saying 'Well done' to the umpires? Yet without their good offices no game can be well played.

Special occasions

A CRICKET dinner is a very special occasion and most clubs celebrate in this way from time to time, but a competition dinner is an even more joyous reunion of men with a common bond. The competitions' first event of that kind was at Churt Village Hall in October 1935. All the clubs were represented, A.J. Stevens was in the chair, four competition secretaries – A.E. Kent, R.L. Robinson, H.M. Edmead and H.J. Knight – were there, and the guest of honour was P.G.H. Fender, of Surrey and England.

Fender has been described as the best captain who never led an England side, and those who heard him that night will not forget his speech. When he rose to his feet glasses were clinking in the bar, the sound mingling with laughter and the hum of conversation. In a matter of seconds there was silence. For 40 minutes he ranged in an intimate yet authoritative way over the whole field of English cricket. Those who had gone out crept back and stood round the door. There was not a sound in all that large company. Time stood still, and when the speech ended the applause for a great player echoed to the roof. On that evening, too, A.E. Kent described how the I'Anson Competition started.

The next dinner was at the Whitehill Club in 1937, with A.J. Stevens, elected a few months previously as the first president of the competitions, in the chair. H.D.G. Leveson-Gower, president of the Surrey County Cricket Club, was guest of honour, and K.C. James, the New Zealand player, also attended. The occasion found 'Shrimp' in cracking form, and his speech set the seal on a gay, delightful evening. J. Broadwood, JP, a vice-president of Whitehill, who had then been connected with village cricket for over 40 years, brought down the house with the story of his first club match as a small boy. 'After the game I had my first glass of home-brewed ale. From that day to this I have always considered that cricket is the finest game in the world.'

Three more Surrey stalwarts, E.W.J. Brooks, R.J. Gregory and J.F. Parker, together with K.C. James, were at the 1939 dinner, held at Headley. Once more the president occupied the chair in his usual genial manner, and each of the three Surrey professionals gave the company the benefit of some shrewd advice and amusing reminiscence. This was the second memorable dinner at Headley. There had been another in March 1935, when the competitions were strongly represented at the farewell gathering for G.M. Hubbuck, and the guests included the Hampshire captain, W.G. Lowndes, who at one time lived at Newton Valence, and for some years played for Alton.

War brought such festivities to an end and, owing to catering problems and the difficulty of finding a hall large enough for the purpose, the dinners were not afterwards revived, though it is hoped to celebrate the Diamond Jubilee in the time-honoured way. Happily, The Bourne continue to hold the dinners with which they have always marked the winning of the trophy, and members of the other clubs are invariably invited.

The competitions were able to repay in some measure the debt to their professional guests by taking a leading part in arranging local matches for them during their benefit years.

Time for reflection: V.F. Ealand, then captain of Surrey II, E.M. Sprot, former Hampshire captain and president of The Bourne, and A.J. Stevens, competitions president, pictured in the 1930s.

CRICKETERS' FRIEND

This is an appropriate place to mention a great friend of the competitions, who, although he never actually played for a local village club, gave much valuable help behind the scenes, Captain (later Major) V.F. Ealand, of Farnham. He skippered the Surrey Second XI in 1936 and 1937 – in the latter year they lost to Lancashire Second XI in the Minor Counties challenge match – and he was captain of the Surrey Club and Ground side from 1932 to 1938. He was instrumental in securing the attendance of many of the distinguished guests at the dinners and was responsible for players from the Farnham district taking part in representative games at The Oval. A friend to all cricketers, he presented the I'Anson Cup to The Bourne when they won the trophy in 1935.

An event which proved of great benefit to the competitions was the opening in 1935 of the Farnham School of Cricket, a venture launched by Frank Moulding. H.D.G. Leveson-Gower was there to take the first ball from A.F. Gover, and A. Sandham demonstrated the art of batting to an appreciative audience. The school ran for several years in premises at the St Cross Estate, off East Street, and most of the clubs attended in a body on winter evenings. Among the professionals were Robert Relf, of Sussex, K.C. James, A.F. Gover and J.F. Parker, and their coaching had a marked effect in improving the standard of play.

In July 1936, part of an I'Anson Cup match at Tilford was broadcast by the BBC, and no setting more typical of an English village could have been chosen. The game coincided with the second Test Match against India at Manchester, but there was no doubt on which game the interest of the locality was centred! Commander T. Woodroffe was the commentator, and The Bourne, in the floodtide of their most successful season, were the visitors. The Bourne declared at 128 for 8 and Tilford replied with 66 for 6, the game being drawn.

The match was 'on the air' at intervals throughout the afternoon. The control point was the old forge on the main road between the Barley Mow and the river – the flat roof of the inn having been found unsuitable for the purpose, although a microphone was installed there – and a microphone on the north side of the bridge leading towards the Post Office picked up the sounds of the running waters of the River Wey. There was another microphone at the scoring table by the Institute, and the comments of some of the village critics were also recorded. It was a memorable day.

THE RADIO TIMES, ISSUE DATED JULY 17, 1936 — 11

TILFORD versus THE BOURNE

Today's Cricket Broadcast

The Test Match will not be the only cricket on the air on Saturday, July 25. Periodic glimpses will also be given of the match between Tilford and The Bourne, a Surrey village match, typical of the game played on village greens all over the country.

A general view of the village green at Tilford, Surrey, during a recent Saturday match. The flat roof of The Barley Mow (right) will provide the viewpoint for next Saturday's commentator. A microphone under the bridge will pick up the sound of running waters of the Wey as they tumble over a weir.

ALTHOUGH this article is about cricket, don't imagine that it will deal with leg-theory or Test Matches or anything like that. It is about village-green cricket—which is quite different.

Everyone has heard of the famous Hambledon Cricket Club, in Hampshire, which flourished during the second half of the eighteenth century. The game soon 'caught on' and spread among the surrounding villages, including Tilford, which is just inside the Surrey border between Farnham and Hindhead.

Tilford boasts a fine old church, a school, a shop that sells everything, and two inns. But what concerns us more is the village green, in the middle of which there is a square of very precious turf. Precious because it is here that the village lads indulge in their favourite pastime of cricket. (When I say 'lads' I am using the word in a general sense, for last year when the Tilford team was one short the place was filled by Mr. Charles Bonner, one of the oldest inhabitants. Mr. Bonner first played cricket on the green over fifty years ago!)

This old Tilford supporter rarely misses a game.

The green is triangular in shape and there are roads on each side passing over quaint old wooden bridges across the river, which is not very far from the pitch. It is not unknown for a batsman to hit the ball into the river. There is a pavilion, which is used during the week as the village club, and on the other side of the green stands The Barley Mow, one of the village inns.

It is a rule of Tilford cricket, that if a batsman hits a ball through a window of The Barley Mow he has to pay for drinks all round that evening, so it is an expensive business if one of your mighty swipes goes farther than you intended.

The game was first played on the green way back in the eighteenth century, but it was not cricket as we know it today. For instance, one of the rules was that the fielding side picked the pitch, and they usually put the wickets up in front of some nice big bumps which, of course, made things difficult for the poor batsman. In those days 'over-arm' bowling was unknown; they bowled what we call nowadays 'lobs' or under-arm.

That was in the days of Billy Beldam, who has been called 'the greatest personality in cricket before Grace'. Many yarns have been told of 'Silver Billy', whose cottage still overlooks the ground at Tilford. 'Silver Billy' played for Hampshire, but he also played for England on many occasions. On the English side one day when he was playing for Hampshire, a famous fast bowler walked up to 'Silver Billy', and said, 'Beldam, I can't decide which of your stumps I'm going to knock down today'. 'Silver Billy' answered by simply patting his bat and saying, 'You're going to allow me this bit of wood, aren't you?' 'Silver Billy' knocked 28 off the fast bowler that day—which was quite good, for in those days the batsman did not have such good pitches to play on, nor such good bats.

All the matches in those days were 'friendlies' and if an umpire was unable to decide whether a batsman was out or not, the fielding side would say, 'Let the lad have another knock'. At Tilford they have a book containing all the minutes of the meetings of the Cricket Club for the last fifty or sixty years. On one page of the accounts we find: 'To repairing Barley Mow window . . . 3s. For advice and work on pitch . . . 7s. 6d.'

Nowadays the local cricket is very well organised. There is a league consisting of all the villages in the district, and the club at the top receives the I'Anson Cup. In the first few years Tilford were top of the league three years running and thus won the cup outright. This feat has never been accomplished since, but The Bourne, the next village to Tilford, who were top of the league in 19[illegible] and 1935, are as yet top again this season and excitement is running high. Tilford's opportunity to wreck The Bourne's hopes of winning the cup outright will come next Saturday.

THOMAS H. PEARCE.

The wall of The Barley Mow makes an excellent grandstand from which local critics, without pausing in their refreshment, can follow the course of the game. Some of them are seen in the picture above. Two more microphones will pick up some of their comments. On the left is a closer view of the Village Club, used as cricket pavilion on Saturdays. Batsmen going in or (like the one here) coming out have to keep an eye open for traffic as they cross the main road. Another microphone will be in position on the scorers' table, seen to the left of the picture. The control point for the broadcast is in the village smithy.

A page from the Radio Times *of 17 July 1936, previewing the broadcast by the BBC of the I'Anson Cup match between Tilford and The Bourne.*

Representative matches

THE first representative match played by the competition took place at Grayshott Hall in 1909, when the Guildford, Godalming and District League were entertained. The minutes record that two games were to be arranged with the league in 1909, and two more in 1910, but the scores of only one can be traced. The competition batted first and made 119, A. Bourne and A. Smith getting 30 apiece. The league had half their side out for 20, and the later batsmen sat on the splice. However, nine were out at 6.30, the time arranged for drawing stumps, and, in response to the wish of the spectators, play was continued for a few more overs, but the last pair remained together until the league team had to leave to catch their train at Haslemere with the score 72 for 9. G.E. Chambers (Tilford) took 5 for 32. A. Ingham Whitaker, with his customary hospitality, provided lunch and tea for the teams.

In 1921 a challenge by the Farnham and District League, which had also been running since the early years of the century, led to a series of four all-day August Bank Holiday matches. They aroused a lot of interest and attracted many onlookers. The first three, played at Tilford, were all won by the I'Anson Competition, and the last, at Frensham, by the league. A ball bearing a plate with the names of the winners was the trophy awarded after each game.

The competition took first innings in the opening match and lost seven for 24, but F. Puttick (39) and E. Johnson (25), both of Grayshott, added 52 in partnership, and with M.W. Payne (Tilford) making 20 not out, the total was 108. A.J. Stevens (Bourne) and H. Karn (Blacknest) gave the league a good start with a stand of 44, but the remaining batsmen did little and the whole side were out for 80. In their second knock the competition totalled 98, V.C. Rapley (Thursley) making 30 and W. Willmore (Tilford) 26. Needing 127 to win, the league were 47 for 6, but some spirited batting by the 'tail' saw the score raised to 111. G.H. Boyes (Wrecclesham) made 33.

The following year the league went in first and could do little with the bowling of W.A. Penycate (Shottermill), who took seven wickets at low cost in a total of 47. The competition also had to struggle for runs and were 43 for 8, but managed to lead by 20. L. Goodchild (Bourne) took 5 for 12. W. Thomson (Rowledge) contributed 41 to the league's second innings of 85. Penycate brought his bag for the match to 13 and went on to score 24. A. Carver (Churt) made 41 and the competition won by six wickets, but continued batting and were all out for 109.

R.H. Dorman-Smith (Dockenfield) – later Sir Reginald Dorman-Smith, successively Minister of Agriculture and Governor of Burma – skippered the league in the 1923 match and his 15 was the top score in a total of 67, W.A. Stratford and A. Cox, of Whitehill, bowling well. The competition responded with 96, the Tilford pair, Payne and Willmore, making 25 and 22 respectively. The league's second innings realised 81. Needing 53, the competition totalled 61, Willmore getting 20 and Payne 16.

EXCITING FINISH

The fourth and final match of the series was played at Pierrepont, Frensham, in 1924 and resulted in an exciting four-wickets victory for the league just on time. Payne set a captain's example by hitting 39 in the competition's first innings of 67, and the league were put out for 41, Penycate taking 6 for 14 and Cox 4 for 12. First in and last out, A.J. Stevens was top scorer with 13. In their second knock the competition made 45, Goodchild capturing 4 for 13 and E.J. Lewis (Rowledge) – who had 7 for 22 in the first innings – 3 for 10. This left the league with 75 minutes to get 72 for victory, and they were 81 for 7 at the close, L. Bidwell (Frensham) being out for 21 in the last over after making the winning hit. Lewis was 21 not out and Stevens scored 19. In 1925 The Bourne, who on two occasions won the league four times in succession, re-entered the competition, to be followed some years later by Frensham and Rowledge. There were no more challenge matches, and in the early thirties the league ceased to function.

Another series of games, between sides representing the Hampshire and Surrey clubs in the competition, started in 1935, and continued annually until the war, with the exception of Coronation year, 1937, when a match with Farnham in Farnham Park was substituted. L.M. Mileham (Whitehill) was captain for the Coronation match, but rain put an end to play after Farnham had scored 92 for 2. All the pre-war Hants v Surrey matches were staged at The Bourne and on several occasions there were over 500 onlookers. The series was revived in 1948, and of the seven games played up to 1950 five were won by Hants, one – the first – by Surrey and two were drawn. These fixtures, mostly in midsummer, were very unfortunate in the matter of rain, and hardly one was played in ideal conditions. For the purpose of choosing the teams, Rowledge, partly in Surrey and partly in Hants, was usually, though not invariably, regarded as a Hants club. Nearly 100 cricketers took part in the series and a marked feature was the way in which the form of the leading players compelled their selection year after year. W.A.J. Chuter (Frensham) and F. Kenward (Headley) were both in six out of the seven, including the first and the most recent. W. Poulter (Bourne) appeared in five, including all four played before the war. Others with unbroken pre-war appearances were A. Bellinger (Headley), S. Butcher and L.M. Mileham (Whitehill), R. Coombes (Grayshott) and L. Goodchild (Bourne).

ONLY VICTORY

The last-named player skippered Surrey for their only victory, in 1935. Surrey declared at 166 for 8, S. Corner (Churt) making 52 – the second highest individual score in the whole series – and L. Tanner (Bourne) 35. L. Goodchild retired after scoring 33. Hants, captained by R. Crumplin (Rowledge), were dismissed for 96, the feature of the innings being the batting of Commander R.H. Stokes-Rees (Headley), who went in first and carried his bat for 36. Goodchild took 4 for 16. Rain ruined the 1936 game. Hants, captained by L.T. Pope (Headley), made 112 for 9 declared, and Surrey, with Goodchild again skipper, replied with 41 for 7. One of the captains was top scorer in 1938, B.H. Swinstead (Oakhanger) making 49 of Hampshire's 138, and J. Warner (Tilford) scored 45 not out in Surrey's reply of 118 for 8. S. Briggs (Bourne) was the Surrey captain. This drawn match was perhaps the best of the series. Surrey, under V.C. Rapley (Thursley) were put out for 54 in 1939, P. Barlow (Headley) taking 5 for 22 and Butcher 4 for 13. Hants, led by Mileham, won by five wickets and made 106, J. Kingshott (Grayshott) contributing 31.

There was little of note in the first post-war encounter at The Bourne in 1948. Hants, with R. Goff (Whitehill) as skipper, scored 78, and Surrey (captain, W. Poulter) 54, Kenward taking 5 for 17. The 1949 match was at Grayshott, and again neither side reached the 100 mark. The honours went to Hants, led by P. Barlow (Headley). They totalled 99, W.A.J. Chuter taking 5 for 23, and Surrey, captained by J. Warner, replied with 79. In the 1950 game at Elstead, Surrey, under W. Burchett (Elstead), scored 129 (W.A.J. Chuter 33, Warner 31). Hants, with D.A. Heron (Rowledge) as skipper, won easily, replying with 147 for 7. Kenward made 112 not out, the first century of the series, hitting five sixes and seven fours, and R. Reynolds (Shottermill) – for some years Aldershot's goalkeeper – did not concede any extras.

Grayshott

THE village where the competition was born is also largely the child of the twentieth century. It became a separate ecclesiastical parish just over 50 years ago and had to wait much longer to achieve civil independence, but there was no doubt about the independence of the cricket club. In the early years Grayshott, standing on the pine-crested ridge running up from Headley to Hindhead, was the centre and mainspring of the competition. Today the focus has shifted northwards, though in the minds of all who care for tradition – and most cricketers do – that Hampshire village will always be the home of the I'Anson Cup. Grayshott shares with Churt alone the distinction of never having missed a season in the competition, and the annual meetings have, with a single exception, been held in one or other of those two places.

The ground at Grayshott Hall, a mile or so west of the village, and the Fox and Pelican Inn, standing by the crossroads, were both new when the I'Anson Cup was launched. The cricket club was founded in April 1896; years later Ingham Whitaker told how Oliver Chapman, whom he described as the pioneer of cricket in Grayshott, came to him about a ground, and the pitch opposite the Hall was the outcome of their discussion. When Edward I'Anson gave the cup, Albert Kent was secretary of the Grayshott club and Harry Mitchell the treasurer, and they got off to a good start in the competition. G.F. Campbell made 54, including 13 threes – where boundaries existed in those days they seem to have counted for one fewer – against Churt, and Kent, a splendid all-rounder for many years, took 6 for 3 with his fast swerve bowling. Lynchmere beat them by an innings in the final match, and it is interesting to recall the Grayshott team that day, for some of the names still have a familiar ring: G.V. Cox, W. Edwards, H.F. Richmond, H. Mitchell, A.E. Kent, F. Budd, E. Hecht, W. Johnson, F. Wart, J. Dicker and G. Winchester. The members expressed themselves unanimously in favour of home and away matches for 1902, but they had to wait another five seasons before that came about. One notable feat that year was by R.F. Russell, who made 60 and 73 in the two innings of a match with Blackmoor, and Grayshott's hopes ran high, but once more they lost to Lynchmere by an innings in the final game.

HAPPY GESTURE

Ingham Whitaker was persuaded to take over the captaincy in 1903 and this happy gesture was successful; Grayshott triumphed in the final match at Lynchmere to win the cup for the first time. Sir Arthur Conan Doyle, who had played for them on a number of previous occasions, had a big hand in the result. Tall and very powerfully built, he was an impressive bat. Two masters from St Edmund's School, G.F. Lucas and I. Sant, were also there. A close link has always existed between the village club and the school staff, and J.C. Morgan-Brown, the headmaster, who was associated with the school for over half a century, took the chair at the annual dinner at the Fox and Pelican in 1913. Others in the 1903 team included the manager of the Fox and Pelican, E.J. Searle, and Ben Chandler, for long the genial host at the Royal Huts Hotel, Hindhead. Searle was an all-rounder of uncommon ability, he took 6 for 32 and made top score when Grayshott, as winners of the trophy, beat The Rest in what afterwards became an annual fixture. In all matches that season he captured 116 wickets at five apiece, and on his departure from the village he received a presentation from the cricketers. He afterwards went to Canada. Grayshott had to wait a long time before they won the cup again, but they continued to be formidable opponents, liable to beat the best at any time. It was against Grayshott that Shottermill, the 1904 winners, sustained their only reverse. At the dinner that year G.F. Lucas was reported as saying that the cup committee 'should arrange for the refereeing of matches by impartial gentlemen'. The question of neutral umpires was often raised in after years and shelved, largely on the score of expense. It is only fair to add that the majority of those who wear the white coat have done their difficult job well.

'BATSMAN OF THE YEAR'

A new name came to the fore in 1905, when E. Johnson, playing for 'the next XIV' against the Grayshott cup XI, retired after making 71, prompting the remark by one critic that if he had not had a place in the first team 'we presume that he will be given a trial at an early date!' Sir Arthur Conan Doyle headed the batting averages that year, but Ernest Johnson aspired to the same honour. He made top score for The Rest against Lynchmere in 1907, and two seasons later earned the title of 'batsman of the year'. His 123 not out against Headley remained the highest cup score until the thirties and, although working away from the district and not being able to play in all matches, he finished with an average of nearly 52. Unfortunately, the full figures for this achievement have not been handed down, but he appeared in more than half the fixtures and, of course, made a number of high scores. Sussex-born, he played for Sydenhurst Ramblers, near Chiddingfold, before coming to Grayshott, and in his early years was a wicketkeeper as well as a batsman. Albert Kent won the bat for the best average in 1910, the year Tilford secured the first cup outright. Grayshott beat them in August, Bert Chapman taking 7 for 10 in a total of 42 and Johnson making 39 of Grayshott's 69 for 8. Tilford turned the tables in 1912 when even G. Spearman's 8 for 5 – five with his last six balls – was not enough to swing the balance. In 1913 Grayshott were runners-up, Johnson heading the batting list and P.M. Snow, who afterwards played for Headley, headed the bowling. The fact that Ernest Johnson was skipper in 1920, the first post-war season, when Grayshott lifted the cup for the second time, gave general satisfaction. J. Dicker and A.E. Kent, of those who had been in from the beginning, shared in the triumph, and Grayshott did not lose a match. They put Tilford out for 13 and A.H. Messenger, another great name in Grayshott cricket, took 6 for 15 in a match with Shottermill, who were at that time unbeaten. A fortnight later he and Percy Burrage dismissed Churt for seven, and in the match with Hindhead that clinched the issue Percy Snow made 68 not out. There were two drawn matches, with Shottermill and Churt, and the game with The Rest was also drawn, Kent registering top score. Mrs Whitaker presented the cup in the presence of her husband, and yet another dinner at the Fox and Pelican, with the latter in the chair, revived memories of old times.

That season's success set the seal on Ernest Johnson's playing career, though he did not give up the game for another ten years or so and was a member of the 1929 cup-winning team. Captain for many seasons, he still takes a keen interest in the club and has rendered great service to the competition as both umpire and steward. Absolutely fair and impartial, he set a high standard on and off the field; of his playing days a contemporary has said: 'I never heard him question or grumble at a decision', and that is a fine tribute.

Grayshott, winners in 1920. Standing, from the left: W. Johnson (umpire), P. Burrage, P.M. Snow, R.F. Petter, J. Dicker, F. Puttick, T. Eames (scorer). Seated: A.H. Messenger, E. Johnson, (captain), A.I. Whitaker (president), A.E. Kent, S. Howick. On ground: W. Cotton, J. Budd.

FUN AND LAUGHTER

After World War One Grayshott played on the new recreation ground given by their president, and to most of those still in the game it is the ground always associated with the club. The wicket, with its green, springy turf, has generally been rated one of the best in the competition, especially since water was laid on; the outfield is good and the light perfect. The ground is, perhaps, rather large and impersonal, lacking the intimacy of a smaller arena, but there have been some splendid matches and performances there. The Grayshott players of the twenties and thirties made their mark on the competition and there were outstanding personalities among them. In the middle period of the first decade after the war R.C. Robertson-Glasgow, so well known as a cricket author and broadcaster, often turned out for Grayshott. The Oxford University and Somerset googly bowler was then a master at St Edmund's School, and if his talents never quite received the recognition they deserved in the first-class sphere – he was desperately unlucky not to play for England – the delightful 'Crusoe', by his personality and writings has given as much pleasure to cricket-lovers as any man living. There was fun and laughter whenever he assisted Grayshott, and he made a lot of runs for them. In 1924, for example, his 51 was the club's highest individual score of the season and he had the best bowling average, though he was not often put on 'because', as one former captain explained to the writer, 'most of the wickets were not too good'. Fast-medium in first-class cricket can be very fast in village circles. Once, after taking top score at Tilford, 'Crusoe' was persuaded to show his skill with the ball and promptly took 4 for 1. When Grayshott held a smoking concert in 1927 he showed equal ability as a comedian and had everyone in fits of laughter. He took the chair at another concert when Grayshott won the cup in 1929 and made a speech remarkable for wit and modesty. He gives a penetrating pen-picture of two of Grayshott's bowlers, Burrage and Messenger, in his autobiography, *46 Not Out*, which all cricketers should read, if they have not already done so.

THIRD SUCCESS

Burrage and Messenger were for many seasons the mainstay of the attack and the former was also a useful batsman, a department in which Messenger was often effectively stubborn. No one could have been more devoted to the game. The nature of a policeman's duties made his appearances uncertain, but Messenger seldom missed a match. How he did it was his own secret; the sound of the willow on leather drew him like a magnet. As a bowler he was full of guile and pads that 'obstructed the traffic' seldom got off with a caution. The cup came to Grayshott for the third time in 1929, when the team, led by Fred

Puttick, who was also in the 1920 winning team, lost only once, at Grayswood, where the aggregate of four innings was just over 100. Grayshott beat The Bourne twice, putting them out on one occasion for 18, and finished a point ahead of Whitehill. Their final fixture, with Shottermill, was not played as it fell on the same day as the Winners v Rest match, in which Grayshott made 79 and their opponents 37. Cyril Pratt, who scored 341 runs to head the batting honours, made top score against The Rest, and Len Coombes, who took 6 for 12, was the season's most successful bowler, capturing 88 wickets at 3.4 apiece. Coombes, then at the outset of his career, was as good a medium-pace bowler as the competition has seen. He delivered the ball with a snap of the wrist, moving it a bit both ways and pegged the batsmen down with the accuracy of his length. In later seasons rather too much work fell on his shoulders, but he was always dangerous, and retired from the game too soon. Pratt, who also played for Hindhead, was a stylish and effective bat. Burrage, Johnson and Messenger, with their captain, brought experience to the side. The skipper, who handled his men with tact and skill, was a tower of strength. Initial nervousness made him an uncertain starter, but when he got going no one could hit the ball harder and he had a terrific straight drive. He received the cup from Miss I'Anson, sister of the donor. Another notable member of the team was R.F. Bremner, who was in Churt's winning combination of 1922. The wicketkeeper was Percy ('Snowball') Hicks, now secretary of the club and a great enthusiast, ever-ready to work hard for the game. Claude Triggs, a big hitter, was among others who played. Lewis Robinson was scorer and W. Johnson, whose memories went back to the competition's beginning, umpire.

Grayshott, winners in 1929. Standing, from the left: L. Robinson (scorer), and the second secretary of the competitions, M. Clapham, H. Spencer Moore, R.F. Bremner, Revd E. Garth Ireland (vice-president), H. Bell, Lt-Com. M.R.T. Knight, W. Johnson (umpire). Seated: L. Coombes, E. Johnson, F. Puttick (captain), A.H. Messenger, C. Pratt. The photograph was taken outside of the captain's house following his recovery from a serious illness. Missing are P. Burrage and P. Hicks. (See also page 94.)

WHEN THE SIREN GOES

The men of Grayshott acquired their familiar green, red-peaked caps in 1929, presented to them by Mrs F. Puttick and Miss Binney, and in the following season they came near to lifting the trophy again, still under the captaincy of Fred Puttick. Beating The Bourne by two runs in August, they tied with the Surrey club at the head of the table, but lost the play-off at Churt, despite the bowling of L. Coombes, who took 7 for 20. Since then the cup has eluded them by wider margins, but they have often been in the running. Between the wars their players included R.E. Pollock, a fine batsman who took guard a yard outside the crease – he hit five sixes, three off successive balls from Penycate – and seven fours in making 82 against Shottermill in 1925, S. Howick, W. Cotton, J. Budd and Jack and Tom Puttick, who afterwards turned out for Haslemere. Jack once hit a ball into the trees on the far side of the road. Tom was a wicketkeeper and Percy Watts also did duty in the same capacity. The cousins Tom Oakford, now of Haslemere, a useful all-rounder, and Reg Oakford come to mind, with Tom Madgwick, an opening batsman in the early days, and Harold Madgwick providing continuity through father to son; A.H. Messenger and his son, A.V. Messenger, furnish another instance. Reg Coombes, brother of Len, has also been an asset to Grayshott, making a lot of good scores. Then there were Phil and Jack Kingshott, a gifted pair of brothers. It was Phil Kingshott, who, in 1935, beat E. Johnson's long-standing record with 133 not out against Whitehill. He made his runs in just over an hour, hitting nine sixes and nine fours. That season he scored 488 runs and took 49 wickets. He made another century, 105 against Oakhanger, in 1937, and his aggregate was 524, Reg Coombes, second in the list, getting 386. In the following year Reg Coombes himself made a century, 108 v Churt, and Grayshott passed the 200 mark. A week later they had 200 made against them by Whitehill, and that may be in the nature of an unusual record. Jack Kingshott, a steady left-handed bat, came to full maturity after World War Two and is still giving the club good service. Another pair of brothers of more recent times are Johnny White, now with Headley, and Fred White. Anthony and Roger Hodgkinson, sons of Mr R.J. Hodgkinson, were two good young players. The latter lost his life tragically in a road accident and the former is now serving in the forces overseas. R. Colwell, a neat player with some nice shots, must be numbered among the batsmen of recent years. And what of that enthusiast, R.F. (Bob) Petter, whose career spans the whole period from 1920, when he was in the cup-winning team – an experience repeated in 1929 – down to the present day? Grayshott cricket would not be the same without his cheerful face and determined bowling as he wheels up the overs with the peak of his cap pulled well down. His duties in the fire service sometimes take him away in the middle of an over when the siren goes, but the next match finds him back in the side. Useful with the bat, he has been both captain and secretary in his time, and his father, another Bob, and a good bowler, played for Grayshott before him. He has a son, Alan, following in his footsteps. George Collis, a sound bowler, Harold Langrish, all-rounder who has appeared for Shottermill, W. Finn, Harry Snelling and the brothers George and Harry Edmead, too, have added their quota to Grayshott cricket.

AGAIN TO THE FORE

There was a period of rebuilding after the last war and Grayshott were again to the fore in 1950, when they finished third after an impressive series of victories in the second half of the season. One of their post-war captains was E.G. Wardle, the schoolmaster, a stylish left-handed bat now playing for Haslemere. H. Sharman, formerly of Headley, and Harry Hubbard from Shottermill brought strength to the bowling. In 1950 the latter and W. Loader formed the spearhead of the attack. Loader, who was also prominent before the war, has real hostility in his arm and gets surprising pace from the pitch. If he took his batting more seriously he might well be a fine all-rounder. Popular members of the team are the two Jamaicans, George Bullock and Sid Hibbert. Quick on their feet, they bring equal quickness of eye to their batting. Bullock has been the team's wicketkeeper for the past few seasons, and Hibbert, captain in 1950, is a master in dealing with the leg ball. He would make a pile of runs if he could restrain himself from flicking at the high riser outside the off peg. Taken all in all, the outlook for Grayshott cricket has never been brighter, and if fortune is kind to them no one will be more gratified than their president, Canon Harvey, a most faithful supporter who seldom misses a home match. Their bowling is good and they have enough runs in the bag to bring a broad smile to the face of that methodical and philosophical scorer, E.G. Potts; and that is as it should be in the competition's Jubilee year.

Churt

ONE of the most attractive villages in the locality, Churt lies at the foot of the northern approaches to Hindhead, hilly and well-wooded, with sandy soil, pines and heather and some agricultural land. Geographically, it is the centre of the competition's area, and has had an unbroken association with the I'Anson Cup. The history of Churt Cricket Club goes back to the nineties, and through the years the village has produced some outstanding players. They have not been among the leaders during the past quarter-of-a-century or so, but the gallant way in which the team have carried on year after year in the face of misfortune, relieved occasionally by notable victories, has won general admiration; but the story has another side. There were seasons in the early days when Churt were a power in the land, and they have twice won the cup: a feat which compares well with the records of other villages. The present generation have every reason to be proud of the achievements of their forbears.

The original ground was on the common by the southern shore of Frensham Great Pond, and years later Edward Turle recalled the carefree atmosphere of those days when he was captain of Churt. It was no uncommon thing, he said, to see a fielder diving into a gorse bush to fetch the ball. When the ground was well established a barrel of liquid refreshment was kept on the field and the skipper never afterwards had to fetch players from the Frensham Pond Hotel! Overgrown with gorse and heather, that old pitch, still part of a public recreation ground, is now indistinguishable from the surrounding common. F.C. (Frank) Wattridge was secretary in 1901 and was one of the small band who drew up the first rules of the competition. He and F.C. (Fred) Martin were two of the leading figures in the Churt team. Wattridge was a left-handed batsman of uncommon ability, and the fast swerve bowling of Martin was universally respected. He showed his mettle with the bat for The Rest against Grayshott in 1903, going in last and making top score of 17 not out. His brother, Frank Martin, was another very useful player, and their nephew, H.C. (Bert) Martin, was in the side for a number of seasons. In 1907 Churt were runners-up for the cup and held a supper at the Pride of the Valley Inn, preceded by a match between married and single members, and this soon developed into an annual event. In 1908 H.A. Baker made 43 for The Rest against Tilford. Son of Sir John Baker, for many years Liberal MP for Portsmouth, he lived at Churt for some time, and in the first of the two general elections of 1910 unsuccessfully contested the Petersfield Division against the Conservative member, Colonel W.G. Nicholson. Although in opposing camps politically, they shared a common interest in cricket, and both were in turn honoured guests at the Grayshott annual dinner. Baker was a fine bat, but another Churt player, A.T. Lawrence, took the honours for The Rest versus Tilford in 1909, scoring 51. That season, for the first time for many years, Frank Wattridge did not head the batting averages, the distinction falling to another left-hander, Alf Carver.

NECK-AND-NECK

H.A. Baker was captain in 1910, and a year later, under his leadership, Churt won the cup for the first time. It was a popular victory, for they were the only one of the original clubs still playing – Headley were then out of the competition – who had not lifted the trophy. In July they had a key match with Shottermill, undefeated at that time, and won easily, Fred Martin taking 7 for 16. Later that month Churt made 185 for 1 declared at Grayshott, Baker hitting 13 fours in his 92 and Wattridge contributing 62. Churt and Shottermill were running neck-and-neck all through the season and had identical records. There was an all-day play-off at Grayshott, and Churt won very easily by 10 wickets, scoring 108 and 10 for 0 to 44 and 77. Fred Martin was well among the wickets and H.A. Baker made top score. Churt went on to beat The Rest on the same ground. After nine wickets had gone down for 39, Fred and Bert Martin carried the score to 74, and The Rest were put out for 46, A.R.T. (Andrew) Baker, the young schoolmaster, taking 4 for 6. A member of a celebrated Hale family – one of his brothers opened the innings for Surrey with Tom Hayward – Andrew Baker was then and afterwards a tower of strength to Churt. A supper was held at the Pride of the Valley in November, when due tribute was paid to the fine

Churt, winners in 1911. Standing, from the left: A. Holden, B. Martin, A. Carver, F.C. Martin, A. Karn, W. Carter, J. Kinge. Seated: A.T. Lawrence, Maj. Edwards, H.A. Baker (captain), F.A. Wattridge, F. Martin. On ground: H. Marden, A.R.T. Baker.

batting of the captain and the splendid bowling of Andrew Baker. Other stalwarts of the team included the three Martins, Wattridge, Carver, Andrew ('Peter') Karn – the village blacksmith – H. ('Dee') Marden, Lawrence and Major Edwards. Reference was made to the departure from the parish of Frank Wattridge, who went to live at Tongham and afterwards emigrated to Australia. H.A. Baker was unable to attend the Grayshott dinner and Fred Martin received the cup. The captain afterwards became an Alderman of the City of London and High Sheriff of the County of London, returning to the district in later years, and he died at Haslemere in 1946. Churt had another good season in 1912, finishing runners-up.

AFTER THE WAR

The trophy came back to the village in 1922, the third post-war season. Andrew Baker was then captain, and a very good one. Only a year previously he had made 67 not out against Whitehill. It was that club who were Churt's chief rivals for the cup in 1922. When Churt visited Whitehill for the final match they knew they had to win if the cup was to be theirs, and they made 92, R.F. Bremner and B. Silvester putting on 26 for the last wicket. The home side fought hard for the draw which would have given them the trophy, but were eventually prised out for 54, W. Checkley taking 5 for 13 and Silvester 4 for 16. Churt had lifted the cup by a single point, winning nine of their 14 matches, drawing three and losing two. The only difference in Whitehill's figures was that they drew two and lost three. Churt were put out for 19 by The Rest, who replied with 53. The winners had a fine side that year. The captain and Carver, a powerful hitter, remained from the 1911 team, and Checkley, Carver, Baker and E.H. Ashby headed the batting list with double-figure averages in that order. Baker, Ashby, Checkley and Silvester all had bowling averages of around four, from which the ability of the side may be gauged. The wicketkeeper was F.D. Berridge, who, after leaving Malvern, played for Kent Second XI. He was outstanding behind the stumps in what proved to be his only season in the competition, for he moved to Rowledge, where he still lives, soon afterwards and was unable to spare the time to turn out again. There were other useful men in L. Gardiner Hill, H.B. Davies – a real stonewaller – and the two youngest members of the side, Ben Wonham and W.F. (Bill) Martin, son of Fred Martin. Three members of the team all later appeared in cup-winning teams for other clubs, Wonham for Thursley in 1924, Baker for The Bourne in 1925, and Bremner for Grayshott in 1929. Ben Wonham's brother George also played for Churt for a time. Checkley, a round-the-wicket swerve bowler who opened the attack with Silvester, was also a useful bat with a remarkable shot over his left shoulder to a ball pitched on his legs. Ashby's fast bowling is still remembered, and he was also a good bat. Churt celebrated their success with a dinner at the school where Andrew Baker spent his working hours. He was the complete cricketer, a fine batsman and bowler, and in 1923 he made 90 against Whitehill. Churt lost one of their mainstays when he became headmaster of The Bourne School, but they were well served throughout the twenties by Bert Silvester, whose medium-fast right-hand deliveries caused the downfall of many a batsman. His length was immaculate and his flight puzzling. Churt suffered a blow in 1923 when Alf Carver died as the result of a motorcycle accident. He had always said he would go on playing until he became captain of the team, and he was skipper that year. The cricketers acted as bearers at his funeral and bore the coffin on their shoulders from their captain's cottage near the Pride of the Valley to the churchyard, a distance of well over a mile.

GREAT-HEARTED TRIERS

After the war Churt played on the new recreation ground in the centre of the village, given as a memorial to the fallen, and it has been their headquarters ever since. The pavilion is the largest in the competition, with a wide verandah, dressing rooms and a big central room where the delegates have often held their annual meetings. The ground, pleasantly situated, slopes down slightly in a northerly direction and the wicket has usually been good, despite a tendency to crumble in dry weather, while the outfield is kept well cut. The playing strength of the club gradually declined after their 1922 success, irresolute batting being largely the cause. The story might have been very different had there been a consistent pair of opening bats, backed up by soundness in the middle of the order. Jack Spencer, whose naval duties prevented him from playing very often, had a grand season with the bat in 1927, his average of 31

Churt, winners in 1922. Standing, from the left: W. Voller (scorer), A Harris, R.F. Bremner, H.B. Davies, E.H. Ashby, B. Silvester, K. We[illegible] (umpire). Seated: L. Gardiner Hill, A. Carver, A.R.T. Baker (captain), [illegible] Wonham, F.D. Berridge. On ground: W. Martin, W. Checkley.

being the best ever recorded for Churt. He retired after scoring 63 in a total of 189 for 6 against Hindhead, and a week later took 50 off the Shottermill bowling. Shottermill were then quite a strong side and it is a curious fact that Churt have often done best against the most powerful clubs. The Bourne, in some of their best seasons, have fallen to Churt. In 1930, for instance, they went down by one wicket in a four innings game, and in 1937 the clubs tied at 63 each. In 1935 Churt beat the cup-winners, Tilford, on their own ground. The bowlers have generally done all that was required of them and the men of Churt have the reputation of being great-hearted triers. Bill Martin, whose father wore the umpire's coat long after he gave up playing, was never afraid to attack the bowling and could change the course of a game in a few overs. There were no half-measures about his hitting, and he was one of Churt's most reliable batsmen over a long period. Stan Corner, dour left-handed opening bat, was another prominent player who served as a steward and appeared in numerous representative games. He sold his wicket dearly and was a most difficult man to shift. A third stalwart is Chris Harris, whose experience covers a longer period than that of any other Churt member now playing. His first season was 1923 and through the years he has seldom missed a match. He is a former captain, a useful batsman, and great enthusiast. His uncle, A.H.C. Harris, was on the competition sub-committee in 1923. Chris Harris's brother Ron was also a player at one time. Henry Kimber, another former skipper, was a stonewaller who could be remarkably impassive and keep his end up when others were failing. He afterwards played for Tilford. Totally different in style was Percy Pelling, who hit very hard with a straight bat. He was an able skipper and pleasant opponent. The claims of business prevented him from turning out as often as he would have liked.

DISMISSED FOR THREE

One of the soundest fast bowlers in the locality for some seasons between the wars was Jack West, whose father, K. West, was umpire in 1922. Jack joined the Hampshire Constabulary and has given the county force good service with bat and ball. Now a sergeant stationed at Whitehill, he plays for that club in the competition. The Matthews brothers, Jim, Alan and Ted, have all appeared in the Churt team, and Alan took 5 for 1 in helping to dismiss Oakhanger for three in 1940. Fred Bishop took the remaining five wickets for two. Other well-known names include those of Frank Glaysher, who in a former generation was noted for his habit of changing step in the middle of his run up to bowl; Tommy Remnant, a steady bat and slow spin bowler; Les Voller, useful with the bat and a cousin of Percy Voller, a fine all-rounder who scored 47 at The Bourne a few seasons ago. Percy Voller is a deadly bowler on his day – there are few better – and a most cheerful trier who always gives of his best. Major Caunter, son-in-law of Sir Walter and Lady Napier, played for a period. Norman Stacey, a useful all-rounder; Arthur Henley, a bowler who lost his life in Italy in the last war; George and Ron Williams, two brothers who pulled their weight for the club; Jim Novell and his son, M. Novell; Fred Pattison, the Yorkshireman; H. (Bert) Mills, J. Sheldon, an all-rounder who could swing the ball quite a bit; J.D. Noble, a bowler of some pace; and the brothers E. and F. Boxall, all bear well-known names.

The wicketkeepers have included Bill Martin, the predecessor of F.D. Berridge, Charlie French, Bert Hide, P.E. ('Tug') Charman – a very keen and useful member – and the present holder of the post, Norman Ellsey, who has been known to take off the gloves and bowl. His wife has scored for Churt for some years. George Cross, the 1950 captain, and Roly Burberry, a clever slow bowler, must not be omitted. A noted Churt character is Harry Massey, secretary and treasurer for many years and groundsman for as long as most people can remember. A tireless, good-humoured worker, he has done much for the club. Always on the spot on match days, he is willing to turn his hand to anything, from donning the umpire's coat to pulling the roller. His two sons, Charlie and George, have played for the club occasionally. Another good supporter on the administrative side is W. (Bill) Weatherley, the match secretary, who never played cricket himself, but takes a keen interest and helps the club in many ways. In the list of presidents the name of A. Caro, a generous patron, who did not confine his support merely to being a figurehead, will long be remembered. He often raised teams to play Churt at holiday times, and there was invariably delightful hospitality at such matches.

The spirit of Churt remains high and the day must come when fortune again smiles on this club, which has such a long and honourable tradition. One thing is certain; win or lose, the players will continue to do their best.

Blackmoor and Whitehill

BLACKMOOR and Whitehill were separate clubs, but their history is bound up together, for the one merged into the other. The older foundation was Blackmoor, a village which grew up round the estate of the Earl of Selborne in the last century. Whitehill was part of the outcome of the building of Bordon Camp and the cricket club absorbed Blackmoor after World War One, though Blackmoor again became a separate club following the second great conflict, playing on the original ground opposite the Estate Office. The guiding spirit in the old Blackmoor club was, of course, W.W. Stratford. He was the genial colossus around whom everything revolved. Big in mind and stature, he learned his cricket in Buckinghamshire, being an accomplished player at 15. Coming to Blackmoor as headmaster in 1893, he took over the captaincy five years later and held the office without a break until World War One. A spin bowler, he carried all before him, taking his 100 wickets season after season, not all in the competition, for, with the limited number of matches, that was impossible. In 1904 he set up a new record for Blackmoor with 166 wickets. He had an easy delivery, making full use of the width of the crease and varying his length by not always coming right up to the line, a procedure followed with great effect in later years by A.H. Messenger, of Grayshott. W.W.'s deliveries came deceptively fast off the pitch and few played him with confidence. With his cap, moustache and genial visage he looked an inocuous trundler just tossing them up. 'I hope the old man is on when I go in' was an oft-repeated comment, and the outcome was always the same: a crest-fallen retreat to the pavilion. In 1903, the year Blackmoor made their record 300 for 5 declared, he twice bowled Conan Doyle in a match, and the great man, then at the height of his powers, made a point of congratulating him. He also bowled A.H. Hartwright in the first over of their first meeting in 1907, and that fine batsman was once part of a Stratford hat-trick. There was another occasion when Hartwright had the better of matters at Blackmoor, and went to 99 before the skipper called on his young son Billy, who promptly bowled the visitor. Hard luck for Hartwright; there were no boundaries on that vast field, set in rolling agricultural country, and every hit had to be run out. The 99 had been well earned. It was no disgrace to be bowled by W.W. Like birth and death, it happened to everyone in turn.

CONSISTENTLY SUCCESSFUL

The cup first went to Blackmoor in 1906, when they were unbeaten, and it was characteristic that in the match with The Rest, which they lost, W.W. carried his bat. They defeated Grayshott that year after being behind on the first innings, Stratford taking 9 for 14. In 1910 the Lynchmere umpire described him as the most consistently successful bowler the competition had seen, and two years later he led Blackmoor to their second success. He captained The Rest on numerous occasions and as a wise administrator was without a peer. An able speaker, he was usually on the toast list at the Grayshott dinners and once composed and sang a song about the competition. What men thought of him is perhaps best summed up in an old player's recollection of a tight match at Tilford. It was so close that the scorers disagreed about the result. W.W. strode to the table, picked up a pencil, added the scores, and announced: 'Tilford won by three.' And that was that. Everyone was satisfied; his integrity was absolute. One other story about him; the setting was again Tilford, when he was playing for Whitehill and a stubborn partnership was causing a lot of trouble. W.W. had the outfield well covered, but the batsmen would not be tempted. During one over he called his men in and set a tight field, sending an obviously inexperienced youth into the deep. Immediately the striker rose to the bait. A slam hard and high landed safely in the hands of the lone outfielder to the disgust of the batsman, and the look on the face of the bowler plainly indicated his thoughts – 'You should have known better'. When Blackmoor won the cup for the second time in 1912 they celebrated the event in May of the following year by holding dinner at the Woolmer Hotel. The Earl of Selborne presided and the captain of the team was presented with a gold-mounted walking stick.

Blackmoor's leading batsman of those days was another W.W., Bill Read, whose 117 at Frensham Hill in 1903 was the competition's first century. The straight bat and the straight drive came easily to him. He made his runs in front of the wicket and made them well. Then there were the brothers Hoar, Arthur and Frank, and among others W.J. ('Bloomer') Bone, opening bat and concertina player, who kept the team amused as they drove along in the wagonette. In after years he formed his own band and gave selections in the villages at Christmas until his death in the thirties. There was always a special serenade for his old skipper. One of the younger members of the club was John Broadwood, now chairman of the Whitehill Bench, a capable performer with both bat and ball and a great figure in local cricket. He took 6 for 12 and made top score for Blackmoor in the 1912 Winners v The Rest match. Physical disability brought his playing days to a premature end, but his experience and sage counsel have been tremendous assets to Whitehill for the past 30 years or so, and he also gave much useful service as an umpire. A witty after-dinner speaker, he tells a good story well, and no one has done more to preserve the happy atmosphere of Whitehill cricket.

WELL WORTH WATCHING

For now the fortunes of Blackmoor became those of Whitehill. The Blackmoor pitch was unusable after the war, the shed which served as a pavilion had blown down and the players joined Whitehill in a body, with W.W. Stratford as captain. Cricket on the ground by the Farnham-Petersfield road was well worth watching in those days. There was the table, a grassy mound surrounded by a sea of heather, with the stumps so loose in the sand that any pace bowler was liable to level all three, a satisfying sight to everyone but the victim. The club windows – for the Whitehill pavilion is also a club – then, as now, framed familiar faces (the game would lose much if John Broadwood were not in his accustomed corner), and other spectators sat on the weather-beaten benches in front or on the bank beneath the shade of the overhanging pines on the far side of the road, a perfect vantage-point. The bank remains, but, alas, not the trees. The advent of wireless in later years provided another attraction at Whitehill, for the latest Test scores and other tit-bits of sporting information, not necessarily connected with cricket, were at once relayed to the players, and the facilities for well-earned refreshment on the spot, as it were, after the match have always been appreciated. And where else is it possible to watch a billiards match while changing?

The year 1920 saw the Blackmoor contingent well to the fore, with Frank Hoar taking the batting honours and W.W. Stratford still formidable with the ball. A new star was his son, W.A. (Billy) Stratford, a fast bowler with a well-controlled action and a useful run-getter. He seemed exceptionally fast then, and in memory he seems so still. His chief characteristic was keeping his left arm rigidly to his side on delivery, and he had a habit of cartwheeling the middle peg without fuss or emotion. There have been few better pace bowlers in the competition. Whitehill didn't win the cup that season, but W.W. captained The Rest once more, as he had first done nearly 20 years previously. Frank Hoar made 90 against Hindhead in 1921 and, although Whitehill beat Shottermill four times that year and carried off the Lyndon Cup, Shottermill secured the major trophy. In 1922 Whitehill were well in the running and everything depended on the final home match with Churt. The visitors won the game and the cup, but Whitehill went down fighting, for it took 50 overs, including 30 maidens, to get them out for 54 after Churt had made 92. A. Cox, a Whitehill bowler of no mean pace, who afterwards played for Frensham, with which village he had family associations, showed his quality by taking 5 for 9 for The Rest v The Winners.

OVER THE RAILWAY

Whitehill were not long to be denied, and they captured the cup for the first time in 1923. Successive defeats at Headley and Shottermill in May gave them a poor start, but they recovered magnificently and won 'on the post'. So W.W. Stratford received the trophy for the third time to crown a wonderful career. The club's president, the Earl of Selborne, was at the Winners and Rest match, together with his son, the Hon Lewis Palmer, who had played for Whitehill on occasion. It was really the climax of the Blackmoor era, and the captain had a special word of praise for Bill Read and Arthur Hoar. Jack Mitchell, another Blackmoor stalwart, was scorer, a function he performed for many years, and

Whitehill, winners in 1923. Standing, from the left: H. Chamberlain (umpire), F. Hoar, W.A. Stratford, A. Cox, E.J. Hardy, W. Read, A. Hoar. Seated: G.H. Cox, E. Heighton, W.W. Stratford (captain), the Earl of Selborne (president), H. Luckin. On ground: H.R. Perry, H. Heighes.

Frank Hoar, whose knuckles and midriff seemed steel-plated, was in the team. The wicketkeeper, generally considered to be the best Whitehill ever had, was H.R. Perry, whose work also called for commendation by the skipper. In later years he rendered good service as umpire, an office filled at that period by H. ('Joe') Chamberlain. The batting rested mainly on the shoulders of J. Brown and E. ('Nobby') Heighton. The former, powerfully built, used his wrists better than most of the moderns. He cut with beautiful precision and his driving was crisp and all along the carpet. Heighton's methods were more rough-and-ready, but he could rattle up much-needed runs after early wickets had gone cheaply. Horace Luckin, gay and happy-go-lucky, was the spectators' especial delight. What a hitter! His sixes changed the course of many a game, though he was no wild slogger and, with sleeves flapping he took a lot of wickets, too. In 1930 he scored 602 runs for the club, including 94 at Shottermill. Jack Britton, a great Whitehill supporter, had offered 10s for 50 and £1 for 100. Horace knocked up the half-century in record time, carrying the railway line with a succession of sixes until Tom Larbey flatly refused again to plunge into the aromatic depths beyond. The century didn't quite materialise, but Luckin certainly 'went on for the pound' that day. Others in the 1923 team included E.J. Hardy, a keen player; Harry Heighes, ever-willing and cheerful; and G.H. Cox, always immaculately turned out; as well as Billy Stratford, then secretary and treasurer – he headed the bowling averages. Whitehill celebrated with a dinner at which Lord Selborne presided.

ALWAYS ON THE WINNING SIDE

A serious illness kept W.W. Stratford out of cricket in 1924, and in due course his son succeeded him as captain. After that, the Father of the Competition captained the Miller Cup side for several years, bringing on the young idea, and he held the secretaryship until 1931. Two years afterwards he had the pleasure of seeing his son lead the team to another victory and, despite his great age, he continues to take an interest in the game he adorned for so long. The 1931 team had many new faces. Colin Nichols, who won his spurs with Headley, was the leading bowler, closely followed by Bill Moss, a genial soul who bowled a nagging length most tantalisingly and, holding the bat in what can only be described as a very 'cack-handed' manner, cracked colossal sixes when he connected, which, unfortunately, was seldom. Luckin and Brown were still there to lead the batting, with Harry Heighes a grand fielder. The wicketkeeper, and a very fine one, was Captain (afterwards Lieut-Colonel) T.E. Adlam, VC, who had followed as headmaster of Blackmoor School in 1926. He holds a competition record likely to remain unique. That was his only season for the club and he was on the winning side in every match he ever played for the I'Anson Cup, being absent on the only two occasions Whitehill lost! In the game at The Bourne which decided the issue he hit the ball over the Mission Church. Then there were Leslie Mileham and Jacko Butcher – of whom more later – N. Humphries, whose drooping moustache and mournful mien concealed a sense of humour and real love of the game, and Eric Hunt, Jack Kneller and Geoff Amey, all good all-rounders. Geoff's brother Willy – 'little Willy Amey' – also gave the club good service over a long period.

Incidentally, Humphries never wore pads and was quite philosophical about cracks on the shin. He was known as 'Springbok', being a South African who served with that country's forces in World War One. H.R. Perry was umpire and Jack Mitchell scorer. Lady Selborne presented the cup and Lord Selborne, who sometimes rode up on his pony to watch the matches, referred with pleasure to the laurels of the father descending on the son. The Earl also presided at the celebration dinner.

Whitehill, winners in 1931. Standing, from the left: V. Shadbolt, H.R. Perry (umpire), H. Humphries, H. Heighes, C. Nichols, H. Luckin, J. Brown, L.M. Mileham, E. Hunt, J. Mitchell (scorer). Seated: Capt T.E. Adlam, S. Butcher, the Earl of Selborne (president), W.A. Stratford (captain), W. Moss, J. Kneller, G. Amey.

A PROLIFIC PAIR

Billy Stratford retired after the 1931 season, and for the remaining years until the war Whitehill cricket lost something of its lustre, though by no means uninteresting. The turf wore so badly that a concrete wicket, topped by matting, was laid down and, with the outfield as fast as ever, there was a spate of high scoring never approached before or since. Butcher and Milcham positively revelled in the new conditions and for several seasons scored a very high proportion of the runs made by the team. The latter also shouldered the burden of captaincy. In 1934 Butcher made 97 against Headley, and a year later headed both the batting and bowling, scoring 553 runs and taking 64 wickets. Mileham scored 95 against Grayshott in 1937 – he also made an exactly similar score against Tilford on the Bordon Officers' ground on another occasion – when Whitehill passed the century mark 11 times, and Mileham and Butcher compiled 1,000 runs between them, Butcher getting 79 wickets in addition. Their aggregate was not far short of that in the following season. Mileham carried his bat for 52 against Frensham in a total of 74, the next highest score being five. Leslie Mileham's batting exuded confidence in those years. Always completely assured, some of his shots, which he seemed to have all the time in the world to play, verged on the cheeky. Butcher was less of a stylist, but anything a bit short went over the fence and a length ball dead on the middle stump was liable to receive the same treatment. His left-handed quick bowling was at times brilliant. It is one of the curiosities of local cricket that, with all the fine batsmen they have produced, no player has ever made a century for Whitehill in a cup match.

Bill Moss trundled on, tireless as ever, doubtless deriving sustenance from the blade of grass so often between his lips, and helped at the other end by A. Tull, who had a long and very deliberate run up from regions behind the umpire. Owen Poulter, son of Tilford's captain in the year they won the cup outright, also played, though his cricket career lay mainly with Liss. Among others of that period, and just after World War Two, were Wilfred Kemp, a very useful all-rounder and a good club man, who now plays for Greatham; Ken Britton, also a good all-rounder who would have gone far with a little more confidence in himself; Tommy Murgatroyd, a stubborn batsman; J. Hardy, very efficient behind the stumps and a sound bat; and Charlie Kingswood, a cheerful and courageous trier. E.C. Ashford – 'Ashey' – an excellent organiser and administrator, was an acknowledged expert on matters like framing rules and a tireless worker behind the scenes. He did a fine job as secretary for some years and, on the field, his determined left-handed near-immobility at the crease often held up the opposing attack. A notable umpire and something of a character was George Thudichum, a tall and venerable figure with a long white beard. In one match a ball was hit through his beard and damaged his ribs, but, rather unlike W.G. Grace when he was the victim of a similar indignity while batting, he took it all in good part.

HAPPY ASSOCIATION

The present Earl of Selborne once remarked at a local cricket function that, although not a player himself, he had a son whom he hoped would one day assist Whitehill. In the course of time his second son, now Major the Hon Robert Palmer, who has played for Blackmoor since that club was revived, did turn out for Whitehill, making his first appearance in a cup match when still a schoolboy at Winchester, where he was in the team. Tall and strongly built, he was a fast bowler who could make the ball lift disconcertingly, and he had a lot more pace than his run-up suggested.

In Headley's championship year they were beaten on their own ground by Whitehill largely owing to Palmer's fine bowling. He has also appeared for the club on a number of occasions since the war and, although not so fast as of yore, is still very difficult to play. His sportsmanship and pleasant personality cemented the close and happy association which has always existed between his family and the Whitehill Cricket Club, an association marked at various times by many acts of generosity.

Starting again after the last war, Whitehill were fortunate to have Leslie Mileham to lead them for the first few difficult seasons, and later the reins were taken over by Ron Goff, a most capable all-rounder. A stylish batsman, very pleasing to watch, he is also a hostile opening pace bowler. The brothers Ted and Tom Rooney, too, brought strength to the team with occasional assistance, when RAF duties permitted, from a third brother, J. Rooney. Tom Rooney's early death in 1950 was a real loss to the club. Ted was the better batsman and made a pile of runs. There were, in addition, Norman Disney and Cyril Butcher, brother of Jacko – the latter an effective hitter inclined to impatience – and for a time 'Buster' Hulbert, who played for Oakhanger in pre-war days. A youthful side, Whitehill finished runners-up in 1949 and, while their 1950 showing was not so good, their future is full of promise.

Tilford

'I TRUST Tilford cricket will ever prosper. Its people have a great heritage, and the Green, I believe, is, next to Hambledon, the oldest playing field of all.' So writes a fine batsman, looking back on the days when he delighted the spectators on that loveliest of grounds, a ground steeped in tradition and framed by the oak, the river, the two hump-backed bridges and the Barley Mow; a jewel of the English countryside, unique and almost unchanging. No one who has played at Tilford on a sunny summer afternoon can ever forget the setting or the atmosphere. When the wickets are pitched the onlookers are drawn as if by a magnet. Few motorists pass without pausing along any of the three roads that make the Green an island. There is something in the scene that grips even the most casual; a feeling as old as time.

Cricket has been played at Tilford continuously for well over a century and a quarter, and the village was the home of the immortal 'Silver Billy', William Beldham, who was born at Wrecclesham in 1766. He died in the cottage – one-storied then – hard by the King's Oak in 1862 at the age of 96, and 25 years ago there were people still living who remembered him. There are some now who recall the Surrey cricketer, Jack Carmichael, playing for the village. The cricket club have a minute book going back to 1886, the year the Revd W.H.F. Edge, vicar for many years, became president and J. Carmichael captain. The club had been long established when admitted to the competition in 1904, under the name of Tilford Institute. The word 'Institute' was not dropped for many years, and is, indeed, engraved three times on the original trophy, which Tilford won outright in 1910. The Institute, a familiar and pleasant feature of the Green's surroundings, stands on the west side of the main road and was the gift to the village of the Anderson family, whose associations with the locality are so well known. The building was completed in 1894 and, unlike a great deal of Victorian architecture, has an attractive appearance, well suited to the dual purpose of hall and pavilion, while the recess near the top of the steps forms an admirable vantage-point for the presentation of a trophy. Generations of cricketers have known it and watched the hands of the clock marking the passing of the hours. The seats let into the wall beneath the east window of the main

Tilford Green in the early years of the last century, and just before the cricket club won the original I'Anson Cup outright. The club had laid one thousand turves to make the green suitable for league cricket, and posts and chains had been introduced to stop cattle from straying on to the pitch.

hall are a boon to scorers and privileged spectators when the weather is too chilly to sit under the small trees just inside the fence fronting the road. The seats may well have been placed there for just that purpose. Major Rupert D. Anderson was for many years president of the club and took a lively and generous interest in its progress.

William 'Silver Billy' Beldham in old age. He lived at Oak Cottage beside Tilford Green for 40 years, and died there in 1862. His bat was found by the author in 1983 (see inside back flap).

TRIUMPHANT YEARS

The Tilford captain throughout the early years in the competition was J.G. Poulter, a local farmer who built up a very good side, and the duties of secretary were in the hands of W. (Bill) Willmore, a grand all-rounder and one of the team's mainstays. He was a good fast bowler and dangerous bat with cricket in his blood, and his playing career extended over a very long period. He held most offices in the club, including the captaincy, which he finally gave up in 1928. For the first few seasons Tilford did little of note, but in 1908 they won the cup for the first time. The Revd C.A. Hamilton, a good bat who played in glasses, made 79 in a winning score against The Bourne, and the following week George Lonsdale got 51 not out against Grayshott, and a little later scored 72 at the expense of Churt. He and his brother Percy were very valuable members of the team. Tilford lost but one match, on their own ground at the hands of Lynchmere, and gained 18 out of a possible 20 points. Considered to be the best fielding side in the competition, they had the better of a drawn game with The Rest, scoring 72 for 2 in reply to 108 for 7 declared. G.E. Chambers, who had batted well all the season, made 44 not out. A tremendous hitter and fast-medium bowler, he had previously played for The Bourne. The captain received the cup from Edward I'Anson at the Grayshott dinner, and the ceremony was repeated a year later, for Tilford were again successful. Once more Lynchmere were the one club to beat Tilford, winning the first match of the season, and the only other point the holders dropped was in a draw with Grayshott. The fixture with The Rest was lost, but was notable for a remarkable incident. Tilford scored 72 and The Rest 109. B.W. Bentinck finished off The Rest innings by taking 5 for 0 in 10 balls with underhand lobs after sending down a couple of overs overhand! He was better known for his prowess with the bat and scored 78 not out in the return game with Lynchmere that year, when Tilford avenged their previous defeat. Bentinck, a barrister, and his brother both played for the club and later moved to Alton, where they rendered yeoman service to the town club. In 1910 it soon became obvious that Tilford would try to make the trophy their own property. Willmore got 60 against Grayshott and in July Tilford, at home, dismissed Lynchmere for 84 and responded with 96, B.W. Bentinck carrying his bat for 66. A defeat by Grayshott adversely affected the side's chances and they lost another game besides, but beat Churt in the final match to win the cup. Although weakly represented against The Rest, they put their opponents out for 49, Willmore bowling well, and replied with 85. For the third time Poulter received the trophy from the donor, and the Vicar of Grayshott (the Revd A.E.N. Simms) humorously suggested that the extraordinary twist of the roads through Tilford gave them that awkward twist to their bowling. Major Rupert Anderson presided at a celebration dinner at the Barley Mow and filled the cup with port wine. B.W. Bentinck headed the batting averages for the second year in succession and Willmore was top of the bowling. The umpire at that period was Harry Sanders, later to become chairman of the Farnham Urban District Council and himself to present the cup to Tilford's nearest neighbours, The Bourne, 30 years later.

TWIST OF FATE

There was a twist of fate, too, in 1911, for Tilford failed to win a match. In June, 1913, when Tilford entertained and

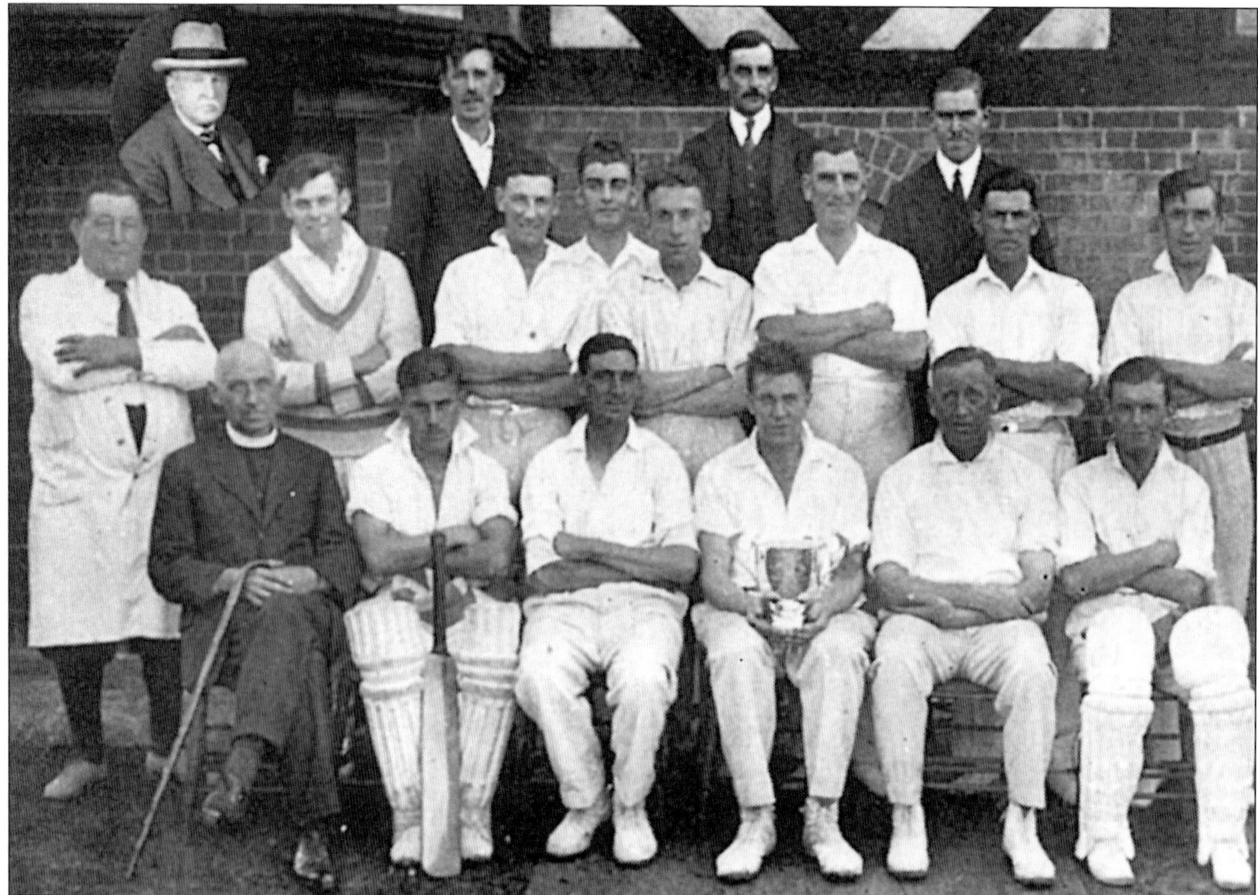

Tilford, winners in 1933. Back, from the left: Maj. R.D. Anderson (president), H. Clifton (secretary), H. Jarrett (scorer), A. Luckhurst (assistant secretary). Middle row: E. Fry (umpire), J. Varney, C. Johns, E. Hall, C. Bessant, G. Wickens, G. Goolding, J. Martin. Seated: Canon M.S. Ware (treasurer), J. Warner, R. Goolding, J. Eddey (captain), W. Stubbs, C. Fry.

defeated Hindhead, a presentation was made to J.G. Poulter, by Major Anderson to mark his ten years' captaincy of the club. Later Hindhead gained their first victory in the competition at the expense of Tilford, who were the only team to beat the champions, Shottermill. Canon Martin Ware, a good batsman and great supporter of Tilford cricket over a long period, scored 73 against Churt and 65 versus Haslemere Working Men in 1914. Another clergyman associated with the club as an active playing member for many years was the Revd C.J. Vernon.

The early post-war period found Tilford cricket still a force in the competition, and W. Willmore made 51 for The Rest against Grayshott in 1920. That was the year M.W. Payne came to live at 'Greyfriars' and he played fairly regularly for the side until 1925. A member of the Cambridge University team from 1904 to 1907, he appeared in four matches against Oxford, being captain in his last year. During that period Cambridge beat Oxford three times and drew the other game. In the Varsity match of 1906, which Cambridge won, Payne went in first and scored all the 45 runs made from the bat in 15 minutes, taking 34 off two overs from one bowler. In half-an-hour he collected 64 out of 73 – 14 fours, a three, two twos and a single. Keeping wicket, he went on to catch six men out and stump one. He also played for Middlesex, but his first-class career was cut short when he went abroad in 1908. His batting was always a delight to watch, cultured and forceful. Old players still talk about a match with the cup-holders at Shottermill in June 1922. Shottermill totalled 148 and Tilford replied with 152 for 5, Payne hitting 102 not out, including three sixes and 11 fours. It was a display marked by magnificent driving at a time when Shottermill were at the zenith of their powers. Payne sent up the 100 with a drive out of the ground, hitting the tree in the middle of Field End garden, and he made more than 50 of the last 60, the next highest individual score being 13. In the late twenties Payne returned to the village and continued to assist the club until 1933, their most recent cup-winning year. Among others of that era were his son-in-law, R. Brooks, the brothers Arthur and Bill Merrett – two useful all-rounders, W. Taverner, a gifted all-rounder; Fred Davis, a former secretary; and Reg Goolding, another all-rounder, now captain of the Second

XI, whose tall figure has surveyed the Tilford scene for several decades. His brother Gordon was a fast bowler. The younger players included John Yarney, a graceful left-handed batsman – one of the best in the locality in his day – and bowler who gave up playing much too soon.

FINE PLAYERS

Jack Warner has made more runs for the club than anyone else, and made them well. He bats with assurance and skill, always looking for the right ball to hit and taking full toll of anything a bit short of a length. Quick on his feet, he has a good defence and is a grand man to open an innings. In 1950 he scored well over 1,400 runs in all matches. He is an excellent captain and sportsman. His father, Bill Warner, was a member of the 1910 team. Jim Eddey is one of the best and most consistent bowlers the competition has known. Cricket is the breath of life to him and he puts his whole heart and soul into every game. He could go on bowling for ever and never lose his length. He holds the ball in both hands at the moment before delivery and his spinners twirl through the air, forcing the batsman back with subtleties of flight until the ball goes off the edge into the waiting hands of the slips or hits the middle stump. A year seldom passes when Eddey does nor get his 100 wickets in the competition, and other matches usually double the number. His son, who bears the same Christian name, has played fairly regularly for Tilford in recent years. Jim Eddey started his long career with Headley and Grayshott before going to Tilford and he well deserved the honour of being captain when the club won the cup in 1933. They had been near to success a season previously, when Frensham won a key match against them and lifted the trophy. In the earlier 1932 encounter, which Tilford won, Payne scored 57. Only three matches were lost in 1933 – all at home – one of them being at the hands of Churt. In a close game with Oakhanger Eddey hit a six when the last pair knocked off the 11 runs required for victory. Tilford lost to The Rest 99 – 35 and, in presenting the cup, Mrs Ware recalled that she was also present when the club last won the cup in 1910. Payne headed the batting averages, followed by Warner and J. Martin, and G. Goolding took the bowling honours, though Eddey captured by far the most wickets, 105 at 5.25 apiece. Yarney took 69 wickets. Eddey, Yarney and Warner all appeared in a trial match at the Oval that year, and Warner afterwards played several times for the Surrey Colts. Tilford celebrated their success in time-honoured fashion with a dinner at the Barley Mow, with Major Rupert Anderson, the oldest member present, in the chair, and no one was more delighted at Tilford's achievement than he. A pleasing innovation was the presence of the ladies, who have always been such keen supporters of Tilford cricket, and tribute was paid to all the club's stalwarts.

THEY ALSO SERVED

Joe Martin, who also assisted Churt and The Bourne, is a cheerful all-rounder still giving good service to the club. Others in the 1933 team not mentioned previously included C. ('Cuth') Johns, a fast bowler and all-rounder still going strong, C. Bessant and W. Stubbs (Lord Snowden's chauffeur), a steady bat and fast bowler, with a broad North Country accent. The wicketkeeper then and now was Colin Fry, who does his job well and is an efficient opening batsman. Time has dealt kindly with him and few would guess, seeing how active he is on the field, that he was for some years a prisoner in the last war. His father, also named Colin, played for Tilford before him. There were two policemen in the side, Ernie Hall, a fast bowler – now a chief inspector – and George Wickens, useful with the bat. A third policeman who played for some seasons and once captained the side was V.B. (Vic) James. Harry Clifton ('Cliffie'), the village baker, a cheerful and tireless worker, was secretary in 1933 and for many years afterwards. He achieved fame in the celebrated broadcast of 1936. Here may be mentioned his successors in office Vic Lowry, Brian Bradbury and the present secretary, R. (Bob) Hooker, a valuable member of the side, usually good for runs when they are needed and a capable organiser. The 1933 umpire, and a noted 'character' who filled that exacting role for a lengthy period was E. ('Prinny') Fry, uncle of Colin Fry. Harry Jarrett, the club's faithful scorer, cannot remember how long he has held the pencil, but he has been recording the runs since the twenties. Talking of 'characters', there was Charlie Woods, from the Barley Mow, whose batting often proved very useful. George Terrell, also from the Barley Mow, played too, and his son Charlie is an effective hitter.

The names of Tilford's players and supporters are legion. Gerard Streatfeild, a staunch upholder of the old traditions, who was a member of the MCC and played for Eton Ramblers and I. Zingari, seldom missed a First XI match, home or away, and was chairman of the committee for some time. L.B. (Les) Gains was a fine batsman, T.A. (Tim) Dimes a dashing left-handed bat and bowler, Percy Rampling an all-rounder, Roy Langley a useful bowler, and Sid Lloyd, another batsman. Then there are Cyril Evans, a young player who went to South Africa; Ken Dutton, a very cheerful player who lost his life serving with the Queen's in the last war; Ron Morrell, who bats left and bowls right; Don Paine, a keen bowler; Tom Foster, all-rounder; and Miles Merrett, son of Arthur Merrett, and an able batsman who scored 103 against Grayshott in 1940 to become the third Tilford player to reach the coveted three figures. And who could forget the gay and generous spirit of Peter Tanner, who lost his life gallantly in the last war? He often brought a side to play the village, and one of these annual encounters, in 1931, was described for the readers of the

News Chronicle by the former England captain, A.E.R. Gilligan. The cartoonist Cumberworth embellished the article with some witty sketches which caused many a chuckle locally.

In the years since they last won the cup Tilford have performed some notable feats and have the reputation of being a most difficult side to beat. They dismissed Churt for five in 1938, Eddey taking 7 for 0. He was in fine all-round form that year, capturing 92 wickets and scoring 291 runs for an average of 14. Tilford were out of the competition in 1946 and 1948, and in August of the following year Eddey accomplished a unique feat in I'Anson Cup cricket by taking 10 for 38 against Shottermill. Warner had a wonderful season in 1939. Starting with not out scores of 47, 34 and 82, he made 102 not out against Grayshott and finished with an average of 57.09, the second best ever recorded in the competition.

OVER THE RIVER

The stories about Tilford cricket are countless. Twenty years ago Leslie Wills, batting at the church end, hit a ball clean over the oak and the river and well into the meadow beyond, a tremendous carry never equalled before or since. In 1934 Charles Bonner, who was in the 1910 team and had not played since 1914, turned out against Whitehill at the age of 75. Going in last, he received three balls. 'The first I played, the second I hit for one run and the third I missed. The other man then got out, so I was one not out!' There speaks the spirit of Tilford. R. (Bob) Morris, another member of the 1910 team, still watches the matches, like many another veteran.

The teas served by the ladies of Tilford in pre-war days were a symbol of hospitality remembered with pleasure. The teams sat down together at the well-laden tables and there was no charge to the visitors. The old traditions of entertainment, with tea as a pleasant social interlude, were maintained at Tilford long after other clubs had adopted the principle of a fixed charge per head, or of the players queuing up and each purchasing such refreshment as he required. The latter system may have been more practical, but there could be no doubt that Tilford's method was more in keeping with the spirit of the game. Post-war conditions compelled the club to fall into line with the other villages in that respect, though generous instincts remain.

Tilford's fame has spread even to the New World. For several seasons past one of their keenest spectators has been Grover Higgins, who annually visits this country from the United States. In 1950 he gave the club a subscription of £100 and a further £50 to buy new caps and a flag. The caps are being worn today and the flag, which flies from the Institute, bears symbols marking the unity of the two countries. The Old World and the New, with cricket, reaching out from one of the villages that gave our national game birth, the connecting link; a happy note on which to close this chapter.

Shottermill

'A NEW form of entertainment was provided by several of the Shottermill supporters going through a series of gymnastic evolutions which were meant to be the manifestation of their delight at the result of the match.' The incident thus quaintly described in a contemporary report was on the Haslemere recreation ground in June 1906. Grayshott scored 103 in a cup game and Shottermill replied with 106, ten being needed when the last pair came together. The scene illustrates something of the essential character of Shottermill cricket, the fierce loyalty of the spectators to their own side and the local patriotism of everyone associated with the club. They have no false inhibitions in those parts and they certainly do know how to enjoy themselves. Those acquainted with Shottermill only in recent years, when fortune has not been too kind to them, may be surprised to learn that during their first ten seasons in the competition they won the cup five times and lost it on another occasion after a play-off. Right up to the early thirties they usually finished in the top half of the table and their ability was acknowledged by everyone. In days when most of their matches were away from home their performances were often brilliant and the third and fourth highest totals ever made in a cup match stand to their credit. Latterly, batting has been their weakness, throwing away the advantage gained by good bowling, and this is largely due to the poor wicket on which they have to play.

Shottermill, winners in 1913. Standing, from the left: R. Rapley, G. Woodward, E.G. Ward, C. Rapson, E. Dicker, R.C. Brown, A.F. Riddle, T.J. Larbey. Seated: W. Pullinger, E. Moorey, W. Balchin, G. Knottley (captain), N. Smithers, W. Dale, C. Pescod. On ground: H. Tickner, P. Booker.

THE FEATS OF 'DUKEY'

Their ground was a problem for Shottermill from the very beginning. The story started well back in the last century. A Tilford minute book of 1887 records fixtures with 'Lyon Green', and Lion Green was the home of the Shottermill club when they entered the competition in 1904 with the proviso that all matches were to be played away. Lion Green today is beautifully kept, though too small for cricket, but then it had a fearsome reputation. Despite the condition laid down, Shottermill duly lifted the cup at their first attempt, losing only to Grayshott and clinching the issue at Blackmoor, where Charles Pescod and Ben Bicknell put the home side out for 20 and then made the two biggest contributions to the Shottermill total. The skipper that year was William Balchin, a grand wicketkeeper, who, like 'Dukey' Moorey, previously played for Lynchmere. 'Dukey' was a great character. He told the writer he was so called because his father's name was 'Dukey.' He was famed for his hitting powers, and once drove a ball against the stone wall on the far side of the Hindhead Road at Lion Green. It rolled down to the bottom of Wey Hill and the batsmen ran 15 – there were no boundaries – before 'Dukey' declared that he could run no more. On another occasion he smashed the tiles on the roof of William Simmonds's house, a huge carry. 'Devvy' Rapson, a notable personality, whose little shop is nearby, asserts that once down Hammer way 'Dukey' lifted the ball on to the roof of another house, where it lodged between the chimney pots. It was not 'lost' because it was still visible, boundaries were non-existent and the batsmen ran 99 while a ladder was fetched and the ball retrieved! Be that as it may, 'Dukey' was a prolific scorer and bowled as hard as he hit.

When the cup was presented at the Grayshott dinner in 1904 J.W. Eele, the assistant secretary, was the only Shottermill representative present to receive it, and he told the gathering that the Shottermill players were agreed that two or three of the grounds on which they played were not one whit better than their own. Shottermill celebrated with a concert at the Working Men's Club, R.S. Whiteway being in the chair. The words of J.W. Eele may have had some effect, because in 1905 Shottermill were allowed one or two home matches, and these took place on the Haslemere recreation ground. Under the captaincy of R. (Bob) Rapley, they beat The Bourne, for whom A.J. Stevens made 36 out of a total of 81. Later, after dismissing Headley for 56, Shottermill scored 215, Moorey getting 76 and B. Bicknell 46. In addition, the latter took 7 for 22. Grayshott, previously unbeaten, were defeated by nine wickets in June, and Shottermill finished the season without a reverse. Against The Rest at Grayshott the captain made top score in a total of 110 and the other side were put out for 91. A.E. Kent declared, at the supper which followed the match, that Shottermill won the cup by good fielding and bowling. Among the stalwarts that season were those previously

Charlie ('Devvy') Rapson, a Shottermill character from the club's early days in the competition, with Ron Reynolds, who kept wicket in the 1950s. Reynolds played in goal for Aldershot before being transferred to Tottenham and then to Southampton, where an injury cut short his career. Picture courtesy of Tim Winter, nephew of Charlie Rapson.

mentioned, including 'Devvy' Rapson, a good all-rounder, George Knottley, F. Madgwick and C. Nightingale. Handing the cup to H.J. Rogers at the Grayshott dinner, A.I. Whitaker remarked that few visitors passing the Lion Green would think that was the home of the cricket champions of the district and thereby they might take to heart the lesson that they must always do the best they could with what they had.

ZENITH OF THEIR POWERS

In the following season Shottermill were again unbeaten until they lost to Lynchmere in July, but the cup went to Blackmoor and 1907 was Lynchmere's year. Shottermill did not compete for the next three seasons, although at the Grayshott dinner in 1909 the hope was expressed that as they were to have a new recreation ground they would return to the competition. The new ground, the one on which they still play, was opened in 1910, and the club made a fine comeback in 1911, losing only two games and figuring in an all-day play-off with Churt at Grayshott. Churt won fairly easily. Next year Shottermill were not quite so successful, but it is interesting to recall that A.H. Hartwright assisted them in several matches. The following two seasons saw them at the zenith of their powers. In 1913, led by George Knottley, they lost at home to Tilford, but won the return, dismissing the home side for 82 and making the highest score put together by Shottermill in the competition, 269 for 5. T.J. Larbey *(55)* and W. Pullinger (38) put on *95* for the first wicket. The veteran C. Pescod, a grand all-rounder, made his highest score (107 not out) with a fine exhibition of batting, and this match decided the destination of the trophy. Next week Pescod made 56 and took 6 for 15 in the final match against Haslemere Working Men. Shottermill lost to The Rest at Grayshott. Pescod had a batting average of 33, nearly double that of anyone else, and also took the bowling honours, his 26 wickets costing 2.80 apiece. The cup was retained by Shottermill in 1914, when Knottley was again skipper. Shottermill won a crucial match at Tilford in July, both sides being undefeated at that time. Pescod made 60 against Churt and hit ten fours in his 42 against Grayshott. The match with The Rest was drawn. All the old stagers were still active and the names of Walter Dale, Pelham Booker and Fred Bargery also appeared in the score-book. The story of the early period would not be complete without mention of C.A. Covington, as fine a wicketkeeper as ever donned the gloves.

'DEVVY'S' VERSES

Then came the break caused by the war. The competition was resumed in 1920 and Shottermill were able to call on a fair proportion of those who had served them so well in pre-war days. They were in the running for the trophy, which eventually went to Grayshott. In July, Hindhead were put out for 27 and Shottermill replied with 263 for 6, T.J.

Larbey making 67 and W. Dale (62) and F. Bargery (45) putting on 122 without being separated. Shottermill that year had an Indian student named Balavavj playing for them, and W.A. Penycate did well with both bat and ball. Balavavj, who opened with Larbey, was a marvellous field, like so many of his countrymen, and moved like lightning. The side finished runners-up, a point behind the winners. The 1921 season was another triumph for Shottermill. They won the cup, their only two defeats being at the hands of Whitehill, and their best performance was at Thursley, where they won with ten minutes to spare after being behind on the first innings. Incidentally, 'Dukey' Moorey donned the umpire's coat that year. When Shottermill played The Rest at Grayshott, Penycate took the first eight wickets for 24 and Bargery bagged the other two. The Rest totalled 48 and Shottermill replied with 73, winning by six wickets. Miss I'Anson presented the cup to the acting captain, William Balchin. Larbey headed the batting averages and Penycate was top of the bowling. A smoking concert was held at the Working Men's Club, with Dr C.W. Jenner in the chair and 'Devvy' Rapson enlivened the proceedings by reciting some verses he had written describing the pursuit of the I'Anson Cup. Medals were presented to G. Knottley, W. Balchin, F. Bargery, W. Dale, T.J. Larbey, G. Hilliard, P. Booker, A.G. Riddle, W. Penycate, J. White, T. Cross and J. Judge.

Shottermill remained a great force in the competition throughout the twenties, nearly always finishing high up the table, but as time passed their batting failed to keep pace with their bowling. They were out of the competition in the 1932-35 seasons, and after they came back they were rather less effective than of yore, though always unpredictable opponents, particularly at Shottermill, where they had a matting wicket for a time. It is unfortunate that they have never been able to find a stretch of turf more worthy of their ability and free from the calls of football in winter, though the recreation ground is not without attraction, except on days when the clay clings to the boots. The surroundings are quite pleasant and the outfield has always been cut.

Most clubs have recollections of good games there and of being very hospitably entertained. The frequency of trains passing the southern end of the ground, where a sharp slope makes sight-screens impracticable, is a cause of frequent hold-ups, usually enlivened by real Shottermill witticisms and visiting batsmen welcome a slight breathing space before again facing up to the deadly local deliveries. The Shottermill men know their plantains, and to stay out there long against them a player has to be good. Speaking generally, attack is the best form of defence and most Shottermill batsmen are seldom reluctant to have a go, though a few of them can stonewall with the best.

SIX IN SIX BALLS

Embodiment of the spirit of Shottermill, Tom Larbey has been a great figure in the club for most of their long association with the competition. His playing career spanned the period from before World War One up to the early thirties and his name figured prominently in representative games. He has held most offices, including the captaincy, and his sound advice is listened to with respect. His cap and drooping moustache are still Shottermill landmarks. He seldom misses a home match and there are many who listen to his shrewd observations on the benches under the hedge. He knows what he is talking about, for there was no broader bat in all the competition when he made his deliberate way out to open the innings. Bowlers heaved a sigh of relief if they could get rid of him cheaply, which they rarely did. He had a sound defence and plenty of strokes, with a partiality for the off drive and the cut. His best-remembered shot was a kind of leg cut under an upraised limb, the whole process bearing a marked resemblance to a canine posture. No matter how many men were posted to block it, he got the ball through for at least a couple. It would be hard to compute how many runs he made in his career or to assess the value of his services to the club. Then there was Walter Dale, who for more than a quarter of a century rendered yeoman service in all departments. He knew the virtues of the straight bat, the straight drive and an impeccable length. Captain and mainstay for many seasons, he had a warm welcome in both senses for visitors and his chuckle was good to hear. Deservedly popular, he possessed a cunning cricket brain. Facing him was a battle of wits. He needed no assistance for the bite he got out of the wicket. A couple just outside the leg peg would tempt the unwary to step in front to the next which looked the same as it left his hand, but turned out to be dead on the middle stump and up would go the umpire's finger. Walter would grin and get the next man with a wicked break-back, completing the hat-trick with a cruel shooter that he seemed able to produce at will and without any apparent change in his easy action. His remarkable six in six balls feat against Churt is recorded elsewhere. He was a true artist with no malice in his make-up. There was not much comfort for the batsman if he got to the other end to tackle Wilf Penycate. He, too, gave nothing away and bowled with his head. An early wicket made him absolutely deadly and he was liable to run through a side. Quick and bustling in the field, he turned the ball quite a bit, flighting it skilfully, and his medium pacers brought him a crop of wickets between the wars. He was still to the fore even after the last great conflict, and his annual 'bag' usually passed the 100 mark. He could make the ball do enough to get through the soundest defence, and over many years the entry in the score-book 'b Penycate' bore witness to his ability. He made runs, too, and made them well, using his wrists and feet. A loyal club man and likeable personality, he has done much for the competition. Some of his most valuable work has been in the leadership of the second team, and young players will not go far wrong if they model their methods on his. His son Max, who bats right and bowls left, follows in his footsteps.

ENJOYED THEMSELVES

Shottermill have never lacked good players and colourful personalities. A few minutes' conversation with 'Devvy' Rapson, ever ready to draw on a fund of reminiscence and produce faded scorecards, is a liberal education in local cricket lore. He enjoyed himself in his playing days, and so did his friends. They found plenty to laugh about and every match was a jolly outing. Once they lost a game at Grayshott because one of their side went off to run in a marathon at Shottermill and got back too late to bat; they could even laugh about that. Like other clubs, Shottermill have their cricket families; the Trimmers, for instance, Reg, Neil, Ern and Ron Trimmer all played at one time, and so did their father, William Trimmer, who skippered the side. A glance at the match records reveals what good all-rounders they were, but does not show their chief characteristic: amazingly quick running between the wickets. When in together they backed each other up, and often a defensive push started as a very quick single and finished up with a boundary overthrow. Then the Woodward brothers, George the batsman, Charlie the fast bowler, Dick, and 'Hobbs' the wicketkeeper and batsman. 'Hobbs' Woodward, slightly stooping and contemplative, was perhaps the best of them. A grand man behind the sticks, he was equally effective with the bat, making 47 when he captained The Rest against Whitehill in 1931. Topping the averages seven years later, he scored 79 against Binsted. Next the brothers H.A. (Bert) and A.G. (Alf) Riddle. The former, a consistently good fast bowler over a long period, has been secretary, and a very cheerful and willing one, for a good many years. Alf was wicketkeeper for some seasons. Their father was umpire and scorer. Fred Bargery's formidable fast bowling was a big factor in Shottermill's successes after World War One and he was captain for a time. Tommy Andrews, another former captain and all-rounder, A. ('Jammy') Bartlett, a round-arm bowler and quick runner between wickets – he had a voice like thunder when he appealed – and 'Ginger' Corrigan, wicketkeeper and stubborn batsman, are another notable trio. So many names: Edgar Rapley, a forcing bat who could also keep wicket; Steve Stemp, all-rounder; R. Carter, a keen player and steady bat; Arthur Masey, the 1950 captain, bowling at a tearaway pace and aiming to hit the ball into the next parish; Ron Reynolds, the present wicketkeeper; R. ('Chiller') Hill; W. Stevenson, the most stylish bat of Shottermill's modern generation, who lost a finger in a shooting accident when captain of the side in 1948; R. Bewley; and that consistent pair of trundlers, Percy Francis and Harry Hubbard. Francis and Hubbard bore the brunt of the bowling in recent post-war years, the former quickish and with a long run and nice action, and the latter a master of guileful deception. There have been times at the beginning and end of the season when Shottermill have been able to enlist the services of Haslemere players, among them that fine batsman Tommy Bryant, and Ken Corbett. Shottermill, as a team, have never lacked variety, and they have made a worthy contribution to the history of the I'Anson Cup.

Headley

THE Rectory Field on a hot summer's day, with buttercups thick in the outfield and sloping down to the long, rather narrow table in the centre, The Holme School at the bottom end of the ground and, beyond, the village green and the pine trees rising from the hills with distant cottages barely visible through the shimmering haze. Most cricketers who have visited Headley over the past half-century will recall that picture. And, looking up from the pitch, the old Parish Church in the background with the clock on the tower chiming the hours, the rather unsightly pavilion with players and spectators crowding the verandah, the little teashop behind, with cups tinkling, and Arthur Stevens leaning over the fence of the Holly Bush garden. A familiar scene, completed by the head of Jack Lickfold – he and his brother Fred were both Headley players – standing on the bank beside his garage, peering over the tall holly hedge right behind the bowler's arm; at the other end the magnificent horse chestnut on the boundary, a challenge to every hitter. The game, like the tree, had roots in Headley well over a century ago, and the club is one of the oldest in the district. Until the thirties, old James Marshall sat under the hedge every Saturday notching the runs on a stick, like the pioneers at Hambledon. He had known and played on the Rectory Field far back in the reign of Queen Victoria. Now the chestnut tree is but a memory and the field altered beyond recognition. Headley have a fine new ground off the Lindford Road, better in every way than the Rectory Field, but lacking as yet the greatest of all attributes, tradition.

Headley, winners in 1938. Back, from the left: H.J. Knight (competitions secretary), A.J. Bellinger, R.P.W. Stevens, L.T. Pope, R.W. Johnstone, T. Lemon. Middle: C. Nichols (umpire), H.A.P. Heaslop, F. Dopson, J. Radford, J. Hudson, W. Dunk, W. North, A. Bellinger (secretary). Seated: E. Turner (secretary), F. Courtnage, Capt R.H. Thackeray (president), E. Nash (captain), G.M. Hubbuck (former competitions secretary and Headley player), H. Blanchard, A.J. Stevens (competitions president).

HAPPY HOURS

It is no accident that. Headley figure so largely among the records at both the top and bottom of the scale. Through the years they have astonished their opponents and exasperated their supporters; brilliant one week, the exact opposite the next. They have beaten The Bourne more times than any other team, yet thrice in 10 years they lost a play-off for the cup with that same club. In all their long history they have won the trophy only once, in 1938, when they held together consistently well as a team right through the season. Success has been in their grasp on at least half-a-dozen other occasions, to elude them in the end. In 1950, for instance, they led all the way, capped a series of high scores with 227 against Tilford, and then, a few weeks later, when requiring one point to secure the cup, were tumbled out for eight at Grayshott, going on to be well beaten in the play-off. They have nearly always lacked the little extra something that makes a good side a great one. Few clubs have produced more outstanding players; equally few have failed so signally to weld their talent into a winning team. Despite all that, the men who have played for Headley have spent many happy hours together. There is a charm and attraction about the cricket there not to be measured in words. Probably no village has supplied more men to neighbouring clubs, but, significantly, most of the players who went elsewhere returned at last to Headley, where some games have brought people near to heartbreak and others furnished memories to give pleasure for a lifetime. One of the original five clubs, Headley were in the competition for fewer than half-a-dozen seasons before World War One. The cause was simple. They had military players and the competition has never favoured outside assistance of that kind. So Headley, with characteristic independence, went their own way, but since their return to the fold in 1921 they have never missed a season.

Their leading figure in the early years was C.E. Fraser, a brilliant batsman and fine sportsman, who at one time combined the offices of president, captain and secretary. Elected life president in 1929, he spent his later years on the Continent, but until his death in 1939 he took a keen interest in the club's progress. Charles Courtnage, stubborn opening batsman, played for Headley for over half-a-century, and seldom missed a match until he died in 1950. He had a fine natural dignity and a shrewdness of observation that made him a unique personality on any ground. Most of Headley's rivals in recent years paid him the tribute, when he visited them, of entertaining him to tea. He wore his earrings with an air and his trim, short figure was to the last as straight as his bat in his playing days, and he enjoyed the respect and affection of all who knew him. His son Fred has long been a stalwart all-rounder for Headley. A third name comes to mind, bracketed with the other two, as typifying the best traditions of the club. Ernest Turner was in the village team when illness crippled him for life at the age of 16, but his devotion to the game never wavered. For 50 years he has helped to hold the club together, as permanent scorer and secretary more times than he cares to remember. There was never a more upright character or more loyal supporter, in good days and bad.

THREE HAT-TRICKS IN A MATCH

In Headley's first match in the competition Churt were dismissed for 12, L.L. Rogers taking 8 for 9. Len Rogers holds a record perhaps unique in the annals of cricket. On the Rectory Field in 1895 he did the hat-trick once in the first innings and twice in the second against the Army Service Corps. The visitors chaired him off the field and C.E. Fraser presented him with a silver badge recording the feat. Rogers played for Headley both before and after World War One. Other great figures of the period included L. Bromley, who made top score for The Rest against Shottermill in 1905; A.W. Stevens, a notable bowler and more than useful bat – as mine host of the Holly Bush he still talks knowledgeably about the game; and Sam Brindley, who used to open with Charles Courtnage. The early twenties produced two outstanding bowlers, Harry Blanchard and Colin Nichols, different in temperament, but alike in their deadly skill. The young Harry Blanchard was a devastating fast bowler. When Churt won the cup in 1922 he played for The Rest and took 4 for 8 in a total of 19. In June of the following year he and Nichols dismissed Hindhead for nine, taking 5 for 2 and 5 for 4 respectively. Next month they put Grayshott out for seven (5 for 3 and 4 for 3). Harry Blanchard bowled with his heart and head and his well-remembered mannerisms made him a character not easily forgotten. Through the years he retained his skill to an astonishing degree, capturing many wickets with his well-concealed slower ball. In 1938, Headley's cup-winning year, his 'bag' was 93. Colin Nichols had a beautiful easy action, with perfect flight and length and was seldom mastered. He did the hat-trick against The Bourne in 1927, when Headley beat them, and both he and Blanchard were to the fore in the following year, Headley defeating both Bourne teams on the same day, the first time the feat had been achieved since the war. Nichols topped both the batting and bowling averages that season. He joined Whitehill in 1929, bore a leading part in their 1931 cup success, and at the close of his playing career returned to Headley to become one of the best umpires the competition has had. His brother Roland also assisted Headley for a number of seasons.

FAMILY OF CRICKETERS

George Barlow's career has covered a long span. Always a stylish bat, and a most useful all-rounder in his heyday, there was never a keener player or student of the game. He has played many great innings, and his undefeated century against Thursley in 1930 was the first made by a Headley man in the competition. His elder son, Philip, has also given the club good service for many years. The complete cricketer, he has all the strokes, bowls skilfully and is an admirable field. The younger son, Dennis, showed great all-round promise and had a trial for Hampshire in the late thirties, but the war cut short his career, a sad loss to cricket. Contemporary with V.G. Barlow, and another evergreen veteran, was P.M. Snow, a swerve bowler of more than ordinary ability, who was in Grayshott's 1920 cup-winning team before joining Headley. Wally North, a steady left-hander, with right foot thrust well down the pitch and a leg hit like the kick of a mule, was one of the mainstays of the batting, crowning his career with a century against Grayshott in 1940. Then there were R.H. Curtis, wise in counsel, a sound player, and captain for some seasons; G.M. Hubbuck, mentioned elsewhere; Tom Lemon, a cheerful utility man; Tom White, who could wheel 'em up tirelessly for hours – his son Bob is a useful all-rounder of the present generation; E.J. (Ted) Warner, an admirable treasurer, always willing to complete a team and bowl well when required; and the four village policemen: M.J. Mileham, a useful player before World War One and father of the Whitehill player, W.H. Ballard, a good batsman, C. Willis, an accurate bowler, calm and deliberate in all that he did, and E. King, an all-rounder of uncommon ability.

Other names recalled are the Hudsons: Joe, Hilton and Gordon (was there ever a more silent, likeable player than Joe Hudson?); S.J. Coombes – 'Gunner' used his bat like a flail and achieved remarkable results with his tearaway bowling; Jim Radford, a grand man in a crisis; Percy Watts, with his stentorian appeals; Bill Dunk, a big hitter; E. (Ted) Croucher, a dangerous left-hander on his day; Clare Eiloart, whose appearances were all too fleeting; Claude Triggs; F.G. Pearce, whose profession took him from the district before he reached his peak; The Holme schoolmaster, V.A. Amos, and his assistant, R.P.W. Stevens, who was killed in the last war and has been sadly missed. There was, too, Commander R.H. Stokes-Rees, who, turning out when not running his own team or playing for the Hampshire Hogs and other prominent sides, gave the club an object lesson in polished batting and wicketkeeping. Where he was, laughter and good fellowship were to be found. Equally notable, in a different tradition, was W. Chesham, an old soldier, wily, keen and utterly devoted to cricket, working long hours on the pitch as groundsman and leading the Miller Cup side to victory on Saturdays. Billy Chesham brought up many young players in the way they should go, and his sons, Ted and Derek, have both been successful players for the club.

TOP SCORE WITH ONE HIT

And what of Ernest Nash, skipper in the victory year and for a good many more seasons besides? An enthusiast if ever there was one, a tremendous worker and an expert at holding a side together. In May 1947, Ernie Nash, going in last, achieved the rare feat of becoming top scorer with one hit. Headley had scored 4 for 9, E. Parratt, of Rowledge, having taken 8 for 1, when Nash hit a ball into the long grass and, while the fieldsmen were searching for it, ran five. That rather spoilt Parratt's analysis, but he had 9 for 6 in a total of 11. How many fieldsmen, like the ball, have shot over the edge of Headley's awkward table into the long grass? There was no fluke about the 1938 win. A defeat for The Bourne at Headley after they had led on the first innings – there was only one wicket in it at the finish – set the stage, the 'double' was completed later in the season and the issue clinched with a little in hand. Headley's 279 against Tilford was the second highest total in the competition and H.A.P. Heaslop took part in a stand of well over 100 with Frank Kenward, whose story is told elsewhere. Hal Heaslop, who had a distinguished military career in the last war, was a great asset to his club that year. So was Fred Dopson, who winds his arm before bowling and usually produces a fizzer in each over. His figures over the years speak for themselves, and they would have been even better if he could have cut out the occasional long hop to leg. He had 89 wickets that year; he, Blanchard and Kenward took 237 between them, a near record for three I'Anson bowlers in one season. R.W. Johnstone's fielding was an inspiration, and his untimely death at El Alamein was another loss to the club. Arthur Bellinger, too, played his part. Anchored to the crease by a disability necessitating a runner, he drove with tremendous power, and in 1936 joined the select band of centurions. His father, Archie Bellinger, then treasurer, was one of Headley's most generous supporters. Since the last war Major W.S.H. Garforth, handicapped in a manner similar to Arthur Bellinger, as the result of war service, has given a grand example of courage and skill, and the batting of K.J. Ridgway has been another feature of post-war Headley cricket. Not forgotten is Ernie Arthur, driver of the club's conveyance for many years, and man of all work besides. He never minded taking off his coat to 'sub'.

R.C.B. (Reg) Thackeray, who succeeded his father as president of Headley and was elected a vice-president of the competitions in 1951.

One honoured name remains. Captain R.H. Thackeray, who succeeded C.E. Fraser as president, did much for the club. In the thirties he invited his friends to join him at tea in the Rectory Field and watch the cricket, and the line of cars along the boundary and the increase in the number of spectators, and incidentally, subscriptions, testified to the success of the innovation. Captain Thackeray helped in other ways, too, to make the village more cricket-conscious. After his death his son, R.C.B. Thackeray, took over the presidency to continue a family tradition. A player with a keen sense of humour and remarkable hitting powers on occasion, Reg Thackeray, now a Justice of the Peace, has always enjoyed the game, and such is his height that a bat looks a mere toy in his hand. His voice matches his stature ('Pretty to watch', he roars from the pavilion when one goes off the edge) and it is quite certain that as long as his association with the club continues, Headley cricket will prosper.

The Bourne

DOWN in the hollow the match is on. Along the west side of the recreation ground the crowd, keen critics and students of the game, line the rails bordering the Old Frensham Road, and there are other onlookers with their feet in the sand of Dene Lane away to the east by the Mission Church. Players cluster round the pavilion. Out in the middle the men in the faded blue caps move purposefully towards another victory amid applause and an occasional ripple of laughter. It is a scene which never pales, repeated year by year as The Bourne add further chapters to their fine story. They have won the I'Anson Cup 14 times since 1925. No other club can boast more than five successes in the 50 years. For the greater part of 25 years The Bourne have been the best village team in the locality and far beyond. Their lean seasons have been few, their triumphs almost monotonously regular. Twice they have won the cup four years in succession and their skill has set a standard hard for others to attain. No club can secure the trophy without beating The Bourne and, in fact, only six other villages have gained the honour since 1925. Six times since 1930 The Bourne have been concerned in a play-off and lost but once.

THAT LITTLE EXTRA SOMETHING

How do they do it? Most certainly not by chance. It has been said that they are lucky. If skill can be called luck, then they are lucky; but not otherwise. Their striking successes have come to them, like success in most other fields of human endeavour, through grit and hard work. They have just that little extra something in a crisis that makes all the difference. Never admitting defeat until stumps are drawn, they seldom lose. Others may give up the fight when things are going wrong, but not The Bourne. Every game to them is a friendly battle, calling for the best that is in them, ball by ball. They may relax in the pavilion; when the game is on it is different. See them take the field together, every man in white, each knowing his position and the part he has to play. Watch their batsmen attacking the bowling, secure in the knowledge that if they fail there are equally good men to follow. They look a team in the best sense of the word, and such they are. They carry their successes with modesty and are generous in defeat. Rowledge alone of all their opponents in recent years have completely matched their fighting spirit and skill, and that for two seasons only. So perhaps it is not unfitting that the turf with which the first pitch was laid out on The Bourne recreation ground in 1898 came from Rowledge. In those days the chairman of the committee was George Sturt, perhaps better known under his pen-name of George Bourne. The Bourne were admitted to the competition in 1905, 'subject to their

A view of The Bourne's ground in the early years of the 20th century.

ground being suitable'. Evidently it was suitable, for they duly played that year. They won more games than they lost, their captain, A.J. Stevens, being in fine form and finishing with a batting average of 25. Lewis Ireson, captain later on – he was killed in World War One – topped the bowling, and his brother, Harry Ireson, who also had a spell as skipper, gave the club good service. Among others prominent in the side in the early years were Ted Trimmer – a familiar figure on the recreation ground with his little dog in more recent times – his brother, Bill Trimmer, Harry Purchase – twice joint captain and a celebrated 'character' who played long-stop in a bowler hat and braces – and tall Jim ('Skimmer') Stapley, an all-rounder and another war casualty. His uncle, Stephen Stapley, was secretary for a good many years. Then there were G.E. Chambers, later of Tilford, Charlie West – an excellent wicketkeeper, seven times captain and Arthur Arnold's predecessor behind the stumps – Jim ('Pompey') Fry, Johnny Wells, Ernie ('Curley') Golding, a left-hander, and his brother Tom Golding. William Goodchild, Lewis Goodchild's elder brother who was killed in the war, the brothers Tony and Walter Smith – the latter a wicketkeeper – Johnny Darlow, Harry Brooker, headmaster of West Street School, Farnham, and his assistant, W. Rackham, were also among the early stalwarts. The players travelled to away matches in a two-horse brake driven by Tom Goddard, of the Railway Hotel, Farnham.

'WE DON'T KILL A PIG EVERY DAY'

Surprisingly, in view of their later success, The Bourne did little of note during their first period in the competition. In 1908 they entered a team in the Farnham and District League and withdrew from the competition midway through the season, though they were back again in the following year. That was the season Stephen Stapley resigned the secretaryship which he had held since 1898. He resumed the office for a short period in 1919. The club's name disappeared from the competition in 1910, and they went on to do great things in the Farnham League, twice being champions for four years in succession, before again competing for the I'Anson Cup – and winning it for the first time – in 1925. Their captain when they returned was George Arnold, first appointed in 1921. A shrewd tactician, he was a man of fine character who always laid special emphasis on the team spirit, and both his own club and the competition in general are indebted to him for much of their success. Ever ready to dip his hand into his own pocket for a good cause, he was, and is, a great enthusiast and wise administrator, with a keen sense of humour and a fund of good stories about the game's local personalities. He has held practically every office in the club, including the treasurership, which has been in his hands for many years, and is a steward of the competition. He was a stylish bat and

The Bourne, winners in 1925. Standing, from the left: S. Hine (scorer), A.J. Stevens, J. Martin, E. Thurston, G. Prior, L. Goodchild, A. Moon (umpire). Seated: A. Arnold, E. Beresford, G. Arnold (captain), A.R.T. Baker, H. Culver. On ground: H. Hack, L. Tanner.

good fielder and four times led the team to victory in the competition. He is in his most benign mood after a celebration dinner for, as he explains, 'We don't kill a pig every day'. His brother, Arthur Arnold, who was in the 1925 side with him, was the best wicketkeeper the competition has known in modern times. He did his work without flourish and, standing right up to any type of bowling, could whip the bails off with either hand. A sound right-handed bat, he was also a fine slip field. An enthusiastic and loyal club member, he has been groundsman for many years, an appointment also held for a period by another brother and player, W. (Bill) Arnold. George and Arthur Arnold captained winning teams in both the I'Anson and Miller Cups, a distinction shared by J.G. Caesar. In Arthur Arnold's year of captaincy the First XI averaged 128 runs per innings. Top of the bowling averages in 1925, a feat repeated on many other occasions, was Lewis Goodchild, whose story is told elsewhere. Len Tanner, who headed the batting list, is another bearer of a name famous in Bourne cricket history. A good right-handed batsman and bowler with a nice off-break, he was at one time on the Kent ground staff and has rendered yeoman service to the village club. Cheerful and determined, he would go anywhere for a game of cricket, and retains his ability to an exceptional degree. H. ('Len') Hack, also right-handed, was a very good opening bat and useful change bowler, who played for many years and scored a lot of runs. Harry Culver, the other opening bat in 1925, was a useful all-rounder who later left the district. Andrew Baker's career comes under review in the chapter on Churt, and Joe Martin's longest associations have been with Tilford. Eric Beresford was a useful right-handed bat who bowled a little and is still a spectator at most of the club's matches. Eric Thurston was a good stroke player and sportsman. G. Prior was the brother of E. Prior, a former secretary, who at an earlier date was taken on the Hampshire ground staff on the recommendation of

The Bourne, winners in 1930. At this time the club had withdrawn their first team from the competitions and the second XI had moved into the I'Anson Cup. The captain, Sid Briggs, is seated to the right of E.M. Sprot, the president. The wicketkeeper is Bill Poulter, whose son Michael was to take up the gloves and grandson Neil is the current custodian. Bill Poulter died, aged 89, in February 2002.

J. Broadwood. A good player, he afterwards joined the Hampshire police, and now lives in retirement at The Bourne. The 1925 umpire was Alf Moon, a useful player in his day, and the scorer then and for many other seasons was Sid Hine. His successor, F. ('Nobby') Clark occupied the scorer's table until recent times.

THROUGH THE YEARS

In 1925 E.M. Sprot, former Hampshire captain, became president of the club and continued in office until his death 20 years later. The pavilion on the recreation ground was opened in 1926, when the club again won the cup. The match with The Rest at Grayshott – The Bourne won the previous year's encounter – was abandoned as a draw when F. Bargery, of Shottermill, was unfortunately injured by the ball. The Bourne secured the cup for the third time in 1927, The Rest being soundly beaten, and G. Arnold again led them to victory in the following year, when, for the first time, the Winners v Rest match was played away from Grayshott. Mrs F.C.D. Haggard presented the trophy at The Bourne, where The Rest were heavily beaten and The Bourne's total of 217 stood as a record for many years. In his four years of successful captaincy, G. Arnold received the cup from a different person on each occasion; in 1925 from A.I. Whitaker, in 1926 from Miss I'Anson, sister of the donor, and in 1927 from the Revd E. Garth Ireland. The club acquired their blue caps in 1928, the year the president gave them sight-screens on wheels. The Bourne withdrew their First XI from the cup in 1929 to play non-competitive matches and the former Miller Cup side went into the I'Anson. They did not win, but lifted the trophy under the captaincy of S. Briggs in 1930, after a play-off with Grayshott at Churt. The next few seasons were rather poor ones by Bourne standards. They again started to run teams in both competitions in 1931, and S. Briggs led the senior side to success in a play-off with Rowledge at Churt in 1934. That started another four-year cycle of victory and in 1937 both trophies were won, as they had been in 1927-8. There was another innovation, a game between the First and Second XIs, instead of the customary Winners and Rest match in 1937.

The Bourne's next cup-winning year was 1939, and they beat Headley in a play-off at Frensham in 1940. Six years later, when the competition was resumed after the war, they won again, lost a play-off with Rowledge at Grayshott a year later, beat Headley in a play-off at Rowledge in 1948, and again captured the cup in 1950 after their third successful play-off with Headley. They have accomplished so much that it is impossible to deal with all their achievements in detail. Club and individual feats which would be very notable in other villages have been almost commonplace to them.

UP THE LAMP POST

Great of heart and small of stature, Sid Briggs – sometimes known as 'Tiggy' – was an outstanding player for a long period. At number 11 he probably holds the record for not out innings. There were few better right-hand bowlers and he had a long tally of wickets in both the I'Anson and Miller Cups. In 1938 he and Goodchild captured 196 wickets between them. He was a captain who never lost his head, and it was typical of him that, going in last, he made the only double-figure score – 10 not out – in the four innings of the memorable 1934 play-off with Rowledge. He did not take his pleasures sadly, and was once discovered, after celebrating the winning of the cup, perched on top of a lamp post grasping the trophy he had done so much to win! His brother, Freddie Briggs, was an exceptionally good fielder. Contemporary with Sid Briggs was A. ('Bandy') Crow, the second best all-rounder The Bourne has produced – and they are noted for their all-rounders. When he opened the innings he gave the impression that he intended to stay there, and usually he did. His powerful forearms enabled him to crack the ball with tremendous force, and he had a terrific square cut. Always looking for runs, he was not afraid to go out to drive, and his defence was very sound. He was, too, a cunning slow bowler, with the ability to hold one back and to produce a special ball in a crisis. In the field he had few superiors, especially close in. Crow hit seven sixes in making 92 against Whitehill in 1929, and in the following year he missed a century by only one run at Grayswood. That season he headed the averages with 507 runs and took 70 wickets. In 1935 he scored 119 at Whitehill, totalling 358 runs that season and capturing 70 wickets. Since the war he has played for Rowledge. E.W. (Ted) Newman, secretary for many years past, was an efficient right-hand opening bat and left-arm bowler, an excellent worker in a quiet way, a former steward, and now a most capable umpire. Henry Hewitt was an occasional umpire and, while on the subject, mention must be made of the high standard set by a recent wearer of the white coat, Stan Ellis, whose judgment is excellent. Jack Knight, a good all-rounder with a powerful drive, gave up playing for The Bourne much too soon. Fred Hazell, who left the neighbourhood when in his prime, was a good right-hand bat and fielder. Ernest Wakeford, of an earlier day, was a batsman who continued to be an excellent supporter of the club after his playing days were over. Alf Parsons was a useful all-rounder, Ernie Wells, a powerful hitter, played regularly for some years, and Albert Yarney, a good all-rounder, was a brother of John Yarney, Tilford's talented left-hander. Fred Beagley was a steady bat and wicketkeeper, 'Snowy' Audsley a hard-hitting batsman and Bill Audsley a fast bowler. W. Hampton was a very strong hitter, and R.C. (Bob) Radford, now a member of Farnham Urban Council, was a good bat who afterwards gave long service to Hale. V.E.D. Haggard, who just failed to get into the team at Winchester and narrowly missed his blue at Cambridge, was an elegant forcing bat and fast bowler. J.O.J. Stevens, who was in the team at Eton, also played for the club on occasion. Son of A.J. Stevens, he was a fine batsman and gave up the game on account of the calls of business.

AN OUTSTANDING PLAYER

The outstanding Bourne cricketer of recent years and the most consistent and prolific scorer the competition has seen is W. (Bill) Poulter, whose I'Anson Cup career extends back over 20 years. When it comes to run-making, there is a touch of Bradman about him. He reaches 50 and settles down for the 100 – he has made more centuries in the competition than any other player – and had time permitted, doubtless he would have compiled even higher scores. He has an air of assurance at the wicket all his own and hits the ball very hard. Even his defensive strokes are made forcefully. In his best form he can completely demoralise a fielding side with the rate of his scoring. The appendix shows the number of times his average has passed the 30 mark; and it has to be remembered that few players average even 20 in the competition. The full record of his feats would entail a separate chapter. The details of his five centuries up to the end of the 1950 season will be found later. His highest aggregate was 699 in 1938 and his best average 37.82 the following year.

He has made many scores of between 50 and 100. The better the bowling the better he plays. His technique is sound, he has a stroke for every ball, and he picks the right ball to hit. If the situation demands it, he can play a defensive innings as well as anyone, and is at his best in a tight corner. His bat looks to fieldsmen to be as broad as a barn door, and when, rarely, he chances to send a catch in their direction the ball is travelling so hard that seldom can they hold it. There have been few better wicketkeepers to any type of bowling than Poulter. His taking of the ball on the blind side was masterly, and he was quite fearless. He can field with distinction in any position. In the thirties he played for the West Surrey village clubs against the East Surrey clubs at the Oval, when West Surrey, under the captaincy of V.F. Ealand, won for the first time. Poulter made 82 not out, the highest individual score. In 1949 an accident at work cost him the partial loss of the sight of one eye, and it seemed that his playing days were over. He was out of the game for a season, but with remarkable tenacity and courage he made a comeback and was soon batting with all his old skill, though he no longer keeps wicket. A capable captain, he has led the side to victory in the competition twice since the war. He has by no means passed the peak of his ability with the bat, and it is safe to say that he will delight The Bourne supporters with many more runs and probably create new records.

RECORD CENTURY

E. ('Croppy') Poulter, Bill Poulter's brother, would be a good all-rounder in any village side. He bats and bowls well and fields splendidly, all with cheerful assurance that becomes more pronounced the lower he pulls his cap. Jim Voller, an opening batsman with a very nice style, has made a lot of runs since the war. Though not blessed with a long reach, he punches the ball very hard and, when well set, takes a deal of shifting. He made 85 not out against The Rest in 1946, and his 141 not out at Shottermill in the following summer is the competition's highest individual score. He reached his century with three consecutive fours and altogether hit four sixes, a five and 16 fours. Later that season he and H.C. Bicknell enabled The Bourne to declare at 158 for 0 against Headley. 'Micky' Bicknell, fair-haired and cheerful, made a century that day, and in 1938 he also reached three figures against Binsted in the Miller Cup, in which centuries are rare. He is also a good opening bowler. The other opener of the attack is fast bowler Frank Cordier, who runs up like a happy, stampeding camel. He gets a crop of wickets and deserves them, for there is no more willing and cheerful trier. He regularly 'retires' at the end of each season, but turns up again in the spring. Charlie Spender gave useful all-round service for several seasons after the war. J.G. (Dick) Caesar, who bears a name famous in the early annals of cricket, was skipper of the side that won the 1948 play-off. Many hold the opinion that it would be impossible to find a better captain. He knows the game from A to Z, has done much for cricket, and is a former steward of the competitions. He now leads the Miller Cup team. H.J. Knight, the 1950 wicketkeeper, bears comparison with any of his predecessors. His namesake, George Knight, quiet and unassuming, is a keen all-rounder with plenty of 'ginger' in his play and complexion. Ken Bicknell, who has also kept wicket, is potentially a very good player, and R. ('Patsy') Bridger fields well in any position, bowls medium-pace off-breaks with marked effect, and can hit very hard. He made 98 in the second innings of a cup match a few years ago. Dr John Seddon's batting is always a pleasure to watch, correct and effective. His bat is very straight and he gets his head right over the line of the ball. A former Leeds University player, he was Bourne skipper in 1949. Possessing a good range of strokes, he headed the averages in 1950 and his style is a model for any young player. John Stonard bids fair to become one of the leading players of the future. A left-handed batsman and bowler – a rarity at The Bourne – he has captured many wickets, especially since he changed from round to over the wicket, and batsmen find it difficult to score off him. E. (Ted) Warner is an all-rounder of whom the best has yet to be seen, and Charlie and Fred LeClercq have both done enough to show that their ability is in the true Bourne tradition. Ron Hole, left arm round the wicket and useful with the bat, can be relied upon when a special effort is needed. Harold Arnold, son of George Arnold, is a left-handed bat and an excellent field with big potentialities. Young and talented is John Tanner, son of Len Tanner, a right-hand bat and slow bowler with a bright future. Graham Elsmore would have done extremely well as a batsman had he been more consistent, and was a useful change bowler. He now lives in Scotland. Joe Rivers, always willing at short notice to fill a gap in the First XI, must not be forgotten. Such good sportsmen are the backbone of any club.

The Bourne, winners in 1950. Standing, from the left: F. Hole (Rowledge, umpire), F. Clark (scorer), F. Cordier, H.J. Knight, G. Elsmore, J. Stonard, E.W. Newman (secretary), J. Miles (Tilford, umpire). Seated: J. Tanner, Dr J. Seddon, E. Poulter, W. Poulter (captain), J. Voller, G. Knight, R. Hole.

MANY SUPPORTERS

The Bourne have no keener supporter than their president, the Revd Æ.H. Hudson, once a player himself, whose genial and friendly personality makes him an admirable chairman at the annual dinner. His witty speeches strike just the right note in any sporting gathering, and he follows the fortunes of the club with real interest. Another enthusiast was G.W. Chennell, former headmaster of The Bourne School, who was chairman of the club for a lengthy period around the beginning of the century, and Frank Turner is remembered as the organiser of several social functions for the funds. The list of those who have worked in the cause of cricket at The Bourne could be continued indefinitely. There are few residents who, at one time or another, have not taken more than a passing interest in the club, and therein may be found part of the secret of success. All the other clubs in the competition are indebted to The Bourne for the high standard of play and sportsmanship they have so consistently maintained, and local pride in their achievements is shared by many whose allegiance lies with other teams. The true spirit of cricket is safe in their keeping.

Thursley

ONE of the most attractive villages in the competition, Thursley lies among the foothills of Hindhead, set above the surrounding countryside, beautiful, remote and very English. Here agricultural land blends with the commons and the cricket ground, where the game has been played for close on a century – there is a minute book going back to 1865 – is a natural arena commanding extensive views. Crooksbury Hill, in the distance, dominates the valley below. The soil is sandy and quick-drying and the altitude tends to keep the rain away in summer, with the result that often play is possible at Thursley when the heavens weep over the lowlands, blotting them from sight. The boundaries are rather short in three directions, particularly by the road. The ball has been known to drop first bounce on to the highway and go rolling down the steep and winding hill as far as the stream several hundred yards away. A drive along the carpet in the same direction is killed by thick heather well short of the boundary, and there are frantic scurryings by the fieldsmen to find the elusive leather while batsmen tear madly up and down the pitch with a wary eye on the operations, well knowing that sudden discovery of the ball will probably mean a run out. That's just part of the fun of cricket at Thursley, where the players never take themselves too seriously and laughter and good fellowship mean more than points, though no game is ever given up for lost until stumps are drawn. The Thursley team have a well-deserved reputation for sportsmanship and members of other clubs look forward to their annual visit. For many years before the last war the village was the home of Sir John Squire, the eminent author, poet and critic, whose writings have a special charm. He lived at Bowlhead Green and, as the founder of the Invalids, a noted team of literary cricketers, it was not surprising that he took an interest in the Thursley club. He played for them in a few matches and local men were sometimes in his own team.

WHEN THEY WON THE CUP

One of the most remarkable features of Thursley cricket has been the way in which a small village, where the limited employment available leads to the migration of the young men, has managed to turn out a team, and sometimes two, year after year. There were times when the struggle was temporarily given up, but not for long, and soon the flag would be flying again. For generations the game has revolved round one family, the Rapleys, and in V.C. Rapley, whose story is told in another chapter, Thursley produced one of the finest all-rounders in the district. His father, M.C. Rapley, captained the club for many years, being followed in that office by another son, M.L. (Lionel) Rapley, who was skipper in the cup-winning year. Lionel Rapley was a good slow leg-break bowler and a very useful bat. Thursley came into the competition in 1921 and soon made their mark. Three years later they lifted the trophy, losing only one match. Lionel Rapley led them splendidly, heading the bowling averages and batting well, and V.C. was in brilliant form, scoring a century and taking many wickets. A cousin, Felix Rapley, gave useful assistance as a steady bat. Henry Rushbrooke opened the innings with V.C. making a lot of runs. In one match the opening pair put on 84. Henry Rushbrooke's brother John was also a run-getter and both were brilliant in the field. A third brother, Lt-Col. W.P.H. Rushbrooke, has been president of the club for many years, as his father, Captain W.H. Rushbrooke, was before him, and the village owes much to this Cosford family. Colonel Rushbrooke, who played occasionally for the club, though not in cup matches, has always taken a keen and generous interest in the game, and his tall figure is part of the Thursley landscape on match days. Henry Swallow, the schoolmaster, was wicketkeeper in 1924. He afterwards went to Witley School, and still lives in that village. Others in the side included Bob McCullough, a useful all-rounder, who emigrated to the United States, Fred Howard, George Warner and Tom Wisdom, a good left-hand round-the-wicket bowler, who later lost his life in a motor-cycling accident. He once took five Headley second innings wickets in five balls, fetching Geoffrey Hubbuck back post-haste from feeding his poultry! His cousin Charlie was very handy with the bat, and Charlie's father (another Charlie) was the 1924 umpire. The scorer was H.S. Tozer, Thursley's sub-postmaster for many years.

Thursley, winners in 1924. Standing, from the left: C. Wisdom, F. Howard, H. Rushbrooke, C. Wisdom jnr, J. Rushbrooke, G. Warner, F. Rapley, H.S. Tozer (scorer). Seated: R. McCullough, M.L. Rapley (captain), T. Wisdom, V.C. Rapley, H. Swallow.

NOTABLE PLAYERS

Thursley did not again touch that peak, but they have put up some notable performances through the years and their players have made an impression on the competition. There was, for instance, Lt-Col. G.E. Badcock, RASC, captain of the Bordon Officers, who lived at Thursley and assisted the local team whenever he could. His batting was strong and elegant and he was a guileful slow bowler. Ben Wonham, the present sub-postmaster and proprietor of the village stores, was in the Churt 1922 cup-winning team, and his batting served Thursley well in after years. The names come swiftly to mind – A.J. (Jim) Edwards, stalwart secretary for a couple of decades; the present secretary, W.J. (Jack) Norman, a cheerful player and methodical and tireless worker, always on hand at representative matches and on other occasions when assistance is needed; bespectacled Ern Ware, carefully playing several balls and then suddenly lashing a six and piling up the runs; and Jim Gale, by contrast a stone-waller and left-arm bowler.

Then that happy Scot, Jock Davidson, keeping his end up with the bat and trundling steadily with native canniness. He had the pleasure of leading the team to victory in the Miller Cup in 1947. His son Alastair, a fine bat and good bowler, is now in the RAF. Also not forgotten is A.

Bert Williams was for many years Thursley's groundsman and umpire, having been a player from 1925-49. His wife Nellie prepared the teas from 1938 and their son David played from 1947, and was a member of the team that dominated the I'Anson Cup at the start of the 1970s. In July 1973, on his 70th birthday, Bert was presented with a cake made and iced in the form of Thursley cricket ground, complete with pitch, balls, stumps, roller, two rabbits and Bryan Karn's dog! Bert's daughter Mary was married to the late Ron Rapley, and their son Barry keeps alive the names of these two great Thursley cricketing families. Picture courtesy of Eddie Gale, whose death occurred as this book was being produced.

Bundy, the village policeman, who made a lot of useful scores in the past few years. In 1946 he shared in a century partnership with V.C. Rapley against Whitehill, his score being 61. A slow bowler, he also kept wicket. Frank Keen, who combined the roles of wicketkeeper and hitter, and Jack Keen, useful with the ball; A. Ayres, a very keen player in his day; Fred Fosberry, present landlord of The Three Horseshoes – a pull-in favoured by cricketers – a former secretary who has made some shrewd blows with the bat; and W. Housden, another innkeeper – he was at The Red Lion before the war – are others in the list. Housden, who had played very good cricket in his time, had plenty of strokes. He also had his own theories about bowling to a field, packing the on side and sending down accurate slow leg-breaks until the batsman, hitting out in desperation, duly paid the penalty. E. (Ted) Winter, a good batsman and bowler, is another valuable member of the side, like E. Voller – a good bat – C. Karn, R. Gillard and Jim Gale, whose old father, Arthur Gale, has long been one of the team's most faithful supporters. The father has never been known to miss a match. Ever ready with a word of encouragement, when a young boy plays for Thursley for the first time he offers him sixpence for every run scored, a valuable inducement to those hoping to win their spurs. Talking of supporters, a keen and regular spectator is the present vicar (the Revd H.G. French).

CHIP OF THE OLD BLOCK

Happily, there are young players in the Thursley team and they bear honoured names. One of the best of them is R.C. Rapley, V.C.'s son, a real chip of the old block, with fine flowing strokes and a tendency to rashness which time will cure. When he is seeing the ball well the runs soon come and he is also very quick in the field and a capable bowler. Another of the younger generation is the 1950 vice-captain, Albert Rapley, a batsman and bowler of ability, and son of Felix Rapley. His brother Wally now plays for Elstead.

This chapter began with a reference to a literary figure. Another, who works in a rather different medium, ends it. The 'thrillers' of John Creasey are enjoyed by thousands who perhaps know nothing of his other great interest, cricket. Coming to Thursley a few years before the last war, he took a tremendous interest in the club and was appointed captain and secretary. He set about raising funds for a new pavilion to replace the old thatched structure which, facing the elements on the edge of the bluff, had done duty for many years. His initiative and drive resulted in the necessary sum being obtained – he was himself a generous subscriber – and in 1939 the new pavilion was up and in use. There was always a flutter of interest when John Creasey arrived on the ground in a large chauffeur-driven car and those who had known him previously only through his books found that he possessed a fine sporting instinct as well as an inventive mind. He thoroughly enjoyed his cricket and was very popular with the players. There was general regret when he had to leave the district just before the war on account of his wife's health. He now lives at Bournemouth, but it is a safe conjecture that he has not forgotten Thursley. The old pavilion, used as a store-shed, was burned down during the war, but its successor remains a permanent memorial to the man who did so much to bring it into being.

Frensham

'PLAY the game as men' was the motto on the Frensham fixture cards at the beginning of the century, and that was the guiding principle of those early stalwarts. In the nineties the Pierrepont Cricket Club flourished under the patronage of the lord of the manor, Richard Henry Combe, father of the Richard Combe who was for so many years the Frensham president. What may be termed the modern club was formed in 1900 and for a time played in a field belonging to Morton Latham on the Hollowdene Estate. Later they moved to Pierrepont and entered the I'Anson Cup competition in 1902, largely on the initiative of the schoolmaster, W.H. Gower, who was then secretary. They had three seasons in the competition, and in 1903 opposed Blackmoor in the famous high-scoring match referred to earlier in the book. When Gower left the district Frensham withdrew from the competition, and for many years afterwards were in the Farnham and District League.

The Chuter family have always been prominently associated with the club, and in the early days one of the outstanding members was T.H. (Tom) Chuter, a clever slow bowler, useful bat and splendid field. He was captain for nearly 20 successive seasons, excluding the war years, and treasurer from 1901 until 1936, serving the club loyally and well in all three capacities. His brothers Harvey and George also played for a period, and his nephews, W.A.J. Chuter and J.A.L. Chuter, have carried on the family tradition and both captained the club. Skipper in 1902 was Harry Newman, father of C.J. Newman, who was in the Frensham XI 30 years later, and in the following year W.H. Bailey, sound batsman and good field, took over the reins. Tom Chuter began his long tenure of the office in 1904. Among others in the team during that period were Jack Aslett, batsman and bowler; Arthur Gibbons, left-arm bowler and batsman; Frank Hiscock, another all-rounder; the brothers Ernie and Edgar Fulbrook – the latter a big hitter; and PS Matthews, a pillar of the law.

'HE'S COMING ROUND AGAIN'

Tom Chuter tells a good story of one of those veterans, long since passed away, who, in the hostelry after the match was wont to buttonhole him with the remark, 'I don't want to praise anybody or run anybody down, Tom, but I reckon you and me were two of the best there today'. We have from the same source an amusing sidelight on the hospitality dispensed by the squire of Grayshott on big match days. 'When we sat down to a meal during the game we were waited on by the butler and footmen,' Tom Chuter recalls. 'The beer was brought round in jugs and as one of our men saw more refreshment approaching he used to nudge me and say, "Drink up; he's coming round again". '

Frensham, winners in 1932. Standing, from the left: H. Newman (umpire), A. Cox, H. Holdaway, W.A.J. Chuter, H.J. Knight, A.F. Swan, L. Bell (secretary). Seated: C.J. Newman, J.G. Caesar, G. Alder (captain), F. Farr, C. Jarrett, J. Farr.

When Frensham returned to the competition in 1932 they won the cup with bowling and fielding of a standard seldom if ever excelled locally. Their batting was rather uncertain, but a score of round about 50 usually proved sufficient. It was not so much a case of making runs as saving them. Nothing was given away; no loose balls, no catches put on the carpet, not a return fumbled. Many batsmen were run out in dazzling fashion. The whole performance was an object-lesson in grand team-work. They began with a score of 146 for 8 declared against Hindhead – who withdrew later in the season – and put their opponents out for 43. Then they drew at Headley and, by a curious twist of fortune, the Hampshire club had to wait six years before they took another point from Frensham. Defeat by The Bourne, who dismissed them for 16, a draw with Whitehill, and another defeat at Tilford, for whom M.W. Payne made 57, put Frensham well in the lower half of the table, but they rallied magnificently and won their last eight matches off the reel. They scored 120 at The Bourne and in a crucial game at Pierrepont beat Tilford by four, dismissing two of the visitors, including Payne, in the first over. They finished the season by defeating The Rest and the Lady Constance Combe presented the well-earned trophy to Guy Alder.

LEAPT OVER THE SEATS

The club's president, Richard Combe, gave a dinner at The Mariners Inn to celebrate the event, and this was just one more instance of the practical interest he took in the game.

Millbridge, Frensham, looking towards Tilford, in the early years of the 20th century. I'Anson Cup cricketers have passed this way for one hundred years.

Always delighted to see Frensham playing at Pierrepont, he and the Lady Constance often watched the home matches, and their appearance at the front door of the mansion, framed by two huge china dogs which have long since disappeared, is an abiding memory. The ground, framed by the trees of the park, had a most attractive approach and setting. There was no pavilion and tea was served in a thatched barn nearby. The wicket might be described as sporting; in other words, a real knuckle-rapper. The springy turf concealed small stones and the local rabbits were in the habit of getting to work just where the ball pitched. On the other hand, there were no boundaries to hamper the batsman. It was a case of all run as the ball sped off past the pump – still a mournful sentinel brooding over past glories – and away into the blue. In another direction fieldsmen had to leap like gazelles over the seats occupied by spectators. A lengthy innings at Pierrepont was a true test of courage, and it could be fun, too, for the Frensham men were always good sportsmen.

Guy Alder, the 1932 captain, was a real live wire, intensely absorbed in every shift and turn of the game. He handled his side well, set them an excellent example in the field, and was a very good change bowler. The spearhead of the attack was A.F. ('Driver') Swan, a deadly fast bowler with a vicious nip from the pitch. His power came from his shoulders, and in his prime he would almost knock the bat from a man's hands. His length was perfect, he bowled to hit the stumps and he could maintain his hostility for an indefinite time. There was no question of wearing him down on any wicket that gave him the slightest help. Of a quiet and sunny disposition, he appealed seldom, and with reluctance and was popular with everyone. His grin when he had beaten and bowled a stubborn opponent was delightful to see and his apology for the occasional bumper caused by the wicket was invariably genuine. A true sportsman and a great bowler.

Hardly less deadly, in a different way, was W.A.J. (Bill) Chuter, chief executioner at the other end. Medium-paced right hand, he studied the batsman and bowled with his head and to his field, skilfully varying flight and pace, quick to exploit a weakness and getting through an over more rapidly than any other bowler in the competition. He was, too, the mainstay of the batting, the one Frensham player to finish the 1932 season with a double-figure average. Moving his feet well, and with a good half-cock defensive stroke for the really dangerous ball, he was always looking for runs. It is wrong to write of him in the past tense, for after nearly 20 years he is still all these things, Frensham's mainstay past and present. There have not been many better all-rounders, and certainly none more heart and soul in the game. He is the only Frensham player who has made a century in the competition, 100 not out in a total of 192 for 8 declared at Whitehill in 1936. He won a bat given by Frank Moulding for that feat, and H.J. Knight (57) shared in a stand of well over 100. Year after year Bill Chuter gets an impressive quota of runs and wickets and, bearing in mind that there have been seasons when he has had to play practically a lone hand in both departments, his consistency has been astonishing. It is a fair comment that if he could have batted and bowled at both ends – and he would have been willing to try – Frensham would have won the cup more than once. Yes, he certainly deserves a paragraph to himself.

LIGHTNING RETURNS

The 1932 wicketkeeper was H.J. Knight, who stood up to all the bowlers, including Swan, and once actually brought off a stumping from one of his fastest deliveries. Quick and skilful, he was sound in all he did. He, like Chuter, has retained his form through the years and kept finely for The Bourne when they won the cup in 1950. He has also played some very useful innings and his batting is better than he thinks. J.G. ('Dick') Caesar, who also performed behind the sticks at one time, was brilliant at cover in 1932 and achieved a number of run-outs with his lightning returns. He opened the innings that year and when firmly set was most difficult to dislodge. He was, and is, a grand worker behind the scenes. A. (Cliff) Cox, formerly of Whitehill, was a hard hitter, sound field and more than useful change bowler, keen enough to cycle over from Longmoor for the matches. He made top score in the vital match with Tilford. His namesake, F. Cox, was a left-handed batsman. B.J.E. ('Sammy') Veale, a steady bat, and his brother Christopher, a fast bowler, were assets to the team, and, like their father, E.W. Veale, one of the vice-presidents, devoted to the game. Another valued member of the side was Freddie Farr, all rounder and fine field, later killed tragically in a motor-cycling accident, and his brother Jack also played. Then there were Cliff Jarrett, a nice bat, Sid Dadson a former wicketkeeper, who often roared up on his motorcycle at the last minute cheerfully to fill a gap; Tom Chuter, whose mobility did not seem to diminish with the passing of time; and H. (Bert) Holdaway, the safest of fields, who took many a skier out by the pump. He would have made a lot more runs if he could have curbed his desire to have a go too soon, and he has played some good innings on occasion. Jack Stock, a cheerful trier who afterwards played for The Bourne, Jack Ralph and C.J. ('Gussie') Newman, who died young as the result of an accident on the football field, were others of the period. Secretary and umpire in 1932, and for a number of years afterwards, was Lawrence Bell, whose cap – set at a jaunty angle – plus-fours and shooting stick were seen on most grounds. He had decided ideas on the proper conduct of the game, and a brusque manner of speaking which failed to conceal a kindly spirit and real love of cricket. He did much for the Frensham club and his advice was eminently sound.

HAPPY GRIN

There have been some colourful personalities at Frensham; for example, Andrew ('Lurcher') Parratt, a tricky slow bowler and big hitter. His son Bernard was an opening bat. There was no keener player in the years before the war than F.W. ('Sweat') Parratt, whose round-arm fast deliveries, sent down with a happy grin, often scattered the stumps. Ben Hopwood was a nice bat, E.G. (Eddie) Glynn had some attractive strokes and Leslie Pink, who bowled left-arm round the wicket, once took 5 for 5 at The Bourne; he lost his life in the war. Others who come to mind include W. Norton, W. Powis, who can make runs and keep wicket, J.A.L. Chuter, a sound bat and good captain, C. Badland, R. Fathers, the brothers B. and D. Wells, Dennis Searle, Desmond Hopkins, whose good style would have paid higher dividends on a better wicket, K. Goldsmith, wicketkeeper, R. Hutchings, a bowler always liable to run through a side, and V.W. Croucher, a left-handed stone-waller. Croucher, formerly of Binsted, has monumental patience and turns the ball a lot when he bowls.

The cup has not returned to Frensham since 1932, but they have often surprised the leading teams, and lack of success has been no bar to the players' enjoyment. In 1934 they beat Whitehill after being put out for 16 in the first innings. In that year, too, they were twice beaten by Oakhanger with identical scores, 39 to 24, and the same bowlers took the wickets in both matches. The club scored 202 against Churt in 1938. There was a droll incident in 1947. Both Frensham and Grayshott thought their first team were playing away and acted accordingly, with the result that on both grounds the I'Anson and Miller Cup teams were ready to do battle with each other. The captains conferred by telephone and decided that the game at Frensham should be regarded as the I'Anson fixture. The two First XIs, not unexpectedly, won.

When the last war broke out Frensham moved to Hollowdene, a recreation ground acquired some years previously through the farsightedness of H.J. Baker, joint author of *Frensham Then and Now*. After the war strenuous efforts were made to improve the pitch and an ambitious levelling scheme, still in process of completion, greatly extended the playing area. This has naturally resulted in a good deal of improvisation, including a matting wicket over grass on the football field in 1949, but the ultimate result should well justify the temporary inconvenience. Two essentials previously lacking are now in sight, a good wicket and a pavilion, and with those advantages Frensham will doubtless again become a formidable power in the cricket world.

Rowledge

THE cricketers of Rowledge, with their distinctive red and black caps, have twice won the I'Anson Cup since the war. Those successes are fairly recent history, but the club is a very old one, with roots deep in the past. A Tilford minute book of 1886 records fixtures with Rowledge, and the game has been played in this Hampshire and Surrey border parish for many generations. Since 1924 Rowledge has been part of the Farnham urban district, but there is nothing urban about its cricket, which, in fact, has a strong rural flavour. The county boundary runs by the recreation ground, and before that ground was opened in 1914 the club played their matches at Holt Pound, close by the Forest Inn, on one of the oldest pitches in the country. Rowledge recreation ground has changed but little with the years. The present pavilion was erected in 1924, and before that the scorers sat under the oak trees on the north side. There is a definite 'atmosphere' about the ground on match days, with children enjoying the swings at the west end, tennis in progress on the hard courts to the east, and the spectators clustered on the other two sides. The men playing bowls near the pavilion are mostly old cricketers, and also pause to watch. No one can be in any doubt as to which club the onlookers support, and they are very ready with comments and advice, all given in good part. Both spectators and players enjoy their cricket and there is seldom a dull moment when Rowledge are batting, for they never were a side to sit on the splice. 'Get on with it, or get out' might well be their motto. Most of the players are all-rounders and their bowling is always good. Visitors find run-getting no easy matter against a team who play hard and keenly, giving nothing away. The quality of the wicket sometimes varies with the weather, but it is usually good for runs and is well looked after, like the close-mown outfield. Now the long-contemplated extension of the ground is an accomplished fact and football will no longer be played over the cricket square. This is bound to benefit the summer game, notwithstanding the loss of some of the trees and the shade they provided on a really hot day. The groundsman for many years was Bert Raggett, who was succeeded by his son Alec.

LIKE A PAGE FROM NATURAL HISTORY

Rowledge first applied for admission to the competition as long ago as 1907, but were unsuccessful, as their ground was considered unsuitable. They played in the Farnham and District League for many years and eventually entered the competition in 1932. They did nothing of note in the first two seasons, but in 1934 won their last nine matches in a row to qualify for a play-off with The Bourne at Churt. The game went to four innings, and in gathering darkness The Bourne won by 27, despite some fine bowling by the Rowledge skipper, Reg Crumplin, who took 7 for 10 in the second innings. The scores were remarkably low, 46 and 21 by the winners and 25 and 15 by the losers. The Rowledge team, in order of batting, was: E.R. Parratt, G. Boxall, W. Parratt, N. Miles, A. Parratt, F. Parratt, S. Miles, R. Crumplin, W. Thomson, C. Nash and A.W. Lee. The skipper and E.R. ('Chick') Parratt, all-rounders and two of the finest sportsmen who ever wore flannels, have been outstanding figures in the club during their whole period in the competition. Crumplin, a free-hitting left-hander, usually opened both the batting and the bowling, and Parratt shared the attack with him. Their medium-paced deliveries, pitched on a tantalising length, were never loose, and they both used their heads. Crumplin often beat the bat and the wicket, too, and Parratt was perhaps the more deadly trundler. He had a vicious break-back, and on his day was almost unplayable. His grin when an opponent had had a particularly narrow escape from a good ball was delightful to see, and he never appealed for lbw unless absolutely certain. He was also most useful with the bat, going in at number seven or eight and hitting sixes and fours with cheerful abandon. Like Crumplin, he was captain for a number of seasons; and his early cricket was played at Dockenfield. His namesakes in the 1934 team were F.W. ('Sweat') Parratt, later of Frensham, W. ('Chokey') Parratt, a big hitter, and Arthur Parratt, a steady bat and 'Chick's' brother. Time was when the Parratts could put a full team into the field, and a good side they were. Talking of names, there was a recent season when the Rowledge team read like a page from natural history, with a swan, a heron, a crow, several 'parrots' and some peaches thrown in for good measure! George Boxall, a stubborn opening bat and a bowler who flighted the ball well, later played for Farnham. It is interesting to recall that the present captain of the town club, A.J. Hillyer, occasionally turned out for Rowledge in the late thirties. Norman Miles, a good all-rounder for many years, and his brother Sid, a very fast bowler, were in the 1934 side, together with Bill Lee, a fine bowler and a leading figure for a great number of seasons, who captained the Miller Cup team when they won the trophy in 1938. Others were Cecil Nash and W. ('Jock') Thomson, the wicketkeeper. Very keen and a real 'character', Thomson came to the village in 1907 after a spell in northern league cricket, and his career extended right up to the last war. He went on playing until he was 65, and scored hundreds of valuable runs for Rowledge. A sound wicketkeeper, he was in the habit of keeping up a running commentary, the purport of which, Scotch accent not withstanding, no batsman could mistake. Cricket meant everything to 'Jock', and he was anxious to have all his opponents back in the pavilion as soon as possible. He would puff his beloved pipe during the intervals and his query, 'Got a match?' was a very familiar one.

William ('Jock') Thomson, right, was the author's grandfather, who kept wicket for Rowledge until he was 65. He is pictured with Harry Parrott, a member of a large local family, whose surname is more usually spelt with a second 'a'.

SECRETARY FOR TWENTY-FOUR YEARS

The man chiefly responsible for Rowledge entering the competition was E.B. (Edgar) Wilkinson, one of the best workers the club ever had. Quiet and unassuming, with a twinkling eye and keen sense of humour, he held the office for 24 years, and when he resigned on the re-formation of the club in 1946 appreciation of his services was recorded in the minutes. He later became a member of the Farnham Urban Council and now lives at Petersfield. In his playing days he sometimes opened the innings with Dr Francis Caldecott, another faithful supporter of the game and a batsman with a very correct and pleasing style. He has done much for the game and served as a steward in the competition. In the old days he used to get up at six o'clock in the morning and mow the outfield with his own machine. A.H. (Arch) Wilkinson, Edgar Wilkinson's brother, also played, as did Tom Crumplin, Reg Crumplin's brother. There was, too, F. ('Mac') Hoare, a big hitter and noted 'character', Harry Eade, a dashing bat who in 1938 made 98 against Thursley, incidentally the nearest any Rowledge player has come to three figures in the competition – Sid Carter, a steady bat whose playing career extended over the period between the two wars, D.K. Marwick, who played mainly in the Miller Cup side, and George Ayres, brother-in-law of Norman Miles. A fast bowler, Ayres lost his life gallantly whilst serving in the RAF during the last war. Playing in a match at Shottermill, he sent a ball between the too widely-spaced stumps without removing the bails, and the ball travelled on to the boundary!

After 1934 Rowledge cricket suffered a brief relapse, but they were third in 1938 and fourth a year later, when Reg Crumplin made 94 against Whitehill. The resumption of play in 1946 saw a great revival and the team finished runners-up under the captaincy of Norman Miles. Three brothers from London – they lived near Lord's – Arthur, Jim and Ben Peach, brought a considerable accession of strength to the side. Arthur Peach, a sound and attractive opening bat with a nice range of strokes, made 82 against Thursley and passed the half-century mark on another occasion to head the batting averages. Jim Peach, an effective fast bowler, also proved useful with the bat, and Ben Peach, though he did not often play, was a gifted all-rounder. Jim Peach was captain when Rowledge won the cup for the first time in 1947 and became the only side ever to beat The Bourne in a play-off. The team that year was one of the best the competition has seen. The batting was powerful, the bowling strong and varied and the fielding excellent. D.A. (Dennis) Little, now in Australia, a free-scoring left-hander and one of the mainstays of Rowledge over a long period, and Reg Crumplin both made half-centuries. Major P.C. Britten, a Grenadier Guards officer, tall and a fine batsman, scored 75 against Binsted. The team were undefeated after eight matches. Then a hat-trick by Jim Peach just failed to avert a reverse at The Bourne, and Rowledge also went down to Frensham, their 'bogy' team in post-war years. However, Arthur Peach got 80 against Headley and followed up with 43 not out and 5 for 19 in the return game in which The Bourne were beaten and a play-off ensured. This took place at Grayshott in the presence of a large crowd, and Rowledge were worthy winners by 107 to 52. Britten headed the batting honours with an average of 31 and seven other men had double-figure averages. Arthur Peach got over 300 runs, and Crumplin and Little more than 200. H. Rawson, a fine left-hander from Frensham

Heights School – another good friend of Rowledge from that school was H. Le F. Counsell – 'Chick' Parratt, H. Mackintosh and J. Peach also did well. In addition, the last-named took 70 wickets at something over four apiece, and 'Chick' Parratt 50 at 5.5 each, and this despite ill-health. The wicketkeeper was C.A. ('Son') Watkins, a stubborn bat, and Eric Maidment, a hard hitter, Johnny Cheeseman now secretary and a sound all-rounder who can also keep wicket, D.A. (Doug) Heron, a good bat, Norman Miles and Arthur Parratt were among others who played.

WON A SILVER BOWL

The club were third the following year, their most notable achievement being a win over The Bourne, who were put out for 24. The star of Rowledge was in the ascendant in 1949, when they lifted the cup again, this time without a play-off. Several of the 1947 members were still playing and the skipper was Reg Crumplin, whose son Les was in the side. Reg Crumplin, who began his career with Bentley and Blacknest, has two other sons who have played for Rowledge, Derek and Dick, and all his offspring are, curiously enough, right-handed, except that Dick bowls left. Arthur Peach was in grand form, registering three half-centuries, two in successive weeks. The Bourne were defeated at Rowledge in the last over after leading by one run on the first innings, Heron twice passed the half-century mark, but a couple of defeats narrowed Rowledge's lead. They restored their advantage with a four-wicket victory at The Bourne after facing a total of 139, Arthur Peach and John Remnant putting on 72 in an opening stand. It was Remnant's initial appearance in the side, and he soon established his position. Earlier in the season B. Peach had done some effective work in a number of games. Towards the end Watkins scored an undefeated half-century and Rowledge finished four points ahead of Whitehill. The Rest made 91 and the champions replied with 230, the highest total ever made in one of these encounters. Arthur Peach scored 80 to bring his tally to 447 for an average of 22. Appropriately, the bowling honours of the match were shared by the evergreen Reg Crumplin, and 'Chick' Parratt, though the latter's health had again been troubling him. A.F. ('Driver') Swan, formerly of Frensham, returning to cricket after a long absence, bowled splendidly throughout the season to take 71 wickets at 4.92 apiece, and he won a silver bowl presented by Miss Ayre. Jim Peach took most wickets, 89 at 5.61 each, and Heron scored over 300 runs. Reg Crumplin received the cup from Sir Henry Chitty, himself an active player. E. ('Toddie') Parratt, 'Sweat' Parratt's brother, and Johnny Cheeseman were in the side, and Sam Bone and Fred Sillick, one of the most promising of the younger players, also appeared in the team during the season. Rowledge have several other useful young players, including Harold Henwood. It is interesting to record that during the four seasons 1946-9 Rowledge won 49 of their 67 I'Anson Cup matches and lost only 11, beating The Bourne, their neighbours and great rivals, five times. Crumplin was still captain in 1950, notable for the appearance in the side of A. Crow, who won fame at The Bourne, and they finished sixth, but will doubtless 'come again'.

Rowledge, winners in 1949. Standing, from the left: F. Hole (umpire), J. Remnant, J. Peach, J. Cheeseman, D.A. Heron, R. Glastonbury (scorer). Seated: A. Peach, E. Parratt, E.R. Parratt, R. Crumplin (captain), C.A. Watkins, A.F. Swan, L. Crumplin.

No account of the activities of the Rowledge Cricket Club would be complete without reference to G.R. (George) Farr, who 'stood' for many years, and his successor, Sid Swan, and the cheerful presence of Reg Glastonbury, a most methodical scorer, is always welcomed at the club's matches. Rowledge have played a worthy part in both competitions for nearly 20 years and all will wish them the best of luck in the seasons yet to come.

Lynchmere

THERE is no club in the district with a finer cricket tradition than Lynchmere. The game has been played in that Sussex parish for well over 100 years; for the first 80 on the Marsh, a stretch of open land on the Fernhurst road near Shulbrede Priory, and in wet weather it does no belie its name. Many men still living learned their cricket on that damp turf.

The present fine ground by Lynchmere House came into use after the formation of what might be described as the modern club in 1899. The squire at that time was Frank Pratt Barlow, and he took a very keen interest in both the club and the ground, establishing a tradition of gracious hospitality and good fellowship which has survived to this day. The wicket was always a good one, where batsmen could reap the full reward of skill and bowlers had to work for their wickets. The thatched pavilion in one corner of the ground was a prominent feature of the delightful setting.

The captain for the whole of the ten years Lynchmere were in the competition was Walter Harding, the squire's bailiff. A sound all-rounder, the measure of his success may be gauged from the fact that during that period the club were always either winners or runners-up, and it was not unfitting that theirs was the first name to appear on the original trophy. Walter Harding's two brothers, William and Arthur, both good players, were also in the team. The outstanding batsman in a very fine side was G. Madgwick, who bore the nickname 'Ranjhi'. He took his time over his runs, but he had plenty of strokes, and his sound defence made him a difficult man to dislodge. His play was once highly commended by B.J.T. Bosanquet, inventor of the googly.

Then there was C. Madgwick, a fine right-hand slow bowler and a stalwart of the club for a long period of years. Until Shottermill came in, Lynchmere also had the services of William Balchin, an excellent wicketkeeper, and E. ('Dukey') Moorey, whose terrific hitting turned the course of many a match. A.W. Smith was an enthusiastic secretary and student of the game. Several of the team came to the notice of the county authorities, and might have been professionals, but they were hard-headed men and preferred a safer, if possibly less spectacular, living. One of them recalls how Hayward and Lockwood, of Surrey, came down to try out the paces of some of the Lynchmere men on the old ground by the Royal Huts Hotel at Hindhead. How the residential difficulty would have been overcome had any of the Lynchmere men turned professional for Surrey is not quite clear.

YORKSHIRE OF THE COMPETITION

Lynchmere gave a taste of their quality early in the 1901 season when they dismissed Churt for 20, Walter Harding taking 8 for 6, and replied with 201 (A. Harding 80). In their final game with Grayshott 'Dukey' Moorey made 54 and Walter and Arthur Harding shared the wickets, the combined product of Grayshott's two innings only just exceeding Moorey's effort. Showing their powers of recovery in 1902, Lynchmere, after succumbing to the wiles of W.W. Stratford, of Blackmoor, and being behind on the first innings, were able to declare at 116 for 6 in their second knock (Walter Harding 58 not out) and won by 72. Moorey's versatility was demonstrated by a hat-trick. So to the final match at Grayshott Hall, to which reference is made elsewhere. A.N. West, a young player destined to take many wickets for the club, despite his lack of inches, had a big hand in Grayshott's innings defeat. At the presentation that year Walter Harding heard W.W. Stratford describe the team as the Yorkshire of the competition. 1903 saw the celebrated match with Grayshott and the end of Lynchmere's long immunity from defeat but, although less successful in the next few seasons, they did not falter.

The advent of A.H. Hartwright took Lynchmere right to the top again in 1907. He came to the district as headmaster of Camelsdale School with a great reputation, having played for the Sussex Gentlemen and the Priory Park club at Chichester. Priory Park were sorry to lose him, for he had a batting average in the region of 70. He could have assisted Haslemere, but friendship with Walter Harding turned the scale in favour of Lynchmere, and it quickly became obvious that he was in a class by himself. Tall and well-built, he was a forcing and attractive batsman. When set, all bowling came alike to him and he was himself a most effective bowler. In July he got 108 not out against Grayshott, the highest individual score made on the Lynchmere ground up to that date, and followed it up by taking 8 for 39. The next week brought another century from his bat, 102 in a total of 213 for 5 declared in a match with The Bourne.

That is still the only century ever made against The Bourne in the competition. Lynchmere duly won the cup, losing only one game – to Blackmoor – beat The Rest without Hartwright's assistance, and afterwards met Shottermill in the final game. Lynchmere declared at 174 for 4, Hartwright scoring 116 not out and hitting 20 fours in the process. He went on to take 6 for 10 and Shottermill were out for 52. Hartwright had made over 500 runs in nine innings in the competition for an average of 73.85 and captured 63 wickets at under four apiece. It remains the highest batting average recorded in the cup. The full figures are given in the appendix. Never again did Hartwright reach quite such heights, although he achieved many other grand performances in after years.

In the three following seasons Tilford won the trophy outright and Lynchmere were their bogy team, beating them several times. After the 1910 season Lynchmere decided to enter a higher class of cricket and, to the regret of the other teams, withdrew from the competition and the spirit of Sussex departed with them. They went on to further triumphs, which form no part of the subject of this book, and although over 40 years have elapsed since they played for the cup their prowess is still fresh in many memories. They certainly kept their side together, for eight of the 1901 team were still playing in 1910.

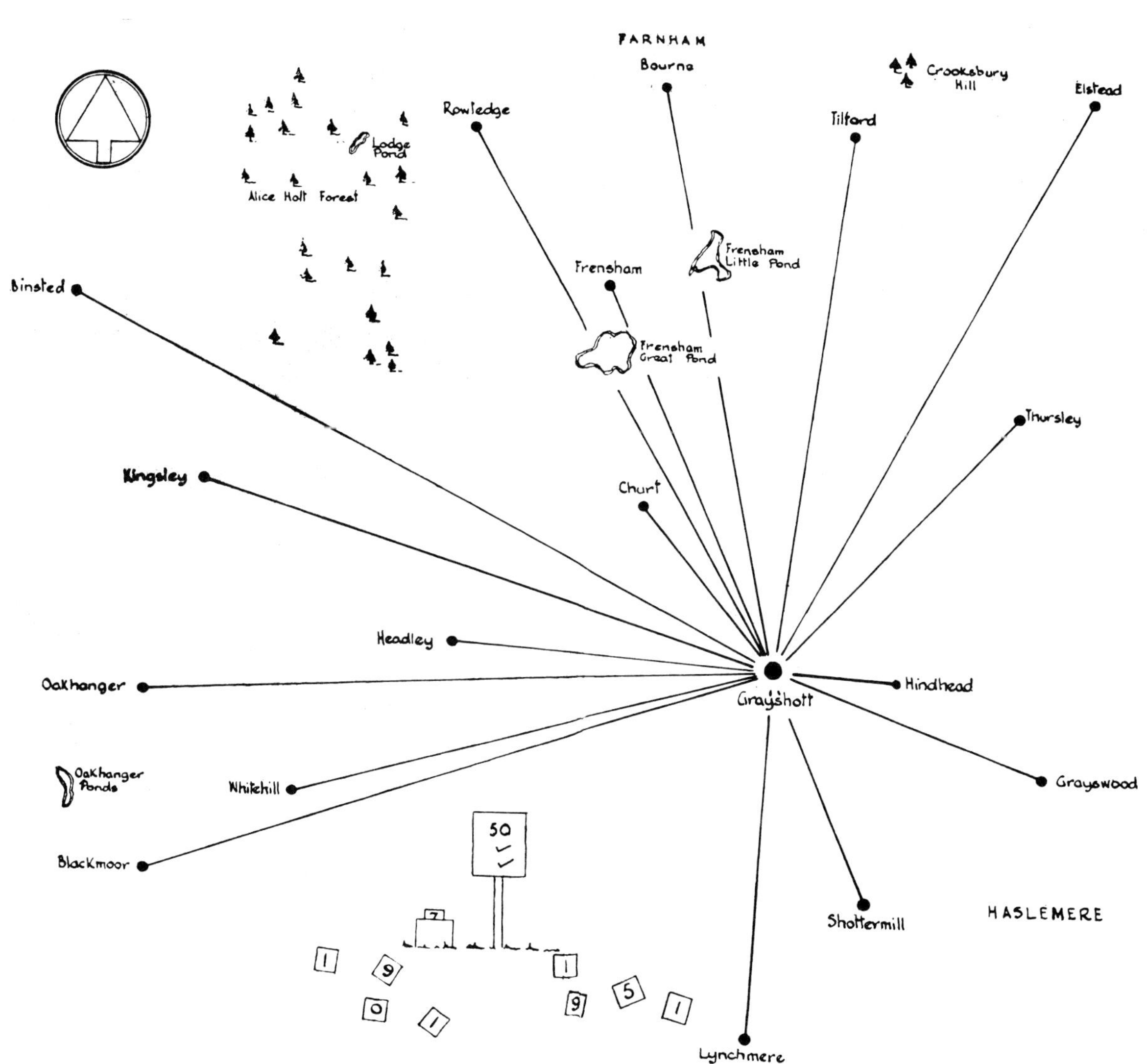

Kingsley and Oakhanger

THE story of Kingsley and Oakhanger in the I'Anson Cup competition is largely that of one man, Maurice Mercer. His accomplishments were a minor epic. Passionately devoted to cricket, he had his own playing career cut short by the effects of gas in World War One, and thereafter he bent his energies, despite constant ill-health, to organising the game for others.

At Kingsley he laid out a ground to compare favourably with any in the district, tending the turf with loving care. It was a delight to see him, towards the end of March, thrusting his thumb into the outfield and observing with a grin, 'The grass is on the move'. Then, as soon as it was on the move, he would hurry off to cut it. When he took over the secretaryship, together with a balance of 1s 8d, he set about building up the organisation known as the Kingsley Sports and Social Club, which embraced tennis and football, as well as cricket. Hundreds of pounds were raised, with willing co-operation, and the effort culminated in the erection of a fine new hall. A pioneer of Sunday cricket away back in the twenties, when to play on the Sabbath was still thought to be slightly scandalous, he gathered around him most of the leading players of the neighbourhood, and there were few in the years between the two wars who did not number him among their friends. They flocked to the attractive Kingsley ground – where the large playing area and the pavilion came into being through Maurice's initiative – for the good cricket, the equally good fellowship and the strawberry teas in season. He built up a formidable Sunday side, playing strong club teams from London and elsewhere. The one essential qualification for admission to that circle was skill at the game. Maurice was never satisfied with less than the best, and a man had to be above average to hold his place. The club competed in the Kingsley and District League for some years, but Maurice had another ambition. Admission to the I'Anson Cup was his goal, and in 1933 he succeeded in getting Kingsley elected.

Now that was a feat above the ordinary, because, although they were all village players, not all the team were Kingsley residents, but they were a fine side and Maurice Mercer had a very forceful personality. What he wanted he usually managed to achieve and, despite some initial misgivings, there was no doubt that Kingsley were an asset to the competition. It happened to be Tilford's year, but the newcomers ran them very close for the cup, under the captaincy of V.G. Barlow. The issue really depended upon the second meeting of the two clubs, at Tilford, and not until their last pair were together did Tilford win. Kingsley were not beaten on their own ground until the last day of the season, when they lost to Frensham. Even so, they finished runners-up.

STARTING AFRESH

That winter Maurice Mercer faced a set-back that would have broken a lesser man. Circumstances arose whereby his years of work at Kingsley came suddenly to an end. Undaunted, he secured a field at Oakhanger and, with his players supporting him to a man, started building up another club from scratch. Almost daily in all weathers he walked several miles to the new ground, worked on it for hours, and then walked back. The players helped him at weekends, and when the 1934 season started the ground and pavilion were ready, a wonderful achievement in the face of enormous odds. Kingsley withdrew from the competition and the new club – the same team under another name – were admitted. They were third that year and the next, and continued to do well until war came in 1939. The traditions of Kingsley were transferred to Oakhanger, the Sunday cricket flourished as never before, and when he died prematurely in 1937 Maurice Mercer knew that his work had been crowned with success. A great 'character', he inspired loyalty and affection to an amazing degree, and countless tales are told about him. He was more than a secretary; he was the club's inspiration and his memory remains green. His shrewd, kindly countenance under a flat cap, his laughter and his eternal optimism will never be forgotten. He was always discovering players with big reputations, and when sometimes the reputation proved but a bubble, he was not a whit abashed, but went on looking for fresh talent. He lived for cricket and all that it means, and to him nothing was impossible. His summer days and the evenings at the Red Lion after the close of play were filled with fun and wit.

Of course, he had his willing lieutenants. There was Fred Stairs, a worker if ever there was one, ready to complete a team or stand down and assist in another direction as required. The ball seldom passed him on the field and he could keep his end up in a tight corner. Then the Swinstead brothers, E.A. (Peter), R. (Dick) and B.H. (Bernard) and their uncle, Percy Southam, who turned out for a match not so long ago at the age of 76; all good players. Dick Swinstead has captained Liphook since the war, and Bernard, one of the best all-rounders the competition has known, skippers Blackmoor. Bernard Swinstead usually headed the Oakhanger batting averages, and in 1935, one of The Bourne's cup-winning years, he put up a memorable performance on their ground. The Bourne made 73 and the visitors passed that score for the loss of five wickets. When Bernard Swinstead left, the score-board read: 85-5-71. He made his runs in half-an-hour, killing a chicken with one drive for six. It was a splendid exhibition of forceful batting. In 1937 he scored over 500 runs in the competition and throughout the years took many wickets with his medium-pace bowling, varied with a cunning slower ball. Dick Swinstead was a sound opening bat and useful change bowler. After Maurice Mercer's death he took over the secretaryship of the club and did the job most successfully. The third brother, Peter, was not able to play as often as he would have wished, but he had cricket in his blood.

PILLARS OF THE TEAM

The cousins R.J. (Jim) and S.H. (Stan) Clements from Binsted – for which village they now play – were also pillars of the team, both all-rounders, with Jim, a shrewd tactician, the steadier of the two. He had a knack of breaking up dangerous partnerships. Stan was an attractive, free-scoring bat when he got going. The main attack was in the capable hands of R.A. Goodyear, from Froyle, and W.A. Clark. Bert Goodyear, a bowler of moods and deadly in his day, had a nip from the pitch reminiscent of Maurice Tate, and many a good batsman, meeting him for the first time, was surprised to see his middle stump knocked out with a ball that did not look fast through the air. Walter Clark, by contrast, bowled right arm round the wicket, keeping an impeccable length and claiming a lot of victims with the ball that went away and the one that came back. He could keep an end going for hours, if necessary, and sometimes bowled several overs without the batsman getting as much as a touch; he had an astonishing record of maidens. His son, also named Walter, gave promise of following in his footsteps as a keen player, and his father, Charles Clark, umpired for a long period with the dignity befitting an ex-police sergeant. These duties were shared with Harry Lamport, another veteran, who would stand apparently lost in thought after an appeal and then suddenly shoot up his finger. Everyone was fond of Harry. E. Lake, from Worldham, was a hitter with strong forearms and good intentions and a capable bowler. The story of V.G. Barlow really belongs to Headley. A convivial wicketkeeper and able skipper, his best score in that period was 79 against Thursley in 1933. E. Bicknell and R. Bicknell, both Oakhanger residents, were two other brothers who served the club loyally in the early days. Ted Bicknell was a sound bat when able to overcome initial hesitancy.

Oakhanger in 1936. Standing, from the left: W. Wadham (scorer), F. Osgood, F. Stairs, R. Swinstead, M. Mercer (secretary), B.H. Swinstead, C. Clark (umpire). Seated: W.A. Clark, V.G. Barlow, R.J. Clements (captain), E. Hulbert, R.A. Goodyear. On ground: E. Lake, S.H. Clements.

FORECAST HIS SCORE

Among the younger players none showed greater promise than E. ('Buster') Hulbert. He had plenty of patience, when he got over an early tendency to rashness, and a nice range of strokes. Improving season by season, he had the distinction of being the only Oakhanger player to score a century in the competition, 106 against Binsted in 1939. Possibly the most remarkable player was one who appeared only for a single season, at Kingsley in 1933. W. O'B. Wilks learnt his cricket in the hard school of the northern leagues. He could usually forecast his score before he went in; 'I think I will get about 50 today', and he did, incredible though that sounds. He would play only on good grounds, making a preliminary inspection during the week and then, carefully adjusting his glasses, he would score almost precisely the number of runs he predicted, large or small. He began with 57, made 45 not out and 66 not out in successive weeks and after four innings had an average of over 100. He didn't continue in quite the same vein – he didn't say he would! – but his final average was 31.27, and that was never bettered for Kingsley or Oakhanger.

Last, but not least, there was old Walter Wadham, the scorer sitting on the verandah with the book, a stub of pencil and his own brand of philosophy. Never late for a match, he liked to linger, after stumps were drawn and most of the players had departed, for a chat about his beloved native Sussex. He, too, was a good player in his day, assisting Blackmoor in the early years of the competition. The memory of him moving slowly up the road with his stick at the close of a long, sunny evening, the shadows stealing across the pitch and the smell of new-mown grass in the air may well conclude this chapter.

Binsted

A TYPICAL Hampshire village, set high on the ridge beyond Bentley to the south of the Farnham-Alton road, Binsted has an old cricket tradition. The civil parish is surprisingly large and includes the whole of the Alice Holt Forest, Bucks Horn Oak, Rowledge Parish Church and all the buildings on that side of the road, and Holt Pound. Its boundary runs with the Surrey border for several miles, and hard by the Forest Inn, just within the parish, lies Holt Pound recreation ground, one of the oldest cricket grounds in the country, where All-England played well over a century ago. Blacknest, in the shadow of the Forest, was the home of a rural cricket club in the not very distant past, and in Binsted village there was a flourishing team, with headquarters at the King's Arms, some years before the close of the 19th century. One of the founders was George Karn, grandfather of two of the present members, S.H. (Stan) Clements, the 1950 captain, and N.G. (Nelson) Clements, the present umpire. Their father, George Clements, clerk to the parish council, was a noted player in his day and has been associated with the club for more than 50 years. He was umpire when Binsted came into the competition. The club played on various grounds, including the field opposite the parish church, before moving to the present recreation ground about 20 years ago. One of the leading figures in the early days was G.G. (George) Chalcraft, who bore a name honoured in Alton cricket circles; and another was a former vicar, the Revd W.G.G. Thompson, who was ordained in the United States and was at Binsted for over half-a-century. His successor's son, G.R. Taylor, captained Hampshire. E.R. Remnant, the all-rounder who qualified for Hampshire when chauffeur to the Revd W.G.G. Thompson, provided an earlier link with the county. A season or two ago Binsted had the assistance of P.M. Studd, a former captain of Cambridge University, whose family were then at South Hay.

MEMORABLE MATCH

Binsted competed in the Kingsley and District League during the twenties and early thirties, twice winning the runners-up shield under the leadership of R.J. (Jim) Clements, who is still in the game. The club entered the Miller Cup competition in 1936, finishing fourth, and were promoted to I'Anson Cup status a year later. The first match they ever played in the I'Anson Cup was against Whitehill and their team comprised the Revd F.A.W. Wilkinson (captain), V.W. Croucher, J.G. Miller, C. Barnes. W. Burden, T. Smith, T. Warner, H. Chappell, C. Chappell, H.J. Penn and G. Retallack. They started with a series of seven defeats and then beat Thursley, who had met with a similar misfortune, in the middle of June. They had to wait until their final match, with Headley, before they gained another victory, winning with the last pair together. Tom Warner took 8 for 20 in that game. The following year they had an improved record, winning five of their 22 fixtures. There was a memorable victory over Whitehill when the vicar's son, J. Wilkinson, made 58 not out and Hector Chappell did the hat-trick twice in the innings. In 1939 they started well by beating Whitehill, Tom Warner taking 7 for 12, but they won only twice more. The return encounter with Whitehill provided a very close finish, Whitehill declaring at 134 for 4 and Binsted replying with 133. Then came the war and a long break before Binsted again competed in 1947. They won three of their first five games, and with six successes in 18 matches had their best season up to that time. W. Trigg made 51 in a drawn match at Whitehill and, under the captaincy of J.G. (Jack) Miller, Binsted registered six totals of over 100, four of them in May and June. For the next two seasons they competed only in the Miller Cup, but came back to the I'Anson competition in 1950, with Stan Clements as skipper, and won seven of their 20 matches, defeating both the two top teams, The Bourne and Headley. They won at The Bourne by six wickets, their first success against that club, Fred Knight taking 8 for 24. In June they made their highest total in the competition, 180 for 9 declared against Tilford, who replied with 141 for 4. Tilford won the return game, although Miller carried his bat through the Binsted innings. There was a most exciting draw at Frensham, when the home side declared at 153 for 7 and Binsted replied with 133 for 9. The story of the club in the competition is one of continuing improvement.

VICAR WAS CAPTAIN

Binsted's pre-war captain, the Revd F.A.W. Wilkinson, now vicar of Holybourne, was a popular figure in the competition and served for three years as a steward. He led The Rest team against Headley II when they won the Miller Cup in 1936 and also played for The Rest when Headley won the I'Anson Cup two years later. He was a fine bat who required a good wicket to reveal his best form, and his son gave useful assistance to the club when available. The other outstanding figure in Binsted's association with the competition has been Jack Miller, secretary of the club for many years past, a grand wicketkeeper and opening batsman who has made many runs for his side and saved many, too; a cheerful and very sportsmanlike player. The opening bowlers in pre-war days were Tom Warner, fast-

Binsted in 1950. K. White, C. Collins, G. Bone, P. Clements, F. Knight, R. Paul, N.G. Clements (umpire). Seated: J. Collins (scorer), P. Hudson, R. Woods, J.G. Miller (captain), R.J. Clements, A. Brooks.

medium leg-break, and Tom Smith, right-hand medium off-break and swerve bowler, who had a knack of finding his opponents' weaknesses. This pair took a crop of wickets between them. Jim and Stanley Clements, Oakhanger stalwarts in pre-war days, both have sons following in their footsteps. R.T. (Bob) Clements, Jim Clements' son, is useful with bat and ball, and Stanley Clements' son, Mark, is also coming on well. Nelson Clements, in the white coat, keeps a humorous eye on everyone. George Chandler, a fine field and useful bat, has been with the club for many years, and W. Burden's quick scoring has sometimes got the side out of difficulty. The brothers Hector and Cyril Chappell, the former fast right-hand with a vicious nip from the pitch, and the latter a batsman and keen slip fielder, have always been well worth their place. Two other brothers are W.V. (Vic) Croucher, a monumental stone-waller who also bowls slow off-breaks – he is now with Frensham – and Tom Croucher, treasurer for some years and a cheerful and willing club member. Fred Hutt, H. Watts and W.E. Wood made their mark as all-rounders, Wood being an effective right-hand slow bowler like Sid ('Kiya') Othen, who took a lot of wickets. E.W. Holford, a master at Eggar's Grammar School, Alton, was prominent for several seasons with his wily spin bowling, able to break the ball both ways. George Gillen and Tom Durman were bowlers of note, and E. Lake, bowling a little above medium pace and a terrific hitter, has put in a lot of good work for the club, as he did for Oakhanger in former times. Others who have taken their full share in Binsted's progress are the brothers Fred and John Fisher, Charlie and Jim Collins and Eddie and Fred Knight. Fred Knight bowls left and bats right, and so does Arthur Brooks, another sound player. W.A. Clark, so well known at Kingsley and Oakhanger, was in the side for a period after the war. Among the members of recent times Rodney Paul and R. (Bob) Woods come quickly to mind, Paul being a batsman and Woods an all-rounder.

The club's president and keen supporter for many years was A. Manwaring Robertson, now of Frensham, whose son, Straun Robertson, played a few times in the Miller Cup, and the office is at present filled by the Hon T.H. Brand, who has also played occasionally. A visit to Binsted is always good fun, even when a cold wind is blowing across the recreation ground. The wicket is true and fast on the belt of 'malm', a mixture of sand and clay, running from the Telegraph to Selborne, and a well-trimmed and unusually fast outfield is an inducement to heavy scoring. However, the Binsted bowlers give little away and the team can be relied upon to put up a good fight in any circumstances. They are keen players and sporting opponents, and long may their club flourish.

Friends old and new

THERE remain three clubs who competed in bygone years: Grayswood, Haslemere Working Men and Hindhead. They never won the trophy and the Haslemere Working Men were in for only three seasons before World War One put an end to their existence. Grayswood took part for six seasons up to 1930 and Hindhead for 13 up to 1931, withdrawing in the following year after playing a few matches.

Admitted in 1913, the year Haslemere achieved urban status, the Working Men were not, strictly speaking, a village team, but they were a keen band of players and their home matches took place on Sir Richard Garton's ground at Lythe Hill. It is interesting at this distance of time to recall the names of those who represented them in their first match, which was against Grayshott: W. Boxall, J. Madgwick, E. Mansfield, R. Cobb, C. Nightingale, G. Clements, C. Snelling, F. Best, E. Bridger, D. Welland and W. Maggs. They gained their first victory in July of that year, when they beat undefeated Blackmoor by 39 runs to 27, F. Tull taking 7 for 9. They held their third annual dinner at the King's Arms, Haslemere, in 1913, when H.J. Rogers presided and T. Oakford was secretary. J. Madgwick and T. Maides received awards for the best batting and bowling averages respectively. They had one more season in the competition before the war, but the club was not afterwards re-formed. Their successors, the Haslemere Comrades, were invited to join the competition in 1920, but the invitation was not ratified by the delegates of the competing clubs, on the ground that the Comrades were not a village team.

HINDHEAD

Hindhead came into the competition in 1913, playing on a ground behind the Royal Huts Hotel, bounded by the London-Portsmouth Road, the Farnham Road and Tower Road. The team for their first match, in which they were beaten by Shottermill, the cup-winners, comprised: J. Kinge, W. Denyer, A. Carver, W. Carter, A. Goddard, A. Denyer, W. Stratton, J. Harris, A. White, W. Moore and W. Grover. They won their initial victory, at home to Tilford, in August. A year later A. Carver made 49 not out for The Rest against Shottermill. When cricket was resumed in 1920 Hindhead were without a ground and had to play all their matches away, losing every game; but they were not disheartened. They had their ground back the following season, and it was often the scene of Miller Cup Winners v Rest matches during the twenties. Although they met with little success in either competition – they ran a Miller Cup team for some seasons – the men of Hindhead always enjoyed their cricket and were most sporting opponents. Their stalwarts included H.M. Edmead, secretary of the competition for some years. He was captain for a time and also played for Grayshott, as did C. Pratt. Frank Martin, who was in the Churt team before World War One, turned out for them, as well as Ben Chandler, but perhaps their best-known player was W.J. Punter, a fine bowler and skipper, aptly described by G.M. Hubbuck as 'the Lion of Hindhead'. A. Worsdell, a stolid left-handed batsman of the old school, who later assisted Liphook, M. Clapham, F. Rowberry, C. Prior and T. Peskett were among others who played.

They took their defeats with a smile, but Hindhead's team had their moments of triumph, too. At a period in 1923, when Shottermill were well in the running for the cup – they eventually finished only a point behind Whitehill – their hopes were dashed by a home defeat at the hands of Hindhead. The visitors made 103 (K. Barker 50) and Shottermill 96. Hindhead withdrew from the competition in 1929, when the lease of their ground ran out, but they managed to acquire a splendid new playing field close to the Tilford Road in time for the 1930 season. That year they defeated The Bourne, Headley and Tilford in successive weeks, and had an unbeaten home record until the end of July. They finally left the competition in June 1932. Their departure was regretted, for they always played the game in the right spirit and their new ground was the equal of any in the locality. When it was first used only the concrete basement of the pavilion had been erected and players had the curious experience of diving down into a dressing-room below the level of the pitch. After completion – it was formally opened in the summer of 1932 – the pavilion was almost good enough for a county ground, superbly

Remenham in Tilford Road, Hindhead, the school previously run by Edward Turle, who was Churt's captain before becoming the driving force in the building of Hindhead's pavilion when the Marchants Hill ground opened in 1932.

appointed in every way and a worthy memorial to Edward Turle. Reference to his connection with Churt will be found in another chapter. Among Hindhead's outstanding players at the close of their association with the competition were G.D. Echlin, headmaster of Hindhead School, a grand all-rounder who played in crepe-soled boots – quite a novelty in those days – and J.T. Comber, a fine left-handed batsman who made 72 against Grayshott in 1930.

Two stories illustrate the gay spirit of Hindhead cricket. A player went through the whole season without scoring a run, and C. Grinstead, father of one of the present members of the club, solemnly presented him with a brace of ducks! There was no more enthusiastic member in competition days than the local constable, PC Clutterbuck. Once, as so often happens with members of the force, he had to leave for duty before the match on the old ground was over. He was on patrol at the Huts corner when an urgent message came. Hindhead had made a recovery, had a chance of victory, and needed him. He hurried down the road on his bicycle, flung off his helmet and tunic, seized a bat, dashed in, made the winning hit, and sped back to his post. Yes, they were happy days. It is pleasant to know that the Hindhead club continues to flourish, and any member of the competition who played against them in former times can be sure of a welcome from some of the veterans, should he chance to visit the ground on a summer Saturday or Sunday afternoon.

GRAYSWOOD

Grayswood were a formidable bowling side, particularly on their own ground, and teams who came away from there with two points considered themselves fortunate. The ground, a large one bounded on the north by the railway line, was on the outskirts of the village in the Brook direction. There were times in mid-summer when the grass was high everywhere, except on the actual wicket, and the scoring of runs was anything but easy, especially against an accurate attack. In 1929, for instance, the year Grayshott won the cup, they were beaten at Grayswood by scores of 40 and 25 to 20 and 27. Such totals were by no means rare. The Grayswood bowlers, who included B. Denyer, H. Smithers and H. Weekes, took a crop of wickets, and had their batting been powerful they would have been strong contenders for honours. Members of the team in their first year in the competition, 1925, included, in addition to those mentioned above, V. Johnson, J. Clear, A. Bicknell, J. Judge, Captain Nation, H. Smithers, G. Puttock and G. Heims. Entertaining The Bourne in June, Grayswood lost only by 35 to 34, and in a second innings the visitors made 54 for 8. The following season was Grayswood's best in the competition, and they finished joint runners-up with Shottermill and Whitehill, ten points behind The Bourne. They won 11 of their 18 games. They beat The Bourne by 58 to 41 and lost the return only by 63 to 55, Shottermill being the one other side to defeat the winners. In 1927 Grayswood were concerned in two ties, then a record. They made rather a habit of beating The Bourne, and did so once in 1928 and twice in the following year. Although they were bottom of the table in 1930, their last season, the skipper, N. Smithers, met with considerable personal success. The cause of their withdrawal from both competitions – they ran a team in the Miller Cup, too – was lack of players. In recent years Grayswood cricket has been well supported and the club now possess an excellent pitch in ideal surroundings on the village green. One of their present players, R. Moorey, provides a link with competition days.

ELSTEAD

Elstead, welcomed as newcomers to both competitions in 1949, are a club with a long cricket tradition and many playing members. They have a fine blend of experience and youth and so keen is local interest in the game that they find it possible to turn out two teams even on Sundays. The wicket on the recreation ground is a good one, there are plenty of spectators at home matches, and the men of Elstead are very sporting opponents. It took them a little time to find their feet in the competitions, and they won only five I'Anson matches in their first season, finishing well down the table. In 1950 they were successful in their five opening fixtures, beating The Bourne, and headed the table for a time. Although unable to maintain that position, they won 11 matches in a programme of 20 and were fourth, an improvement which augurs well for the future. The annual game between the Hampshire and Surrey clubs in the competition was staged on their ground in 1950, and they went to great trouble to make the occasion a success, even erecting a marquee.

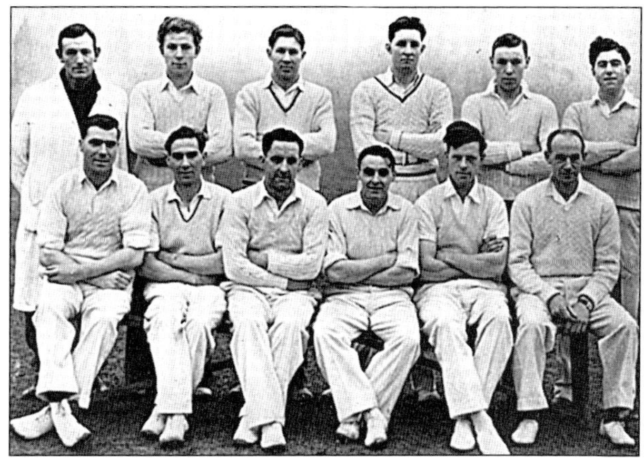

Elstead in 1950. Standing, from the left: R.P. Hedger (umpire), B. Payne, G. Steer, R. Pryce, B. Karn, B. Ford. Seated: R. Reffold, R. Burchett, A. Burchett, C. Reffold (captain), W. Rapley, A. Bagwell (secretary).

The Elstead club have a strong ambition to win the I'Anson Cup, and with the wealth of talent at their disposal they may well do so before very long. There is plenty of variety in the batting and bowling, and in W. Burchett they possess one of the best all-rounders in the locality. C. Reffold, captain for the first two seasons, and B. Payne bring pace to the attack and are well supported by R. Reffold and W. Burchett. The last-named had a batting average of over 20 in 1949, and if he gets going at the start of an innings the runs soon come, for he has a good eye and a sound defence and hits very hard. G. Steer is a good all-rounder, and among the younger players of note are D. Hardy, R. Pryce and the brothers A. and B. Karn. The wicketkeeper is R. Burchett and W. Rapley, member of a well-known Thursley family, is also in the side. A. Bagwell was the enthusiastic secretary in the period under review and his successor, B. Ford, is another enthusiast.

Elstead's story in the competition is as yet a short one, but they bid fair to write many long chapters of achievement.

Three great all-rounders

THE most admired player in the game is the all-rounder, the complete cricketer, and during the past quarter of a century three of the outstanding men in that category have been V.C. Rapley, L. Goodchild and F. Kenward, all different in temperament and style, but alike in their modesty, ability and the touch of greatness without which no one reaches the top, either at Lord's or on the village green. What constitutes greatness in any class of cricket is hard to define, but we all know it when we see it, and these three will have their place among the competition's immortals.

V.C. RAPLEY

Vernon Cheasmar Rapley, always known by his initials V.C. – which somehow fit the heroic stature of the man – was born in 1895. He was the son of a Thursley farmer-cricketer, M.C. Rapley, who captained the village team and taught his family to play at an early age by bowling to them on the garden path. V.C. showed a natural aptitude, with fleetness of foot and a keen eye, and in his teens was already doing great things both as a batsman and fast-medium bowler. His enthusiasm and energy were unbounded. He made his mark as soon as Thursley entered the competition in 1921, scoring 110 at Hindhead in July of that year. Two seasons later, in June 1923, he made 107 in a score of 209 for 6 against Churt, the highest Thursley total since V.C.'s father also made 107, out of 207, 40 years previously. Then came Thursley's cup-winning season, when V.C. reached his peak. His 7 for 14 against the powerful Shottermill team did not save his side from defeat, but they won the return easily enough, and Rapley made 83 against Churt, Henry Rushbrooke helping to put on 84 for the first wicket. In August V.C. scored 113 in a total of 159 at Whitehill before being run out, and when Thursley won the cup under the captaincy of his brother, M.L. Rapley, they beat The Rest, V.C. getting top score. He headed the batting honours with 588 runs for an average of 42 – more than twice as good as anyone else – and was also top of the bowling, his 65 wickets costing 3.2 runs apiece.

V.C. Rapley: member of a Thursley dynasty.

V.C. continued to be the club's mainstay in the years that followed. Cheerful and keen, he almost carried the side on his shoulders through good seasons and bad, Never a man to sit on the splice, he attacked the bowling from the start, and when well set scored with a flow of graceful strokes all round the wicket. He could go yards up the pitch, change his mind, and get back to convert an intended drive into a cut. When he did hit, the ball fairly hummed along the ground to the boundary. No one was faster between wickets, and he was the same in the field, moving like quicksilver. In a few overs, with bat or ball, he would change the trend of a game. His run up combined easy style and menace, and he could swing the ball both ways, sensing a batsman's weakness and playing on it; pitching one well up, the next a little shorter, cleverly disguising changes of pace. Perhaps his most deadly ball was the slower one, pitching on the middle and leg and going away towards the slips. Few could resist the temptation to nibble at the bait, and how he would grin as the catch followed the snick. He fielded to his own bowling wonderfully well and got through an over with no loss of time. Rapley first became captain of Thursley in 1936 and led The Rest to victory against the cup-winners for the second successive time. The passing of the years seemed to have no effect on his form, and when the game was resumed in 1946 after the war period he made 111 not out against Whitehill in a score of 189 for 5. It was 22 years since his previous century. Typical of his character was the innings he remembers with most pleasure, a winning second innings knock of 60-odd in 20 minutes against Frensham, when he went down the wicket to A.F. Swan. Today, at the age of 56, he is still playing with unimpaired zest, making his runs with briskness and certainty and keeping the batsmen quiet with his bowling, a model for all young cricketers. For 30 years he has given of his best to the competition, and those who love the game applaud him.

LEWIS GOODCHILD

Lewis Goodchild was born in 1901 in the village with which his name is so closely associated. His brother, W. Goodchild, played for The Bourne before World War One, and his uncles, L. and H. Ireson, were at one time captains of the club. In his schooldays at The Bourne he showed remarkable aptitude for the game. He recalls with amusement that once one of the masters, himself a cricketer, and the other boys tried in vain during play periods on several successive days to dismiss the youthful Lewis Goodchild as he defended a wicket chalked on the wall. During the war he and other lads received valuable coaching from Basil Trusler, an ex-soldier invalided out of the forces. Once at Rowledge, when an army team failed to turn up, the boys took on the village side and beat them. Playing for The Bourne after the war, Goodchild did well as a medium-pace bowler in the Farnham League, and his batting developed rapidly. When the club entered the competition in 1925 he experienced four seasons of unparalleled success, capturing during that time 442 wickets for 3.9 apiece and scoring 1,869 runs for an average of 18. His 757 runs in 1928 constituted a record aggregate for a season. [See appendix.] It was not surprising that The Bourne lifted the cup four times running. On the occasion when The Rest were dismissed for 23 in 1925 he took 7 for 9. Two years later he made scores of 98 at the expense of Churt and 84 against Hindhead, following this up with 87 against Hindhead in 1928, the year he and H. Hack put on over 100 for the first wicket in a match with Tilford, a record for The Bourne ground at that time. The first century of his career was in the game with The Rest in 1928. It was the only 100 ever made in these encounters, and he also took 7 for 24.

After that he was out of the competition for some years, playing for Farnham Gas Company, where he was employed, but he returned to the side when The Bourne won a play-off with Rowledge in 1934, taking 9 for 14 in the two innings. A full season next year saw him back in his old form, and in 1936 he captained the club when they won the cup without defeat, although they lost to The Rest. He was captain when they won again the following season; W. Wells helped him to put on 84 for the last wicket versus Headley. He took 75 wickets, increasing the number to 112 in 1938 and also scoring 104 not out v Thursley. He led the team to victory for the third time in 1939, his tally of wickets being 75, and when The Bourne beat Headley in the play-off of 1940 he had been skipper of four cup-winning teams – equalling a record. A road accident early in 1945 nearly cost him his life, ended his playing career and left him permanently incapacitated, but his interest in the game was undimmed and he remains a keen supporter of the team for which he did so much.

Lew Goodchild presents the I'Anson Cup to the Tilford captain, Alf Farnfield, in 1958.

The memory of Lewis Goodchild as a cricketer is unforgettable. He was, beyond doubt, the most formidable player of his generation in the competition. An admirable captain and fine field, he was a brilliant bowler with an immaculate length, and there were times when it seemed he could do anything with the ball, except make it talk. No batsman was ever really comfortable against him. When he went to the wicket himself he was a delight to watch. Cultured and correct, he had a sound defence, his bat was straight, and he possessed a full range of strokes. All his movements bore a natural grace. Almost invariably he bowled in plimsolls and batted in boots. He was the soul of modesty, generous in his appreciation of the merits of others and incapable of a mean action. When he appealed for lbw, which was seldom, the batsman could be quite sure he was out. He enjoyed his cricket and others enjoyed playing with him, for he was both a fine player and a fine man.

FRANK KENWARD

Frank Kenward, youngest of the trio, was born at Headley in 1914. He had no cricket background. Other members of his family did not play, but when he was a schoolboy someone lent him a book on the game by that great Indian batsman, K.S. Ranjitsinhji. He studied it carefully and practised the strokes, sometimes with the aid of a mirror, until he developed a technique which marked him out as a

Frank Kenward: best of the lot.

youngster of unusual promise when he began to play for the Headley Miller Cup team in the late twenties. A right-handed bat, like the other two, he was also, unlike them, a left-arm fast bowler, and it was apparent, after he joined the I'Anson Cup XI, that a new star was rising. It is impossible to assess his ability in terms of figures, though they are impressive enough. He has always been, in cricket, a law unto himself. Like the little girl in the nursery rhyme, when he is good, he is very, very good. There is about him an authentic touch of genius; on his day he rises to great heights. In pre-war years a curiously diffident manner sometimes cloaked his skill; there were days when he seemed to lose interest, and but for that he would almost certainly have played for Hampshire. Once in the late thirties at Liphook he had the Club and Ground batsmen groping for the ball like novices, but the great occasion has not always found him at his best. Throughout the thirties he usually topped the Headley batting averages without effort and the winning of the cup in 1938 was largely due to his work. He made 127 not out in a total of 279 at Tilford, scored 722 runs – the second highest aggregate the competition has known – for an average of 34 and took 55 wickets. In 1946 he went to Germany and was not seen in the competition again until 1948, when his 7 for 19 in the play-off with The Bourne failed to win the cup for Headley. The following season he twice took nine wickets in an innings and had a bag of 91, besides heading the batting. In 1950, the year of his captaincy, his ability came to full flower. At Tilford again he made 136 of a total of 185 in 50 minutes, hitting nine sixes and ten fours in a glorious exhibition. For the Hampshire Clubs against the Surrey Clubs at Elstead he scored 112 not out. His 53 out of 101 against Frensham and 50 of a total of 93 and 7 for 10 versus Whitehill were other notable feats in a vintage year which brought him 648 runs – 400 more than anyone else in the side – for an average of 32, and 93 wickets – over 50 more than the next best – at five apiece. Despite that great feat, Headley lost the cup in yet another play-off with The Bourne. Kenward hit 1,366 runs (average 34) and took 154 wickets at 4.87 each in all matches, recording three centuries.

Those who have played with him for many years know the passion for the game that animates Frank Kenward, and have a great affection for him. He may stand in the slips apparently regardless, but the ball will never pass him and his catches there and in the deep sometimes border on the miraculous. He makes it all look so easy. His batting is attractive to watch and his strokes have no flaw. His fast bowling, over or round the wicket, can be devastating. He has uprooted the middle stump of the best batsmen more violently and more often than most of his contemporaries. The silence of the onlookers when he bowls down the hill at The Bourne has often provided eloquent testimony to that. A shrewd judge of the game has said he could, had he been so minded, have been the finest slow bowler in the competition. In any match he is an unknown quantity, but when the spark of genius flares many will echo the words of the writer, 'May I be there to see'.

The rules

EVOLVED by the process of trial and error and careful revision from time to time, the present-day rules of the competition differ widely in detail from those framed originally, but the fundamentals are largely the same.

The first rules, some 20 in number, specified the villages eligible to compete and provided for one match with every other club. Drawn matches were to be re-played, the village losing the fewest matches to hold the cup for a year. In the event of two or more villages losing an equal number of matches, additional games were to be played on neutral ground. 'Such matches shall not be decided (as in the case of the others) on the first innings, but shall be played out according to the rules covering two-day matches.' Play was to commence at 2pm, or earlier, according to mutual agreement, and stumps drawn at 6.30pm in May and August and 7pm in June and July. 'If either team be not ready to begin play within half-an-hour of the appointed time, their opponents may claim the match, subject to the approval of the committee.' A fair and competent umpire was to be appointed by each village and 'any player guilty of using bad language towards another player or an umpire during the progress of a cup match' was to be reported to the committee, who had power to suspend offenders. Incidentally, the committee comprised the secretary of each competing village. Players had to reside in the parish of the club for which they played, or within a radius of three miles from the ground. No one could play for more than one club in the same year, and military officers and men were ineligible, unless permanent residents. Professional cricketers, while employed as such, were also barred, 'but may be engaged as umpires'. Also, players had to reside in a village for three months before becoming eligible.

ON THE MAP

Twenty-five years later the villages eligible were still specified. The points system, with home and away matches, had long since been incorporated in the rules, and the trophy still went to the team losing fewest matches. The committee had grown to two representatives from each village. One rule now read: 'That play commence at 3pm, allowing 20 minutes for tea; stumps drawn after four hours' play.' The entrance fee for each club was still, as in the beginning, 2s 6d, but the residential qualification period had been reduced to six weeks. It was laid down that 'no club shall protest against any umpire except after the match is over, and then only in case of any unfairness'. Somewhat curious was the rule which read: 'That any club playing an ineligible person in the competition, except with the consent of the opposing captain, forfeit the match.' The Bourne were made an exception to the rule about parish residence and, in fact, had the 22nd and last rule to themselves: 'The Bourne players shall be eligible who reside in area shown on map in hon secretary's possession.' This was the outcome of friction between The Bourne and Tilford in pre-World War One days, and at the competition annual meeting in 1909 the boundary between the two clubs 'regarding players' was agreed and a map prepared showing the respective areas. The rule and the map have long since disappeared.

The 1950 rules were much more clearly worded and only 12 in number. They began: 'All clubs within a radius of eight miles of Grayshott Village Hall shall be eligible to make application to compete in the competition.' Quite a masterpiece of phrasing. The final decision in all matters of substance now lay with the delegates' annual meeting or the stewards, and the entrance fee had risen to 10s. Rule 3 ran: 'All players must reside in the parish or within three miles of the club's ground. No player may play for more than one club in a season, but a player may continue to play for his old club, even if he changes his residence and is no longer within the required three-mile radius, provided that permission is given by the stewards. Serving soldiers, unless qualified as civilians, and professional cricketers, while employed as such, are not qualified. Every player must have four weeks' residential qualification as a civilian, but birth or long family residence qualifies immediately. Any club playing an ineligible player shall forfeit the match.' There is a footnote by the stewards: 'When considering applications from clubs who desire to play members living outside the three-mile radius the stewards will base their deliberations on the fact that I'Anson and Miller Cup Competitions were instituted to foster village cricket.'

HOURS OF PLAY

The MCC received mention in rule 4: 'Matches as arranged by the stewards shall be played according to MCC one-day rules. Win counts two points; draw, tie or abandoned game one point each. The club with the highest number of points shall hold the cup for one year. In the event of a tie for first place, a deciding match shall take place on a neutral ground, the venue to be decided by the stewards. Umpires for such matches shall be appointed by the stewards.' Rule 5 was particularly interesting: 'Play shall commence at 3pm (September, 2.30pm), with four hours' play. There shall be an interval of five minutes between each innings. If tea is taken between innings, the interval shall be dispensed with.

Intervals and tea interval shall be excluded from four hours' play. Interference by rain shall be included in the four hours, once play has commenced, but not otherwise. Match shall be abandoned unless commenced by 5.30pm, and stumps must in all cases be drawn by 8pm. After tea interval, captains and umpires shall arrange time of drawing of stumps. If a team is late, their opponents shall have the option of claiming extra time, notice of which must be given before the last over is called.' Other provisions included those for the election of five stewards annually, the appointment of a fair and competent umpire by each club – 'the competency of any umpire shall be decided by the stewards' – a match between the Winners and The Rest on the former's ground, and an addition proved necessary by experience, 'Incoming and outgoing batsmen shall cross at or before the pavilion'. Another clause laid down that if two clubs tied for first place 'the deciding match shall supersede the Winners versus The Rest fixture'.

The day of the week on which matches shall be played has never been stated in the rules and in bygone years games took place occasionally on Wednesdays and Bank Holidays (all day), but in modern times they have been confined to Saturdays. In deference to the view that the donor of the cup never envisaged play on the Sabbath, cup matches are not permitted on Sundays, and, despite a few applications from clubs to the contrary, this ban has met with general approval. It does not apply to representative games, as distinct from cup matches. The rules have worked very well through the years and, generally speaking, they have been faithfully honoured. Protests have been rare and the essential spirit of the game has been preserved.

The Miller Cup

THE Miller Cup was given in the spring of 1922 by Mrs Alexander Miller, of Stoatley Hall, Haslemere, to encourage the Second XIs and other junior teams of the district. She was a friend and patient of Dr Arnold Lyndon, of Grayshott, and it was on his suggestion that she gave the trophy, although not herself particularly interested in cricket. Each year up to the last war she also provided a replica of the trophy for presentation to the captain of the winning team. Despite some forebodings, the new competition was an immediate success and for more than a quarter of a century it has done much to develop the skill of young players and has enabled many veterans, no longer able to command a place in the First XI, to keep in touch with the game. This blend of experience and youth has often produced good teams. The competition has always been run in conjunction with the I'Anson Cup, with the same rules and officials, and on more than one occasion both trophies have been presented together.

Half-a-dozen teams took part in 1922 and the first winners were Shottermill II, under the captaincy of W. Trimmer. They finished level on points with Grayshott II and there was a play-off at Hindhead. Grayshott were a little unlucky. They made 27 and 39, and Shottermill, after topping their first innings score by four, were 22 for 9 in the second innings, when stumps were drawn. It is interesting to recall that one of the young Grayshott players was J. Eddey. Dr Lyndon presented the cup, a task he also performed on several other occasions. Shottermill II (captain, C. Snelling) were top again in 1923, winning 13 of their 14 matches, but rain prevented a Winners v Rest fixture. In 1924 Grayshott II were leading by one point when they entertained Whitehill II in the final match. Whitehill, well led by A.J. Chiverton, a good wicketkeeper despite physical handicap, beat them and won the cup. Next year Grayshott II had a play-off with The Bourne II at Hindhead. Rain interfered with the game, but Grayshott put their opponents out for 21 and replied with 28 for 6. Mrs Miller handed the cup to H. Langrish when Grayshott met The Rest on the same ground, and this was the only occasion on which she presented her own trophy to the winners. In other years she was usually in Scotland or abroad at the end of the summer and someone else deputised for her. Mrs Miller died at Haslemere in 1941.

TROPHIES PRESENTED TOGETHER

After the 1925 play-off no other was necessary until 1950, when the competition was run in two sections. Shottermill II (with C. Snelling again captain) were undefeated in 1926, winning 13 matches and scratching the other. There could be no Winners v The Rest game, as the Hindhead ground was needed for football, and both the I'Anson and Miller Cups were presented at Grayshott. The Bourne II, after being runners-up for two successive years, lifted the cup in 1927 and 1928, with Jack Knight as captain, the First XI also winning the I'Anson Cup in both those seasons. The Winners v The Rest game in 1927 saw a notable feat, for after The Bourne II had been dismissed for 24 they got rid of The Rest for 18, S. Briggs taking 4 for 9 and W. Arnold 4 for 7. In the next two seasons the Miller Cup went to Headley, under the captaincy of W. Hodgson and B. Glaysher. Grayshott II won the cup and all their matches in 1931, and their captain, R. Oakford, was again skipper when they lifted the trophy for the third time in 1934. In the two intervening years The Bourne II, under G. Arnold, and Headley II, led by J. Radford, were the winners. J. Radford received the cup from C.E. Fraser, the Headley president, who was on a visit from the Continent. It was a period of ascendancy for Headley II, as they won again in 1935 and 1936 – W. Chesham was skipper – and thus triumphed five times in the course of eight seasons. Both The Bourne teams won their respective cups in 1937, E.W. Newman being the Miller Cup captain. Rowledge II (captain, A.W. Lee) were the 1938 champions, and in the following season the competition was unfinished owing to the outbreak of war.

Not until 1947 was the Miller Cup again played for and, with nine teams in, the popular winners were Thursley, captained by J. Davidson. A. Arnold led The Bourne II to victory in 1948, with one team more competing. This number had grown to 13 when, in 1949, Shottermill II, under L. Oliver, gained their first success for 23 years. Fixtures were limited to 18 for each team. There were 15 entries in 1950 and the competition was run in two sections, The Bourne II (captain, J.G. Caesar) heading one and Kingsley (captain, F. Edwards) the other. It was Kingsley's first post-war season in the competition. The Bourne II won the play-off at Whitehill and, for the fourth time, the club became the holders of both trophies.

Unlike the I'Anson Cup, the Miller Cup could be won outright, for there is no proviso to the contrary, but so far no club has been successful three times running. In fact, only seven of the 19 teams competing through the years have won the trophy. The Bourne II have done so more times than any other club (six), and they are also the only club who have secured both cups in one season. Another Bourne record is that three of their players, G. Arnold, A.

Arnold and J.G. Caesar, have each captained winning teams in both competitions.

ALL OUT FOR TWO

Generally speaking, the competition has not produced many big individual scores or high totals, though there have been some very low ones. This is largely because players who show good form are usually promoted to the First XI. In May 1937, The Bourne II dismissed Binsted II for two, including one extra. The only run from the bat was off a snick through the slips which should have resulted in a catch! B. Karn, for Thursley II against Churt II in May, 1925, took 8 for 0 in a total of 14. There were three hat-tricks in a match at Tilford in August 1931, one in each innings by S. Butcher – then aged 17 – of Whitehill II, and the other by A. Westbrook, of Tilford II. Butcher took 9 for 10 and 9 for 12 and also made the winning hit. Probably the most curious coincidence the competition has known occurred in June 1948, when Churt II and Frensham II each made 58 in their first innings and Churt again scored 58 in their second knock, Frensham replying with 49.

Several clubs taking part in the Miller Cup Competition at various times never competed for the I'Anson Cup. Among them were Lythe Hill, one of the original entrants. The members were from the estate of Sir Richard Garton and played on his ground at Lythe Hill, Haslemere, now occupied by the Admiralty Signal Establishment. They remained in for the first four seasons and did quite well. Lindford competed for several years in the thirties and returned to the competition in 1949. A keen, sporting team, they have put up some very useful performances. Weyburn Sports, a side drawn from the Elstead engineering works of that name, were in for three seasons in the years before the last war, and many teams found them doughty opponents. Kingsley and Oakhanger, too, consist almost entirely of men who have not competed for the I'Anson Cup and their enthusiasm for the game is an asset for the competition. Churt II and Grayshott II, as in the I'Anson Cup, are the only two teams who have never missed a season in the Miller Cup.

Brief mention must also be made of the Lyndon Cup which Dr Arnold Lyndon gave for competition among Wednesday clubs. This, too, was run in conjunction with the I'Anson Cup. In the first season, 1914, Haslemere Working Men were the winners and Mrs Lyndon handed the cup to their captain, G. Egerton, at a Winners v The Rest match.

Five other teams took part: Grayshott, Headley, Hindhead, Shottermill and Whitehill. Shottermill, captained by T.J. Larbey, were the winners when the competition was resumed in 1920, Whitehill (captain, F. Boulton) were successful in the following year, and the trophy returned to Shottermill (captain, C.A. Covington) in 1922. Only three teams took part in 1923, when Whitehill won the Lyndon Cup and the I'Anson Cup as well. A.E. Jeeves was captain of the Lyndon Cup side. Owing to lack of entries, the competition then fell into abeyance and was never afterwards revived.

To the ladies

THE story of the competition is concerned mainly with the feats of men, but without the help and interest of the ladies – mothers, wives, sisters and sweethearts, yes, and even grandmothers – the game could not be played. How many week-end outings have been sacrificed only the ladies know. The summer offers so many other diversions, and no man goes off to the match Saturday by Saturday without some self-denial on the part of his womenfolk. The immaculate appearance of the great majority on the field is a constant tribute to their industry. Many of the ladies take more than a passing interest in cricket. Others confess that it holds no attraction for them, but one and all have a smile and a word of encouragement for the players who so often set off after lunch as optimists and return as pessimists. How consoling are wives and mothers when things go wrong, and how uncritically appreciative of a good score or fine bowling performance. And where could a man find a better audience for his story of what would have happened if –?

When the tea cups tinkle on any ground the ladies are there to serve the players and to do the washing-up afterwards. They are among the keenest of spectators and well to the fore at social functions. Some act as scorers, and very efficient scorers, too. Mrs John Chuter, of Frensham, and Mrs Ellsey, of Churt, are among those now serving in that capacity. Teams have their faithful band of feminine supporters and cricket is the better for their presence. So may the writer, on behalf of all the players, voice a heartfelt 'thank you' to that great anonymous sisterhood whose names never figure in the score-books or among the records, but who, season by season, make such a vital contribution to cricketers' enjoyment.

Never-ending story

NOW the tale is told, imperfectly, it is true, and doubtless with many omissions, for cricket is a never-ending story. Every man who has played it has his own fund of reminiscence, growing larger with the passing of time. 'He didn't mention so-and-so' or 'I could have told him –.' Such thoughts are inevitable. The author makes no claim to infallibility. The aim has been to place on record some of the outstanding and interesting features of the competition during the past 50 years, and if the book gives pleasure and revives pleasant memories the attempt will have been well worth while. 'Happy hours do not count themselves.' Indeed they do not, but men do well to remind themselves of the things that made them happy. Andrew Lang once wrote that the game draws all the brethren together, and one might add that in the heart of every cricketer there is always another spring!

Appendix

THESE statistics are as complete as possible, but records of some matches, particularly in the early years, have not been preserved. Tables were not published regularly or even at the end of the season, with one exception, until after World War One.

Complete continuity in that respect dates from 1924, and careful examination will reveal that several of the early tables printed here are not correct in detail, but after such a lapse of time they cannot now be adjusted. No tables were printed during the 1940 war-time season. Records and outstanding feats have been included only in cases where they could be checked by contemporary reports.

The batting achievements listed can be seen in proper perspective if it is borne in mind that cup matches are limited to four hours' play. Hence the comparatively few centuries, all of which were scored in very quick time. Many players were approaching three figures when the innings had to be declared closed.

Seasons in competition

(Possible 40)

*Churt	40
*Grayshott	40
Tilford	35
Shottermill	31
*Headley	30
Bourne	25
Whitehill	25
Thursley	18
Frensham	17
*Blackmoor	14
Rowledge	14
Hindhead	13
*Lynchmere	10
Grayswood	6
Oakhanger	6
Binsted	5
Haslemere WM	3
Elstead	2
Kingsley	1

* Original members

1901

Winners: Lynchmere (unbeaten).
Others: Blackmoor, Churt, Grayshott, Headley.

1902

Winners: Lynchmere (unbeaten).
Others: Blackmoor, Churt, Frensham, Grayshott, Headley.

1903

Winners: Grayshott (unbeaten).
Others: Blackmoor, Churt, Frensham, Lynchmere.

1904

Winners: Shottermill.
Others: Blackmoor, Churt, Frensham, Grayshott, Headley, Lynchmere, Tilford.

1905

Winners: Shottermill (unbeaten).
Others: Blackmoor, Bourne, Churt, Grayshott, Headley, Lynchmere, Tilford.

1906

Winners: Blackmoor (unbeaten).
Others: Bourne, Churt, Grayshott, Lynchmere, Tilford, Shottermill.

1907

Winners: Lynchmere. P12 W10 D1 L1
Others: Blackmoor, Bourne, Churt, Grayshott, Shottermill, Tilford.

1908

Winners: Tilford. P10 W9 D0 L1
Others: Blackmoor, Churt, Grayshott, Headley, Lynchmere.

1909

Winners: Tilford. P10 W8 D1 L1
Others: Blackmoor, Bourne, Churt, Grayshott, Lynchmere.

1910

Winners: Tilford. P8 W5 D1 L2
Others: Blackmoor, Churt, Grayshott, Lynchmere.

1911

Winners: Churt, after play-off with Shottermill.
Both clubs P8 W6 D0 L2
Others: Blackmoor, Grayshott, Tilford.

1912

Winners: Blackmoor. P10 W7 D0 L3
Others: Churt, Grayshott, Haslemere Working Men, Shottermill, Tilford.

1913

Winners: Shottermill. P12 W11 D0 L1
Others: Blackmoor, Churt, Grayshott, Haslemere Working Men, Hindhead, Tilford.

1914

Winners: Shottermill. P12 W11 D1 L0
Others: Blackmoor, Churt, Grayshott, Haslemere Working Men, Hindhead, Tilford.

1920

Winners: Grayshott. P10 W8 D2 L0
Others: Churt, Hindhead, Shottermill, Tilford, Whitehill.

1921

Winners: Shottermill. P13 W11 D0 L2
Others: Churt, Grayshott, Headley, Hindhead, Thursley, Tilford, Whitehill.

1922

Winners: Churt P14 W9 D3 L2
Others: Grayshott, Headley, Hindhead, Shottermill, Thursley, Tilford, Whitehill.

1923

Winners: Whitehill P14 W10 D1 L 3
Others: Churt, Grayshott, Headley, Hindhead, Shottermill, Thursley, Tilford.

1924

	P	W	D	L	P
Thursley	14	12	1	1	25
Shottermill	14	11	0	3	22
Grayshott	14	8	1	5	17
Whitehill	14	8	1	5	17
Tilford	14	4	2	8	10
Hindhead	14	4	1	9	9
Headley	14	3	1	10	7
Churt	14	2	1	11	5

1925

	P	W	D	L	P
Bourne	18	15	0	3	30
Whitehill	18	14	1	3	29
Grayshott	18	12	0	6	24
Shottermill	18	12	0	6	24
Thursley	18	8	1	9	17
Grayswood	18	8	0	10	16
Hindhead	18	7	0	11	14
Tilford	18	6	1	11	13
Headley	18	3	1	14	7
Churt	18	3	0	15	6

1926

	P	W	D	L	P
Bourne	18	16	0	2	32
Grayswood	18	11	0	7	22
Shottermill	18	11	0	7	22
Whitehill	18	11	0	7	22
Headley	18	9	0	9	18
Grayshott	18	9	0	9	18
Churt	18	7	0	11	14
Hindhead	18	6	0	12	12
Tilford	18	6	0	12	12
Thursley	18	4	0	14	8

1927

	P	W	D	L	P
Bourne	18	15	1	2	31
Whitehill	18	12	2	4	26
Shottermill	18	11	2	5	24
Headley	18	10	2	6	22
Grayshott	18	7	2	9	16
Tilford	18	6	3	9	15
Thursley	18	7	1	10	15
Grayswood	18	4	4	10	12
Churt	18	5	3	10	13
Hindhead	18	2	2	14	6

1928

	P	W	D	L	P
Bourne	16	13	0	3	26
Whitehill	16	10	0	6	20
Headley	16	8	1	7	17
Grayswood	16	8	0	8	16
Tilford	16	7	1	8	15
Hindhead	16	7	0	9	14
Churt	16	6	2	8	14
Grayshott	16	6	0	10	12
Shottermill	16	4	2	10	10

An alternative picture of the Grayshott team with the cup in 1929 to the one accompanying the section on the club in A Cup for Cricket. *Missing from the other shot were Percy Hicks and Percy Burrage, who are shown here, respectively, to the left of skipper Fred Puttick.*

1929

	P	W	D	L	P
Grayshott	15	10	1	4	21
Whitehill	16	10	0	6	20
Bourne	16	10	0	6	20
Grayswood	16	9	0	7	18
Shottermill	15	8	1	6	17
Headley	16	8	0	8	16
Thursley	16	6	0	10	12
Tilford	16	4	0	12	8
Churt	16	3	0	13	6

1930

	P	W	D	L	P
Bourne	18	14	0	4	28
Grayshott	18	14	0	4	28
Tilford	18	13	0	5	26
Whitehill	18	10	1	7	21
Shottermill	18	10	0	8	20
Churt	18	9	0	9	18
Headley	18	8	0	10	16
Hindhead	18	6	0	12	12
Thursley	18	3	1	14	7
Grayswood	18	3	0	15	6

Bourne beat Grayshott in the play-off

1931

	P	W	D	L	P
Whitehill	14	12	0	2	24
Tilford	14	10	1	3	21
Bourne	14	9	0	5	18
Shottermill	14	8	1	5	17
Grayshott	14	5	0	9	10
Churt	14	4	1	9	9
Headley	14	4	0	10	8
Hindhead	14	2	1	11	5

1932

	P	W	D	L	P
Frensham	14	9	3	2	21
Tilford	14	8	1	5	17
Grayshott	14	8	1	5	17
Whitehill	14	7	2	5	16
Headley	14	6	2	6	14
Bourne	14	7	0	7	14
Rowledge	14	5	1	8	11
Churt	14	0	2	12	2

1933

	P	W	D	L	P
Tilford	18	13	2	3	28
Kingsley	18	11	2	5	24
Bourne	18	11	1	6	23
Frensham	18	10	1	7	21
Headley	18	9	1	8	19
Whitehill	18	8	1	9	17
Churt	18	7	1	10	15
Grayshott	18	7	1	10	15
Rowledge	18	6	1	11	13
Thursley	18	2	1	15	5

1934

	P	W	D	L	P
Bourne	18	15	0	3	30
Rowledge	18	15	0	3	30
Oakhanger	18	13	0	5	26
Headley	18	10	0	8	20
Frensham	18	9	0	9	18
Tilford	18	9	0	9	18
Whitehill	18	6	1	11	13
Grayshott	18	6	0	12	12
Churt	18	4	0	14	8
Thursley	18	2	1	15	5

Bourne beat Rowledge in the play-off

1935

	P	W	D	L	P
Bourne	20	16	2	2	34
Tilford	20	15	1	4	31
Oakhanger	20	13	2	5	28
Grayshott	20	12	2	6	26
Headley	20	11	1	8	23
Frensham	20	8	1	11	17
Churt	20	7	2	11	16
Rowledge	20	7	1	12	15
Thursley	20	5	2	13	12
Whitehill	20	5	1	14	11
Shottermill	20	3	1	16	7

1936

	P	W	D	L	P
Bourne	20	19	1	0	40
Tilford	20	13	2	5	30
Headley	20	13	0	7	29
Grayshott	20	10	1	9	22
Whitehill	20	7	5	8	21
Rowledge	20	8	1	11	18
Oakhanger	20	7	2	11	16
Frensham	20	7	1	12	15
Churt	20	7	0	13	14
Shottermill	20	6	1	13	13
Thursley	20	5	2	13	12

1937

	P	W	D	L	P
Bourne	22	17	1	4	35
Grayshott	22	14	5	3	33
Tilford	22	15	2	5	32
Headley	22	13	1	8	27
Rowledge	22	13	1	8	27
Whitehill	22	12	3	7	27
Frensham	22	9	3	10	21
Oakhanger	22	9	3	10	21
Shottermill	22	8	1	13	17
Churt	22	5	4	13	14
Thursley	22	2	2	18	6
Binsted	22	2	0	20	4

1938

	P	W	D	L	P
Headley	22	19	0	3	38
Bourne	22	17	0	5	34
Rowledge	22	14	1	7	29
Frensham	22	13	1	8	27
Oakhanger	22	11	1	10	23
Tilford	22	11	1	10	23
Grayshott	22	11	0	11	22
Whitehill	22	10	1	11	21
Thursley	22	6	1	15	13
Churt	22	6	0	16	12
Shottermill	22	6	0	16	12
Binsted	22	5	0	17	10

1939

	P	W	D	L	P
Bourne	20	18	0	2	36
Tilford	20	15	0	5	30
Headley	20	14	0	6	28
Rowledge	20	12	1	7	25
Frensham	20	11	0	9	22
Oakhanger	20	10	1	9	21
Grayshott	20	9	1	10	19
Shottermill	20	7	2	11	16
Whitehill	20	7	1	12	15
Thursley	20	6	0	14	12
Churt	20	5	0	15	10
Binsted	20	3	0	17	6

1940

The Bourne and Headley finished level, each winning all but two of their matches, and The Bourne won the play-off at Frensham. Other teams: Churt, Frensham, Grayshott, Oakhanger (who withdrew during the season), Thursley, Tilford, Rowledge, Shottermill.

1946

	P	W	D	L	P
Bourne	16	14	1	1	29
Rowledge	16	11	2	3	24
Grayshott	16	9	2	5	20
Headley	16	9	2	5	20
Shottermill	16	7	1	8	15
Frensham	16	6	0	10	12
Churt	16	5	1	10	11
Whitehill	16	3	2	11	8
Thursley	16	2	1	13	5

1947

	P	W	D	L	P
Rowledge	18	15	1	2	31
Bourne	18	15	1	2	31
Shottermill	18	11	2	5	24
Tilford	18	11	1	6	23
Grayshott	18	9	1	8	19
Headley	18	8	1	9	17
Binsted	18	6	2	10	14
Churt	18	3	2	13	8
Frensham	18	3	1	14	7
Whitehill	18	2	2	14	6

Rowledge beat Bourne in the play-off

1948

	P	W	D	L	P
Bourne	14	10	2	2	22
Headley	14	10	2	2	22
Rowledge	14	7	4	3	18
Whitehill	14	5	3	6	13
Frensham	14	4	4	6	12
Grayshott	14	4	3	7	11
Shottermill	14	4	3	7	11
Churt	14	0	3	11	3

Bourne beat Headley in the play-off

1949

	P	W	D	L	P
Rowledge	18	15	0	3	30
Whitehill	18	13	0	5	26
Bourne	18	11	1	6	23
Headley	18	11	0	7	22
Tilford	18	11	0	7	22
Shottermill	18	8	0	10	16
Grayshott	18	7	1	10	15
Elstead	18	5	1	12	11
Frensham	18	5	1	12	11
Churt	18	2	0	16	4

1950

	P	W	D	L	P
Bourne	20	16	1	3	33
Headley	20	16	1	3	33
Grayshott	20	12	2	6	26
Elstead	20	11	1	8	23
Frensham	20	9	3	8	21
Rowledge	20	10	0	10	20
Binsted	20	7	3	10	17
Tilford	20	7	3	10	17
Whitehill	20	7	2	11	16
Shottermill	20	4	2	14	10
Churt	20	2	0	18	4

Bourne beat Headley in the play-off

Representative matches

Farnham League v I'Anson Competition

Played at Tilford on August Bank Holiday, 1921, this was the first of a series of annual matches.

I'Anson Competition

V.C. Rapley (Thursley) b Goodchild 5
F. Hoar (Blackmoor) c and b Alderton 0
A.E. Kent (Grayshott) b Alderton 2
M.W. Payne (Tilford) not out 20
M.L. Rapley (Thursley) c West b Alderton 2
W. Willmore (Tilford) st West b Alderton 5
Capt. P. Jones (Tilford) b Goodchild 7
F. Puttick (Grayshott) b Alderton 39
W.A. Stratford (Whitehill) c and b Goodchild 0
E. Johnson (Grayshott) c Tanner b Bidwell 25
B. Silvester (Churt) c Bidwell b Alderton 0
Extras 3
Total 108
Second innings: 98 (V.C. Rapley 30, Willmore 26, Jones not out 17, Payne 12).

Farnham League

A.J. Stevens (Bourne) b Stratford 25
H. Karn (Blacknest) b Stratford 13
H. Hack (Bourne) b Kent 6
L. Tanner (Bourne) c Hoar b Stratford 7
W. Thomson (Rowledge) c and b Stratford 0
W. Alderton (Blacknest) b Kent .6
C. Rutter (Blacknest) b Stratford 0
G.H. Boyes (Wrecclesham) c Puttick b Kent 0
L. Bidwell (Frensham) not out 8
L. Goodchild (Bourne) run out .0
C. West (Bourne) b Stratford 0
Extras 15
Total 80
Second Innings: 111 (Boyes 33, Alderton 18, Hack 14, Goodchild 12, Bidwell 11).

Surrey Clubs v Hants Clubs

Played at The Bourne on 6 August 1938, this match was generally considered to be the best of the series.

Hants

L.M. Mileham (Whitehill) c Pelling b Johns 22
F. Kenward (Headley) lbw b Parratt 5
R. Coombes (Grayshott) b Parratt 0
P. Kingshott (Grayshott) st Woodward b Parratt 5
S. Butcher (Whitehill) lbw b Goodchild 0
A. Bellinger (Headley) b Parratt 19
W.A. Clark (Oakhanger) b Johns .0
B.H. Swinstead (Oakhanger) c W. Poulter b E. Poulter .49
P. Barlow (Headley) not out 21
J. Hardy (Whitehill) c Little b E. Poulter 10
H. Blanchard (Headley) b Briggs 7
Total 138

Surrey

C. Woodward (Shottermill) b Butcher 1
L. Goodchild (Bourne) b Blanchard 6
W. Poulter (Bourne) b Butcher 4
J. Warner (Tilford) not out 45
P. Pelling (Frensham) c Bellinger b Clark 9
E. Poulter (Bourne) c Kenward b Blanchard 17
D.A. Little (Rowledge) b Swinstead 1
C. Johns (Tilford) c and b Barlow 16
A. Arnold (Bourne) st Hardy b Coombes 15
Extras 4
Total (for 8 wkts) 118
E. Parratt (Rowledge) and S. Briggs (Bourne) did not bat.

Other notable matches

Lynchmere v Grayshott – July 1903

Lynchmere, unbeaten since the competition started, needed to win this match to secure the cup outright.

Lynchmere

G. Madgwick st Chandler b Searle 0
C. Madgwick c Chandler b Lucas 1
P. Madgwick c Doyle b Searle 6
G. Puttick b Searle 8
Walter Harding b Lucas 6
A. West c T. Johnson b Lucas 4
A. Harding c Mitchell b Doyle 16
E. Moorey st Chandler b Lucas 6
W. Balchin c and b Lucas 11
H. Farminer not out 7
William Harding b Lucas 3
Extras 8
Total 76
Bowling: Lucas 6–24.

Grayshott

Sir A. Conan Doyle b G. Madgwick 37
I. Sant run out 4
G.F. Lucas b West 30
H. Mitchell c West b A. Harding 4
E.J. Searle b West 0
B. Chandler run out 3
A.E. Kent c and b A. Harding 9
W. Johnson c A. Harding b West 3
R. Petter b West 4
T. Johnson b West 2
A.I. Whitaker not out 8
Extras 6
Total 110
Bowling: West 5–25.

Grayshott v Churt – 12 August 1911

Churt

F.C. Martin retired hurt 23
H.A. Baker st E. Johnson b Moore 92
F.A. Wattridge not out 62
Extras 8
Total (for 1 wkt dec) 185
A.R.T. Baker, Major Edwards, A. Carver, H. Marden, B. Martin, A. Karn, F. Martin and W. Carter did not bat.

Grayshott: 101 (E. Johnson, P. Burrage, B. Chapman, M. Moore, A. Spearman, F. Puttick, W. Johnson, T. Madgwick, G. Halstead, R. Petter and A. White).

Tilford v The Bourne – Saturday, 25 July 1936

This match was chosen by the BBC for a broadcast commentary as being typical of village cricket.

The Bourne

A. Crow b Eddey 30
J. Goolding b Eddey 12
W. Poulter b Eddey 8
J. Knight lbw b Eddey 30
E. Poulter lbw b Johns 1
A. Arnold c Johns b Eddey 1
L. Goodchild c Goolding b Paine 27
L. Tanner c Johns b Eddey 9
F. Briggs not out 4
S. Briggs not out 0
Extras 4
Total (for 8 wkts dec) 126
W. Arnold did not bat.
Bowling: Eddey 6-36.

Tilford

J. Warner lbw b Goodchild 36
R. Morrell b Goodchild 2
K. Dutton c A. Arnold b E. Poulter 14
W. Kimber c A. Arnold b Goodchild 5
W. Waller b S. Briggs 0
J. Eddey b S. Briggs 0
R. Goolding not out 5
J. Martin not out 2
Extras 2
Total (for 6 wkts) 66
D. Paine, C. Johns and C. Fry did not bat.
Bowling: Goodchild 3-28.

Highest totals

Frensham v Blackmoor
11 July 1903
Blackmoor

W.W. Stratford lbw b Harding 9
W. Bone c and b Hiscock 47
C. Knight c Hiscock b Harben 53
W. Read c Burrage b Hiscock 117
A. Golder not out 43
A. Dawson run out 1
G. Oliver not out 10
Extras 20
Total (for 5 wkts dec) 300
G. Chiverton, A. Hoar, G. Cozens and J. Mitchell did not bat.

Frensham

H.F. Capper not out 80
H.D. Harben b Knight 32
W. Burrage lbw b Read 9
F. Hiscock c and b Read 6
F. Chapman b Read 11
Extras 9
Total (for 4 wkts) 147
W.S. Harding, J. Aslett, G. Veasey, Matthews, W. Bailey and H. Newman did not bat.

Tilford v Headley
23 July 1938

Tilford: 47 (J. Martin, C. Fry, W. Waller, J. Warner, D. Paine, J. Eddey, C. Johns, R. Bridger, R. Langley, R. Goolding, R. Morrell).

Headley

F. Courtnage c and b Paine 17
H.A.P. Heaslop c Johns b Goolding 79
W. North b Langley 10
F. Kenward not out 127
L.T. Pope b Goolding 3
A. Bellinger lbw b Goolding 3
J. Hudson lbw b Goolding 5
F. Dopson run out 14
P. Barlow b Goolding 2
E. Nash c and b Warner 4
H. Blanchard run out 8
Extras 7
Total 279

Tilford v Shottermill
26 August 1913

Tilford: 82 (W. Willmore, W. Merrett, C. Woods, Revd M.S. Ware, L.J. Sturge, G. Wakeford, A. Merrett, J. Poulter, C. Fry, F. Turner, W. Warner)

Shottermill

T.J. Larbey b A. Merrett 55
W. Pullinger c W. Merrett b Willmore 38
W. Balchin c Wakeford b A. Merrett 16
G. Knottley b A. Merrett 0
C. Pescod not out 107
H. Tickner c sub b Poulter 29
W. Dale not out 17
Extras 7
Total (for 5 wkts) 269
E. Moorey, P. Booker, N. Smithers and R. Brown did not bat.

Shottermill scored 263-6 declared (T.J. Larbey 67, W. Dale 62, F. Bargery 45 not out) against **Hindhead** in 1920.

The Bourne made 250 (W. Poulter 104 retired) v **Whitehill** in their first post-war cup match in 1946.

Twenty-nine instances of totals between 200 and 250 are recorded, ten of them by **The Bourne.**

Highest total in a Winners v Rest match was 230 by **Rowledge** in 1949, and the next highest 217 by **The Bourne** in 1928.

Lowest totals

Three by Oakhanger v Churt, 4 May 1940. At Churt. Oakhanger, batting first, made 57 and Churt replied with 49. In their second innings Oakhanger were dismissed by A. Matthews (5 for 1) and F. Bishop (5 for 2), nine players failing to score. The home team made 12 for 7 in their second innings.

Five by Churt v Tilford, 4 June 1938. At Churt. Tilford scored 91 and Churt were put out by J. Eddey (7 for 0) and R. Langley (2 for 1), the other man being run out. There were four extras, and the only run from the bat was scored by the village policeman, W. Storey. Eddey did the hat-trick. In their second innings Churt made 56.

A great many other instances of teams totalling fewer than 10 are recorded.

The century-makers

Year	Batsman	Score	Opponent
1903	W.Read (Blackmoor)	117	v Frensham
1907	A.H. Hartwright (Lynchmere)	108*	v Grayshott
1907	A.H. Hartwright (Lynchmere)	102	v Bourne
1907	A.H. Hartwright (Lynchmere)	116*	v Shottermill
1908	E. Johnson (Grayshott)	123	v Headley
1913	C. Pescod (Shottermill)	107*	v Tilford
1921	V.C. Rapley (Thursley)	110	v Hindhead
1922	M.W. Payne (Tilford)	102*	v Shottermill
1923	V.C. Rapley (Thursley)	107	v Churt
1924	V.C. Rapley (Thursley)	113	v Whitehill
1928	L. Goodchild (Bourne)	100	v Rest
1930	V.G. Barlow (Headley)	101*	v Thursley
1935	W. Poulter (Bourne)	115*	v Churt
1935	P. Kingshott (Grayshott)	133*	v Whitehill
1935	A. Crow (Bourne)	119	v Whitehill
1935	A. Bellinger (Headley)	100	v Shottermill
1936	W.A.J. Chuter (Frensham)	100*	v Whitehill
1937	P. Kingshott (Grayshott)	105	v Oakhanger
1938	W. Poulter (Bourne)	109*	v Rowledge
1938	F. Kenward (Headley)	127*	v Tilford
1938	R. Coombes (Grayshott)	108	v Churt
1938	L. Goodchild (Bourne)	104	v Thursley
1939	E. Hulbert (Oakhanger)	106	v Binsted
1939	J. Warner (Tilford)	102*	v Grayshott
1940	W. Poulter (Bourne)	127	v Grayshott
1940	M. Merrett (Tilford)	103	v Grayshott
1940	W. North (Headley)	102*	v Grayshott
1946	W. Poulter (Bourne)	104 ret	v Whitehill
1946	V.C. Rapley (Thursley)	111*	v Whitehill
1947	J. Voller (Bourne)	141*	v Shottermill
1947	H. Bicknell (Bourne)	104*	v Headley
1948	W. Poulter (Bourne)	101 ret	v Grayshott
1950	F. Kenward (Headley)	136	v Tilford
1950	F. Kenward (Headley)	112	v Surrey Clubs

* Denotes not out

Jim Voller, whose 141 not out for The Bourne in 1947 was the highest individual score in the first half-century of the competitions.

Best batting averages

A.H. Hartwright (Lynchmere) – 1907

I	NO	Runs	HS	Average
9	2	517	116	73.85

(In that season Hartwright also bowled 99.1 overs, including 15 maidens, for 232 runs and 63 wickets, average 3.68).

J. Warner (Tilford) – 1939

I	NO	Runs	HS	Average
17	6	628	102*	57.09

E. Johnson (Grayshott) – 1908

Average 50 (details not recorded).

Most runs in a season

L. Goodchild (Bourne)	757	1928
F. Kenward (Headley)	722	1938
W. Poulter (Bourne)	699	1938

Notable averages

Batsmen who have averaged 30 or more in a season include: C. Pescod (Shottermill), 33.40 (1913); J. Spencer (Churt), 31.00 (1927); W.O'B. Wilks (Kingsley), 31.27 (1933); W. Poulter (Bourne), 37.43 (1935); S. Butcher (Whitehill), 32.57 (1938); W. Poulter, 36.78 (1938); W. Poulter, 37.82 (1939); J. Voller (Bourne), 38.80 (1946); W. Poulter, 34.00 (1946); Major P.C. Britten (Rowledge), 31.42 (1947); W. Poulter, 30.91 (1948); Dr J. Seddon (Bourne), 39.41 (1950); F. Kenward (Headley), 32.40 (1950).

Best bowling averages

It has not been possible to compute these, as published averages often include figures for non-competitive matches and in reports of many games analyses were not given. The feat of taking over 100 I'Anson wickets in a season has been achieved on numerous occasions. The only recorded instance of all 10 wickets in an innings was by J. Eddey (Tilford) at Shottermill in 1949. Many bowlers have taken nine wickets in an innings.

Notable feats

In 1937, L.M. Mileham and S. Butcher (Whitehill) provided the only instance of two batsmen at the head of the averages aggregating over 1,000 runs between them.

	I	NO	Runs	HS	Ave
Mileham	22	0	540	95	24.54
Butcher	24	4	479	73	23.95

(Butcher also took 79 wickets)

In 1937 L. Goodchild (47) and W. Wells (31 not out) put on 84 for The Bourne's last wicket against Headley.

In 1938 L. Goodchild and S. Briggs (Bourne) took 196 wickets between them:

	O	M	R	W	Ave
Goodchild	229	74	541	112	4.83
Briggs	207.3	44	595	84	7.08

In 1925, C. Wisdom (Thursley) took the first five Headley second innings wickets in five balls, when Headley required 17 to win and lost nine wickets getting them.

In 1937, W. Dale (Shottermill) finished off the Churt innings for 32 by taking six wickets with successive balls.

All-round performances

For the four seasons 1925–28, L. Goodchild (Bourne) had the following figures:

1925

I	NO	Runs	HS	Average
22	1	157	24	7.47
O	M	R	W	Ave
212.3	69	327	117	2.79

1926

I	NO	Runs	HS	Average
25	0	372	49	14.80
O	M	R	W	Ave
221	65	366	96	3.81

1927

I	NO	Runs	HS	Average
31	3	583	98	20.82
O	M	R	W	Ave
318.1	122	529	111	4.76

1928

I	NO	Runs	HS	Average
28	1	757	100	28.04
O	M	R	W	Ave
292.4	111	504	118	4.27

In 1924, V.C. Rapley (Thursley) had the following figures:

I	NO	Runs	HS	Average
17	3	588	113	42.00
O	M	R	W	Ave
Not recorded		208	65	3.20

In 1950, F. Kenward, captain of Headley, scored 404 more runs and took 58 more wickets than any other member of the team:

I	NO	Runs	HS	Average
24	4	648	136	32.40
O	M	R	W	Ave
260.3	83	482	93	5.18

(He scored, in addition, 112 for the Hants Clubs v Surrey Clubs and made over 1,000 runs in all matches).

Miller Cup

Seasons in competition

(Possible 22)

Club	Seasons
*Churt	22
*Grayshott	22
Headley	21
*Shottermill	18
Bourne	17
*Whitehill	16
Rowledge	12
Frensham	11
Tilford	11
Thursley	9
*Hindhead	8
Binsted	7
Grayswood	5
Lindford	5
Kingsley	4
*Lythe Hill	4
Weyburn Sports	4
Oakhanger	3
Elstead	2

* Original members

Winners

Year	Winner
1922	Shottermill II (After play-off with Grayshott II)
1923	Shottermill II
1924	Whitehill II
1925	Grayshott II (After play-off with The Bourne II)
1926	Shottermill II
1927	Bourne II
1928	Bourne II
1929	Headley II
1930	Headley II
1931	Grayshott II
1932	Bourne II
1933	Headley II
1934	Grayshott II
1935	Headley II
1936	Headley II
1937	Bourne II
1938	Rowledge II
1939	Unfinished
1947	Thursley
1948	Bourne II
1949	Shottermill II
1950	Bourne II (After play-off with Kingsley)

Chairmen of Annual Delegates' Meeting

1901	W.H. Bailey
1902	A.E. Kent
1903/04	W.W. Stratford
1905	F.A. Wattridge
1906	W.W. Stratford
1907	F.A. Wattridge
1908/12	W.W. Stratford
1913	R.J. Petter
1914	W.W. Stratford
1920	A.R.T. Baker
1921	W.W. Stratford
1922	A.R.T. Baker
1923	W.W. Stratford
1924	R.H. Curtis
1925/29	W.W. Stratford
1930	G. Arnold
1931	W.W. Stratford
1932/33	G. Arnold
1934/35	H.J. Knight
1936	G. Arnold
1937/38	A.J. Stevens
1939	E. Wilkinson
1940/41	G. Arnold
1946	L.M. Mileham
1947	G. Arnold
1948	L.M. Mileham
1949	A.J. Stevens
1950	G. Arnold

Standing sub-committee

1921/22	A.R.T. Baker, T.J. Larbey
1923	R.H. Curtis, A.H.C. Harris
1924/25	E. Johnson, T.J. Larbey, F.C. Martin
1926	E. Johnson, T.J. Larbey, F.C. Martin, G.M. Hubbuck
1927	T.J. Larbey, E. Johnson, G.M. Hubbuck
1928/29	E. Johnson W. Dale, G.M. Hubbuck
1930	W. Dale, E. Johnson, W. Punter

Stewards

1931	W. Dale, E. Johnson, W. Punter
1932/33	G. Arnold, S. Corner, C. Woods
1934	J. Broadwood, L. Bell, J. Eddey, E. Newman, Dr F. Caldecott
1935	J. Broadwood, S. Corner, E. Johnson, E. Newman, Dr F. Caldecott
1936	E. Johnson, Dr F. Caldecott, E. Newman, S. Corner, L. Bell
1937/39	A. Bellinger, Dr F. Caldecott, E. Newman, E. Johnson, Revd F.A.W. Wilkinson
1940/41	A. Bellinger, E. Newman, E. Johnson, C. Woods, P. Pelling
1946	C. Woods, E. Johnson, P. Pelling, E.W. Newman, E.C. Ashford
1947/48	G. Arnold, E. Nash, J.G. Caesar, E. Johnson, E.C. Ashford
1949/50	G. Arnold, E. Nash, W.A. Penycate, J. Eddey, E. Johnson

This concludes the reprint of *A Cup for Cricket.*

Anniversary dinners

Golden Jubilee

THE dinner to mark the golden jubilee of the competitions was held in the Memorial Hall in Farnham on Monday, 19 November 1951. The *Herald* reported that the company of 170 people spent a 'very happy evening renewing old friendships and recalling the events of the past 50 years'.

The highlight of the speeches was a tribute to village cricket by John Arlott, who expressed the hope that in due course his son might be present at the centenary dinner. The district was not unknown to him; he remembered being caught off his shoulder at The Bourne, and recalled a football match at Binsted 19 years earlier when his team from the Basingstoke area went home 'with legs kicked from under us'. He continued: 'As far as cricket is concerned, I stand on extremely historic ground.' He said that 'Silver Billy' Beldham had once said, 'I can tell you when Hambledon club was founded because, when we beat them in 1780, the squire said, "Have I been raising this team for 30 years to be beaten by a mere parish?" '

Mr Arlott added: 'This is a dinner after 50 years. If I were asked to propose a toast I would do so to those gentlemen who played in this competition and who are not alive to be here tonight. We are told that the tradition is that son follows father. I wonder if it is possible for the secretary to put in the minutes that I would be very grateful if at the centenary my boy could be asked? If he lives a better life than his father he should be still alive! I should very much like to think he might be here, and with some of your sons.'

He said that village cricket did not really need encouraging. 'You cannot always raise a great side, but I have the firm belief that in the villages you will never stop kids from playing with a bat and ball. Winning cups, like winning the tests, does not matter much. The important thing is to remember it is just a game.

'If you are a good player you may play for vanity, or to blind your girlfriend with science, or to gain self-respect you don't get in any other way. If you are a bad player you play for only one reason – because you like it. I hope you will never be so keen on winning a competition that there is no place for a bad player. Otherwise who is going to provide the cars to take the good players to matches?

'There are 20 Test players and 200 county players, but there are thousands of bad players who love it just as much. When bad players cannot enjoy a game of cricket it ceases to be a game. If this dinner is held again at your centenary, the years that are coming won't be as bad as some people think. If I knew the centenary dinner would be held here, most of my fears would be dispelled.'

I'ANSON CUP COMPETITION

1901 - - 1951

GOLDEN
JUBILEE
DINNER

MEMORIAL HALL
WEST STREET, FARNHAM

19th NOVEMBER, 1951

Chairman :
MR. A. J. STEVENS
(President).

Golden Jubilee dinner menu card.

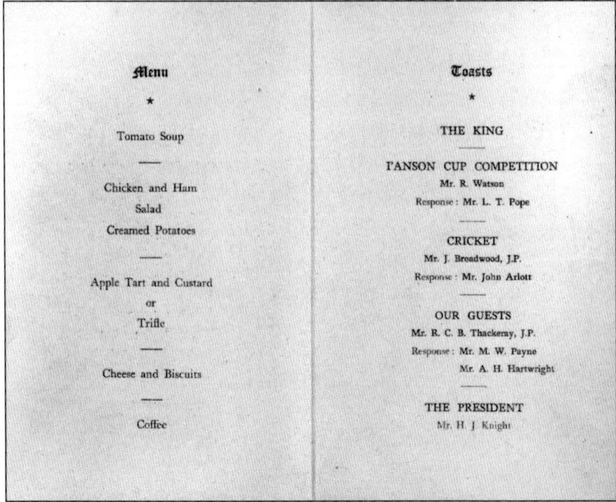

Menu

★

Tomato Soup

Chicken and Ham
Salad
Creamed Potatoes

Apple Tart and Custard
or
Trifle

Cheese and Biscuits

Coffee

Toasts

★

THE KING

I'ANSON CUP COMPETITION
Mr. R. Watson
Response: Mr. L. T. Pope

CRICKET
Mr. J. Broadwood, J.P.
Response: Mr. John Arlott

OUR GUESTS
Mr. R. C. B. Thackeray, J.P.
Response: Mr. M. W. Payne
Mr. A. H. Hartwright

THE PRESIDENT
Mr. H. J. Knight

Menu and toasts at the Golden Jubilee dinner.

The *Herald* reported that the dinner was 'admirably' organised by a committee comprising H.J. (Harry) Knight (competitions secretary), G. (George) Arnold, P. (Percy) Hicks, S.R. (Bob) Hooker and J.G. ('Dick') Caesar, and that it had been the wish to stage it in one of the villages but no hall was large enough. (The annual delegates' meeting had agreed to hold the dinner in Grayshott.) The 12 clubs in membership – Binsted, The Bourne, Churt, Elstead, Frensham, Grayshott, Headley, Rowledge, Shottermill, Thursley, Tilford and Whitehill – were all represented and gave financial support (two guineas each) to the venture. There were also a number of generous anonymous donations. It was later reported that the event made a profit of £8 19s 11d.

Lynchmere, the first winners of the cup, were represented by one of their most outstanding players of former times, A.H. Hartwright, who, in replying to the toast to the guests 'on behalf of the old boys who played in the early games', recalled the days when boys of his generation challenged those of the neighbouring villages. As befitted a former headmaster, he considered that cricketers did not practise like they used to, and he urged that more attention should be given to this matter.

The link between past and present generations, said the *Herald*, was the theme of an attractive painting, executed specially for the occasion by an anonymous well-wisher, which depicted a cricketer of former times shaking hands with a player of the present day beneath the symbol of the I'Anson Cup and with a gaily adorned pavilion in the background. There was also a display of cricket equipment, and the two I'Anson Cups were on the table in front of the president, A.J. Stevens.

A number of veterans who were playing at the beginning of the century attended, among them W.W. Stratford, 86, of Whitehill, known affectionately as the 'Father of the Competition'. Tribute was paid to the great part he had played in shaping the destiny of the competition in the early years. Bill Read (also W.W.), who played in the old Blackmoor team with Mr Stratford, was another honoured visitor. He had lost a leg in a road accident the previous winter but, at the age of 79, had overcome the handicap with immense courage, commented the *Herald*. He was given an ovation when mention was made of the fact that he scored the first century ever recorded in the competition (117 v Frensham at Frensham Hill on 11 July 1903).

M.W. (Meyrick) Payne, who played for Tilford in the 1920s and before World War One won four successive Blues at Cambridge and appeared for Middlesex as an amateur and for the Gentlemen against the Players, was among the speakers. He said: 'Teach the game to your sons and grandsons. See they are imbued with the fine spirit and that they will use it not only in play, but in dealings with their fellow men. I think when cricket dies, this country will die – but not before.'

One man who was unable to be present was A.E. (Albert) Kent, the first secretary of the competitions, who was unable to leave his home at Seaford because of ill health. In a letter he said: 'I had for many years looked forward to this event, and cannot say how disappointed I feel at not being with you all. It still gives me a great deal of pleasure to look back and think I have done one good deed in giving pleasure to so many who partake in the grand old game of cricket. Give them all my kindest regards. I shall be with you all in spirit – whisky for choice – with the toast of success to the I'Anson Cup Competition.'

There was also a letter from H.S. Altham, who wrote: 'I hope it may not be inopportune for the president of Hampshire County Cricket Club to send the cricketers of the I'Anson Competition congratulations and best wishes on the occasion of their golden jubilee dinner. May I also, as chairman of the MCC Cricket Enquiry Committee, take this chance of asking them to do everything they can to help the boys of the next generation to learn to love the game. We all know what cricket has meant, and still means, to us. The more it can mean to them the better, I believe, for England.'

The toast to the competition was proposed by R. ('Dickie') Watson, of Farnham Cricket Club, who said it had survived two world wars and had had a match broadcast by the BBC – the finest achievement, administratively, in his opinion.

In reply, L.T. (Theo) Pope said it was always pleasant to have the goodwill of senior clubs like Farnham and Haslemere. He said there had been only five secretaries, and two of the former holders of the post, Harry Edmead and Lewis Robinson, were present. The secretary for the past 16 years, H.J. Knight, had announced his impending retirement but there was reason to believe he would continue if a capable assistant could be found. Mr Pope referred to 'this commonwealth in miniature' of different clubs in villages with different ways of life, but with the common bond in cricket. He also appealed for encouragement for young players, saying: 'When Mr I'Anson gave this cup he never thought his unusual name would be perpetuated by what he did. I am sure that if he could see us tonight he would be happy that the competition was still flourishing. The best tribute to him is to carry on the competition with that same spirit of friendship and good fellowship that has always characterised us in the past, and to keep in the forefront the aim written on the cup – to encourage village cricket.'

Among the guests included in a toast proposed by R.C.B. (Reg) Thackeray, president of Headley CC, was Jack Parker, the 'great Surrey all-rounder who would probably have had a place in the England side but for the war'. He was a coach at the Farnham School of Cricket in pre-war days and had helped to raise the standard of I'Anson cricket. At his benefit match in Farnham Park the previous August, between Surrey and a Farnham and District side, the sum raised was the second largest in the county. (According to the competitions' minutes, the figure was £243 6s 7d [£243.33], which was an 'outstanding result considering the inclement weather'.)

Diamond Jubilee

The competitions were again in celebratory mood when the diamond jubilee dinner was held in the TA Centre in

Diamond Jubilee dinner menu card.

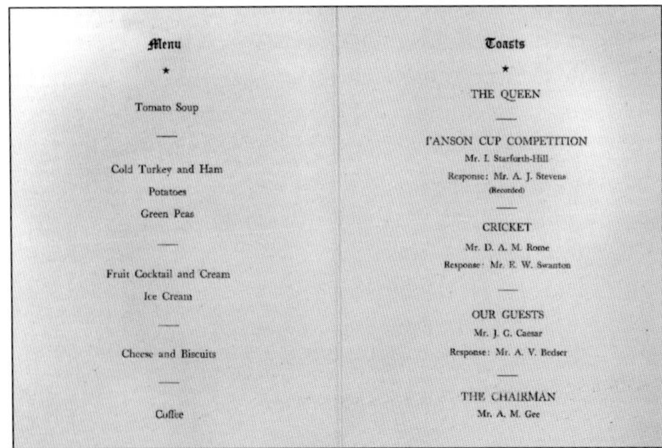

Menu

★

Tomato Soup

—

Cold Turkey and Ham
Potatoes
Green Peas

—

Fruit Cocktail and Cream
Ice Cream

—

Cheese and Biscuits

—

Coffee

Toasts

★

THE QUEEN

—

I'ANSON CUP COMPETITION
Mr. I. Starforth-Hill
Response: Mr. A. J. Stevens
(Recorded)

—

CRICKET
Mr. D. A. M. Rome
Response: Mr. E. W. Swanton

—

OUR GUESTS
Mr. J. C. Caesar
Response: Mr. A. V. Bedser

—

THE CHAIRMAN
Mr. A. M. Gee

Menu and toasts at the Diamond Jubilee dinner.

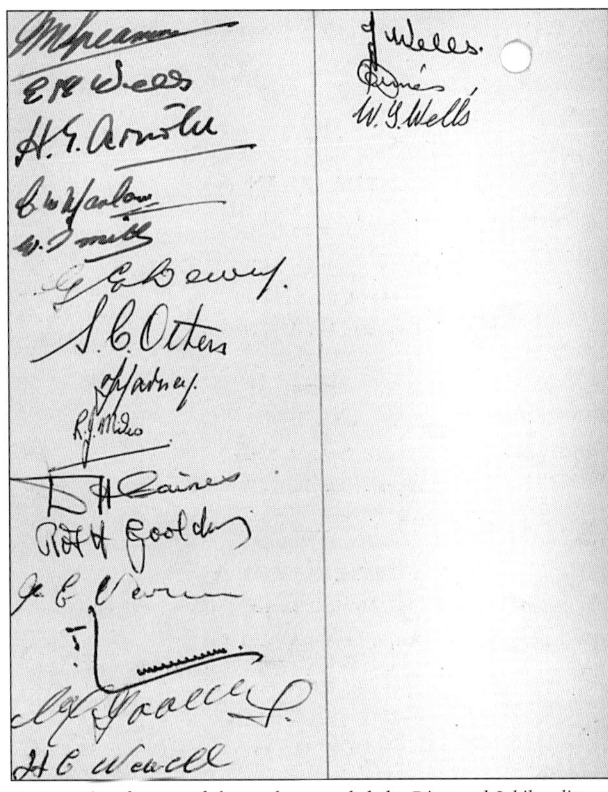

Autographs of many of those who attended the Diamond Jubilee dinner, including E.W. Swanton and Alec Bedser.

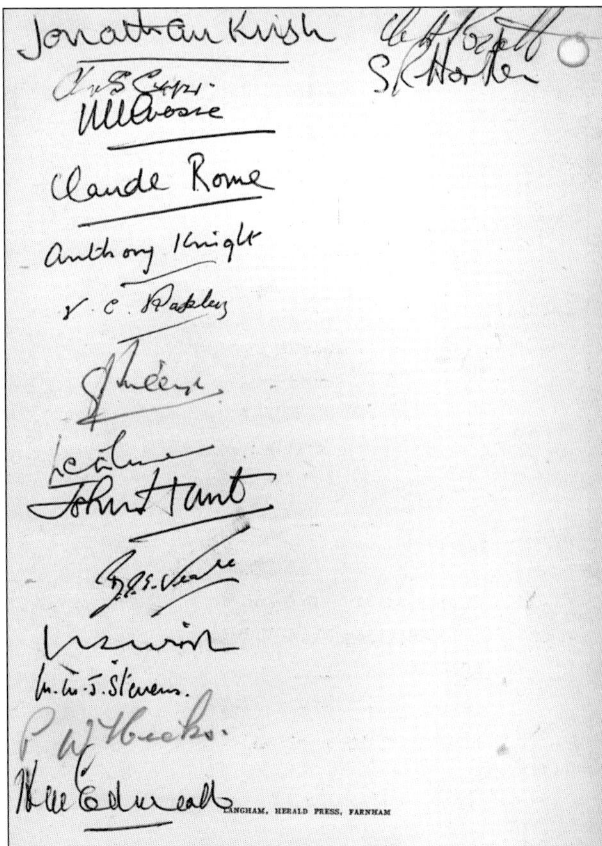

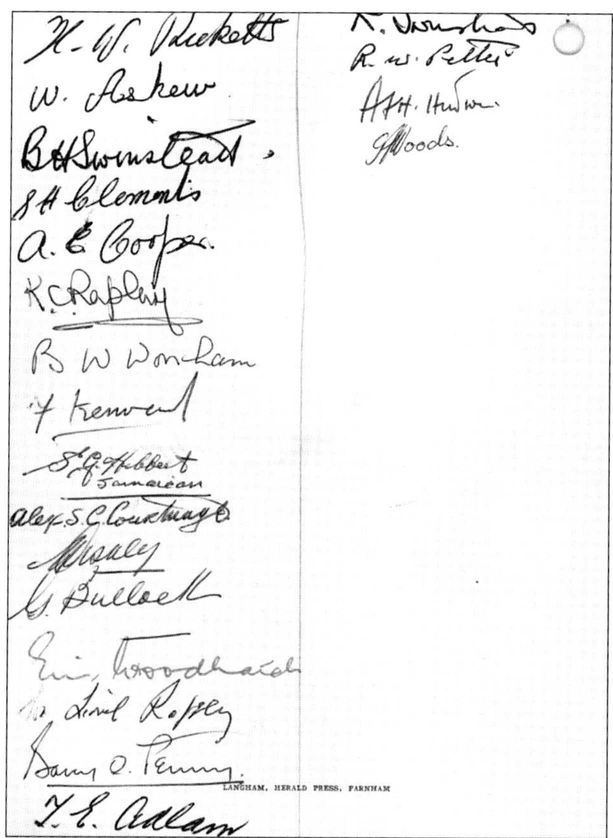

LANGHAM, HERALD PRESS, FARNHAM

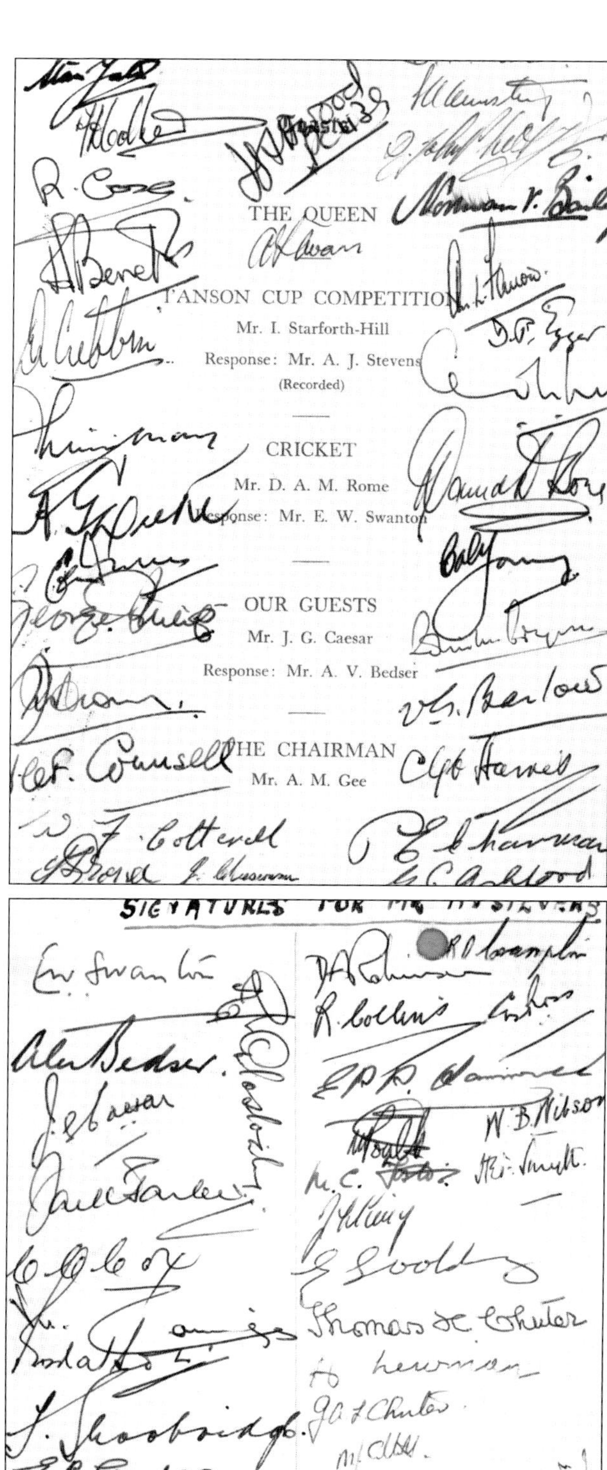

THE QUEEN

I'ANSON CUP COMPETITION
Mr. I. Starforth-Hill
Response: Mr. A. J. Stevens
(Recorded)

CRICKET
Mr. D. A. M. Rome
Response: Mr. E. W. Swanton

OUR GUESTS
Mr. J. G. Caesar
Response: Mr. A. V. Bedser

THE CHAIRMAN
Mr. A. M. Gee

LANGHAM, HERALD PRESS, FARNHAM

E.W. Swanton and Alec Bedser, flanked by J.G. Caesar (right) and H.J. Knight, at the Diamond Jubilee dinner.

S.R. ('Bob') Hooker, the former Tilford player and secretary, left, and B.J.E. ('Sam') Veale, right, who played for Frensham in their 1932 victory and who lived at Bridge Farm, Tilford, at the Diamond Jubilee dinner.

The Bourne's table at the Diamond Jubilee dinner included Bill Poulter (left) and, next to him, Lew Goodchild.

More guests at the Diamond Jubilee dinner, including the Wrecclesham scorer Charlie Marlow (right) and, next to him, H.G. (Harold) Arnold of The Bourne.

Farnham on Friday, 14 October 1960. The guest of honour was E.W. Swanton, cricket commentator and writer, and also among the 200 diners were Alec and Eric Bedser, the Surrey twins who always gave great support to the competitions, Vic Cannings, the Hampshire bowler who began his career with Farnham, Tom Clark, the Surrey opener, who was to have a benefit year in 1961, and Jack Parker.

The two I'Anson Cups occupied pride of place, along with the Miller and Stevens Cups, and there was the added interest of two of Alec Bedser's England blazers, a number of caps and two cricket balls presented to him, one with which he took his 150th Test wicket.

The president, A.J. Stevens, was unable to be present, but diners heard a tape-recorded message from him. (A 10in record of the speeches at the dinner was sent to him at Christmas 1962, with the good wishes of the competitions.) H.J. Knight, the former long-serving secretary, then a vice-president, steward and the treasurer, was in the chair, and the secretary of the day, Peter Warman, was the toastmaster. Canon Aelfric Hudson, rector of Compton and former vicar of The Bourne who was a great supporter of I'Anson cricket, said grace.

Ian Starforth-Hill, of Frensham who later became a judge, in proposing the toast to the competitions, said: 'All of us ought to know a lot more about the I'Anson Cup.' He then proceeded to relate the history of the competitions and praised officers, past and present, for their hard work and devotion to the cause. 'No competition like this could work unless they were prepared to put in hard work,' he said.

Mr Starforth-Hill mentioned that Arthur Hoar, who had played for Blackmoor in the first season, and Harry Newman and Tom Chuter, captain and vice-captain of Frensham in 1903, were present, as was Bob Morris, who had played for Tilford as long ago as 1890 although he had not taken part in the competition's earliest matches. Three stalwarts of a later generation who were mentioned were Lewis Goodchild (The Bourne), V.C. Rapley (Thursley) and Frank Kenward (Headley). 'They were the forerunners of what will be going on for years and years. Here is the backbone of the I'Anson Cup, and you can look to yourselves for the rest,' he said.

The competition was not designed entirely for fun, he added. It tried to help people who were in trouble. From time to time there were benefits for people who were in financial need. As for the spirit that existed, one just had to look at the number of people who were wearing the I'Anson tie to see that nothing was lacking in that direction. There were three good things about village cricket: 'It brings us all together; it gives a chance to younger people; and it is nearly always played in the right spirit. What we want is a good game of cricket, and for that there is nothing to beat village cricket.'

In his recorded reply, Mr Stevens said: 'The I'Anson Cup and its fellow competitions provide youngsters with games and keeps flying the flag of the greatest summer game.' Cricket demanded devoted, dedicated service. He hoped the competitions would be celebrating their centenary in 40 years.

'Jim' Swanton, replying to the toast to cricket proposed by D.A.M. (David) Rome, a prominent Farnham resident and Surrey official, said: 'I never thought I would have the privilege of sitting down to dinner with a gentleman who played for Tilford in 1890. It practically takes one back to Beldham and the earliest days of cricket of which your part of the country is the very cradle.' He said that the people who played in the competitions were the envy of a lot of other cricket organisations because the I'Anson competitions were so successful. 'There is no decline in the cricket in which you play. It took root here and the tree is as strong, or stronger, than it was before…' Cricket, he said, started as a primitive game, but it was now one of the most complicated games. 'We are inclined to forget that it is a game. But you play it for what it is, which is a fine thing. I wish you success in 1961 and all the years in which you play this great competition.'

Alec Bedser, replying to the toast to the guests, proposed by J.G. Caesar, said players who had had benefit matches in Farnham, against district sides which included I'Anson players, really appreciated them. 'The keenness here is far in excess of anywhere else in the country,' he said.

H.J. Knight, in replying to a toast to himself as chairman of the dinner, said: 'I think you would all do well to remember the stalwarts of the past, many of whom made great contributions, who, unfortunately, are no longer with us in this proud moment of our history. It can truthfully be said that we are enjoying the fruits of their labours.' He paid tribute to past secretaries, in particular Leslie Mileham who was responsible for getting the competitions under way again after World War Two, and who had come from his home in Sandbanks for the occasion. Referring to close friends, including 'Dick' Caesar, who had been intimately concerned with many of the new ideas put into operation, Mr Knight said: 'I personally feel we have been one big happy family, with a great father in AJ, and yours truly as a sometimes ruthless nursemaid.'

In the *By the Way* column in the *Herald*, Theo Pope wrote: 'A moving moment at the dinner came when Peter Warman called the roll year by year up to 1925. First to stand was Arthur Hoar, of Blackmoor, who responded to 1901. Then came Tom Chuter, of Frensham (1902). Others who started playing in the first decade of the competition included Harry Newman (Frensham), George Arnold (The

Bourne), Harry Edmead (Grayshott and Hindhead), who was secretary of the competition from 1927-30, and Arthur Taylor. George Barlow (Headley) started in 1913, Bob Petter (Grayshott), who stood when 1920 was called, was still playing for the same club. The remarkable thing about all these veterans was their apparent youthfulness and zest for reminiscence. Oldest of them all was Bob Morris, of Tilford, who started playing in 1890... The gathering included Lt Col T.E. Adlam VC, of Blackmoor, who played cricket until he was 65.' The piece concluded by saying that the Stevens family was represented by one of AJ's sons, Michael, and two of the president's grandsons, John Hunt and Brian Stevens.

The diary piece included an anecdote concerning the name I'Anson. A former Churt wicketkeeper, P.E. ('Tug') Charman, while on a motoring holiday in the North of England the previous month, had been surprised to discover that the name of the licensee of the Crown Hotel in Grewelthorpe, near Ripon, was Mr H. I'Anson. The latter was very interested in the I'Anson tie which Mr Charman produced, but could not claim that his family was connected to the donor of the cup. However, he showed Mr Charman a report in a local newspaper published that week that recorded the sale of Hill House in Richmond, Yorkshire, once the home of Frances I'Anson, who had inspired the song *Lass of Richmond Hill*.

There was a postscript to the dinner in the form of an exchange of letters to the *Herald* by two former players who had attended. On 4 November 1960, B.H. Swinstead, of Blackmoor, having paid tribute to the organisers 'for all their hard work and good intentions', said the event turned out to be reminiscent of a first-class cricket match. 'We arrived to find car park chaos, milling crowds at the bar, through which we had to fight our way to the lavatories where we met a few old friends for a brief chat, then fought our way back to the bar just in time to get a pricey drink before the umpires' bell rang. We exchanged a few glassy stares with the teams, then sat down to watch while the field was set and the batsmen came in.

'These preliminaries over, the opening batsmen took guard, then proceeded to stay in for half an hour without scoring before being run out. The remaining batsmen stayed in for varying lengths of time, we applauded one or two good cracks and stood occasionally to rest our weary behinds, while the screens were moved or to see who dropped a catch. There was a certain amount of barracking from the direction of the bar towards the end of play, spectators started to drift away before play had finished and some of the players left the ground after having their innings. There could be no result other than a draw as only one side batted and above all there was rain. This was not village cricket, but town and county cricket.'

A reply the following week came from E.C. Ashford, formerly of Headley and Whitehill and then living in Gloucestershire. 'I attended the dinner by virtue of the fact that for many summers I was allowed to carry a bat out to the crease (and carry it back again to the pavilion shortly afterwards) on Saturday afternoons. The committee which invited me had, I understand, been given full powers by the general meeting of the I'Anson and Miller Cup Competitions to make all the necessary arrangements. I quite agree that some of the speakers went on too long, but that is something that I was prepared for. But what can one do about it?

'I noticed that Mr Swinstead complained of the crowd around the bar. Was this crowd specially imported by the committee to prevent guests from getting a drink? The crowd I recall was composed of players and ex-players from Headley, The Bourne, Frensham, Thursley, Whitehill, Churt, and they pushed and they shoved and they drank and they laughed as they did and still do at the Barley Mows, the Cricketers, the Shants, the Holly Bushes in the I'Anson country. For a spell I was back in the past and I could see other faces in that crowd – Chappie Messenger, Old Man Stratford, Walter Dale, Charlie Courtnage to name a few. Happy faces of a past age! May the memory of this "hostile" crowd remain green in my memory for many years to come!

'In conclusion, may I point out that I, like Mr Swinstead, have really no right to rush into print, nor have I any way of airing a grievance for I, like Mr Swinstead, do not now belong to any club of the competitions. I felt, however, that some sort of reply to his letter was necessary to remove the nasty taste that it left in our mouths.'

Mr Swinstead returned the following week and said the intention of his parody was to compare it with a first-class match not to air grievances. 'I did not "rush" into print, I gave a good deal of thought to the subject and heard other opinions as well, and we all have a perfect right to express our opinions. One can do something about long-winded speakers; it is common knowledge that after-dinner speeches should be limited to about 10 minutes each. Earlier "bar-racking" would have helped. No mention was made in my letter of any "hostile" crowd at the bar; they were a very cheery and boisterous lot. Players and ex-players from many more clubs than those mentioned by Mr Ashford were present at the dinner. I will now retire!' And to that, the editor added that 'stumps will now be drawn'.

The Seventieth

A third dinner was held in the Memorial Hall in Farnham on Friday, 26 March 1971, to mark the 70th anniversary. Nearly 170 people were present, including Arthur Hoar, aged almost 90.

In introducing John Arlott to propose the toast to 'Cricket', the president, J.G. Caesar, said: 'He talks a language we understand in this part of the country.'

I'ANSON CUP COMPETITION

1901 1971

70th Anniversary Dinner

MEMORIAL HALL
WEST STREET, FARNHAM
26th MARCH, 1971

President:
MR. J. G. CAESAR

Seventieth anniversary dinner menu card.

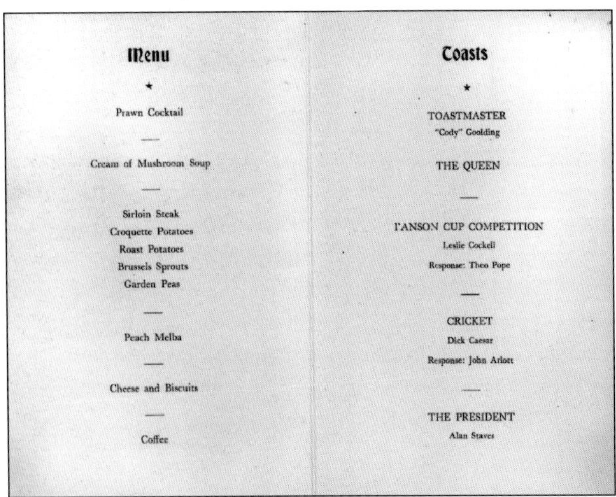
Menu

Prawn Cocktail

Cream of Mushroom Soup

Sirloin Steak
Croquette Potatoes
Roast Potatoes
Brussels Sprouts
Garden Peas

Peach Melba

Cheese and Biscuits

Coffee

Toasts

TOASTMASTER
"Cody" Goolding

THE QUEEN

I'ANSON CUP COMPETITION
Leslie Cockell
Response: Theo Pope

CRICKET
Dick Caesar
Response: John Arlott

THE PRESIDENT
Alan Staves

Menu and toasts at the 70th anniversary dinner.

Mr Arlott, by then the voice of cricket, recalled that he had said to the organisers 20 years ago, 'if you ask me again 20 years in the future, the answer will still be "yes".' He described the district as 'cricket country', and spoke of the days when Farnham, Fleet and Hartley Wintney had the greatest teams in England. 'We are in a place where this game belongs.' It was a game that would never stop because, in a way, it gratified the simplest of urges. 'It started in these parts – in the churchyards and on the greens, and it will never be stamped out.'

Leslie Cockell, treasurer, and subsequently president, of Farnham CC, who had played for Frensham, proposed the toast to the competitions, and said the I'Anson Cup conjured up in his mind a picture of a friendly, peaceful game of cricket on the village green – 'a sacred heritage'.

L.T. Pope, in response, recalled the secretaries of the competitions from Albert Kent, who served for the first 24 years. The oldest surviving former secretary was H.M. Edmead, aged 83 and living in Guildford, who had been prevented by ill health from being present, and the good wishes of the dinner were to be sent to him. The late H.J. Knight had served for 23 years during which the competitions 'attained great popularity'. L.M. Mileham, who had restarted the competitions after World War Two, when Mr Knight was unavailable, had travelled from Poole to be present, but another former incumbent, P.C. Warman, was unable to attend because of a business engagement. H.C. Bicknell, who had barely taken over from Harry Knight when he resigned and moved to Australia, was now back in the area and was present, while Lt-Col. J. Cornwell was now living in Australia. The current secretary, Alan Staves, had already done a tremendous amount of work for the competitions, Mr Pope said. The game in 1971 was as good as ever it had been and the youngsters were jolly good players, he added. 'Village cricket has gone on all our lives and long may it continue to do so,' he said.

The menu card contained the following verse, by Herbert and Eleanor Farjeon, entitled *The Game that's Never Done:*

Soft, soft the sunset falls upon the pitch,
The game is over and the stumps are drawn,
The willow sleeps in its appointed niche,
The heavy roller waits another dawn –
Bowled is the final ball again,
Hushed is the umpire's call again,
The fielders and the batsmen cease to run –
But memory will play again
Many and many a day again
The game that's done, the game that's never done.

A.J. Stevens and the Stevens Cup

ALFRED Julius Stevens, whose background is described in *A Cup for Cricket*, was elected the first president of the competitions in 1936. From his marriage in 1905 until his death in 1968 he lived in The Bourne. When he had completed 21 years as president, the competitions presented him with a garden seat bearing the following inscription: 'Presented to A.J. Stevens Esq, MA, by the clubs and officers of the I'Anson and Miller Cup Competitions, as a token of their affection and respect for a generous friend and patron of cricket, and to mark his completion of 21 years as their president – Autumn 1957 – "Happy hours do not count themselves".'

In a letter to Harry Knight, who himself had just completed 21 years as secretary and treasurer, Mr Stevens thanked the competitions for the gift 'that has been made me for having contrived to live on for 21 years after having been elected president and thoroughly enjoying it! This in fact is the case, and I can only say that I have been very proud and gratified to have occupied the position for so long.

'You will appreciate as much as I do that the very efficient officers and committee are entirely responsible for the high position the competition has attained in something beyond the sphere of local cricket. They have achieved this by working harmoniously together for its benefit, though, as in all forms of sport, differences of opinion inevitably arise, especially on rules and regulations and, indeed, add much of interest to their administrative work, and the continuous high reputation of the competition is doubtless largely due to the tactful solution of such differences as have arisen. All the good work that has been going on over so considerable an area seems to have caught up your president in the general feeling of gratitude for the achievement, small though his personal part in it has been. I am therefore justified in feeling that this token, so deeply appreciated by me, is also a tribute to all those with whom I have been associated.

'The form of this generous gift is most apt for several reasons. First, I have in any case been turning over lately in my mind the happiest way to contrive a seat in my garden of a type really matching the surroundings. Secondly, I have been personally working on a little glade in the wood, which was crying out for just such a seat from which a viewer could enjoy the scene in comfort, shade, and with the light behind him (or her). Incidentally, the seat is delightfully suited to three to four persons' comfort, or perhaps best of all for two when two's company and three's a crowd. Lastly, as I frequently potter in this glade myself, I equally frequently wish to rest my legs as they have just about arrived at the age of four score years and begin to creak a bit.

'Further, I much appreciate the very kind inscription with its apt quotation, for it's true I began to be a cricket fan in 1885 (particularly of village cricket) and still am, and that, coupled with gardening and its serene hours, is as pleasant a background to the routine of work as can be found.

'My last wish is that neither you, nor any other interested member, should let the year pass without paying a visit to this seat as sited and drinking to its health with me.'

A.J. Stevens was then elected life president, and at Christmas 1962 the competitions sent him greetings in the form of a 10in record of the speeches at the Diamond Jubilee dinner of the I'Anson Cup on 14 October 1960, when E.W. Swanton was the guest of honour.

Little Twynax, off Shortheath Road, The Bourne, the home of A.J. Stevens. Originally three cottages and about 300 years old.

Lindford, second winners of the Stevens Cup in 1954. Standing, from the left: W. Dunk (umpire), G. Putman, W Broadbent, J. Geering, P. Viney, H.W. Merrett, J. Burton, A.S.C. Courtnage (umpire), R.A. Viney (scorer). Seated: H. Warburton, C. Butcher, J. Lambley, who had broken a leg while fielding earlier in the season, A W. Cooper (captain), A.J. Stevens, N. Disney, the current competitions life president, E. Rooney, D. Fear.

Mr Stevens, then in his 90th year, died on 24 January 1968, and at the annual meeting at the end of that year, the acting chairman, Arnold Gee, described him as a true gentleman and a generous supporter of cricket, adding, 'I have not known a finer man'. The meeting stood for a moment in silence, and later J.G. ('Dick') Caesar was elected the new president.

The competitions' connection with the Stevens Cup can be traced back to September 1952 when, at a special delegates' meeting in Churt Village Hall, it was agreed to adopt the recommendation of the stewards and form what was in effect a second division of the I'Anson Cup. This was proposed by The Bourne, and seconded by Shottermill, after it was decided that a separate competition would not be a good idea. Clubs within eight miles of Grayshott were to be approached and the new division would be open to First XIs. It was anticipated that some Miller Cup sides would wish to join, and the Miller competition would then be restricted to Second XIs of I'Anson clubs. In time, there would be promotion and relegation between the two divisions, but not in 1953. It was suggested Binsted, Lindford, Thursley and Wrecclesham compete in the new competition, and to recruit further clubs. It was reported that Bentley, Blackmoor, Grayswood and Northchapel had showed an interest in joining in 1954.

The move was ratified at the ADM in December 1952 when it was announced that Binsted, Kingsley, Lindford, Thursley and Whitehill would play each other four times for a trophy donated by the president and to be known as the Stevens Cup. Wrecclesham, who had only been in the Miller Cup until then, were elected to replace Whitehill in the I'Anson Cup, and 10 teams would compete for the Miller Cup, including Wrecclesham II.

The first two matches in the Stevens Cup were played on 25 April 1953, Binsted beating Kingsley by nine wickets and Lindford defeating Whitehill by eight wickets. Thursley, who were to be the first champions, had a bye. The following Saturday, Thursley found Kingsley's Fred Edwards in particularly fine form, and his 9-9 remains a Stevens Cup record.

C. Butcher, of Lindford, who made 106 and shared an opening stand of 127 with A. Cooper (40) at Whitehill on 4 July 1953, scored the competition's first century.

Thursley often fielded five members of the Rapley family, and it was Albert who was handed the trophy by the donor on 29 August. It did not matter that they lost to Lindford that day, because the league had been won the previous weekend when the skipper had whipped out Binsted with figures of 8-5, including four wickets in as many deliveries.

Thursley thus became the first club to win all three trophies, having won the I'Anson Cup in 1924 and the

Miller Cup in 1947. Mr Stevens said three of the 1924 team were the brothers M.L. (Lionel) Rapley, the captain, and V.C. Rapley, plus a cousin, Felix Rapley. Albert and Walter were sons of Felix, and also in the 1953 team were Lionel's son, M.C., and R.C. (Ron) Rapley, the son of V.C. and whose son Barry keeps alive one of the I'Anson Cup's most celebrated names.

V.C., whose story is told in *A Cup for Cricket*, saw the Stevens Cup presented for the first time and indeed made several appearances in the season. One of the umpires that day was 'Jock' Davidson, captain of the 1947 Miller side, who had moved to Scotland but found the call of Thursley too strong and had returned to the village.

Mr Stevens said he had given the trophy with the object of broadening the basis of the competitions. He looked forward to the time when it would be possible to introduce a system of promotion and relegation. He had kept the cup under wraps until the evening before the presentation when he entertained many of the stewards of the competitions to dinner at the Coffee House in Farnham. Present on that occasion were George Arnold, J.G. Caesar, R.J. Clements, Jim Eddey, H. Massey and Harry Knight, together with L.T. Pope. There were apologies presented by E.R. Parratt and R.C.B. Thackeray, both indisposed, and E. Nash and E.A.M. Gee, who were on holiday.

Thursley celebrated their success with a dinner in the Red Lion in the village on Friday, 30 October, and at which Mr Stevens was the guest of honour. It was always a great pleasure to sponsor cricket, he said, because he was so fond of the game. 'I don't know how one starts liking cricket, it seems to be in the blood when one is quite small, and it grows as one gets older.' It started with hero-worship, and later came the small boy with all his statistics. Cricket had an extraordinary attraction that could not be explained, but one of its joys was that one never knew what was going to happen next. 'I don't think you need worry about it. I think one really likes cricket just because one likes it.'

The chairman, Major Anthony Knight, said: 'Cricket is the one game in the world that has made England what it is. The game of cricket is the centre of the English way of life, and it starts on the village green.' He added that the importance of the game was such that in Thursley they must ensure that whatever happened there would always be a cricket club in the village. At the moment they struggled along against high prices of bats and balls, and the expense of travel which was the greatest financial worry of all and one that killed many clubs. 'Luckily we have a certain amount of funds in hand,' he added. 'Nevertheless, there are certain things we want to do. We want to do a bit more to our wicket and we really want to do something to our pavilion so that we can make somewhere to have tea.'

For the 1954 season, Kingsley withdrew and Shottermill and the newly formed Alexandra Park (Bordon) were elected. Kingsley's decision was no surprise as many of their players were agricultural workers and found it impossible to play regularly. Alexandra Park, having spent £165 on playing equipment, crockery and cutlery, started the season with three wins. The captain in their opening game against Shottermill was F.S. Dagwell who, at 63, wondered if he was the oldest cricketer in the district. Formerly the headmaster at Selborne school, he was now the librarian for the Royal Engineers at Longmoor Camp. He told a story of when he was bowling for a south Hampshire village against an obviously talented young batsman, and had two appeals for catches peremptorily turned down. Later, spreadeagling the stumps, he inquired sarcastically, 'Well, how's that, then?' The umpire, a delightful old son of the soil, hitched up his corduroys and blandly replied, 'No ball', adding, 'That there's the squire's son down from Eton. We'm come to see him a-batting, not you a-bowling.'

Jim Kneller, who died in October 2001, was the Park's

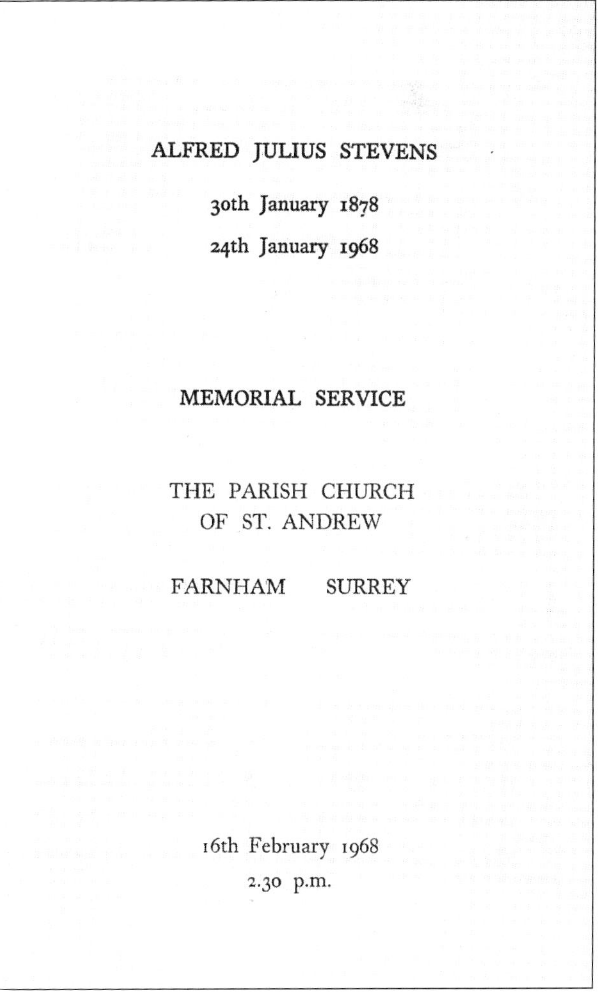

ALFRED JULIUS STEVENS

30th January 1878

24th January 1968

MEMORIAL SERVICE

THE PARISH CHURCH
OF ST. ANDREW

FARNHAM SURREY

16th February 1968

2.30 p.m.

Card for the memorial service for A.J. Stevens in February 1968. He died, aged 89, on 24 January that year.

key bowler, and on 14 August 1954 he took five wickets in successive balls to hand champions Lindford their first defeat of the season, and to ensure second place for the newcomers.

But all was not going according to plan and at the annual meeting in December 1954 it was reported that Binsted and probably Whitehill had withdrawn. Alexandra Park had applied to play in both the I'Anson and Miller Cups but withdrew from the senior competition on hearing the earlier news. With only four clubs left, the meeting was in a quandry, but it was agreed to attempt to keep the competition alive, and the second XIs of The Bourne and Rowledge, as Miller winners and runners-up, agreed to move for one year only.

This at least kept the fledgling competition alive, but any thoughts of promotion and relegation would have to wait until the decision taken at Tilford 35 years later in 1989. However, it did demonstrate that the administrators were willing to be innovative. The Bourne II won the trophy in 1955, when Lindford's E. Rooney took five wickets in an over against Rowledge II, and Albert Rapley did the hat-trick in successive matches.

The decision to call a halt was made at the annual meeting in January 1956 when it was learnt that Alexandra Park had withdrawn. Thursley declined an invitation to join the I'Anson Cup, which left the competition with nine teams, and instead joined Lindford and Shottermill in a Miller Cup comprising 12 sides.

There were two representative fixtures, both against Hindhead, played by a Stevens Cup XI. In the first, in August 1954, Hindhead won by seven runs. Hindhead made 104 (J. Mattock 32, L. Owen 23; K. Burton 4-33, J. Kneller 3-15, W. Rapley 2-19) and dismissed the visitors for 97 (J. Miller 42; H. Snelling 3-27, H. Hubbard 3-39). The following year Hindhead's winning margin was two wickets. Stevens XI 105 (N. Disney 19, M. Ricketts 18; H. Hubbard 5-15), Hindhead 106-8 (M. Reese 29no, Hubbard 22; E. Winter 5-35, J. Kneller 2-29).

Points mean prizes

THE award of points, which began with a simple two for a win and one for a draw, has been changed on a number of occasions throughout the last 50 years. And now, as the competitions enter their second century, there is, perhaps, the most fundamental of changes taking place, with league positions being assessed by average points per completed fixture rather than by a cumulative total, which has always included awards for matches either cancelled or abandoned through inclement weather.

It was in 1954 that the original points structure was first changed, with Elstead's proposition of four points being awarded for a win on the first innings if a match was not played out, plus one bonus point for a victory by an innings or over four innings. There were two points each for a draw, tie, or abandoned game. Rowledge seconded this proposal and it was carried by 12 votes to one (Tilford) at the ADM.

Elstead's Duncan Whittaker, a newcomer to the I'Anson Cup from northern league cricket, said the idea was to increase interest in the game, but Bob Hooker, the Tilford stalwart, argued that run-scoring was easier on some grounds and suggested that, if adopted, the rule would lead to less care being taken in the preparation of wickets.

The irony was that Tilford won the I'Anson Cup that year, and would have done so under the old system in any case. In fact, in the first two seasons of the new system only one club would have finished in a different position had the original points award still been in place – Elstead would have moved up one place to fourth in 1955.

By and large the points structure changed little after that, until bonus points were first introduced in 1979. Frensham put the system forward and everyone seemed surprised when it was voted in 7-5. Teams were awarded one batting point for reaching 100, 135 and 170 runs and one bowling point for taking three, six and nine wickets. With six points for a win, it was possible to take a maximum 12 points from a match played over two innings.

However, the system was flawed from the start because sides batting second and winning could keep the losers in the field while chasing further points. The scheme was abandoned after five seasons, and it was not until 1994 that the present version of bonus points was accepted.

The Stevens Knockout Cup

THE competitions paid their respects to A.J. Stevens when the life president died in January 1968, and almost 12 months later, at the annual meeting in Churt, a fitting memorial was agreed. The chairman of the meeting, Arnold Gee, the competitions' senior vice-president, described Mr Stevens as a true gentleman and a generous supporter of cricket. 'I have not known a finer man,' he said. During the meeting, it was said that the stewards were very conscious of the feeling in most clubs that something tangible was needed in order to commemorate the great contribution 'AJ' had made to the competitions. They felt that it would be appropriate to use the Stevens Cup, which had been in mothballs since 1955, for this purpose and, after much discussion, the meeting opted for an evening knockout tournament in which the winners would be presented with the old trophy. Tilford made the proposal and agreed to help with the organisation, but there was not unanimity and two of the 12 clubs were not in favour.

The first contest for the Stevens KO Cup took place in 1969 and, fittingly, it was Grayshott who were the first winners when they beat Headley by 32 runs in the final at The Bourne. Grayshott made 160-5 in 16 overs (G. Baker 82no) and Headley replied with 128-7. 'Dick' Caesar, who had been elected president in succession to Mr Stevens, handed the cup to Harold ('Spud') Murphy. This was to be Grayshott's season as they went on to win the I'Anson Cup for the first time in 40 years.

The following year, Grayshott retained the evening cup when they defeated The Bourne by eight wickets, and 'Spud' Murphy accepted the trophy from Mrs Brian Vesey-Fitzgerald, the daughter of A.J. Stevens and a person who had reached international standard in women's cricket. The scores were: The Bourne 105-9 (R. Pharo 34; R. Lawry 3-25, G. Tribe 2-20, J. Sinclair 2-22), Grayshott 106-2 (Tribe 41, P. Clapham 25, B. Lillis 23no; A. Ralph 2-21).

Details of subsequent finals are:

Grayshott, first winners of the Stevens Knockout Cup in 1969. Standing, from the left: C. Dodge, J. Sinclair, W. Richards, E. Gulliver, D. White. Seated: P. Clapham, G. Baker, P. Jones, H. Murphy (captain), B. Lillis, G. Tribe.

1971: It was the turn of The Bourne who beat Rowledge by 53 runs with Charlie LeClercq ending the match by taking a hat-trick. Alistair Ralph received the cup from 'Dick' Caesar. Scores: The Bourne 122-8 (M. Poulter 42, W. Steward 20; P. Prior 3-35), Rowledge 69 (R. Piper 31; J. Arnold 3-6, C. LeClercq 3 20).

1972: The Bourne held on to the cup when they beat Thursley at Headley. Scores: Thursley 91 (D. Hardy 27; C. LeClercq 5-24), The Bourne 95-8 (L. Knight 46; G. Pilbeam 4-19, R. Walker 3-31). The president made the presentation, as he did in 1973-75.

1973: Big hitting in the last three overs by Whitehill took the score from 41-6 to a winning 87-6 against Tilford at Churt, Les Parkins receiving the cup. Scores: Tilford 86 (P. Cooper 34; R. Woodward 3-11, J. Kneller 2-10), Whitehill 87-6 (D. Cooper 27no, J. Kneller 19no; J. Gould 2-13).

1974: Rowledge won the first of three successive finals. Rowledge 85 (B. Silver 32no, R. Piper 23), Tilford 54-9 (P. Prior 3-20, J. Kersley 2-5, C. Silver 2-6).

1975: The Bourne 82-9 (A. Prior 4-19, J. Kersley 2-15) lost to Rowledge 86-5 (R. Simpson 26, A. Prior 25no; A. Ralph 3-14) at Elstead.

1976: Churt 108-5 (K. Brown 38, B. Burberry 20no, P.J. Slinger 20; J. Kersley 3-20) lost to Rowledge 112-3 (G. Bayly 54, C. Yates 43no). Chris Yates received the cup from Cliff Jarrett, the competitions secretary.

1977: Whitehill 76 (B. Dewey 25; R. Birch 3-9) lost to Churt 78-3 (K.Brown 25, B. Burberry 25), skipper Richard Kemp accepting the trophy from J.G. Caesar.

1978: The first final to be sponsored, by Harp Lager, was played at Churt and Grayshott made 103-6 (E. Gulliver 45) to easily beat Headley 51 (C. Dodge 4-10, A. Shrubb 3-18). 'Dick' Caesar presented the cup to Mick Greathurst, and Eddie Gulliver was named man of the match by Jack Warner, who was to become president that year, and received a bat from the sponsors. The competitions received a cheque for £250 from the sponsors, who also quenched the players' thirst during the evening. In the second round that season, Churt's Ken Brown (94no) and Peter Allatt (34no) put on 144 in 16 overs for the first wicket against Tilford.

1979: Harp Lager returned again and Headley made amends when they beat Tilford at Thursley, Barry Woodger receiving the cup. Tilford made 103-8 (M. Pryce 26, M. Russell 23, R. Pike 22; R. Holden 3-17) and Headley 106-5 (A. Rooney 36; S. Goolding 3-24). Dick Holden was named man of the match and received a bat. Jack Warner presented a radio to 'Dick' Caesar to mark his 10 years as president. The evening was rounded off by the presentation of an I'Anson Cup cap to competitions stalwart Bob Burchett, the last of the 24 people to receive the honour.

1980: Rowledge 100-7 (R. Simpson 20; J. Ingram 3-13, C. Dodge 3-16) beat Grayshott 64 (C. Yates 4-6, B. Silver 3-15) at The Bourne. Jack Warner presented the cup to Alan Prior.

1981: There was sponsorship from Pace Petroleum when Grayshott beat Tilford in the last over at Churt. The cup was presented to Eddie Gulliver by Cliff Jarrett. Tilford 107-4 (C. Wilson 35, M. Pryce 21), Grayshott 108-4 (Gulliver 72no).

1982: Rowledge 135-6 (A. Prior 37no, R. Simpson 20, J. Burton; C. Dodge 2-28) beat Grayshott 103-9 (R. Lake 30, E. Gulliver 24; C. Yates 3-32, A. Field 2-10) at Kingsley. Leslie Cockell, president of Farnham in that club's bicentenary season, handed the cup to Alan Prior.

1983: Rowledge retained the cup when they beat Thursley by five wickets at Whitehill. Thursley 130-2 (P. Connor 38, K. Tilson 31no, R. Walker 31no, M. Taylor 26), Rowledge 133-5 (N. Dunbar 38, R. Simpson 29, J. Dunbar 28no).

1984: Rowledge completed their second hat-trick of wins when they beat Thursley again, this time by seven wickets at Wrecclesham. Thursley made 95-7 (K. Tilson 29; A. Field 2-12, B. Silver 2-22, A. Prior 2-28) and Rowledge replied with 98-3 (J. Dunbar 35, N. Dunbar 20; S. Connor 2-29). Jack Warner handed the cup to Alan Prior, as he had done the previous year. Earlier in the season, Martin Pryce (73no) and Noel Hume (69no) put on 131 for Tilford's second wicket against Churt, who needed two runs off the last two balls to overhaul the home side's 149-1, and were all out for 148.

1985: Unstoppable Rowledge beat Tilford by 38 runs at Thursley, Prior receiving the trophy this time from former Thursley player Ron Rapley. Man-of-the-match Chris Yates had played for British Telecom earlier in the day. Rowledge 125-8 (Yates 74, P. Offord 23), Tilford 87-8 (B. Silver 3-21, Yates 2-27).

1986: Tilford beat Grayshott at Lindford when Alistair Macdonald struck five huge sixes. Grayshott 114-7 (E. Gulliver 52; M. Stoker 3-42, N. Martyn 2-23), Tilford 119-5 (A. Macdonald 37no, H. Macdonald 26). Martin Pryce received the cup from Norman Disney and halted a run of five times on the losing side in a Stevens final.

1987: In a repeat final, played at The Bourne, Tilford again beat Grayshott. Grayshott 55 (N. Martyn 3-15), Tilford 57-5 (R. Grogut 23; M. Sobey 3-17). Jack Warner presented the cup to Chris Cobbett.

1988: Elstead 45 (R. Ward 4-17, A. Culham 3-15) lost to The Bourne 46-6 (R. Elgie 4-8) at Churt. Hot sun on a wet pitch produced difficult conditions for batsmen and Elstead, in their first final, were 29-6 and all out in 12 overs. Man-of-the-match Roger Elgie made The Bourne nervous with his left-arm slow-medium bowling, but they got home in 14.7 overs. Ron Allatt, the Churt president, presented the cup to Mick Hoy. In the second round, Grayshott openers Mike Absolom (126no) and Neil Elisha (73no) put on 217 v Whitehill.

1989: Grayshott beat Churt by two runs at Headley when the veteran Frank Kenward presented the cup to Neil Elisha. Churt needed 17 runs in the last two overs with eight wickets in hand, but lost six wickets in an action-packed finish. Grayshott 128-3 (M. Absolom 71no, R. Baker 20), Churt 126-8 (P. Allatt 46, S. Griffin 28, A. Mayson 20; G. Clapham 3-28, M. Sobey 2-23).

1990: Grayshott again when they scored 139-4 (R. Baker 43, M. Sobey 35, S. Whitley 30) and restricted Tilford to 137-9 (H. Macdonald 35, D. Hounsham 34, D. Jervis 24; Whitley 3-19) at Frensham. Tilford needed nine off the last over from Mark Sobey, and Denis Hounsham was bowled as he tried to hit a four off the last ball. President Norman Disney made the presentation.

1991: Frensham won the cup for the first time when they beat Grayshott by 31 runs at Lindford. The trophy was presented by Alan Prior to John Storey as regular skipper Ray Clarke and a number of other Frensham players were on tour in Holland. Frensham 131-7 (J.G. Storey 48, J.H. Storey 24no), Grayshott 100-9.

1992: Aldershot West Indians became the first new club to reach the final, but Grayshott beat them by 39 runs at Churt. Grayshott made 119-8 (A. Wheble 37, M. Absolom 29; D. Stephenson 4-29) and AWI replied with 80-7 (J. Kharki 23). Neil Elisha received the cup from Christine Brannaghan, widow of Peter Brannaghan, the Churt and Farnham League administrator who had died at the end of the previous year. Earlier in the season, Frensham's 'Rusty' Moorcroft had taken a hat-trick against Tilford, and John Storey junior had hit six sixes in his 61 for Grayshott against Wrecclesham.

1993: Grayshott beat Headley by 25 runs at Thursley in a repeat of the first final. Grayshott 142-5 (R. Baker 62no, A. Wheble 47; R. Leonard 2-40), Headley 117-5 (R. Shergold 26, G. May 21; G. Clarke 2-29). Norman Disney presented the cup. In the first round, Peter Hammond scored 89 off 39 balls in a stand of 107 for Frensham v Tongham, and in the semi-final Lindford skipper Mark Hoban fell while fielding on the boundary against Grayshott and ruptured an achilles tendon. He was taken to hospital by ambulance and was operated on the following morning.

1994: Frensham beat The Bourne at Elstead. Frensham 147-3 (S. Dickinson 40, J. Willson 28no, J. Kohler 24), The Bourne 132-9 (G. Senior 31, I. Rosher 24; R. Moorcroft 4-19, R. Clarke 3-35). In the second round, Matt Barnes of Badshot Lea made 119 (seven sixes) off 70 balls against Tongham.

1995: A thrilling climax saw Tilford hold off Frensham. Tilford 83 (D. Jervis 36, P. Knight 15; D. Coldicott 3-16, T. Falkiner 3-19), Frensham 80-9 (B. Maxwell 14, N. Thayer 13; P. Knight 2-18, N. Martyn 2-21, A. Macdonald 2-24). Tilford bowled and fielded like tigers at The Bourne, with Phil Knight holding two catches off his own bowling, in murky light, to determine the result. The cup was presented by Bert Holdaway, 91, who was believed to be the I'Anson Cup's oldest surviving former player. He first played in 1919 and died in May 1996. In the first round, James Huntley (Headley) hit a century v Badshot Lea.

1996: Headley 131 (Gavin May 54, A. Cook 45; D. Coldicott 3-29) beat Frensham 84 (M. Potter 25, D. Coldicott 24; C. Thomas 4-13, W. Scott 3-16, G. Badland 2-22) at Grayshott. Brian Spencer, president of Grayshott in their centenary year, handed the cup to Alan Rooney. In the third round, Will Gear of Tilford scored his second Stevens Cup century of the season when he made 106 v Wood Street. Sandy Meyer took four wickets in the last over, including a hat-trick, for Tongham v Witley.

1997: Witley 165 (D. Penny 43, N. Mansbridge 34, S. Hobson 23; B. Cervi 4-37, M. Crawley 3-35) beat The Bourne 47 (J. Gartland 5-13, A. Kelly 3-18) in a one-sided game at Dogmersfield, where Norman Disney presented the cup to Neil Mansbridge. In the first round, John Taylor (81no) and Matthew Barnes (54no) put on 151 for Badshot Lea to beat Tongham by 10 wickets; in the second round, Paul Collyer did the hat-trick for The Bourne at Milford.

1998: Grayshott beat Tilford by three wickets at The Bourne. Tilford 144-6 (M. Barnes 100; A. Wheble 3-30), Grayshott 145-7 (S. Whitley 44, M. Sobey 31no, A. Lang 26; N. Martyn 3-10, S. Mitchell 2-60). Barnes hit the first century in a Stevens Cup final. Grayshott started the last over needing 28 runs off eight balls. Mark Sobey, who struck four sixes, and Graham Sampson brought the scores level with one delivery left and everyone knew that a 'dot' ball would give Tilford the cup by virtue of having lost fewer wickets. Skipper Nigel Martyn called the fielders into run-saving positions, Stuart Mitchell bowled just short of a length, Sobey got some bat on it, Sampson hurtled down the pitch and a misfield in the excitement saw Sobey home safely at the other end. Mike Poulter, president of The Bourne in their centenary year, presented the cup to Andy Wheble. In a quarter-final replay, Milford beat The Bourne with Steve Rowe (81no) and Dave Richardson (64no) putting on 144 for the second wicket.

1999: Grayshott 117-3 (P. Coleshill 43no, A. Wheble 37) beat Division Three Puttenham 115-9 (J. Crouch 28; A. Lindsey Clark 3-25) at Hindhead, whose president, Audrey Mattock, presented the cup to Andy Wheble. In the semi-finals, Grayshott defeated Frensham by seven wickets, the match starting sensationally when, off the first ball, Frensham's Ben Maxwell was run out by James Tomlinson's 80-yard throw.

Grayshott, centenary year winners of the Stevens Cup. Standing, from the left: Geoff Tribe (president), Phil Coleshill, James Tomlinson, Paul Roberts, Alastair Lindsey Clark, Simon Whitley, Richard Baker. Kneeling: Andy Wheble, Lee Conway, Paul Osborn (captain), Mark Sobey, Andy Lang.

2000: Tilford 140-6 (A. Macdonald 27, J. Hunt 25no, S. Crawte 21no) beat Witley 135-6 (K. Ritchie 63, J. Phillips 26no, I. Munday 21) at Thursley. Keiron Ritchie and James Phillips put on 99 to bring their side to a position from where they could still win. Needing 23 off the last over from Steve Crawte, Witley scored only four off the first five balls and lost their fifth wicket. Then new batsman Matthew Whiddett hit two straight sixes and Witley needed another off the last ball to level the scores and take the cup on fewer wickets lost. Whiddett tried but failed. Pat Hastings, long time Thursley and competitions administrator, presented the cup to Hamish Macdonald.

2001: Grayshott 130-4 (P. Osborn 60no, S. Whitley 28no) beat Elstead 126-8 (J. Crutcher 37, J. Allen 25, S. Wade 22; A. Lang 4-52) in the centenary year final held on a Sunday afternoon at Fernhurst. Life president Norman Disney presented the cup to Paul Osborn who was also named man of the match.

Paul Osborn, the Grayshott captain, receives the Stevens KO Cup from life president Norman Disney in 2001. Herald *sports editor Carl Obert checks the scores.*

Playing in the rain

CRICKET in the rain in the I'Anson Cup is common-place, but it has led to many a squabble and dispute down the years. The management bodies have often had to make important decisions regarding the award of points, and the *Herald* has also been known to comment forthrightly on the subject.

Take 1951, for instance. A wet Saturday in May caused the newspaper to admonish certain clubs for their inability to follow the rules with regard to timings. The rule on the point was perfectly straightforward, the newspaper said. 'Play shall commence at 3pm (Sept 2.30pm) with four hours' play…Interference by rain shall be included in the four hours once play has commenced but not otherwise. A match shall be abandoned unless commenced by 5.30pm and stumps must in all cases be drawn by 8pm.'

The situation in most cases on the previous Saturday, it stated, was that no play was possible until about 4.15, therefore the time lost to rain did not count in the four hours and stumps should not have been drawn before 8pm. However, the rule was not complied with in every case and several of the matches were to be the subject of consideration by the stewards.

'Consequently, it is not possible to publish the tables this week,' the *Herald* stated with a degree of tetchiness. Copies of the rules, which could hardly be phrased in clearer language, were in the hands of every club, and it was astonishing how often they were either not known or misinterpreted, it commented.

And it has been a matter of déjà vu on numerous occasions in the intervening half a century.

L.T. Pope and the Pope Cup

THE Pope Cup, like the Stevens Cup, recalls the name of one of the great servants of I'Anson Cup cricket. L.T. Pope was a Headley player before and after World War Two but, more importantly, he was connected with the *Herald* newspapers. This ensured that the cricket competitions received superb treatment on the sports pages. But Theo Pope was an eminently fair man and it was not just I'Anson and Miller Cup cricket that received excellent coverage, but all cricket. Indeed all sport.

L.T. Pope (seated second left) in the Headley team beaten by The Bourne in the 1948 play-off. Immediately behind him is Frank Kenward, probably the greatest all-rounder in the history of the competitions. Standing, from the left: F. Dean, H.A.P. Heaslop, K.J. Ridgway, F. Kenward, E. King, F. Dopson, P. Barlow. Seated: F. Courtnage, L.T. Pope, A.J. Bellinger (captain), D. Chesham.

He joined the *Herald* from Eggar's Grammar School in Alton in the late 1920s and, except for war service, he served the paper faithfully until he retired in 1975. For the last six years he was the editor and prior to that, since the war, he had held the almost equally onerous position of news editor.

Before the war he and his family lived at Conford, near Liphook, and in those days he represented the *Herald* over an area covering Liphook, Headley, Bordon, Alton and Bentley. He became well known but made another wide circle of friends through cricket while playing for Headley, sometime as captain. When the war came he was one of the first to join the Anti-Aircraft Battery formed in Farnham. He also served in Belfast and attained the rank of captain.

After the war he returned to live in Farnham and took over executive duties at the *Herald* with F.O. Meddows Taylor, son-in-law of the newspaper's founder, E.W. Langham. Theo Pope played a valuable part in the expansion of the *Herald*, which today numbers five editions under separate titles. The *Herald* series continues to offer unrivalled coverage of the competitions and was the main sponsor of the centenary year.

Theo Pope's obituary notice in the *Herald* stated that his 'lasting contribution to the game locally was writing the history of the I'Anson Cup Competition for the golden jubilee in 1951. *A Cup for Cricket* entailed a tremendous amount of research and interviewing in which his journalistic experience and his love of the game stood him in good stead. The book was very well received and copies today are not easy to find. He was often asked to write a sequel, but it was a daunting prospect and certainly not to be undertaken while he was giving all his energies to the *Herald*.

'Well, not quite, for he was involved in the management of the competition and at the time of his death (on 11 May 1979) he was a vice-president. In the winter he was in demand as a speaker at annual dinners. As a regular subscriber to *Wisden* his general knowledge of the game was encyclopaedic; a day at a county match with Theo would produce a wealth of information.'

Theo Pope was elected a vice-president of the competitions in 1952 and his opinion on the running of the two leagues was often sought. He formed one element of a strong management team that also included J.G. ('Dick') Caesar and H.J. ('Harry') Knight, both formidable administrators. Theo often took the chair at the meetings and it was at the annual delegates' meeting in Churt Village Hall in 1977 that he agreed to donate a trophy for a subsidiary evening competition to be competed for between first and second round losers in the Stevens Cup.

It may be our smallest trophy but its name ensures that the memory of Theo Pope, administrator, historian and chronicler of so much of the I'Anson Cup Competitions, remains with us.

In a *Herald* sports page tribute, following his death, competitions secretary Cliff Jarrett said that Theo Pope was always ready to give encouragement and advice. 'Unassuming and never seeking the limelight, Theo was, I suppose, almost unknown to many of the young men taking part in our competitions today. But the success and continuity we enjoy is due to a large extent to the interest stimulated before and during his period as editor of the *Herald* – and, happily, continued under his successors.

'It was on his express instructions that the *Herald* began to follow the fortunes of our youngest players by reporting every match played in the Two Counties Youth Competition; and he was always to be found on the ground when the boys were playing one of their big matches.

'His passing is particularly sad to those of us left who played cricket with or against him during his playing days

SERVICE
OF
THANKSGIVING

for the life of

LOUIS THEODORE POPE

ST. ANDREW'S PARISH CHURCH
FARNHAM

MONDAY, JUNE 4th, 1979

Card for the thanksgiving service for Theo Pope in June 1979.

with Headley. He was a keen competitor and a great sportsman, playing a straight bat straight down the line in every sense of the word. He will be greatly missed by those no longer playing as well as by those now taking part in our great English game of cricket.

'How better to end this short tribute than to quote that well-known saying: "When the last great scorer comes to write your name, it matters not who won or lost, but how you played the game". Farewell, Theo, and thanks.'

At all league grounds on 12 May 1979, one minute's silence was observed before the start of matches as a mark of respect to one of the competitions' closest friends.

The current secretary, and compiler of the second half of the history of the competitions, could not have had a better and more caring journalism mentor than Theo Pope. When he joined the *Herald* in 1960, at the age of 16, Theo was still the news editor, but his command and authority was such that the young reporter believed him to be the editor. In fact, Oliver Meddows Taylor was both managing director and editor under the ownership of his father-in-law, but Theo was the journalist and it was to him that any budding young scribe approached for advice.

The inaugural competition for the Pope Cup took place in 1978, and the donor was at the final at Elstead to present the trophy to the Tilford captain, Chris Aust, after they had beaten Thursley by 33 runs thanks to some useful bowling from Sid Goolding (3-21) and Noel Hume (2-14).

The final in 1979 was played shortly after Theo's death, and president Jack Warner handed the cup to Rowledge, whose all-rounders Chris Yates (69 not out and 3-17) and Alan Prior (25 and 2-15) simply dominated proceedings at The Bourne against the luckless Thursley.

Headley were awarded the trophy in 1980 when opponents Whitehill got themselves tied up in a fixtures knot. Headley objected to a suggested new date for the final, so that Whitehill could fulfil a fixture in another evening competition, and the stewards supported them. It was not the manner in which the donor would have wanted his old club to win the cup for the first time.

Mrs Joan Pope agreed to present her late husband's cup in the 1981 final at Elstead, and handed it to Alan Prior after Rowledge had again thrashed Thursley, this time by nine wickets. Tony Field had bowled fast and straight to take 5-12, and was assisted by Steve Huckle (3-16) and Chris Yates (2-16), and then Huckle (36no) and Bob Simpson (23no) did the rest.

Details of subsequent finals are:

1982: Paul Slinger led Tilford to a one-run victory over his old club Churt at Headley. Tilford 108-6 (R. Grogut 45no; M. Warner 3-14), Churt 107-7 (I. Ferguson 33no, M. Warner 22; N. Cowell 2-24). Former Headley player Bob Shergold, captain of Farnham, presented the cup.

1983: There was a large crowd at Lindford's new ground on Broxhead Common to watch Tilford retain the cup by beating Grayshott. Reg Hatt, who had worked alongside Theo Pope for many years, and who had succeeded him as editor, handed the trophy to Martin Pryce, whose score of 70 was the highest in the competition to date.

1984: In spite of an all-round performance by 14-year-old Graham Thorpe (31 and 2-37), Wrecclesham lost to Headley at Frensham. Dick Holden received the cup from Robin Radley, the new editor of the *Herald*, who said of Theo Pope: 'As an ex-Headley man he would have approved of their success. He did a great deal for the cup competitions and he had a feeling for the underdog.'

1985: Headley retained the cup when they beat first-time finalists Lindford by six wickets. Max Reese, a former *Herald* reporter and colleague of Theo Pope, and a much respected cricketer with Hindhead, presented the trophy to Kevin Williams.

1986: Frensham beat Elstead at Thursley to win a trophy for the first time since 1932. Sheoghan Dickinson (99) and John Storey junior (54) put on 134 for the second wicket in a massive total of 182-8 (M. Absolom 4-46), and Elstead made 111-6 (Absolom 52; R. Clarke 3-5) in reply. Bert Holdaway, a survivor of Frensham's 1932 I'Anson Cup winning side, presented the trophy.

1987: Thursley beat Headley at Frensham. Headley 131-5 (G. Bridger 43no), Thursley 134-5 (B. Karn 35, A. Phipps

28, R. Walker 21; T. Lee 3-29). Norman Disney presented the cup to Barry Rapley.

1988: Whitehill 106-7 (J. Mace 28, D. Mann 28; B. Woodger 3-13) beat Headley 103-7 (R. Vernier 29, D. Cook 23; W. Scott 4-18) by three runs at Elstead. Capt M.G. 'Pinkie' Haworth, the Elstead president, handed the cup to Ron Woodward.

1989: Tilford beat Whitehill at Lindford thanks to good performances by Roger Grogut (66no), Alan Coates (4-8) and Nigel Martyn (4-21).

1990: The Bourne defeated Elstead by four wickets at Tilford.

1991: Churt just edged out Lindford by two runs at The Bourne, John Daddo's 60 being an important knock.

1992: In spite of another good innings by Australian opener Daddo (47no), Churt were beaten by 19 runs by The Bourne at Headley, where new I'Anson Cup treasurer Keith Mayson presented the cup to Ron Neil.

1993: Farncombe Wanderers became the first of the new breed of I'Anson clubs to win a trophy when they beat fellow newcomers Witley by 40 runs at The Bourne. Strong Wanderers batting saw them to a big evening score of 162-7 (Andy Nye 41no, Phil Miles 36, Tim Gorringe 24, Colin Puttock 24) and Witley, apart from an undefeated half-century from Dave Penny, could not respond against some good bowling by Gorringe (3-39), Puttock (2-20) and Sean Bidwell (2-21). Mike Poulter, president of The Bourne, presented the cup.

1994: Lindford got their hands on a trophy for the first time since being re-formed in the early 1970s, but then had it taken away when they admitted they had played an ineligible player. Opponents Frimchett subsequently declined to accept the cup and the final was declared void.

1995: Witley got their revenge against Farncombe Wanderers, and current *Herald* editor Peter Thompson, newly appointed, presented the cup. The talking point of the season was the 136 that Matt Barnes scored for Badshot Lea against Kingsley in an earlier round. It remains the Pope Cup's only century.

1996: Chiddingfold sprung a surprise when they beat Grayshott at Wrecclesham, where the cup was presented by Dennis Stone, then the vice-chairman of Herald newspapers and a former colleague of Theo Pope.

1997: Grayshott bounced back when they easily defeated Thursley at Kingsley.

1998: Frensham's veteran skipper Ray Clarke received the trophy from Tilford president and league fixtures secretary Ian Webster after a 10-run win over Lindford.

1999: Man-of-the-match Paul Marden (61no) steered Chiddingfold to a seven-wicket win over Thursley at Frensham, whose centenary year president, Bob Campbell, presented the cup.

2000: Grayshott headed off a gallant Cranleigh St Andrews. Phil Coleshill, who hit three sixes in his 53 and shared a second-wicket stand of 77 with skipper Paul Osborn, handed his man-of-the-match bat to his side's youngest player, Mark Richards.

2001: Cranleigh St Andrews 70-1 (R. Samways 30no, Y. Senior 30) beat Fernhurst 69-8 (A. Stone 3-22, S. Ketley 2-11, S. Hook 2-14) in the centenary year final on a Sunday afternoon at Fernhurst. Stuart Ketley, the Saints' captain, received the cup from life president Norman Disney, and was named man of the match for his two wickets and four catches.

Cranleigh St Andrews, winners of the Pope Cup in 2001.

If the cap fits...

WHEN Arnold Gee, who gave outstanding service to the competitions, agreed to present caps to players appearing in representative matches, it was considered to be a wonderful gesture. In fact, the stewards decided that the dark blue caps with a badge replica of the cup and the word 'I'Anson' prominently displayed, would be awarded to players who distinguished themselves in representative matches. In all, 24 caps were awarded, the last in 1978.

W. ('Bill') Crebbin, the Churt captain who was one of the first players to be awarded an I'Anson cap.

The first were awarded when the stewards met at Mr Gee's home in Rowledge on Thursday, 11 June 1953. The recipients were Bill Crebbin (Churt), Frank Kenward (Headley), Basil Payne (Elstead), Bill Poulter (The Bourne), John Seddon (The Bourne), Jack Warner (Tilford) and Duncan Whittaker (Elstead). All but Seddon and Payne received their caps from the president, A.J. Stevens, during the tea interval in the then annual inter-club Surrey v Hampshire match at The Bourne on Sunday, 28 June 1953. Mr Gee, unfortunately, was unable to attend. Seddon and Payne received their awards from Mr Stevens at the Winners v The Rest match at The Bourne at the end of the 1953 season.

The following year Les Crumplin (Rowledge), Gladstone 'Ken' Bullock (Grayshott) and Bob White (Headley) were nominated, and then followed Ray 'Patsy' Bridger (Tilford), Robin Pryce (Elstead) and Albert 'Driver' Swan (Rowledge). Jim Eddey (Tilford), George Williamson (Wrecclesham), Bryan Karn (Thursley) and George Knight (The Bourne) were awarded their caps in 1958.

G.O. (George) Williamson pictured wearing his I'Anson cap at the centenary exhibition at Farnham Maltings in March 2001. The Wrecclesham all-rounder was honoured in 1958.

There was then a gap of 10 years before the Grayshott veteran Bob Petter, who first played for the club in 1919 and was in the I'Anson Cup winning side the following year, received his from J.G. Caesar in July 1968, two years after retiring from the game. In the same year, 'Joe' Piper of

R.W. ('Bob') Burchett, player, umpire and administrator, who was the last person to be given an I'Anson cap. He is pictured in 1995 with the Chiddingfold team, who were the first to win the Division Four trophy bearing his name.

Rowledge was nominated, and Alan Young (The Bourne) received his award in 1969 after scoring a magnificent century in taking the representative side to victory against Farnham.

In 1971, 'Dick' Caesar was awarded a cap for outstanding service as a player and an administrator, the presentation taking place at the 70th anniversary dinner of the competitions.

Norman Disney, the current life president, who played with distinction for Whitehill, Lindford and Headley, where he continues to be the president, and the Rowledge all-rounder Alan Prior were honoured in 1977, while Bob Burchett, the long-time Elstead player, competition official and umpire, became the last recipient the following year, the presentation taking place at the final of the Stevens Cup held at Thursley.

The eligible player

ELIGIBILITY has always been a bone of contention and, if rules have been challenged by the clubs, the management committee and, in earlier times, the stewards have had the power to control who can and cannot play in the competitions.

From the outset, the founding fathers were troubled by where players resided, and in 1903 drafted the following: 'That all players... be bona fide members of their respective clubs, and that all players reside in the parish of the club to which they play, or reside within a radius of three miles from the cricket ground of their club, and that no player may play for more than one club during the same year in the competition.' And on the matter of military personnel, with Bordon camp on the doorstep, it was agreed that 'all military officers and men be considered ineligible, unless permanent residents of those villages taking part in the competition'.

In a further effort to make the rule watertight, the committee decreed that all players 'must reside in the village three months before being eligible to take part in the competition'.

The fact that the question of eligibility continued to cause a problem can be seen in a 1954 attempt to clarify the clause that stated that 'all players must reside in the parish or within three miles of the club's ground' by the insertion of the word 'ecclesiastical' before 'parish'. This did little to settle the issue, and two years later it was agreed that serving soldiers living in private residences could play in the competitions.

The rule on eligibility then read, somewhat clumsily: 'All players must reside in the ecclesiastical parish or within three miles of the club's ground. No player may play for more than one club in a season, but a player may continue to play for his old club even if he changes his residence and is no longer within the required three-mile radius, provided that the stewards give permission. Every player must have four weeks' residential qualification, other than in barracks or military married quarters, but birth or long family residence qualifies immediately. Any club playing an ineligible player shall forfeit the match.'

Such discrimination was rife and, in time, led to many clubs finding it difficult to select two competent sides every week. It was not until the format changed in the 1990s that the competitions' archaic rules on residence were completely overhauled.

Players have always changed clubs, of course, but in 1960 the stewards went as far as rejecting an application from a well-known player to join one of the strongest clubs at the start of the season. Such a restraint has never been applied again, and for many years player movements, both between member clubs and clubs inside and outside of the competitions, have been controlled by rules agreed to by the clubs themselves.

Twenty years ago, at the ADM in 1981, Churt's respected official, Donald (now Sir Donald) Limon, made what he called an 'extreme statement' when he said: 'My committee has been troubled by the behaviour of Rowledge, a very strong team. We do not approve of their practice of trying to take players from other clubs. We feel it is not in the spirit of the competition. We therefore suggest that Rowledge should not play, so that this meeting is aware of our displeasure at this practice.' To which Alan Prior of Rowledge replied: 'Nobody at Rowledge takes other players. There is only the usual chat after matches. It is purely a matter for the individual if he wants to play for Rowledge.' In spite of the fact that no delegate was prepared to support Churt publicly, there was the feeling in the hall that there was sympathy for Churt's sentiments.

Size matters

THE only forum for changing the rules is the Annual Delegates' Meeting (ADM) or, in certain circumstances, a Special Delegates' Meeting (SDM), and down the years there have been some memorable disagreements among clubs as to how they wish the competition to be run. Traditional rivalries between clubs have often been behind such disputes.

This might well have been the case at the ADM in 1951 when, with Binsted and Thursley withdrawing from the I'Anson Cup and Wrecclesham applying to join, Rowledge proposed that the competition be limited to ten clubs, so that byes were avoided and the season could end in August. Tilford seconded this proposal and it was carried by seven votes to two.

'Harry' Knight, the secretary, said it had taken almost every night for three weeks to work out the previous season's fixtures, and the committee did not want to burn the midnight oil arranging matches that would not take place (a reference to the fact that Shottermill had failed to fulfil their first three matches). 'We have made it difficult to get into the competition, and the only things we look for are good grounds and good standards of play,' he said. Thursley, Binsted and Wrecclesham were elected to the Miller Cup, but Kingsley were not because of the state of their ground.

Robin Pryce, stylish batsman who captained Elstead to their only I'Anson Cup title in 1952, and then played for Tilford. He was an early advocate of promotion and relegation.

Wrecclesham did not take too kindly to what they saw as a snub, their delegate at the ADM, Cyril Watkins, referring to Rowledge's proposal as 'selfish and inconsiderate' when he spoke at the club's annual meeting, which was reported in the *Herald*. This provoked an exchange of letters to the newspaper. Robin Pryce, then of Elstead and later of Tilford, wrote: 'If, as the delegates decided, it is for the good of the competition to restrict the number of teams to ten, then I see very little prospect of any other club getting a place for some time to come.' He made a suggestion that the bottom side in the I'Anson Cup be relegated to the Miller Cup if the Miller winner was a 1st XI; and that the bottom team in the Miller Cup seek re-election. This would give delegates the chance to elect a new club. In a footnote, Theo Pope said the question of forming an I'Anson second division for 1953 was under consideration.

'Harry' Knight wrote that he thought the move to reduce the number of teams was sound. There would not be encroachment by football. He said The Bourne had originally proposed a reduction to ten at the ADM in 1950, but it was defeated. Then 12 clubs were seeking election. The Rowledge proposal was entirely different since only 11 clubs wished to be elected. He did not share the same pessimistic view as Mr Pryce because of the second division consideration.

He said: 'There have been occasions when I have taken the opportunity of pointing out to delegates that as our organisation is the only one of its kind on the Surrey and Hampshire borders, every endeavour should be made to increase the scope of the competitions and thus further the interest in village cricket which is our paramount function.' He added that the stewards were to prepare a report for consideration at a SDM. He said Mr Pryce's proposals fell short of what was really required as a long-term policy.

Soon, there was a brief attempt to accommodate extra clubs with the introduction of a second division (without promotion and relegation) for the Stevens Cup, and thrice in the 1980s clubs were re-elected by a secret ballot, so charged was the atmosphere at the ADM. However, it was not until the monumental decision taken at Tilford in 1989 that the age-old problem of offering additional clubs a home was solved. But, in spite of this, the issue of the number of teams in a division continues to be discussed, although a league questionnaire and a recent ADM both came down in favour of each of the top three divisions comprising 12 teams.

The delegates who attended the Tilford meeting set the competitions on an entirely new course, which, the majority observed at the time, and still more in subsequent years, was to save the oldest village cricket league from probable oblivion. But as bold and brave as the decision was, the seeds of change had been sown almost 40 years earlier, principally by H.J. Knight.

He was nothing if not forthright and the competitions, with which he had been connected since the late 1920s, had a place in his heart. When he spoke it was with the deep feelings of a man absolutely committed to the cause. So, when, under Any Other Business at the conclusion of the annual meeting in Churt Village Hall on Monday, 17 December 1962, he asked delegates to consider two points for the future there could have been no doubting his motives.

The questions he asked were: Is the radius of eight miles from Grayshott realistic in this age? Is the three-mile radius imposed on players required by the clubs?

The minutes of the meeting state that the points were discussed at length and that it was felt that: ten teams was an ideal number for the I'Anson Cup; that two more teams were needed for the Miller Cup; and that it would be to the advantage of both competitions if the Stevens Cup (the so-called second division that had lasted only three seasons in the 1950s) could be restarted.

Clubs were asked to put forward their suggestions on the two points to Mr Knight by 31 March the following year for examination by the stewards prior to a special delegates' meeting being called. Sadly, 'Harry' Knight died on that very deadline day and the competitions quite naturally entered a period of mourning for a man who had brought village cricket out of the abyss of World War Two and on to the road to recovery.

His frustration at not being able to achieve what he believed to be right for the future of the I'Anson and Miller Cups was to go with him to his grave.

There was little appetite in 1963 for anything other than to get through the season. The Bourne's proposal that the three-mile radius clause be deleted from the rules was declared to be out of order at the annual meeting, while a proposition from Rowledge that a club could register up to three players residing outside of the prescribed radius, subject to scrutiny and approval by the stewards, was allowed. This, at least, was a step in the right direction, but perhaps the biggest single acknowledgement that 'Harry' Knight was right was when the meeting agreed to immediately restart the Two Counties Youth Competition under the administration of the competitions. Fittingly, the proposal came from The Bourne, with whom he had enjoyed so much of his cricket.

And so the huge blow felt by the early death of such an I'Anson stalwart was softened in the best way possible – by taking local competitive cricket forward and offering it to the next generation of players. For a couple of decades there was little requirement for further change.

Batting records

IN the first 50 years of the competition there were four individual batting milestones: Bill Read's 117 for Blackmoor against Frensham at Frensham Hill (now Frensham Heights School) in 1903; Ernie Johnson's 123 not out for Grayshott against Headley in 1908; Phil Kingshott's undefeated 133 for Grayshott against Whitehill in 1935; and the 141 not out by Jim Voller for The Bourne against Shottermill in 1947.

Bob White, of Headley, had the class and the power to beat the record, as did several other batsmen in the 1950s, but it was not until 11 May 1957, that Voller's best was overtaken.

The Hollowdene ground at Frensham is, of course, ideally suited to high scoring, and in making 151 not out White needed only a little over an hour to put together his chanceless innings.

When he joined 'old firm' partner Frank Kenward with three wickets down for only six runs in reply to Frensham's 62, the home side might have allowed themselves thoughts of a victory. But by the tea interval White and Kenward had pulled the game round and, after the break, with Kenward playing second fiddle, they took the score to nearly 200 before Stan Armstrong bowled the latter for 52.

According to the *Herald*, White scored 98 in boundaries but in truth he struck eight sixes and 15 fours to give him 108 runs by the short route. His most productive shot was the straight drive over the bowler's head, and his only piece of luck came early on when a ball from Frensham skipper Frank Agar shaved a stump. 'Which side of the wicket did that one go?' inquired the modest White.

When Kenward was out, Headley, in normal circumstances, would have declared, but they delayed their decision so that White could break the I'Anson record. The stoppage came at 225-4, and there was still time to dismiss shell-shocked Frensham again for 25, with Basil Payne adding 4-12 to his first innings haul of 7-35.

Bob White: broke down a barrier.

Other Headley players that day were Peter Lee (whose son Trevor was later to play for the club and now appears for Lindford), K. Ridgway, A. Gandy, P. Bemrose, who was 10 not out and helped White get to the record, J. Gates, F. Courtnage, E. Chesham and I. Oakley. Headley's score was their best since the 279 (then the second highest total in the competition, behind Blackmoor's 300-5 declared against Frensham in 1903) they made against Tilford in 1938, when Kenward was undefeated on 127.

John Storey jnr: holder of the record.

White continued to play for Headley until the 1970s, and saw his record survive until 1 September 1990, when Sheoghan Dickinson scored 182, The twist here was that Dickinson was playing for Frensham against Headley, and those same short boundaries at Hollowdene undoubtedly helped. One who admired Dickinson's knock was Frank Kenward, who was an umpire in the match, while White, when told that his record had gone, said: 'Good luck to Sheoghan. It's about time someone beat it.' Bob White died, aged 61, the following August.

Dickinson's 182 was the penultimate three-figure score in the old-style I'Anson Cup competition, and remained as the overall record until the first day of the 1995 season, April 22, when Matthew Barnes made 206 not out for Badshot Lea at The Bourne in a Division One match. Later that year, on 1 July, and on the same ground, John Storey junior cracked an unbeaten 211 for Wrecclesham in a Division Two fixture against The Bourne II, to claim the outright record for the highest score in the competitions.

Matthew Barnes: first to 200.

Michael Allen, of Fernhurst, and Jack Harris, of Hindhead, are the competitions' only other double centurions. Allen scored 200 not out against Crown Taverners II in August 1997 and Harris made 203 away to Tilford II in July 2001. Since Bob White broke through the 150 barrier 45 years ago, his score has been either equalled or beaten on 22 occasions.

1,000 runs in a season

TWO batsmen, in the history of the competitions, have scored 1,000 league runs in a season.

The first was Sheoghan Dickinson, of Frensham, who, in 1984, amassed 1,020 runs in 22 innings in the I'Anson Cup.

Thirteen years later, Michael Allen, of Fernhurst, scored 1,021 runs in only 12 innings in Division Four.

Dickinson's season will long be remembered because he dominated the bowlers in a matchless performance of batsmanship. His captain was Peter Chuter, a player steeped in the traditions of the competitions, who, although in every way a Frensham clubman, subsequently enjoyed league cricket with Thursley and The Bourne before returning to his roots.

Dickinson, a teacher, first appeared for Frensham in 1973 and immediately impressed with his cultured style of batting. The *Herald* in August of that year referred to him as a 'promising newcomer' when he scored 27 and shared a sixth wicket stand of 48 with David Bone against Headley.

Sheoghan Dickinson: a season to remember.

He subsequently scored many elegant runs as Frensham began to assemble themselves into a side capable of taking on the stronger teams in the I'Anson Cup. The following season he headed the first team's batting averages with 30.4, having scored 213 runs in eight innings.

On 16 August 1975, he recorded his first century for Frensham, an unbeaten 102 at Churt. It was only the third century in the I'Anson Cup by a Frensham player, the previous two having been scored by Frank Agar (100 not out) in 1956 and John Bennington (126 not out) in 1974. Dickinson again topped the club's batting averages.

However, his days with the club were numbered, though, as his profession called, and a Sunday century on 30 May 1976 to all intents signalled his departure. Although the club benefited from occasional appearances it was not until the 1980s that he returned and became a pillar of the side, which he was to captain.

It was the 1984 season that catapaulted Dickinson to a place in the record books. His 1,020 runs came from 22 innings (nine of which were not out), an average of 78.5. His highest score was 94 not out. He reached his 1,000 when making an unbeaten 50 at The Bourne in the last match of the season. All told, he scored 12 half-centuries, seven in succession. In that final game he and John Storey put on 107 in a carefully composed third-wicket partnership as he looked for the magic 1,000 runs.

Ironically, Dickinson's season started with a duck against Whitehill, but there followed 85 v Churt, 12 (Thursley), 94 not out (Tilford), 67 not out and 72 not out (Elstead, who were beaten by an innings), 63 (Headley), 89 not out (Grayshott), 80 (Lindford), 70 (Wrecclesham) to give him a mid-season tally of 604 runs, 46 (The Bourne), 26 (Whitehill), 36 not out (Churt), 51 (Thursley), 19 (Tilford), 4 (Rowledge), 58 (Elstead), 57 not out (Headley), 0 (Grayshott), 4 (Lindford), 37 not out (Wrecclesham), 50 not out (The Bourne). The first match against Rowledge was cancelled because of the weather. Behind the stumps he held 18 catches and made six stumpings, and he even took a wicket in a rare appearance as a bowler.

Michael Allen's golden summer came in 1997 when he took the Division Four bowling apart in a display of powerful hitting. His 1,021 runs were scored in only 12 visits to the middle and his three not outs gave him an average of 113.44. His record was: 32 (Peper Harow), 54 (Frimchett II), 96 (Rowledge III), 108 (Elstead II), 45 (Wrecclesham II), 131 not out (Tongham II), 60 (Grayswood), 87 not out (The Bourne III), 22 (Frimchett II), 164 (Peper Harow), 200 not out (Crown Tavs II), 22 (Elstead II).

Michael Allen, second from the right, at the end of his record year, when Fernhurst won Division Four. Keith Mayson presented the Bob Burchett Shield to skipper Nick Ralph. Allen's father John, who is a member of the competitions management committee, is third from the left.

All ten wickets

THERE have been 15 recorded instances of a bowler taking all 10 wickets in an innings in the competitions.

At senior level, Jim Eddey, the legendary Tilford player, was the first to record the feat when he took 10-38 at Shottermill on 13 August 1949. Bowling his immaculately flighted slow-medium right-arm deliveries, from which he derived considerable spin, the Tilford skipper took the last five wickets in 14 balls for six runs as Shottermill slumped to 90 all out in response to Tilford's 92. History does not record his full analysis.

Jim Eddey: 'I took 'em all'.

Eddey, who died in 1964, aged 60, took the best part of 20,000 wickets in his career, and it made headlines when he did not take 100 in a season. His colleague, the late Bob Hooker, recalled in the 1980s the day Eddey skittled Shottermill. 'As we were walking off,' he said, 'Jim said, "I took 'em all". It was then that a cheer went up.'

The Shottermill scorecard from that day was:

T. Andrews b Eddey	10
E. West st Fry b Eddey	0
A. Heather c Terrell b Eddey	14
A. Massey b Eddey	11
P. Francis b Eddey	26
H. Woodward c Baker b Eddey	0
H. Hubbard not out	15
J. Trimmer st Fry b Eddey	0
A. Moorey b Eddey	3
H. Riddle lbw b Eddey	0
R. Bewley lbw b Eddey	2
Extras	9
Total	90

Bowling: Eddey 10-38

That long, hot summer of 1949 belonged to Eddey who would have bowled all day and every day, and at both ends, if it had been possible. In all, he took 268 wickets at 5.25 runs each and trundled down 548 overs. One weekend in August he bowled unchanged through four completed innings, taking 28-120 in 40 overs.

Walter Loader: 'real hostility'.

Seven years later, on 26 May 1956, Walter Loader, of Grayshott, a formidable fast bowler with what Theo Pope called 'real hostility in his arm' and 'surprising pace from the pitch', became the next bowler to take all 10 in the senior competition. His figures of 10-33 were against Frensham at Grayshott. Loader died in 1991, aged 71.

The Frensham scorecard in that match, which Grayshott won by three wickets, read:

A. Wells c Cowie b Loader	5
J. Ramsay c Birch b Loader	4
F. Agar lbw b Loader	5
M. Abbott c Bullock b Loader	20
D. Wells b Loader	31
H. Holdaway c and b Loader	0
C. Badland not out	15
S. Armstrong b Loader	0
D. Loat b Loader	5
F. Turney c Tickner b Loader	0
J. Farr c Goodes b Loader	0
Extras	7
Total	92

Bowling: Loader 10-33

Tony Peach, aged 20, of Rowledge, returned 10-21 in 11.2 overs (four maidens) in the second innings at home to Frensham on 5 August 1961. The scorecard has not been preserved but the details of the match were Frensham 71 (Les Crumplin 5-24) and 85 (Peach 10-21) lost to Rowledge 143-6dec and 18-1. Peach, the son of former Rowledge player Ben Peach, bowled off a short run and used a drying pitch to devastating effect. Fifteen years later, he was captain of Rowledge when they won the Miller Cup, and made a weekly round trip of 380 miles from his home in South Devon to play.

Tony Peach: drying pitch.

The best senior 'all-10' haul came the following year when Peach's clubmate Les Crumplin took 10-19 in the second innings at Wrecclesham on 14 July. Sadly, there are no further details.

Finally, in the I'Anson Cup bowling hall of fame, comes The Bourne's Dave Knight, who ran

Les Crumplin: best senior haul.

through Whitehill to give the visitors an unfriendly welcome to the new season on 30 April 1983. Knight, who, like his father George before him, has given wonderful service to the only club he has known, took 10-48 and Whitehill were put out for 94. In reply, The Bourne made 128 (C. Fry 28, M. Hoy 21; Woodward 5-40, Stroud 4-29) and won by three wickets.

The important Whitehill scorecard read:

P. Offord b Knight	14
N. Parkins c M. Poulter b Knight	16
R. Burton c May b Knight	13
K. Stroud c and b Knight	0
J. White st Thomas b Knight	8
D. Mann b Knight	7
A. Chalkley c May b Knight	7
R. Woodward not out	17
N. Smith c L. Knight b Knight	4
L. Parkins b Knight	7
R. Smith c M. Poulter b Knight	1
Extras	0
Total	94

Bowling: Knight 17.1-3-48-10

The best bowling figures of all time in the competitions are 10-3 by Arthur Yeomans, of Kingsley, against Frensham II on 4 August 1951. He took 15-13 in the match, which Kingsley lost by 25 runs, and it was played on the club's new (but not current) ground at Lode Farm.

The first recorded 10-wicket haul in the Miller Cup was on 30 July 1932, when Fred Courtnage took 10-34 for Whitehill II against Headley II. Six years later, on 13 August 1938, S.J. 'Gunner' Coombes, captaining Headley II away to Shottermill II, took 10-30.

Other bowlers who ripped through an innings in the Miller Cup are:

Peter Crow (Rowledge II), 10-24 in 12 overs against Frensham II on 1 August 1959; Ken Huckle (The Bourne II), 10-25 v Headley II, in 1963; Alan King (Whitehill II), 10-24 v Wrecclesham II on 21 June 1964; Mick Cane (Rowledge II), 10-17 in the second innings against Elstead II on 9 July 1966; Alec Liddicott (Frensham II), 10-50 in 20.5 overs v Rowledge II, on 31 July 1982; and Dave Harfield (Wrecclesham II), 10-23 when visitors Kingsley II were dismissed for 49 on 5 July 1986.

Dave Knight (left), 17 years on from his 'all-ten', pictured with his Bourne III colleagues after they had received the Division Five trophy from Cyril Crawte (second from the right) in 2000. At right is John Fullbrook, former Tilford and The Bourne opening batsman.

The only other recorded full hand is by Glen Woodward, who took 10-21 in 16.4 overs for Kingsley II at home to The Bourne II in a Division 2 match on a slow, unpredictable pitch and into a strong wind on 27 June 1998.

The best match figures in the I'Anson Cup, when fixtures were played over four innings, were 17-39 (8-18 and 9-21) by D.J. ('Joe') Piper for Rowledge against Frensham on 24 August 1963.

In the Miller Cup, the 18-22 (9-10 and 9-12) by S. Butcher, aged 17, for Whitehill II away to Tilford II in August 1931 is thought to be unparalleled, and included a hat-trick in each innings for good measure.

Highs and lows

THE highest innings total in the competitions is 400-8dec scored in 46 overs by Frensham II (Richard Doran 131) at home to Wrecclesham in Division Two on 21 September 1996.

Other totals of 300 or more are:

334-5dec in 45 overs by Fernhurst (Michael Allen 200 not out and an opening stand of 169 with Martin West, 53) at Crown Taverners II in Division Four on 23 August 1997.

320-6dec in 44 overs by Frensham (John Storey junior 100 and an opening stand of 144 with John Turbard) at Thursley, who fielded 10 men, in the I'Anson Cup on 10 September 1988.

315-9 in 48 overs by Frensham at home to Kingsley in Division One on 31 August 1996.

306-6dec in 47 overs by Wood Street at Chiddingfold in Division Three on 22 June 1996.

304-4dec in 36 overs by Wrecclesham (John Storey junior 211 not out) away to The Bourne II in Division Two on 1 July 1995.

303-4dec by Frensham III (Paul Hammond 162 and Ian Mason 116 not out in a second-wicket stand of 252) at home to Badshot Lea II, who fielded nine men, in Division Three on 20 September 1997.

303-8dec in 45 overs by Farncombe Wanderers at DERA in Division Two on 21 September 1996.

300-5dec by Blackmoor (Bill Read 117) v Frensham at Frensham Hill (Heights) in the I'Anson Cup on 11 July 1903.

The lowest innings total in the competitions is two by Binsted II v The Bourne II in May 1937.

The lowest total in the I'Anson Cup was three by Oakhanger in the second innings at Churt on 4 May 1940. Alan Matthews (5-1) and Fred Bishop (5-2) did the damage after Oakhanger had snatched a lead of eight runs on the first innings. Churt won the match by scoring 12-7 in their second innings.

Previously, Churt had held the record with five at home to Tilford (Jim Eddey 7-0, including a hat-trick) on 4 July 1938.

In the 1950s, Churt twice featured in single-figure totals. They were put out for five, again, by Frank Kenward (5-2) and Bob White (4-2) in the second innings at Headley on 5 May 1956 (they fielded 10 men), and on 19 May 1951, they were dismissed for nine on their own ground in the first innings against Elstead.

The highest innings total in the Miller Cup was 252-3dec in 29 overs by Frensham II (Paul Hammond 151 and a second-wicket stand of 222 with Mick Fathers, 79 not out) at home to Churt II on 5 May 1990. This beat the 250-9dec by Rowledge II (Roy Piper 105) away to Frensham II on 1 June 1957.

The lowest total in the Miller Cup was the two scored by Binsted II, mentioned above, and followed by four by 10-man Churt II against Tilford II on 26 July 1958. They were replying to Tilford's 124-3dec and were dismissed a second time for 16 (Jim Eddey 5-1 and 5-11, Ron Morrell 4-3 and 4-5).

Other single-figure totals in the Miller Cup:

Seven by Oakhanger at home to The Bourne II on 30 June 1951 (F.W. 'Sweat' Parratt 7-0 in 8.3 overs); by Elstead II (and 12 in the second innings) at home to Rowledge II on 14 June 1958 (A.F. 'Driver' Swan 11-3 in the match and Jim Peach 8-14); by Wrecclesham II v The Bourne II on 11 July 1959 (Frank Cordier 6-4, including a hat-trick, Ron Hole 4-2); and by Headley II at home to Rowledge II on 12 May 1962.

Eight by Shottermill II in the second innings v Rowledge II on 27 June 1959 (P. Crow 6-1); by Tilford II (the holders) v Rowledge II in the first game of the season, 26 April 1964 (Barry Guest 5-2, Alan Prior 5-6); by Grayshott II in the second innings v The Bourne II on 3 May 1964 (Ken Huckle 5-1, Frank Cordier 3-2); and by Whitehill II in the second innings v Frensham II on 30 May 1981 (George Pither 6-3, Alec Liddicott 3-5 and one batsman 'timed out').

Nine by Rowledge II away to The Bourne II on 4 May 1957 (Ron Hole 6-2, Frank Cordier 4-7); by Churt II v Elstead II in 1961; and by Kingsley II (10 men) away to Churt II (Alan Lang 7-1), 31 May 1986.

The record for the most runs scored in a match is 573 by Farncombe Wanderers (303-8 in 45 overs) and DERA (270-9 in 45) at DERA's ground at Pyestock in Division Two on 12 September 1996.

The presidents

A.J. Stevens presenting the Farnham and District League shield to the Rowledge captain, Reg Crumplin, who continued as skipper when the club re-entered the competitions in 1932. The author's mother took this photograph.

1936-68 A.J. Stevens, whose story is told elsewhere.

1968-78 J.G. ('Dick') Caesar. He was elected at the annual meeting at the end of 1968, almost a year after the death of A.J. Stevens. The membership needed no introduction to 'Dick' Caesar, whose name had been synonymous with the competitions since before the war. He had played for Frensham when the club first won the I'Anson Cup in 1932, and after war service with the RAF skippered The Bourne to the I'Anson Cup in 1948.

Julius Gurney Caesar was a member of an old, local family, probably with connections back to 'Silver Billy' Beldham. Ben Caesar was with his grandfather 'Silver Billy' the night before the grand old cricketer died at Tilford in 1862, aged 96, but 'Dick' would not confirm to this writer that he was a descendant. An auctioneer and estate agent in Farnham, he played for Wrecclesham and Rowledge before joining Frensham. He was well known in sporting circles, and was a director, chairman and finally president of Aldershot FC. He had been treasurer of the competitions for two years when he was elected the president, and held both positions until stepping down as president after ten years. He then became a life vice-president but continued to hold the purse strings until his death on Easter Monday 1983.

In *A Cup for Cricket*, Theo Pope wrote: 'Many hold the opinion that it would be impossible to find a better captain. He knows the game from A to Z.' When he was elected president, Mr Pope wrote: 'He was a fine fielder, sound wicketkeeper, tenacious batsman and astute captain, and this was never seen to better advantage than when he led The Bourne to victory in 1948.' The then secretary, Alan Staves, picked up that theme at the 70th anniversary dinner in 1971, when he proposed a toast to 'Dick' Caesar as president. Mr Staves said that 'Dick' opened the batting and was difficult to move once he got set. He was also a fielder of renown and not many batsmen would attempt a quick single when they played the ball in his direction in the covers. Mr Staves added: 'His cricketing brain possibly

J.G. Caesar presents the I'Anson Cup to Rowledge captain Alan Prior in 1975. Picture courtesy of Mrs June Tanner.

stems from the great Julius Caesar of Surrey and England fame, of whom 'Dick' is a descendant. His story is like an iceberg; only a very small part is visible in just a quick look at the surface, but there is so much more that he does in the background. He is a tireless worker.'

On his death, former competitions secretary Cliff Jarrett, a contemporary in the 1932 Frensham side, recalled that his friend was 'a great disciplinarian on and off the cricket field'. And the *Herald* noted that 'he was another product of the old Farnham Grammar School who served the town and district well and which is the poorer for his passing, but which benefited immeasurably by his living'.

Jack Warner, who had succeeded 'Dick' Caesar as president, unveiled a memorial seat at Wrecclesham recreation ground on 2 July 1983. Frank Cordier, chairman of Waverley District Council, who was soon to become the first mayor of the newly designated borough, recalled his playing days at The Bourne when 'Dick' was captain of the 1948 side. Among those present at the unveiling were Reg Crumplin, aged 80, and his son Les, both former captains of

'Dick' Caesar presented the I'Anson Cup on many occasions, this time to Tilford captain Chris Aust in 1978. Brian Turner, who later played with newcomers Farncombe Wanderers, is immediately behind the cup, with Martin Pryce behind him, and immediately to Mr Caesar's right is Noel Hume, who continues to give good service to Tilford.

Rowledge; F.W. 'Sweat' Parratt, who played for Frensham and The Bourne; Cliff Jarrett; Norman Disney, the current life president; Bill Poulter, veteran star batsman with The Bourne and Wrecclesham, who recalled the days when pigeons were taken to away games so that the score could be sent back at regular intervals, and when trips to Grayshott and Shottermill usually meant getting out and pushing the transport up the hill to Hindhead; John Tanner and Charles LeClercq, who were able to link their playing days alongside 'Dick' to the present, for both were still playing for The Bourne. Subsequently, the seat was complemented by the planting of a tree in memory of Reg Harris, the Wrecclesham potter and cricket umpire, and in 1985 Surrey Playing Fields Association donated a seat in memory of 'Dick' Caesar at The Bourne recreation ground.

1978-88 J.E. (Jack) Warner. His father Bill was in the Tilford team that won the first I'Anson Cup outright, and Jack made his debut for the club in the competition in the 1920s. He captained the side to the I'Anson Cup in 1954 when A.J. Stevens, in presenting the trophy, described him as small but audacious, and always trying to sever point's left hand or perforate short leg if he came too close. Nine years later, aged 50, he led the Second XI to the Miller Cup. Jack became an umpire when he retired and first appeared as a steward in 1969. He chaired his first stewards' meeting on 1 April 1976, when he stepped in for J.G. Caesar, who was unwell. He had been elected a vice-president of the competitions at the ADM the previous November, and became the president in 1978 when 'Dick' Caesar stepped down. He said it was one of his greatest honours. The scorer of many thousands of runs, he was a good judge of the game and liked nothing more than to talk about it, more often than not with a pint in one hand and his pipe in the other, in that quiet, unassuming manner that made him such a friend around the grounds. Jack Warner died on 5 November 1988, aged 75, and as a memorial Tilford presented the Jack Warner Cup for the Cricketer of the Year. His sons Mick and Terry played for Tilford, and Mick later continued his career at Churt, while Mick's son Stephen played for Kingsley and Churt.

Jack Warner (left) walks to the middle at Tilford with Alf Farnfield.

1988- N.G. (Norman) Disney. He became the second life president in the history of the competitions when, in 1991, he was re-elected president 'for as long as he wishes'. Norman enjoyed a long career as a wicketkeeper-batsman, appearing in two spells for Whitehill, between which he had success at Lindford when they won the league version of the Stevens Cup in 1954, and then at Headley where he helped to win the I'Anson Cup in 1962. Norman chaired his first I'Anson meeting on 7 September 1972, having been a steward since 1964. He was elected a vice-president in 1978, and was elevated on the death of Jack Warner 10 years later. He has chaired all but one of the last 16 annual delegates' meetings, and has, as the *Herald* once put it, a reputation for 'stern authority'. At Headley he has fulfilled most roles over the years, and continues to be the president. A firm believer in the 1989 changes, Norman continues to be a great supporter of the competitions, and his pragmatic approach to decision-making is built on the standards set by those who have held the top office in the past. At the centenary dinner, he was presented with an inscribed silver salver to mark more than 50 years of service as a player and administrator.

Life vice-presidents
1978-83 J.G. Caesar
1998- C.A. (Cyril) Crawte

Vice-presidents
1951-74 E.A.M. (Arnold) Gee (he retired from office)
1951-65 R.C.B. (Reg) Thackeray
1952-79 L.T. (Theo) Pope
1953-64 J. (John) Broadwood
1958-63 H.J. ('Harry') Knight
1960-70 G. (George) Arnold
1960-68 J.G. ('Dick') Caesar (he then became president)
1968-92 E.W. (Ted) Newman
1968-80 Brig H.E.F. Smyth
1968-88 E.J. (Ted) Turnbull
1975-78 J.E. (Jack) Warner (he then became president)
1978-88 N.G. (Norman) Disney (he then became president)
1980-92 C.G. (Cliff) Jarrett (resigned)
1982-99 R.W. (Bob) Burchett
1988- A. (Alan) Staves
1989- L.E. (Lou) Cannons
1990- C. (Charles) Kemp
1991- P. (Pat) Hastings
1992-97 P.D. Clark (resigned)
1992- A. (Andrew) Fry
2001- K.G. (Ken) Williams

Chairmen of the ADM
1951 G. Arnold
1952 A.J. Stevens
1953-54 E.A.M. Gee
1955 L.T. Pope
1956-68 E.A.M. Gee
1969-76 J.G. Caesar
1977 L.T. Pope
1978-85 J.E. Warner
1986-97 N.G. Disney
1998 C.A. Crawte
1999-01 N.G. Disney

Norman Disney is presented with an inscribed silver tray to mark his long service to the competitions, by former England captain Chris Cowdrey at the centenary year's gala dinner in Farnham Castle. Picture courtesy of Herald Newspapers.

Cyril Crawte (left) was appointed a life vice-president in 1998. He and his wife Barbara are pictured with former Prime Minister John Major, who attended a centenary reception as president of Surrey County Cricket Club, together with Lou Cannons, a vice-president since 1989, and his wife Ros. Picture courtesy of Herald Newspapers.

Crisis, what crisis?

IN a century of competitive cricket there are bound to be crises, and the most difficult one for the competitions to resolve occurred in 1971 when the president and the secretary were on the brink of resigning.

The *Herald* of 9 July reported that the stewards had overturned a decision of the president, J.G. 'Dick' Caesar, and had taken two points from I'Anson Cup leaders Thursley. Mr Caesar had earlier agreed that the Elstead v Thursley match could be switched to Thursley because the Elstead pitch was unfit for play, but by a majority decision the stewards had rejected this and declared the game cancelled, with two points to be awarded to both sides. Thursley had thus remained on top by four points, having hauled themselves up from the bottom with seven straight wins.

Alan Staves, the secretary who came close to resignation, and his wife Sheila pictured in 2001.

The minutes of an extraordinary stewards' meeting at Tilford on 8 July reveal that it was called because the competitions secretary, Alan Staves, wished to resign, because the stewards had not backed the president. He had had long discussions with both Mr Caesar and senior vice-president L.T. Pope.

'Dick' Caesar said he fully understood the reason for Mr Staves's proposed action and said that he was of a similar mind. This clearly shook the stewards and on the proposition of John Chuter (Frensham) the meeting unanimously agreed that in future the president (who also acts as chairman) and secretary of the competitions be empowered to make any decision they were called upon to make in the knowledge that they would have the full backing of the stewards.

John Chuter, whose proposition saved the day.

The secretary was asked if he would carry on, and Jack Warner (Tilford) offered his apologies for what had occurred at the previous meeting. He was sure other stewards would agree with him and now saw that they were in the wrong.

Mr Staves, who was a Thursley player, agreed to continue if he was given a 100 per cent vote of confidence. The stewards responded and also asked Mr Caesar to continue. Both agreed.

Secretaries and Treasurers

A.E. (Albert) Kent 1901-24

Much detail concerning the founding secretary appears in *A Cup for Cricket*, and the following was contained in his obituary in the *Herald* on 12 December 1952, headed, 'Pioneer of sport'. It recorded that Albert Kent, aged 81, had died at midday on Tuesday, 9 December, at Seaford in East Sussex, where for the past seven years he had been living with his son and daughter-in-law. In the past few years his health had been failing, but he was seriously ill only for about 10 days before his death.

For 32 years he was the manager of Hindhead Stores, on the London Road (A3) near the crossroads, and a member of various sports clubs. He had moved from his native Kent in 1896 and had worked for Charles Burgess in Godalming before transferring to Hindhead two years later. Always a sportsman, he had won about 100 prizes on the running track in events from 100 yards to 10.5 miles.

A competent all-round cricketer with a particular gift for fast swerve bowling, he became the secretary of the Grayshott club in 1899, and in the following year organised the first of a series of annual dinners. It was as a direct result of a speech he made at that dinner that Edward Blakeway I'Anson presented the first trophy for the competition.

Mr Kent also took an active part in launching the competitions for the Lyndon (Wednesday) Cup in 1914 and the Miller Cup in 1922, and for many years was recognised as one of the local leaders of the game. His retirement in 1924 was marked by the presentation of a silver cup in recognition of his work.

His activities were by no means confined to cricket. He was the first secretary of the Undershaw Football Club, founded in 1902 by Sir Arthur Conan Doyle, a Grayshott team-mate, then residing at Undershaw, close to Hindhead crossroads. So little was known of football in the village in those days that Mr Kent and Sir Arthur used to get the men together and mark out the positions for them on the billiard table at Undershaw. Mr Kent played centre-forward or outside-right for Undershaw, and he persuaded Conan Doyle to give the first trophy for the Surrey minor cup competition. He also founded and led gymnastic classes at Grayshott for men and boys; the Grayshott branch of the Tunbridge Wells Equitable Friendly Society; was actively associated with the Grayshott Village Hall for nearly 30 years; was president of the men's club; the first president of the bowls club and gave a trophy for annual competition; a member of the first committee of Undershaw Rifle Club;

Undershaw, the home of Sir Arthur Conan Doyle when he played for Grayshott, and well known to A.E. Kent and other local sportsmen. Albert Kent is pictured in the Grayshott team of 1920.

for some years on the Beacon Hill Village Club management committee; a member of Grayshott Parish Council; and of the Onslow Lodge of Freemasons.

A staunch Conservative, he founded the Hindhead Conservative Association in 1902 and became its first secretary. When he became too old for cricket he took up golf and for several years was captain of the Hindhead and Churt Village Golf Club. He did good work as secretary of the Hindhead Recreation Club and was largely instrumental in getting the Friary Brewery Company to allow the use of the ground behind the Royal Huts Hotel for cricket and football. He helped to raise funds to prepare the field for play and later for the erection of a pavilion.

Mr Kent left Hindhead in October 1930 to take over a grocery business in Egham, and on his departure he received numerous tokens of remembrance and appreciation. His wife died in October 1939.

R.L. (Lewis) Robinson 1924-27

Another Grayshott man and a colleague of Albert Kent, he played for the club for many years and later was the scorer. Extremely thorough in everything he did, he carried out the task of competitions secretary during a difficult interim period. He later lived at Headley Down. His name is recorded in Grayshott parish church as a resident who served in World War One. He is pictured with the 1929 Grayshott team.

H.M. (Harry) Edmead 1927-30

The captain of Hindhead for a number of seasons when the club played on the ground behind the Royal Huts Hotel, he was a good wicketkeeper. He also played for Grayshott, which enabled the link with the founding club and the administration to be maintained through the first 30 years of the competitions. His business later meant he needed to live in Guildford and for one season he ran the cricket from that town, no easy job in an age before mass communications became the norm. He continued to take an interest in the competitions, and was at Grayshott in 1969 to see his old club presented with the I'Anson Cup for the first time in 40 years.

G.M. (Geoffrey) Hubbuck 1930-35

A tower of strength in the Headley club, being at one time captain and secretary, and a man who was steeped in village cricket lore. He always had the donor of the I'Anson Cup in mind when running the competitions, and perhaps his lasting memorial was an overdue revision of the rules, which saw the introduction of a radius clause that halted a drift towards Farnham. The clause has since been modified, but essentially the work of Geoffrey Hubbuck holds good today. He was presented with a silver-plated inkstand and a silver pen at a farewell dinner at Headley. He is pictured with the 1938 Headley team.

H.J. ('Harry') Knight 1935-58

Henry James Knight was the second of the three long-term secretaries in the first 100 years. He was also the first appointed treasurer. He had wanted to stand down at the 1950 annual meeting but agreed to continue in the golden jubilee year. Thereafter, 'Harry' Knight, who was a local government officer in Farnham and was involved in many community organisations, continued to be re-elected annually, while still saying he wished to step down, and had assistance, first, from W.G. (George) Steer, an opening batsman with Elstead, and then Miss Alison Gordon, a work colleague. However, in 1958, 'Harry' Knight at last got his way and resigned, but only as secretary. In the absence of a new treasurer coming forward, he continued until his early death in 1963.

H.J. ('Harry') Knight: enjoyed every minute.

At the Winners v The Rest match at The Bourne in 1951, the president, A.J. Stevens, announced that 'Harry' had told him that after 16 years he must retire from the secretaryship. He had had a busy year with the golden jubilee organisation and the benefit match in Farnham for the Surrey player Jack Parker (he was involved in the organisation of all the local benefit matches for Surrey and Hampshire players, including the Bedser twins, Jim Laker, Vic Cannings and Alf Gover, from 1936 to the late 1950s). The president said the competition owed him a tremendous debt of gratitude for the many hours of his not very great spare time he devoted to the competitions. Not only did the office demand a lot of hard work, but also that rather rarer quality called tact.

Mr Knight said he had enjoyed every minute of the job, although during the last two seasons the delegates and he had not seen eye to eye on one point. It had been his contention that the I'Anson Cup should be reduced to 10 teams and the Miller Cup divided into two sections, but he was not resigning on that account alone. There came a time in one's life when one had to look in other directions, and he felt the job was now one for a much younger man full of enthusiasm for the game, and he was sure one would be found. 'If he is not forthcoming I shall not let the competitions down. When you have been secretary for such a long period you begin to think that the competitions are your own. I think for a number of years I have regarded these competitions as my own, and that is quite wrong.'

This report in the *Herald* prompted a letter from Ernest Turner, the veteran secretary of Headley, who wrote: 'No one can realise more fully than the secretaries of competing clubs to what extent Mr Knight has given unstinting time and thought to the competitions and the prompt manner in which he has kept secretaries informed on all matters arising out of them for presentation to their respective clubs.'

At The Bourne's dinner in 1955, the competitions' first vice-president, who for many years chaired the annual meeting, E.A.M. (Arnold) Gee, of Rowledge, said of Mr Knight that he was the pillar of the competitions and 'no words of mine can do justice to all the hard work he does. I am sure that he will go down in history as one of the finest and most able secretaries the competitions have had'.

In 1956, he received a silver salver and a cheque to mark 21 years as secretary, and there was also a cheque and a bouquet of flowers for Mrs Knight. The inscription on the salver recorded that it was given 'by his cricket friends to mark the completion of 21 years in office and in appreciation of his devoted service to the game'. Several past and present Surrey players had contributed to the fund, which had raised £92, and the presentations were made by J.G. ('Dick') Caesar, one of 'Harry' Knight's oldest cricket friends. He said that when he had shown the silver salver to A.J. Stevens the previous evening, he had responded: 'When we chose our secretary 21 years ago we couldn't have made a better choice. It doesn't matter whether it is a cricket club, cricket league, company board of directors or anything else – unless you have a good secretary you can't be successful.'

Mr Caesar said he had known 'Harry' since 1929 when he had first come to Frensham and, through the influence of Jim Chuter, joined the Frensham club. 'Harry' was a batsman and wicketkeeper, and they had played together for Frensham (they were in the 1932 team that won the I'Anson Cup for Frensham for the first time) and The Bourne ('Harry' Knight was a member of I'Anson Cup championship-winning sides in 1950, 1951 and 1953), and on a good many different occasions. 'I can vouch for the splendid way in which he has carried out his work, and I am quite sure that no cricket competition in the country is run better than ours,' 'Dick' Caesar said. 'May you look back, "Harry", from time to time and recall the pleasure that your work has given to so many of us, and may you continue in office even yet for a further long period.'

He and his wife were deeply appreciative of the kindness of so many people, said Mr Knight. 'This is truly a wonderful occasion for both of us and one which we are not likely to forget.' He said he had enjoyed the privilege of the friendship of A.J. Stevens since 1930, and thanked Leslie Mileham, of Whitehill, who as assistant secretary had given him much help and held the fort while he was absent from the district during World War Two.

When he resigned as secretary at the annual meeting in 1958, he said that he was prepared to 'serve these competitions, which have been so near my heart for so many years, in any capacity, except the secretaryship, and all the time I have reasonable health it will be a pleasure to serve you'. At the Tilford dinner that year, the club's president, Col. G.A. Campbell, recalled that A.J. Stevens had told him a short while before that 'if it hadn't been for H.J. Knight these competitions would have crumpled up years ago'.

He was a modest man, and when he took the chair at the golden jubilee dinner in October 1960, in the absence of the life president, Arnold Gee said in a toast to him: 'I am only too pleased to see "Jim" (as he was known to his friends) as chairman at this celebration dinner and not lurking in the background as he has done for many years.' The reply was: 'I have always believed in village cricket and therefore it has been a pleasure to be associated in a small way with an organisation such as ours. The reward, if any is required, is your presence here this evening, coupled with the knowledge that the competition is still flourishing.' It had always been his good fortune to serve with a good team of stewards, all of whom were present. 'We have worked in unison because we all have the same interest – good cricket, sportsmanship and, what is more important, lasting friendship.'

'Harry' Knight died on Sunday, 31 March 1963, aged 56, after a short illness. It was completely in character that, in spite of his weakness, he insisted on attending a meeting of Frensham Parish Council, of which he was the clerk, on the Friday evening. In an appreciation in the *Herald*, A.J. Stevens said: 'His completely unexpected demise has not so much shocked the whole local cricket community as filled it with dismay at the wide gap rent in its administration. Who – who indeed! – can fill his unique place in it? If anything is worth doing, it is worth doing well, might have been his motto.'

There were many warm tributes paid, of course, and the legacy he left the competitions was that he made those who took part aware of the importance of cherishing the heritage left us by the founding fathers more than 60 years earlier. At the annual meeting in 1962, four months before his death, 'Harry' Knight had suggested that all clubs and officials examine the whole structure of the competitions so that they might survive and prosper in the modern age. It was to be nearly 30 years before significant changes were made to breathe new life into our cricket.

A memorial fund was established by the competitions and raised £455 8s 8d (£455.43), of which the bulk was given to his widow. The balance paid for a clock and case to be placed on the pavilion at Frensham, and this continues to be a memorial to one of the great administrators in our 100 years' history.

H.C. ('Mickey') Bicknell 1958-59

He was the secretary of The Bourne and, at the annual meeting of the competitions on 28 November 1958, agreed to fill the gap created by the resignation of H.J. Knight. He had played in the competitions for 25 seasons and was a competitive all-rounder who helped The Bourne to both I'Anson and Miller Cup titles. The late John Tanner described him as 'small in stature but a quick bowler (as well as an opening batsman) who on his day was capable of reducing the opposition to nervous wrecks with his pace and accuracy'. His tenure lasted only a few months before he emigrated to Australia from where, in a letter to the *Herald* in July 1960, he referred to that 'great cricketer and old friend' Frank Kenward. 'I'd love to see Headley win the competition again before he retires,' he wrote (they did, in 1962, and Kenward continued to play on into his 70s). 'Mickey' Bicknell, whose brother Ken kept wicket and opened the batting for both The Bourne and Tilford during his career, returned to England after two years in Queensland, where he captained his local team. When he made his decision to return home, he told a friend it was because the prospects for his three sons were not as good as had been painted by the immigration authorities. He died some years ago.

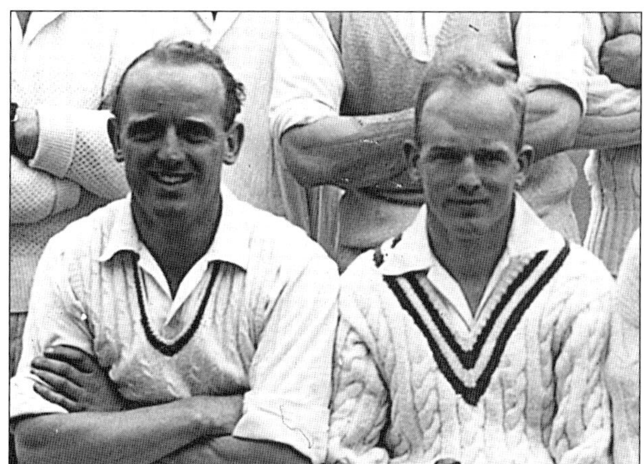

H.C. ('Mickey') Bicknell (right) and his brother Ken.

P.C. (Peter) Warman 1959-66

A Tilford player who, when National Service commitments permitted, played a part in the I'Anson Cup successes in 1957 and 1958. He had joined Tilford in 1950 and had been the treasurer for five years until he was called up in 1957. Back in civvies in 1959, he again became treasurer and was also a member of the successful Miller Cup side that year. An Old Farnhamian, as is the current secretary, he was 25 years old when he stepped into the position abruptly left vacant in July 1959 and served the competitions well until business commitments made it too difficult to continue. 'I feel it more and more difficult to perform the job in the way in which I feel it should be carried out,' he said. 'I no longer have the time available to devote to the affairs of the competitions.' Mr Warman, who lives in Frensham, came to the rescue of the competitions a second time in 1963, with the death of H.J. Knight, and was the acting treasurer until the annual meeting that year, when he was replaced by a club colleague, Lt-Col. J. (Jim) Cornwell, who was later to follow him as secretary.

Lt-Col. J. (Jim) Cornwell 1966-68

Although his stay in the district was brief, Jim Cornwell made many friends and was well respected. He became Tilford's secretary in 1961, and worked hard on behalf of

Lt-Col. Jim Cornwell looked up old haunts in centenary year during a visit from his home in Australia.

local cricket. He was a part of Tilford's Miller Cup winning side in 1963. His last appearance as a player, prior to leaving for a new life in Australia, was as captain of The Rest against Miller Cup winners The Bourne in 1968. He was a stickler for ensuring the rules were adhered to, and was particularly outspoken on the condition of pitches and the provision, or lack of it, of umpires. He felt so strongly about the latter that in his final report he suggested that clubs which did not provide an official should have their application for membership refused. When he stepped down, he said: 'This is one of the greatest village cricket competitions to be found anywhere; it is surely the duty of us all to ensure that standards are maintained at the highest possible level. It calls for constant work and enthusiasm in every club. It is seldom easy to find members prepared, or able, to do all that needs to be done. I would say to all clubs, look to your younger members, many of whom will take on a job and do it well if given an opportunity.' He continues to live in Australia, and returns to this country periodically. He reacquainted himself with the competitions when he visited Tilford during a centenary fixture in June.

A. (Alan) Staves 1968-72

A long-time player with Wrecclesham and Thursley, he was a key member of the latter's side at the beginning of the 1970s when they won the I'Anson Cup in three successive seasons. In 1971 he topped the batting averages, scoring 400 runs in 22 innings. As a bowler, his best return in the competitions was 8-31 for Thursley against Elstead in July 1967, when his match figures were 14-48. When he informed the stewards in July 1972 that he intended to retire at the annual meeting on 30 November, it was at the end of a meeting that had deliberated on a bruising exchange between Tilford and Thursley in connection with the arrangements for a Stevens Cup match. Tilford had cried foul when beaten and had suggested that Thursley be removed from the competition. The stewards declined to agree. Mr Staves said that neither he nor his wife had enjoyed good health in recent times and this had contributed to his decision to step down. However, when a successor failed to come forward at the annual meeting, it was adjourned until 10 January 1973, when C.G. (Cliff) Jarrett, an old friend of president 'Dick' Caesar, offered to fill the position. Mr Staves then acted as assistant secretary and was also a steward from 1974-80. He is now a vice-president.

C.G. (Cliff) Jarrett 1973-80

He was a member of the Frensham team that won the I'Anson Cup in 1932 and was a colleague of 'Dick' Caesar, who was able to persuade his old friend to step into the breach as 1973 dawned. Having returned to the competitions after 40 years, he said he could see nothing wrong with the way I'Anson Cup cricket was now played. When he resigned he said: 'I've done the job for seven years and now I think it's time someone else took over. I hope it will be a younger person – someone who will bring fresh thinking into the running of the competitions. I hope such a person is available. Cricket is changing all the time and we have to keep up with modern trends.' He added: 'It has been a time of great satisfaction for me. I played in the competition over 50 years ago and I feel I have done something useful in return.' There should be changes, he said, but reminded delegates that 'big was not always beautiful'. In 1992 he resigned as a vice-president, saying that he disagreed with the expansion of the competitions and that they no longer resembled those that he had remembered as a player and then secretary. He is pictured in the 1932 Frensham team.

G.R. (Graham) Collyer 1980-2002

The longest-serving secretary, in terms of continuous cricket, who took on the job at the annual meeting in 1980 after the competitions' only ballot for the position. He had recently returned to the area, but was steeped in the history of the competitions, his grandfather and uncles having played for Rowledge between the wars, and he and his father having been connected with Elstead from the mid-1950s. A journalist who began his career with the *Farnham Herald* at the age of 16 under the watchful eye of L.T. Pope, his interest in the history of the competitions began at an early age, with the publication of *A Cup for Cricket*, and was encouraged by Theo Pope. On the death of the latter, he was given much of his cricketing archive material, which has been put to good use in the compilation of this book. Like 'Harry' Knight 30 years earlier, he became acutely aware of the fragile nature of the competitions and towards the end of the 1980s decided that it was time for a radical change. He encouraged his managerial colleagues to follow him, and the result was the monumental decision taken at Tilford in 1989 that has produced the league structure we have today. At the annual meeting in 2001, he indicated his intention to stand down in a year's time.

Graham Collyer: radical changes.

There have been six assistant secretaries: L.M. (Leslie) Mileham, of Whitehill, who restarted the competitions after World War Two, when H.J. Knight was away from the district; W.G. (George) Steer, of Elstead, and Miss Alison Gordon, of Farnham, during the 1950s; A. (Alan) Staves, 1973-80; P. (Pat) Hastings, of Thursley, 1990-98; and Mrs Julie Gibson, of Crown Taverners, 1998-2000.

The treasurers

There was not a designated treasurer in the first 34 years of the competitions, the secretary undertaking the task as part of his overall duties. The first appointment was made in 1935, but in fact the dual role continued as H.J. Knight became both secretary and treasurer. He held both positions until he resigned as secretary in 1958, but continued as treasurer until his death in 1963.

P.C. (Peter) Warman 1963, who was by then the secretary, stepped in as treasurer until the annual meeting at the end of 1963.

Lt-Col. J. (Jim) Cornwell 1963-66, resigned on becoming secretary.

J.G. ('Dick') Caesar 1966-83 (see the section on the presidents).

A. (Andrew) Fry 1983-91. A former treasurer of The Bourne, he joined the competitions' administrative team following the death of J.G. Caesar. A member of a Tilford cricketing family, his brothers David, Peter and Tim continue to play in the league. He stepped down for family reasons (he had become the father of twins) in 1991, and at the annual meeting in November 1992 he was elected a vice-president and presented with an inscribed tankard.

Andrew Fry: cricketing family.

K.E. (Keith) Mayson 1991-. A retired banker, he responded to a brief mention of a vacancy that appeared in the *Herald* and was appointed at a meeting in the Fox and Pelican, the league's birthplace in Grayshott, in December 1991. He attended his first stewards' meeting as treasurer on 5 March 1992, at Lindford. He was a Churt player for three seasons in the 1970s, and played his last match against Whitehill on 20 September 1975, before leaving the district. This was Churt's centenary season, and he fittingly took the last wicket of the match to give Churt a win by 74 runs. He topped the bowling averages with 34 wickets at 10.7. At the club's dinner he was awarded the Jaynson Cup for work on and off the field, and also received a mounted cricket ball. He and Bill Alexander, who was also leaving the district, jointly donated the Cricketer Cup to the club, of which he was chairman until recently. In September 1973, he included a hat-trick in taking 5-17 in the Miller Cup at Rowledge. More recently he has also been the chairman of the centenary committee and has presided over the many meetings that were required to plan the year-long celebrations.

Keith Mayson in celebratory mood.

Over the boundary

BY their very nature, village cricket grounds differ greatly, and there has to be a need for local rules. The competitions default to the Laws of Cricket while adhering to their own set of rules, which are now comprehensive but were once rudimentary.

For instance, in 1955 Headley's proposal that four runs be added to the score for boundary byes on all grounds was approved. Previously only two runs had been given on some grounds.

The following year it was agreed that six runs be awarded for all hits pitching over and clear of the boundary line or fence. Until then some grounds simply had marker posts at intervals without any connecting line. It was a proposal by Grayshott that led to all grounds having their boundaries marked by a continuous white line.

Whether this change was prompted by events in a Miller Cup match at Tilford on the first day of the 1955 season is unknown. Then, Bob Hooker and Henry Ford ran 10 after Hooker had hit the ball into the outfield and the Alexandra Park fielders had failed to find it. No one called 'lost ball' and the batsmen ran on until they could run no more. The tale made the *News Chronicle*, which recorded that Hooker's strike 'fell to earth somewhere between Black Prince and Robin, the Ford family's two horses that were quietly eating the outfield'. By the time the batsmen had completed their tenth run they were reduced to a stroll, and skipper Jim Eddey muttered, 'Glory, no one shouted "lost ball". Darn it, they could have run 50.' As it was, Hooker and Ford put on 143 before the former was out.

Management Committee

THE organisation of the competitions is in the hands of a management committee elected annually. The first meeting of the committee was held at Lindford CC on Thursday, 4 March 1993, when, in addition to the life president, Norman Disney, who has chaired almost every subsequent meeting, those present were Graham Collyer (secretary), Keith Mayson (treasurer), Alistair Ansell (nominated by Kingsley and whose father Martin had been a steward), Tony Cheeseman (Thursley), Cyril Crawte (umpires' secretary), Mark Harrop (Frensham), Pat Hastings (assistant secretary), Frank Lunt (Lindford), Pat Murphy (Elstead), Ian Webster (Tilford) and Ken Williams (Grayshott). Apologies were received from Ron Neil (The Bourne) and Roger Vernier (Headley). The committee members had been elected at the annual meeting in November 1992 following a long debate during which several delegates expressed concern that not enough clubs would be represented. The proposal was for a committee of six, plus officers, but with nine nominations it was agreed that they should all be elected.

Life president Norman Disney (left) in discussion with Ron Neil (right) and fixtures secretary Ian Webster.

The idea of a management committee had been part of the overwhelming change in the organisation of the competitions that had stemmed from the meeting in Tilford Institute in March 1989. It was considered that the controlling body of stewards that had grown from three in earlier times to one member of each club by 1964 would become too unwieldy as more clubs were admitted to membership. The last meeting of the stewards was therefore held at Lindford on 1 October 1992.

Changes in personnel on the management committee in subsequent years have been few. In 1994 David Havenhand (Badshot Lea), a former steward, replaced Roger Vernier, who did not seek re-election. The ratio of officers to nominated members also changed after Ian Webster had been elected fixtures secretary at the 1993 annual meeting.

David Havenhand (left) and Pat Hastings with the president.

By 1995, Alistair Ansell had resigned and no one had taken his place. In October that year, Graham Sampson (Grayshott) was co-opted in place of his father-in-law, Ken Williams, who stood down in order to take charge of the Grayshott club's centenary year celebrations.

There were no more changes until February 1997 when Les Davis (Dogmersfield) and Gareth Saunders (Frimchett, now Tilford) were co-opted as members. At the annual meeting that year, Paul Malpass (Crown Taverners) was elected and he attended the final meeting in 1997.

In 1998 meetings switched from Lindford to The Bourne. Graham Sampson resigned for business reasons after the first meeting, and Mark Harrop, who had also been the competitions' statistician and an umpire, stepped down at the annual meeting.

Since then Paul Malpass has left the committee, and John Allen (Fernhurst) was elected at the annual meeting in 2000.

In addition to the chairman, secretary and treasurer, whose details are recorded elsewhere, the current members of the committee are:

John Allen, who is the latest recruit and continues the trend of representation from the new intake of clubs. He has been a leading member of the Fernhurst club for many years, and is also a member of the competitions' rules committee.

Tony Cheeseman, who began his playing career with Elstead in the mid-1950s, and then followed several of his colleagues to Thursley. He organised the umpires' pool in 1971-72 before stepping down to become secretary of Thursley. He first attended a stewards meeting on 4 December 1980, was ever-present from 1981-86 and has had continuous service since 1992. He is a member of the umpires' pool.

Tony and Sandra Cheeseman, who have given many years of solid service to the competitions. Picture courtesy of the Cheesemans.

Frank Lunt, doyen of Lindford CC.

Cyril Crawte, who has given more than 40 years' service to Wrecclesham and the competitions, and is the chairman of his club. He first attended a stewards meeting on 7 April 1977, and has chaired meetings in the absence of the president. He took over the organisation of the umpires' pool in 1992, and is also the chairman of the rules committee. His contribution to the competitions was recognised at the annual meeting in 1998 when he was made a life vice-president.

Les Davis, who is also a member of the umpires' pool, is starting his sixth year of membership. He was secretary of Dogmersfield in their early days in the competitions. A member of the centenary committee and the competitions' webmaster.

Pat Hastings, who has been associated with Thursley since the 1970s and first attended a stewards meeting on 10 April 1987. He was chairman of the working party that prepared the way for the changes to the structure of the competitions and was assistant secretary from 1990-98. He was elected a vice-president in 1991.

David Havenhand, who is a former player with Rowledge and Tilford, and has vast experience as a cricket and football administrator. He first attended a stewards meeting on 5 March 1992.

Frank Lunt, who has been associated with Lindford since the formation of the present club at the beginning of the 1970s. A tireless worker for his club, and in the centenary season was believed to be the oldest player in the competitions. He first attended a stewards meeting on 6 May 1976. A member of the centenary committee.

Pat Murphy, who has been a player and an administrator with Elstead since the 1980s, and first attended a stewards meeting on 7 March 1991. In 1990, he was the first winner of the Jack Warner Trophy for player of the year and received the cup from Jack's widow Norah. A demanding left-arm bowler, his figures that season were 341-109-782-78. He also hit two half-centuries, and off the field was a member of the reorganisation working party. He is a member of the rules committee.

Pat Murphy and the Elstead pavilion he hopes will be replaced soon.

Ron Neil, who is both president and chairman of The Bourne, and was the captain when they won the I'Anson Cup in 1994 after a barren spell of 26 years. A tireless worker for the competitions, and a member of the centenary committee.

Gareth Saunders, who is the youngest member of the committee and, until he moved to Tilford, his membership of Frimchett was another link between old and new. He is secretary of the rules committee.

Ian Webster, who has been connected with Tilford as player and administrator for almost 30 years. He was the club treasurer in the mid-1970s and is now the president. He was elected the competitions' fixtures secretary in 1993, and is a member of the rules committee. He first attended a stewards meeting on 5 April 1979.

In addition to Messrs Davis, Lunt and Neil, the centenary committee, chaired by Keith Mayson, included secretary Graham Collyer and:

Martin Pryce: long service to Tilford and the competitions.

Heart to heart: Ken Williams and Ron Neil.

Martin Pryce, who has been an outstanding player for Tilford since the 1970s and a solid supporter of the competitions. He is the son of the late Robin Pryce, who was a stylish batsman with Elstead and Tilford until illness forced him to retire prematurely in 1976.

Ken Williams, who opened the batting for The Bourne when they won the I'Anson Cup in 1953. A tireless worker, he has been associated with Grayshott for many years, some as secretary, and left the management committee to organise the club's centenary in 1996. His work on behalf of the competitions was recognised at the 2001 ADM when he was elected a vice president.

Stewards of the competitions were introduced in 1931 and replaced the standing sub-committee that had been in

The centenary is launched. Writer and broadcaster Christopher Martin-Jenkins and competitions secretary Graham Collyer hold the original I'Anson Cup on Tuesday, 23 January 2001 – 100 years to the day that the founding fathers met in the Fox and Pelican public house in Grayshott. Also pictured, from the left, are Ron Neil, Ken Williams, John Sandy (the Mayor of Waverley), Les Davis, Norman Disney (life president), Keith Mayson (treasurer and centenary chairman) and Frank Lunt. Picture courtesy of Herald Newspapers.

existence since 1921. The names of the representatives up to and including 1950 are recorded in *A Cup for Cricket*, and those who followed were:
1951: G. Arnold, J. Eddey, E. Johnson, E. Nash, W.A. Penycate.
1952: The number increased with R.J. Clements, H. Massey and E.R. Parratt joining, and W.A. Penycate retiring.
1953: J.G. Caesar replaced E. Johnson, who retired after 47 years' service to the competitions.
1954: Unchanged.
1955: E. Giles replaced H. Massey.
1956: S. Ellis and J. Radford replaced J. Eddey and E. Nash.
1957: C.C. Cox and W.J. Norman replaced E. Giles and J. Radford.
1958: Unchanged
1959: H.J. Knight replaced R.J. Clements.
1960: Unchanged
1961: C. Harris replaced G. Arnold, who retired after more than 30 years' service.

George Arnold: retired after long service to the competitions.

1962: M. Baulcombe replaced S. Ellis.
1963: Unchanged
1964: After the deaths in 1963 of H.J. Knight and W.J. Norman, the chairman, the annual meeting agreed that each club should nominate a steward. The enlarged group met in Tilford Institute until 1979.
1964: C.C. Cox (chairman), A. Arnold, J.G. Caesar, N. Disney, C. Harris, H. Holdaway, A. Karn, Maj. J. Marriott, E.R. Parratt, R. Petter, R. Read.

Cyril Cox: Elstead player, umpire and official, who became a steward of the competitions in 1957 and was the first chairman when the controlling body was enlarged in 1964.

1965: Marriott (chairman), Arnold, R.W. Burchett, Caesar, Disney, C. Harris, R. Harris, Karn, Petter, J. Sinclair, J. Thayer.
1966: Marriott (chairman), H. Arnold, L. Austin, Caesar, Disney, R. Harris, B. Karn, Petter, K. Pierce, Sinclair, Thayer.
1967: Caesar (chairman), Arnold, Austin, Disney, Harris, L. Jenkins, Karn, Marriott, Petter, Pierce, G. Pither.
1968: Caesar (chairman), Arnold, J. Chuter, Disney, F. Edwards, Harris, Karn, Marriott, Petter, Pierce.
1969: Caesar (chairman), Arnold, R. Barratt, W. Betts, Chuter, Disney, E. Dolton, Edwards, Harris, Karn, F. Norris, Petter, J. Reay, J. Warner.
1970: Caesar (chairman), M. Ansell, Arnold, Betts, Chuter, Disney, Dolton, J. Grover, Harris, Norris, Petter, Tribe, Warner.
1971: Caesar (chairman), Ansell, Arnold, Betts, R.W. Burchett, Chuter, Disney, Grover, Harris, Norris, Tribe, Warner.
1972: Caesar (chairman), Ansell, Arnold, Betts, Burchett, Chuter, W. Crosby, Disney, Grover, Harris, D. Limon, Norris, Tribe, Warner.
1973: Caesar (chairman), Ansell, Betts, Burchett, Chuter,

Crosby, Disney, Grover, Limon, G. Nixson, Norris, M. Poulter, Harris, Warner.
1974: Caesar (chairman), Ansell, Betts, Burchett, R. Dibdin, Disney, Grover, M. Henderson, W. Hodgson, K. Huckle, Limon, Nixson, Norris, A. Staves, Warner.
1975: Caesar (chairman), Ansell, Betts, Burchett, Crosby, Dibdin, Disney, Hodgson, Huckle, Limon, Nixson, Norris, Staves, Warner.
1976: Caesar (chairman), Ansell, Burchett, Dibdin, Disney, Huckle, K. Jones, Limon, F. Lunt, Nixson, Norris, P. Prior, Staves, Warner.
1977: Caesar (chairman), Ansell, Burchett, C. Crawte, Dibdin, Disney, Huckle, Jones, Limon, Nixson, L. Parkins, Prior, Staves, Warner, who chaired most of the meetings.
1978: Caesar (chairman), Ansell, Burchett, Crawte, Dibdin, Disney, Jones, Limon, Nixson, Parkins, Poulter, Prior, Staves, Warner. [Warner, Staves and Disney shared the chairmanship in the year in which 'Dick' Caesar's wife died.]
1979: Warner (chairman), Ansell, Burchett, Dibdin, Disney, P. Hobdell, Jones, Limon, Nixson, Parkins, Poulter, Prior, Staves, I. Webster.
From 1980-83 most of the meetings were held in St Francis's Hall at Rushmoor, Churt.
1980: Warner (chairman), Ansell, Burchett, Dibdin, Disney, Jones, Limon, Nixson, Parkins, Poulter, Prior, Staves, M. Stoker, Webster. [A. Cheeseman attended the last meeting of the year, which was held in Churt pavilion.]
1981: Warner (chairman), Ansell, K. Bone, Burchett, Cheeseman, Crawte, Disney, Jones, Limon, Nixson, Poulter, Prior, Webster, R. Woodward. [One meeting at Churt pavilion.]
1982: Warner (chairman), Ansell, Bone, Burchett, Cheeseman, Crawte, Disney, Jones, Limon, Nixson, Prior, G. Senior, Webster, Woodward.
1983: Warner (chairman), Ansell, Bone, Burchett, Cheeseman, Crawte, Disney, Jones, Limon, Nixson, F. Norris, Prior, Senior, Webster. [Disney in the chair once.]
From 1984-89 meetings were held at Frensham RBL.
1984: Warner (chairman), Bone, Burchett, Cheeseman, Crawte, Disney, D. Emery, Jones, A. Lang, D. Mann, Nixson, Senior, D. Shaw, Webster.
1985: Warner (chairman), Burchett, Cheeseman, Crawte, S. Dickinson, Disney, N. Dunbar, B. Francis, M. Hoy, Jones, Lang, Mann, Nixson, Webster.
1986: Disney (chairman), Burchett, Cheeseman, Crawte, Francis, G. Haytree, Jones, Lang, Mann, G. May, Nixson, M. Poulter, Webster.
1987: Disney (chairman), Burchett, Crawte, P. Hastings, Haytree, Jones, L. Knight, Lang, T. Martin, Mann, G. May, Nixson, Webster. [Burchett in the chair once.]

George Nixson, who played for Grayshott when still in the navy. He became the club chairman and was a long-serving steward and umpire. His quiet affability made him a great favourite among players, who also respected his deep knowledge of the game he loved. He died, aged 71, in September 1992.

1988: Disney (chairman), K. Bevan, Crawte, Hastings, Haytree, R. Holden, Jones, Knight, Lang, Martin, Mann, Nixson, Webster. [R. Burchett in the chair once.]
1989: Disney (chairman), Bevan, Crawte, Hastings, Haytree, G. Hirst, Jones, Knight, Lang, D. Mace, Nixson, K. Williams (Headley), Webster. [P. Hastings in the chair once.]
From 1990-92 the meetings were held at Lindford.
1990: Disney (chairman), Bevan, Crawte, P. Golding, Hastings, Haytree, Hirst, Jones, Lang, Mace, Nixson, Williams, Webster. [P. Clapham, F. Lunt, C. Russell and G. Senior were deputies; Badshot Lea, Dogmersfield, Rowledge and Tongham were represented at the last meeting of the year.]
1991: Disney (chairman), S. Allen, Crawte, Hastings, Haytree, T. Henderson, Hirst, F. Holland, A. Johnston, Jones, Lang, Mace, P. Murphy, Nixson, C. Ray, G. Smeath, A. Watts, Webster, Williams. [F. Lunt was a deputy twice.]
1992: Disney (chairman). All clubs were represented but not all names recorded. Among those known to have attended were C. Ackehurst, A. Ansell, I. Carter, Cheeseman, Crawte, Hastings, M. Harrop, D. Havenhand, Holland, Johnston, Lunt, Lang, Mace, Murphy, D. Newell, Nixson, Ray, R. Baldrey, Webster, R. Vernier. [P. Hastings was in the chair once.]

A matter of discipline

PROTECTING the good name of the competitions and of cricket is the over-riding resolve of the management committee, as it was of the stewards in another era. Instances of unsporting or ungentlemanly conduct brought to the attention of the committee are dealt with swiftly and positively.

The message has been clearly stated on many occasions, and put simply is: No behaviour that brings the competitions and cricket into disrepute will be tolerated, and players or clubs found guilty can expect to receive an appropriate penalty. It had been enshrined in a 1903 rule, thus: 'That any player guilty of using bad language towards another player or an umpire, during the progress of a cup match, be reported to the committee, who will have power to suspend such offender from taking any further part in the competition'.

Fortunately, there have been few occasions when the administration has felt it necessary to act. Until enlargement, disciplinary matters were rare and there was only one recorded instance of a player being suspended by the competitions, as opposed to receiving a ban from his club. Expansion inevitably brought difficulties. As the cricket became more competitive, some players found it hard to stay out of trouble. It is also true that some of the new clubs found it hard to settle into a different environment. League cricket outside of the I'Anson Cup Competitions is a relatively new phenomenon, a child of the seventies. And in cricket, as in life, the last 30 years have been different – more abrasive, more competitive, and certainly more litigious.

In the earlier years of the competitions it is fair to say that players knew their place. Umpires and administrators were usually senior, statesmanlike figures with whom one argued at one's peril. Consequently, one did not argue, at least not to their face.

Now, although umpires and administrators still earn respect, the 'them and us' has, thankfully, disappeared and there is, generally, a closer relationship between the majority of the players and those who run the competitions. The minority who find it hard to accept rules and etiquette spoil the game for the majority, and this is what the management committee will not tolerate.

A code of conduct drawn up by the committee and distributed to all clubs before the 1999 season sought to make everyone who played in the competitions aware of the seriousness of stepping out of line. It led to a noticeable reduction in ungentlemanly and unsporting behaviour, but the measure was further strengthened the following year when club secretaries were required to ensure that each individual player in his club was personally made aware of the content of the code. Subsequently, the updated Laws of Cricket have required captains to exercise even greater control over their players.

Debate and discussion is healthy, but in the right place. What players need to be aware of is that to argue on the field of play is out of order and unacceptable. The target is usually the umpire, whose decision is and must be final. Of course umpires are fallible, but they are called upon to make snap decisions. Some of these, in retrospect, may be wrong or at least borderline, but they are, and must be, final.

The large majority of players will just get on with the game, taking the rough with the smooth. A few will not. These are the players that the management committee seeks to root out.

In his report to the 1993 annual meeting, Graham Collyer said the new management committee had shown its teeth by issuing fines when breaches of the rules had been proved. 'Clubs should take notice that the committee is not prepared to put up with breaches of the rules and it has already grown tired of receiving reports of bad language on the field, harassment of umpires and unsporting and ungentlemanly conduct,' he said. 'If these continue next season, I can predict that the committee will come down heavily. The league is just not prepared to tolerate anything that tarnishes its and cricket's good name.' Punishments could include suspension of players and docking of points, he added.

That message failed to make an impression on a Frimchett player, who was initially suspended for 21 days in 1994 and then barred from playing in the competitions for the whole of 1995. An umpire had reported him for using 'persistent foul and abusive language' during a Division One match against Lindford on 14 May 1994. He was forced to miss three league matches and one cup-tie. Graham Collyer said: 'The league has warned clubs and players to crack down on unsporting and ungentlemanly conduct, or face the consequences. The management committee is not prepared to tolerate behaviour that brings cricket and the I'Anson Cup into disrepute.'

Then, on 10 September that year, the same player was alleged to have used foul and abusive language towards a Frensham batsman after he had had an appeal for a catch by the wicketkeeper turned down. The player was eventually removed from the bowling attack by Frimchett's acting captain before the match was abandoned, because of bad weather, in only the seventh over.

In 1995, a Crown Taverners II player received a 21-day suspension for 'persistent use of abusive language' during a Division Two game with Grayshott II. This player had been the subject of earlier reports and his club had been warned as to the likely repercussions should a similar report be made.

Later that season a Wrecclesham player was removed from the competitions for three weeks for using foul language in a Division Two fixture against Kingsley in which the pool umpire pulled up the stumps, leaving the game abandoned with more than three overs left to be bowled. The player had been no-balled on a number of occasions by the umpire who took exception to the language he received in return. It was a bizarre way in which to resolve the issue, and one that the management committee termed 'precipitate', but it was upheld.

When 1996 passed without the need to reprimand any players there was a belief that the message had been received and thoroughly taken on board. But midway through the next season, in a moment of madness, three players brought the game into such disrepute that it caught everyone by surprise and attracted the attention of the national press. The players, one from Elstead and two from Frimchett, were swiftly dealt with by the management committee and each suspended for 12 months. At the annual meeting that year, Graham Collyer said that the 'disgraceful incident at Elstead on 19 July will remain with me, probably, for the rest of my life'. It was far and away the blackest day in the long, proud history of the competitions, he said, and one that made him question his continued involvement. 'But after due consideration, and with the backing of the management committee which moved swiftly to suspend the players for a year, I realised that the competitions, which had been so much a part of my family for so many years, were bigger and more important than three players who failed to control their tempers.'

What had made matters worse was that the incident had not been reported to the competitions by either of the two clubs or the official umpire, but by a spectator, who had written to the *Herald*. 'The game was turning into an entertaining affair,' he said in his letter to the editor. 'In a split-second of what I can only call madness a fight had broken out between the bowler and non-striking batsman, with both of them on the ground and the umpire desperately trying to separate them. Another fielder ran 20 to 30 yards to join in, throwing three or four punches. Players from both sides intervened and at last so-called peace was reached. So much for friendly village cricket. I do hope the guilty are dealt with severely in the interests of true lovers of cricket.'

The *Herald* led the front page with the story, and reported that the two clubs were intending to deal with the incident in their own committees. However, sports editor Carl Obert said: 'The clubs' action may not satisfy the I'Anson committee which has cracked down hard on incidents of indiscipline in recent years'. He quoted the league secretary as saying: 'We deplore any incidents that blacken the good name of the competitions. The management committee will undoubtedly want to get to the bottom of the matter and take any action it considers necessary.'

It was timely that the monthly meeting of the committee was scheduled for the Thursday following the flare-up at Elstead, and by the time the members came together the two captains and the umpire had responded to the request for statements. The three players involved were invited to attend the meeting, but did not do so. However, two members of the Frimchett team did attend and produced a statement based on observations made by colleagues after the match. Elstead had a representative on the committee, and the umpire in question was also a member of the committee.

The chairman, Norman Disney, allowed a free-ranging discussion before calling for a proposition. This was that the three players be suspended for the remainder of the season. But an amendment sought a 12-month ban, which was carried by a majority vote.

It was a decision that no one on the management committee enjoyed having to take, but one that was necessary if all the statements about stamping out loutish behaviour were to mean anything.

In addition to referring to the matter when he spoke at the annual meeting in 1997, the secretary raised the issue of the 'continued harassment of umpires'. He said: 'One was even called a cheat by a player young enough to be his grandson (which led to the umpire declining to officiate for the remainder of the season). The management committee will not tolerate this behaviour and is determined to cut it out.'

Early in 1998, a Tongham player was barred from appearing in the competitions after an allegation of verbal abuse and harassment towards an umpire in the car park after the final match of the previous season. This matter dragged on and on and the player did not play again in the competitions until 2000.

The sad catalogue of player suspensions continued with a Lindford member receiving a three-match ban in 1998-99, one from Tongham being barred for two fixtures in 1999, and a Dogmersfield player being suspended for three matches at the start of the 2002 season.

A quarter of a century earlier, the principle of accepting an umpire's decision was at the heart of a matter that was referred to the MCC. The incident at Tilford on 7 June 1975, reverberated around the then tightly knit I'Anson community. Against Thursley, a Tilford batsman was given out obstructing the field after the bowler, having fielded the ball, attempted to throw the wicket down. The batsman stopped the ball with his bat – to avoid being hit, he claimed – and the umpire gave him out when the wicketkeeper appealed. Tilford protested to the stewards who met on 3 July under the chairmanship of J.G. ('Dick') Caesar. They heard a report from the umpire who said his decision had been bitterly criticised by the batsman who, after leaving the field, had returned brandishing a scorebook containing the Laws of Cricket. More argument took place at the tea interval during which the umpire decided to withdraw from the match.

The stewards asked for a special meeting to be convened with the player concerned invited to attend. This took place a week later and when the player was called the chairman read the umpire's report to him and asked him to comment. The player said he did not disagree with what had been stated and bitterly regretted taking the action. He could only leave the matter to the judgment of the stewards. In answer to questions, he still maintained the umpire's decision was incorrect and hoped that the MCC could be approached for an opinion.

The chairman said the meeting was not considering whether the umpire had been right or wrong in his decision but rather the principle of accepting an umpire's decision on the field. After the player had left the meeting, some members felt strongly that some form of action should be taken in order to send a signal to other players who might wish to question an umpire's decision, and also to be seen to support the umpire. The secretary, Cliff Jarrett, said he had written to the secretary of the MCC with details of the incident, and he had also taken advice from a county umpire. It was regarded that the umpire had indeed made an error, but that in all cases the umpire's decision was final.

The first proposal was for the player to be censured; an amendment called for a two-week ban but was withdrawn in favour of one seeking a four-week suspension. This was carried by a clear majority with the Tilford steward abstaining. At the following meeting a letter from Tilford asked that the penalty be reconsidered in view of the player's good conduct in the past and his work on behalf of the competitions. The secretary had replied saying that consideration had already been given in this regard and the stewards' decision was final.

In 1974, another Tilford player had been involved in an incident that was referred to Lord's. The result of a Miller Cup match between Churt and Tilford, which had been reported as a draw, was overturned by the stewards after the chairman, 'Dick' Caesar, had taken the matter to the MCC. A Tilford player had left the field in protest after delivering only three balls in the 15th over of the minimum 20 in the last hour of play. Churt claimed Tilford were in breach of Law 24 of the Laws of Cricket and Rule 22 of the competitions. Letters were exchanged between the clubs and the stewards. Tilford said the bowler had taken his action in protest at the umpires acting outside the scope of their authority, but the club would accept the decision of the stewards. Mr Caesar sent a copy of Churt's letter and the rules of the competitions to the MCC, whose reply was to the effect that the matter should be dealt with by the competitions. So it was decided by a majority vote that Churt be awarded a victory. It was further agreed that Tilford should be admonished for the unsporting behaviour of one of their players, but Churt declined to be associated with this stricture, as they had not raised the matter as one of unsporting behaviour.

Dress sense

IN the early 1950s, when clubs and their players were still struggling with the after-effects of the deprivations brought about by the war, money was tight and a club ran its finances on a shoestring. Nevertheless, The Bourne expressed their concern at what they saw was a growing tendency for young players and others to turn out unsuitably dressed for cricket.

The competition president, A.J. Stevens, said that when he first played for The Bourne in 1905 'a great many braces and boots were to be seen on cricket fields'. Bob Burchett (Elstead) thought a set rule would penalise many youngsters who could not afford to buy the correct clothing. But Ted Newman (The Bourne) maintained that as a man was dressed on the field, so he played his cricket. If a man was slovenly in his dress, probably he was slovenly in his cricket.

The secretary, H.J. Knight, thought it was a matter that could be left to the good sense of captains and committees, and the ADM of 1952 concurred.

Today, everyone accepts there is a dress code in cricket and, while there are numerous variations on the theme, it is extremely rare to see a player who is not in whites.

E.W. ('Ted') Newman, who was a long-time steward and vice-president.

The second 50 years

FOUR clubs have dominated the competitions since 1951: The Bourne, Tilford, Rowledge and Frensham. Between them they have won the I'Anson Cup on 36 occasions in the second half-century, and in total 57 times. Overall, The Bourne are the most prolific winners with 20 titles, followed by Rowledge with 15, of which all but two came between 1959 and 1985, when the club left the competitions after claiming the cup in six successive seasons.

There are 15 different clubs named on the two trophies (the original cup was won outright by Tilford in 1910), and just three – Chiddingfold, Elstead and Wrecclesham – have won the title once only. When Chiddingfold took the cup in 1999 they were not only the first of the new intake to win the oldest village cricket league in the country but the first new name to be engraved on the silverware since 1956.

When Elstead, in 1952, and Wrecclesham four years later won the cup it might have appeared that the old order was at last being broken up, but it was not to be and, as The Bourne's dominance began to fade, Tilford and Rowledge emerged and between them won the I'Anson league in nine out of the next 11 seasons. Then came the total supremacy of Rowledge, and, since 1986, the phenomenal rise of Frensham.

What follows in this section is an alphabetical journey through what might be called the 'traditional' clubs. The story of the last decade of the second half-century is dealt with in subsequent chapters.

THE BOURNE

CARRYING on where they had left off, The Bourne began the second half-century of the competitions by doing the double. The golden jubilee year produced one of the wettest seasons anyone could remember with all the rain seeming to be stored up for the weekends and few matches being

George Knight receives the I'Anson Cup from Harold Sanders in 1951.

played in warm, dry conditions. This probably stopped The Bourne's Bill Poulter from breaking the league record of 757 runs in a season set by the club's pre-war giant Lew Goodchild back in 1928. Poulter started like an express train, but after missing several matches he returned and was held back by very soft pitches. In the end he scored 474 runs, and finished second in the averages to John Seddon, who made 455 runs, with Jim Voller, holder at that time of the league's individual best score of 141 not out, making 401. John Stonard, with 64 wickets at 5.3, and Frank Cordier, 59 at 7.1, were the workhorses in attack, with solid contributions also from H.C. ('Mickey') Bicknell and spinner Ron Hole. Skipper George Knight, whose son David has now been a Bourne player in six decades, led a team that seemed invincible, but the next year they were beaten in a play-off by Elstead, still relative newcomers to the I'Anson Cup. 'Dick' Caesar, later to be competitions president and treasurer, was captain of the seconds in 1951, and their leading scorer was Poulter's older brother Ted ('Croppy') and main bowler F.W. ('Sweat') Parratt. The LeClercq brothers, Charles and Fred, were prominent among the batsmen, and while Fred went on to Farnham and then re-entered the competitions with Headley, Charles remained with The Bourne and played on until he was in his seventies.

The Bourne, winners in 1953. Standing, from the left: E.W. Newman (umpire), J. Seddon, H.J. Knight, J. Stonard, E. Warner, R. Hole, L. Tanner (scorer). Seated: W. Poulter, J. Tanner, H. Arnold, G. Knight (captain), H.C. Bicknell, K. Williams. Picture courtesy of John Stonard.

Knight was again the captain in 1953 when the double was achieved for the seventh time, although the seconds had to defeat Rowledge II in a play-off at Tilford. For a club with such a tradition it was surprising that four regular members of the Second XI preferred to play football than to take part in the decider, but skipper Cordier took a hat-trick and ended Rowledge's challenge. Cordier finished with 6-33 in ten overs, and described winning the cup as the proudest moment of his life. He received it from Theo Pope, who had been made a vice-president of the competitions in recognition of his authorship of *A Cup for Cricket*. Frank Cordier subsequently became a leading local councillor, the first Mayor of Waverley and has been the chairman of Farnham's historic Venison Dinner for many years. Seddon, who died in 1991 having given up cricket in his 58th year when he failed to make a score equal to his age, again headed the firsts' batting averages, although Stonard's 201 was the leading runs total. Stonard's left-arm bowling, with movement in the air, accounted for 54 wickets at 5.6, but fellow left-armer Hole took 57, with Bicknell picking up 38.

Jim Voller took over the captaincy of the second XI in 1954 and The Bourne retained the Miller Cup with a 21-point lead, a margin then without parallel in the competition, and brought about by the side having won all 16 matches in a wet summer following an increase in the points allocation. Voller headed the averages with 30.4 (456 runs), from Geoff Harris, 28.86 (433 runs). Charlie LeClercq led the bowling with 25 wickets at 3.48, but Ken Warner, aged 16, took 78 at 5.0, and more than 100 in the season, as he burst on to the scene, while Voller picked up 43 at 5.37.

LIFE MEMBERSHIPS

At the end of the year the club recognised the work of George Arnold by honouring him with life membership. He had served The Bourne for 50 years, and had just stepped down as treasurer. The previous year his brother Arthur, father-in-law of John Stonard, had received a similar award when he retired as groundsman. Lew Goodchild was the club's only other life member. The Arnolds were great supporters of the competitions, and George first became a steward in 1931. He several times chaired the annual delegates' meeting and retired as a steward in 1961. Born in Southampton, he moved to The Bourne before the dawn of the twentieth century and was for a time gardener to A.J. Stevens. He died in May 1970, aged 81.

John Tanner, who had played in the championship-winning sides of 1950-51-53, scored his maiden century in 1954 and was captain the following year when the club pulled off a unique double because the seconds were in the Stevens Cup league. Bill Poulter had gone off to Wrecclesham and all-rounder Ted Warner had joined the police, but there was strength in depth. Tanner's father Len had been connected with The Bourne since the 1920s and he and his brother Doug, who switched to Rowledge where he can still be found among the spectators, had been introduced to cricket at an early age. Young John was the first team's scorer before graduating to the Miller Cup side and then into the firsts at the end of the 1940s. He was an all-rounder in those days, but in time he dropped his off-breaks in favour of the wicketkeeper's gloves. But it was his batting that had always caught the eye, and after two decades with The Bourne he moved to Farnham, but returned to the village side in 1975 and captained the seconds to the Miller Cup three years later. In 1981 he was captaining the firsts when he received a fractured skull from a rising ball by Churt's Rodney Birch. He was taken to the Cambridge Military Hospital in Aldershot where he was detained until the Monday morning. Characteristically, he was not out of the game long. John Tanner died in 1999, and at his funeral service the mourners were reminded of his cricketing prowess and how, as a lad of 16, he had stepped out into the world of work. In those far off days in the offices of A.J. Stevens, the well-known Farnham lawyer, his first task each morning was to clean out the grate and prepare the fire in Mr Stevens's room. AJ, of course, was already a mover and shaker in cricket at The Bourne, and became the first president of the competitions in 1936. John Tanner's formative cricketing years were spent in good company.

In 1955 he won the toss 12 times and always elected to bat first. The title was confirmed in the last game, at Wrecclesham, where former player Bill Poulter was the captain. A large crowd saw The Bourne recover from 43-5 to make 100 and Stonard take 6-17 to have Wrecclesham 39-9. Poulter found a durable partner in number 11 A. Hutchings and they took the score to 81 with the skipper snatching the bowling at the end of most overs. The Bourne became rattled as quick singles were taken, but the match ended with Hutchings being run out for five with both batsmen at the same end, leaving Poulter not out 45. The *Herald* said that in his long and successful career he had never played a more courageous innings. During the season, there was consistent batting, and Ted Warner's 71 was the highest score. No bowler took more than 50 wickets, but Stonard, 'Mickey' Bicknell and Ken Warner exacted a heavy toll on the opposition. The cup was presented to The Bourne for the 17th time since 1925, R.C.B. (Reg) Thackeray, a vice-president of the competitions and president of Headley, saying that the club's unparalleled success had been achieved by consistency, toughness and the ability to withstand shocks. The team always seemed to pull something out of the bag. George Arnold, who had been captain of the winning side when they re-entered the competitions in 1925, unfurled the championship flag.

Stan Golding captained the Second XI and Jim Voller headed both batting and bowling averages. At a celebratory dinner in The Bourne Hall a colour film, shot by William Ricketts, showed the presentation of the I'Anson Cup and the unfurling of the flag. It created a precedent at local cricket dinners, said the *Herald.*

Golding led the seconds again in 1956 when the Miller Cup was retained, and Ron Hole took 100 league wickets at 5.53 (231 overs 61 maidens 553 runs). The firsts had to take a back seat to Wrecclesham, where Bill Poulter stepped forward to collect the cup. This reverse signalled the end of the first team's supremacy, and the I'Anson Cup has gone to The Bourne on only three further occasions. However, the second team continued to dominate the Miller Cup and won the trophy eight more times up to and including 1970. Stan Golding, who was skipper for five seasons, was a man of constant humour, said Tanner, in spite of not enjoying good health. He got the best out of players, not because of his ability but by his rare quality of understanding people. Golding died young, but his son Peter ('Rocky') continues to serve the club. Stan collected his second Miller Cup title in 1957 when Shottermill were defeated in a play-off. There was a hat-trick of successes in 1960-62, and two more triumphs in 1964-65, but in 1963, when Ken Huckle, now better known in football circles, took 10-25 against Headley, they finished third.

Stan Golding: successful Miller Cup captain.

PLAYED INTO HIS SEVENTIES

It was another double year in 1964, with Charles LeClercq and Frank Cordier the respective captains. Cordier had his son David in the team, and there were two other father-and-son combinations in the seconds – George and David Knight and Bill and Michael Poulter. The firsts' secret weapon was the fast bowling of Jack Partridge, who, as John

Storey had done when he first appeared for Rowledge in 1961, got through defences with sheer pace. They also had the talented Michael Ricketts, who played regularly for Surrey II, and the emerging Les Knight, who was to become one of the leading batsmen in the competitions over the next quarter of a century. The firsts won the cup by three points from Rowledge, with both teams losing on the final day, The Bourne at home to Churt, who finished second to last, and Rowledge, who were the holders, against a Headley side with ten players.

Charlie LeClercq's 50 years with the club was marked by a presentation in September 1997. Mike Poulter, the president, recalled his youth cricket at Wrecclesham when he faced Charlie's spin, and then, for 20 years, keeping wicket to him for The Bourne. 'Charlie didn't turn the ball that much, but he was a master of flight and had a wicked arm ball,' he said. 'He and Ron Chambers were superb bowlers over many years and took a pile of wickets.' Charlie, then 73, still turned out for the Third XI and his long service was only matched in recent times by the late Frank Kenward who played for Headley into his 70s. Born and bred in The Bourne, Charlie first played for the village team in 1947 after leaving the army. He started as a medium-pace bowler, but soon switched to off-spin. He was at his peak in the 1960s and he and Ron Chambers were known as the 'spin twins'. Their combination was a decisive factor in The Bourne's I'Anson titles in 1964 and 1968. 'Ron was left-arm slow, I was right arm, so we were a good combination. In those days, we took around 50 wickets a season each and did an awful lot of bowling,' he recalled.

The tenth and final double celebration occurred in 1968 when Alan Young captained the first team with great style. He was a major run-getter and was awarded his I'Anson cap in 1969 after scoring 117 as the league side beat Farnham.

The Bourne stalwarts Charles LeClercq (left) and Colin Ray on the club's stand at the centenary year exhibition in Farnham Maltings.

Other sixties player who are recalled are Alistair Ralph and Robin Frommholz, both wholehearted bowlers, the latter still at the club and a member of the umpires' pool, Ken Park, whose leg-spin was usefully employed, Don Briggs, son of the pre-war great, Sid Briggs, and still playing, Peter Kenward, Alan Thurgood, John Hole, Roger Pharo and Roger Buck, who, recalls 'Rocky' Golding, once hit a six through an open window of a nearby house and into a pot of strawberry jam sitting on a table where the family were having their tea.

MIGHT HAVE JOINED SURREY

Bill Poulter, who died on 4 February 2002, had long since returned to The Bourne when, in 1970, he captained the second team to success and played his last competitive match, in which he made 36 not out against The Rest. Poulter was then 58 and he had played for the club, apart from the four years at Wrecclesham, since 1926. His son Michael was president in the club's centenary year, 1998, and his grandsons, Gary and Neil, have followed in the family tradition. In 1950, Theo Pope said of Bill Poulter: 'When it comes to run-making, there is a touch of Bradman about him. He reaches 50, and settles down for the 100. He has an air of assurance at the wicket all of his own, and hits the ball very hard. Even his defensive strokes are made forcefully. In his best form he can completely demoralise a fielding side with the rate of his scoring. He has a stroke for every ball, and he picks the right ball to hit.' He was also a superb wicketkeeper until he was partially blinded in one eye by a work accident in 1949. After a year out of the game, he returned to score copious amounts of runs, showing why he had been selected for a trial at The Oval in 1935, when he was 23. He scored 81 not out in that match and said much later that had he been three years younger he would have been signed by Surrey, and would have seized the opportunity to become a county player. Poulter scored six I'Anson centuries, second only to Grayshott's Eddie Gulliver, who played on vastly improved pitches.

Players from the previous three decades, such as Harold Arnold, son of George, Frank Cordier, Joe Rivers and John Stonard were involved in the 1970 success, while eight years on, when John Tanner was at the helm, the seconds included, among others, Mick Farnfield, whose father Alf had skippered Tilford to two I'Anson Cup titles in the late 1950s, John Fullbrook, once of Tilford and still a great supporter, Ali Ralph, Ian Laker, a police officer who captained the team in the eighties, Chris Fry, Colin Ray and Graham Senior, then beginning his career which has taken on a new path since his move to Frensham a couple of years ago.

Senior and Dave Knight forged a reliable opening bowling attack in the 1980s, when both led the side, while Les Knight and Mike Poulter were batsmen who would usually get the side off to a good start. But the decade was barren as far as league trophies were concerned, and Dave Knight's 10-48 against Whitehill on 30 April 1983 was the highlight. Eight years later, he captained the seconds to the Miller Cup in that competition's last season before the trophy became the award presented to the Division Three winners. It was the twentieth time The Bourne had won the cup, and Knight's contribution was 63 wickets at 7.3 apiece. Charlie LeClercq, aged 67, took 34 and between them they bowled more than 370 overs. Adrian Thomas was top run-scorer with 511 from 16 innings for an average of 39.3.

CARE OF THE PAVILION

Ted Newman, who had been connected with the club since the 1920s and had first become a steward of the competitions in 1934, died in August 1992, aged 91. He was the longest serving vice-president of the competitions, having been elected in December 1968. His home for 66 years overlooked The Bourne's ground, and his daughter knew that a letter posted to the pavilion was all that was required to convey the news of his death.

The last major title to be won by the club was in 1994 when Ron Neil led the first team to the Division One championship and the I'Anson Cup for the first time in 26 years after a tense last day of the season that was the very essence of this great local cricket league. Frensham and Grayshott were also in the frame at the start of play, and Grayshott were playing at The Bourne. Graham Clarke elected to bat knowing that a win would give his side two bonus points and send them above The Bourne. All would then depend on Frensham who were at Tilford. There, Ray Clarke won the toss and also chose to bat first. Mobile phones kept people in touch between the two grounds, and when news came through that Frensham had been dismissed for 118, The Bourne knew they were in a good position, despite the fact that Grayshott had batted strongly to make 186-9 declared. But the script did not run smoothly after tea, because Tilford soon lost four wickets and then battled for survival. Meanwhile, The Bourne were doing their best to throw away a good season and were quickly 16-4, but Andy Culham and Steve Clarke dug in before there was another slump. In the end, The Bourne scraped through with Neil Poulter, watched by father and grandfather, and Graham Senior guiding the side to a paltry 45-8 but, more important, a precious point while denying Grayshott more than four for the faster scoring rate draw. Skipper Neil was quite new to the club, but has since become a driving force as chairman and president, as well as being a key member of the competitions' management and centenary committees.

CHURT

BETWEEN 1922, when they won the I'Anson Cup for the second time, and 1976 Churt had a very lean time, which

A Churt team from the early 1950s.

included a few years out of the competition. But in the 1970s, and with Donald Limon very much to the fore, the club looked up and back-to-back titles in 1976 and 1977, with the Stevens and Miller Cups also being won in the latter year, indicated their strength in depth.

How different it had been in the immediate post-war years when Churt were so often the whipping boys, and invariably finished bottom or near to the foot of the table, and on to 1966 when they withdrew. In those 20 years they won only 53 of their 356 matches, and in three of those seasons they completed their fixtures without a win. The seconds fared no better and pulled out of the Miller Cup at the end of the 1961 season.

Out with the old: Churt's new pavilion, which cost £3,500, was opened in September 1965.

Their position in the I'Anson Cup had been discussed at the club's annual meeting in November 1950, after they had finished well adrift in the table, and it was only the casting vote of the president, Mr A. Caro, that saved the day after the members present had been divided six votes to six with a further six abstaining. Harry Massey, the secretary and treasurer, said there was enough talent in the village to enable the club to raise a winning team, but there was no co-operation. George Cross, the 1950 captain, said there was no interest in the club, and that in nine out of ten matches non-members were turning out. It was not a matter of selecting a team, but of persuading players to turn up, he said. Mr Caro said he gave his casting vote in favour of retaining the status quo because he thought that if the club was not in the competitions what interest there was would be lost and the club would, in time, cease to exist.

GIRL IN THE TEAM

They finished bottom of both tables in 1951, but made I'Anson history when they included a girl in their first team at Tilford. Joan Bassett, aged 13, the daughter of J.W. Bassett, headmaster of the village school, and whose twin brothers, John and David, 17, were regular members of the side, turned out because Churt were three players short. She had gone along to keep the score, while her father, who was intending to be Churt's umpire, also played, and made highest score. Bill Weatherley, the team secretary, who had not held a bat for 20 years, completed the side. Joan was a pupil at Farnham Girls' Grammar School and had been taught to play cricket by her brothers, with whom she practised. She made two not out but could not prevent Churt losing by six wickets.

Robin Dibdin returned from Frensham to play for Churt in 1952, and topped the batting averages with 10.05 (181 runs). He subsequently went back to Frensham, where he skippered the side, but in the last quarter of a century has been inextricably linked to the Two Counties Youth Competition, whose spiritual home has been Churt through its sponsorship by Rod Berkeley, of Berkeley Sports, and its former president, Donald Limon, who became Sir Donald on his retirement from his position as Clerk to the House of Commons.

As the fifties rolled on, fortunes did not improve for Churt who, with only ten men at Headley in May 1956, were dismissed for five in the second innings, having made 16 in the first (Frank Kenward 11-4 in the match). This score equalled the total they made at home to Tilford in 1938. At that time it was the lowest total in the I'Anson Cup, but in 1940 Churt redeemed themselves by sending back Oakhanger for three. This latest embarrassment led to the club informing the stewards that they wished to withdraw from the I'Anson Cup for 1957 while remaining in the Miller Cup, but they were told that such a decision could only be made at the annual meeting of the competitions. And when that meeting was held at the end of the year, all talk of leaving had been consigned to history and the club were re-elected with a wish that the stewards take note of the improvements made to the square and the hope that this might lead to a representative match being held on the ground. Clearly, there had been some straight talking at the club, but sadly it was not really translated into results out in the middle and Churt bumped along until pulling out in 1966.

A NEW ORDER

When the club were readmitted in 1972 there was a new order at the recreation ground. Young players who had come up through the youth teams in the Two Counties set-up were ready to take on senior responsibilities, and they were players who had a point to make. First to show was the Second XI, captained by Dave Hodson, who brought the Miller Cup to the club for the first time in 1973, beating holders Headley by a single point. Competitions president and treasurer 'Dick' Caesar handed over the cup, but he was not to know that one of the Churt players whom he congratulated was to take his place as head of financial affairs 18 years later. Neither did the player have any inkling, for Keith Mayson, a good all-rounder who scored 297 runs and took 56 wickets at 5.9 apiece, was an international banker and was soon to leave Churt. Fortunately, retirement brought him back to the area, which was not only to the benefit of the competitions but also to Churt, where Keith became club captain and sons Anthony and David players.

Ken Brown's time with Churt was long enough to have a significant influence on Richard Kemp's team, and when he and long-time wicketkeeper Peter Allatt opened the batting at home to Thursley on 8 June 1974, they all but wrote themselves into the record books. Brown cracked ten sixes and 15 fours in an unbeaten 142, which left him nine runs short of Bob White's individual record. There was talk of Churt and Brown having no knowledge of the record, which might have been true since White scored his 151 not out in 1957 and no batsman had got remotely near in the intervening years. Brown and Allatt, who played second fiddle for 26 not out, put on 172 in 90 minutes, which was just two runs short of the then highest opening partnership of 174 not out by Les Knight and Alan Young for The Bourne against Tilford four years earlier. Brown scored 805 runs in 24 innings for an average of 38.3 in the 1974 season and Churt finished fifth.

The next year they were second as Rowledge swept the board, and then came the breakthrough as they clinched the cup for the first time since 1922. They did it in style, with two games remaining, when the fast bowler Mick Harris dismissed the last four Elstead batsmen, Brian Druce, Chris Grant, Mick Jeffery and Fred Aldred, in successive deliveries to finish with figures of 10.4-1-31-9. When Richard Kemp received the cup from J.G. Caesar it was hailed as a popular win, and the skipper had reason to thank his bowlers, for Harris, who had returned to the club after a year's absence, took 85 wickets in the I'Anson and Stevens Cups at 8.8, Stan Clarke picked up 70 at 9.1 and there were 32 for Mick Warner, whose slow bowling had boosted the attack in his first season after severing his ties with Tilford. Harris's brother David had been Churt's main bowler in the 1960s, before moving across the border to Grayshott where in 1968 he took the third nine-wicket haul of his I'Anson career.

MEDALS FOR THE WINNERS

Churt were back and underlined their superiority by doing the treble the following year, Kemp's fifth as captain. Brown again was to the fore, top-scoring in the all-too-easy Stevens win over Whitehill, and scoring more than 1,600 runs all told, including 709 in the league. Mick Harris was the leading bowler again with 82 league wickets, but the attack missed Clarke all season after he had broken a leg while playing football. The I'Anson title was assured when Peter Slinger struck a fierce 89 against Whitehill, an innings that announced the coming of age of this player who continues to enjoy his Saturday cricket to the full. 'Dick' Caesar again handed the trophy to Kemp, but this time he was able to distribute medals to all the members of the winning team. The annual meeting in 1976 had agreed to support a proposal by the stewards that medals be presented to players of the winning league sides, and the accounts showed that the cost was £27.70.

Six years earlier The Bourne had proposed that 15 mementoes be provided for the I'Anson and Miller winners, but the annual meeting had rejected the idea by a one-vote margin. The Bourne's Mike Poulter had said: 'Our motive may well have been jealousy of Grayshott who provided their own mementoes a few seasons ago. But it would be nice to have something to show for a job well done.' The ensuing discussion could be said to be a fair reflection of the progress of an average annual delegates' meeting. Peter Clapham of Grayshott warned: 'You can reckon on £25 for 12 shields.' Mike Poulter: 'We were thinking of perhaps a small medallion.' Headley's Dave Lambert: 'We have nothing to show for a season's hard work, while in football the league presents the winning team with medals as well as a trophy.' Bob Burchett of Elstead: 'We feel the cost should be borne by the club involved.' J.G. Caesar, who was in the chair, recalled that in the past clubs had provided the awards. 'Thursley did so this year,' he added, in a reference to that club's I'Anson Cup success. After the vote, Poulter commented: 'You can see how close it is. It seems a pity that our rules prevent us from referring the matter back to the stewards for further consideration.' Caesar responded and gave a glimmer of hope, which was to materialise in the fullness of time: 'The stewards have discussed this matter fully; we are not against it.'

The Second XI also received medals when 'Dick' Caesar presented the Miller Cup to Donald Limon, and at the club's dinner Mr Caesar made a presentation of a trophy to mark the club's treble. This was to be the beginning of a marvellous run for the seconds, with Alan Lang receiving the cup in 1979 at the start of a hat-trick of victories, to be followed by two more trophy years in 1984 and 1985.

THEY LEAVE AGAIN

While the firsts continued to be a force – they went 43 league matches without defeat under Clarke up to August 1981, when they lost to Tilford, for whom Paul Slinger made 88 and his brother replied with 72 for Churt – they did not again win the league in its old format. Rodney Birch occasionally ripped batting line-ups asunder with some quick bowling, the spin of Ron Chambers bemused some teams, and 1960s all-rounder Joe Lindsey Clark reappeared briefly. When they did lift the trophy again, as the first Division One champions, skipper Chris Barnes and Churt were talking openly of moving on, although many of the members were reported to be far from happy with the decision. As early as 1987, the club's annual meeting had voted 17-7 in favour of joining the Three Counties League, and this was endorsed the following year, but their application was rejected. Then in January 1992, the *Herald* reported that Churt were to join the new second division of the Fullers Surrey League.

'The reorganisation of league cricket in the county has given Churt their chance, although for some time the club

Sir Donald Limon, who worked so hard for Churt and youth cricket. He and a supporter are pictured during a TCYC tour to Kent. Picture courtesy of Robin Dibdin.

Robin Dibdin, former Churt and Frensham player who followed Donald Limon as secretary of the Two Counties Youth Competition.

have made no secret of their ambition to play a higher standard', the newspaper said. 'Although not a surprise, it comes as a deep disappointment to the ancient village league's working party which has restructured the competition and widened its boundaries in the hope of keeping the stronger clubs in the fold.' The article stated that at the annual delegates' meeting the previous November, Churt were critical of the changes, particularly the formation of a third division from the Miller Cup and aspects of the promotion/relegation rule but, in fact, said the *Herald*, their decision had already been taken at the club's AGM in October. 'Although the move was approved by a hefty majority at a well-attended meeting, some senior players were apparently not in favour, notably Rodney Birch, Peter Allatt, John Watson and Jim Allen, four members who have formed the hard-core of the I'Anson team for many a season. Their fear is that Churt will lose its village identity when competing in a league against mainly town and suburban clubs, and travelling as far as London to play their matches, rather than over the way to Frensham or Thursley.'

Donald Limon, the president and a member for 25 years, said on behalf of the club: 'For some years Churt have been seeking a suitable opportunity to move into a higher grade of cricket. The outcome of the recent expansion of the competitions has not found favour with the club's playing membership and this has added impetus to the desire for change. Churt pay particular tribute to the I'Anson and Miller officers and stewards for their signal and continuing services to the cause of local cricket.' The *Herald* said that Chris Barnes had been the key figure behind the push for change and, it seemed, he had the support of the younger players and some older members who no longer played regularly. When the newspaper added: 'Churt will need to increase their playing strength. A dwindling membership caused them to withdraw their well-established third XI and, last season, they struggled at times to put out two Saturday sides,' Limon was quick to respond: 'Last week's coverage appeared to us to fall a little below your usually scrupulous standards of accuracy and fairness in reporting local cricket. It would surely have been odd if no club from our part of the county had sought entry into the second division of the Surrey County League – an important development, which is part of a long-term plan to improve the structure of league cricket in the whole of the county. That the Churt club's facilities and playing record came up to the quite exacting standards required by the new league should be a cause for gratification among fellow members of the I'Anson and Miller Cup Competition. Our aim will be to follow the excellent example set in Hampshire in recent seasons by Rowledge, but this will be difficult unless we have good support, especially from the local press. I can assure you that the decision to recommend this move was taken after the most careful consideration by the club's committee – and endorsed by an overwhelming majority at our AGM when the debate was devoid of acrimony and the decision accepted gracefully by the minority.'

So the club left the competitions, for the second time, at the end of the 1992 season, and the league was the poorer for the loss of players such as Peter Allatt, a leading wicketkeeper since 1972, Jim Allen, a dogged opening bat and former captain, Phil and Nick Bennett, the former a long-time secretary and winning Miller captain in 1985, Rodney Birch, the often flamboyant Australian John Daddo, Willie and Terry Hill, unrelated and both good middle-order run-scorers, Alan Lang, untiring bowler whose son Andy has assisted Grayshott of late, the Mayson brothers, John Watson, former captain and opening left-arm bowler with nagging accuracy, Ian Whalley, who captained the second team in some of their championship-winning seasons, and Quentin Woods, who reappeared with Wrecclesham in 2001. The league was also robbed of one of its characters when Peter Brannaghan died, aged 44, at the end of December 1991. Since 1977 the very efficient scorer for Churt, as well as bar manager, he seldom played cricket (in fact, he made his league debut for the seconds in September 1990) but he proved to be an able administrator and ran the Farnham and District League almost single-handedly when it was revived in the 1980s. 'Local cricket should be grateful for this because several of the Farnham League clubs were well schooled in league cricket when they moved to the expanded I'Anson Cup last year,' said the *Herald*. 'Peter's scorecards were always accurate. He took enormous trouble with club averages and records and liked to produce specially printed menu cards, including individual averages, for league players at the annual dinner. His stern efficiency in running the bar was not always appreciated by visitors, but his serious face disguised a dry sense of humour. There was nothing he liked better than serving pints of real ale from an excellently prepared barrel at prices, which he insisted, were the lowest among local clubs.' Donald Limon added: 'It was an appropriate finale to his all-too-short life that Churt managed to win the I'Anson Cup in his last season, after which he was elected a life vice-president.'

ELSTEAD

THEY may well win the I'Anson Cup before very long, was Theo Pope's prophetic opinion in 1951 of the club who had joined the competitions two years before. Well, 12 months on Elstead pulled off the biggest shock in the history of the competitions when they beat The Bourne in a play-off on Tilford Green in front of more than 1,000 spectators. There were knowing nods when Bill Poulter won the toss and elected to bat, but Elstead's fast bowler Basil Payne quickly dismissed the openers. Then Poulter and Ted Warner put on more than 50 before Robin Pryce, the Elstead captain, introduced Bob Reffold into the attack at the top end of the green. It was a master stroke. Reffold took three quick wickets and The Bourne were on the slide. When, just after tea, Bill Denyer took a spectacular one-handed catch on the boundary to dismiss Poulter for 55, the then strongest club were all out for 108 (Payne 5-40, Bob Reffold 3-13 and his brother Charlie 2-24).

No one was prepared to predict publicly whether the total was enough to hold off the upstarts, but it looked likely to be when John Stonard whipped out the openers and set Elstead on the way to 66-6. But Pryce again found he could rely on Bob Reffold and between them they inched the score along against an increasingly desperate Bourne side. Two further wickets were lost and when 18-year-old David Baldwin joined Reffold for the ninth wicket partnership, 15 runs were still needed. As the crowd in turn cheered every single scampered and every maiden over bowled, the pair stayed together for half an hour to win the cup for Elstead, Reffold off-driving for two on the stroke of 7.15 in a light drizzle. He was 24 not out, Duncan Whittaker made 26 and Pryce 25. Whittaker, who had played as an amateur in the Yorkshire League before moving to the village, did much to win the cup for Elstead in his first season, scoring 582 runs in 17 innings, and his average of 44.76 was then the fourth highest in the competition. At Whitehill he scored 102 not out and, with Aubrey Karn (39 not out), shared a fourth wicket stand of 147. Bill 'Wiggy' Burchett, whose son Chris followed him into the Elstead side before enjoying a good career with Farnham, made 293 runs. Bob Reffold's 64 wickets were at a cost of 5.68, Payne took 44 at 8.84, Charlie Reffold 37 at 8.62 and Whittaker 28 at 6.64.

Elstead, winners in 1952 after a play-off against The Bourne at Tilford. Standing, from the left: D. Whittaker, W. Burchett, R. Reffold, B. Payne, W. Denyer, G. Steer. Front: R. Glastonbury (Rowledge, umpire), A. Davidson, C. Reffold, R. Pryce (captain), D. Baldwin, N. Pride, E. Garret (scorer), J. Miles (Tilford, umpire). Picture courtesy of Elstead CC.

CARRIED BY FEMALE SUPPORTERS

Elstead were joint runners-up the following year, Coronation Year, but have never again won the cup. The loss of Whittaker, who went out of the league, Payne to Headley, and many other star players to Thursley and Tilford left the club in the doldrums for much of the next two decades. There were players, like the fast bowler Ray Jackson and the veteran spinner Charlie Langridge, who were capable of upsetting the strongest of batting line-ups, but all too often Elstead's own batting frailties gave the bowling attack little chance of lasting domination.

However, the seconds kept the flag flying with two play-off victories in the Miller Cup. The first came on 10 September 1955, at Frensham, when they beat Tilford II by two wickets on the first innings, but were close to losing over four innings. Both teams lost only once, to each other, throughout the season, and the scene was set for a good showdown. Tilford, who had Jim Eddey and Ron Miles as their main bowlers, were put into bat by Albert 'Stumpy' Stovold and made 82 (John Fullbrook 27; Ron Burchett 5-25, George Pilbeam 3-28). Elstead lost two early wickets but Tony Tilson made a wonderful half-century and put his side into the lead with a straight six. When Mick Warner bowled him, four female supporters chaired Tilson back to the pavilion. Miles took 5-26 as Elstead took a lead of 16. Tilford's policy, with 105 minutes left, was to get runs quickly, and Eddey's declaration at 67-2 left Elstead with 35 minutes' batting in deteriorating light. He and Miles were almost too good for them, and at 22-5, with Eddey having taken three wickets in an over, there was more than a chance of a Tilford victory. Fielders ran to their positions, and Miles took two wickets with the fourth and fifth deliveries of the penultimate over. Skipper Stovold prevented the hat-trick, which left Bob Burchett to face the last over from Eddey, who had taken 6-9 in six overs. With half a dozen fielders round the bat, Burchett blocked the first four balls, allowed the next to go through to the wicketkeeper, and survived an appeal for a catch off his arm off the final delivery. Elstead had survived at 30-9, 22 behind their target but with the title won on the first innings. As the cup was presented, Stovold thanked the Tilford players, and especially Eddey, for three good games and called for three hearty cheers.

When they beat Whitehill in a play-off at The Bourne in

Elstead, champions of Division Two in 1996. From the left: S. Gaylard, K. Nutt, J. Marsh, P. Murphy jnr, C. Grant, K. White, M. Butler, P. Murphy snr (captain), M. Druce, C. Broome, P. Bright, with Norman Disney and Graham Collyer. Picture courtesy of Elstead CC.

1971, the captain of the seconds was Harold Andrews, a shopkeeper in the village, who received the cup from J.G. Caesar. Another reason to be cheerful occurred three years later when opener Mike Sweeney's 100 not out at Thursley was believed to be only the second century by an Elstead player since the war, the first being Whittaker's in the championship year.

Fortunes began to rise when Pat Murphy and Martyn Gowar arrived in the village, having played cricket at a higher level elsewhere. In 1984, his first season, Gowar, a stylish opening bat, included a century and five half-centuries in his 608 runs in 16 innings, while all-rounder Murphy's nagging left-arm bowling continues to trouble batsmen. These two engendered a new spirit in the club, and although Gowar's career lasted only a few seasons, Murphy continued to lead the resurgence and in 1996 he skippered the firsts to the Division Two title, with son Patrick taking 75 wickets in 15 matches with some pacy bowling that was soon to be seen in Farnham's Surrey Championship attack. Elstead, though, without the edge given them by Murphy junior, who was away at university, were relegated the following season, and although James Crutcher, who had captained the under-15 side at The Oval in 1990, led them back to the top flight in 2000, they dropped straight back again. As *A Cup for Cricket* recorded half a century ago, it may not be long before Elstead do well. There is the talent in the club, although Pat Murphy, opener Simon Wade and evergreen bowler Chris Grant may be heading towards the end of their careers. All that is needed is some cohesion.

FRENSHAM

FRENSHAM are now at the top of the tree, but it has not always been thus. In fact, until Rowledge moved away at the end of the 1985 season, Frensham were always the challengers. They had only won the I'Anson Cup on one occasion, way back in 1932, before Rowledge's withdrawal left the way clear for the club to take over as top dog. The signs of their improvement had been noticeable since 1983 when John Storey, having ended his long, record-breaking association with Farnham, decided to return to the competitions with Frensham, instead of Rowledge, where he had enjoyed three successful seasons in the early 1960s.

Storey, the charismatic talisman of Hollowdene, knew what had to be done to lift the club: invest in youth. Acting in the role of the Pied Piper, the 44-year-old drew youngsters to the ground in ever-increasing numbers for evening practice and matches, and, more than that, their dads came too. In time, Frensham had strength in depth where none had existed before, and the club went onwards and upwards.

But there is a need to take things in chronological order and pick up where *A Cup for Cricket* left off. Theo Pope recorded that Frensham had moved to Hollowdene after the war, and added that 'two essentials previously lacking are now in sight, a good wicket and a pavilion, and with those advantages Frensham will doubtless again become a formidable power in the cricket world'. Again, how prophetic were his words. The new pavilion was used for the first time on 10 May 1952, when The Bourne were the visitors in the opening home match of the season. A ten-man side losing heavily to the defending champions tarnished an auspicious occasion. Since then, of course, the pavilion has been improved and enlarged, and in 1962 was dedicated to Len Heath, a great man of the village who had been a world famous motorcycle trials rider. Now, with its patio overlooking the ground it is a busy venue on match days, and Hollowdene, with its natural banking offering spectators a raised view of proceedings, is a charming spot at which to watch cricket. In 1993, a second square was unveiled adjacent to the main playing surface, and the club now turns out four league sides every week.

How very different to the 1950s when Frensham were known as the Cinderella club. Captains like Frank Agar, a Yorkshireman whose unbeaten 100 at home to Elstead on 30 June 1956, joined Bill Chuter's identical score in 1936 as the only Frensham centuries in the competitions, and Michael Abbott had tried their very best to lift the club, without success. What was lacking was the young talent now seen in profusion. In the 1960s, as the old brigade began to disappear, youngsters such as Ray Clarke, Trevor Jeffery and Mike Fathers did begin to make the selectors think. They learnt their trade from players like Bert Holdaway, who was recalled to the first team at the age of 62, Cyril Badland, Stan Armstrong, Robin Dibdin, George Pither, Ted and George Jones, and Sid Clarke, father of Ray, but more than that, they were also part of the re-invented Two Counties Youth Competition, which was responsible for giving the senior competitions a new lease of life. The youth league eventually emerged into a very large organisation run first by Donald Limon and then by the same Robin Dibdin who had given such sterling service as a forceful batsman to not only Frensham but also Churt. Ray Clarke, always competitive, is now a Frensham institution, but sadly his great friend Trevor Jeffery died in 1988 and has been greatly missed.

THOUGHT THEY WERE CHAMPIONS

It was in 1964, one of the seasons when Dibdin was captain, that Frensham claim they were robbed of the title. Peter Chuter, a delightful raconteur and club historian, recalled in the club's centenary brochure that Dibdin's team had the

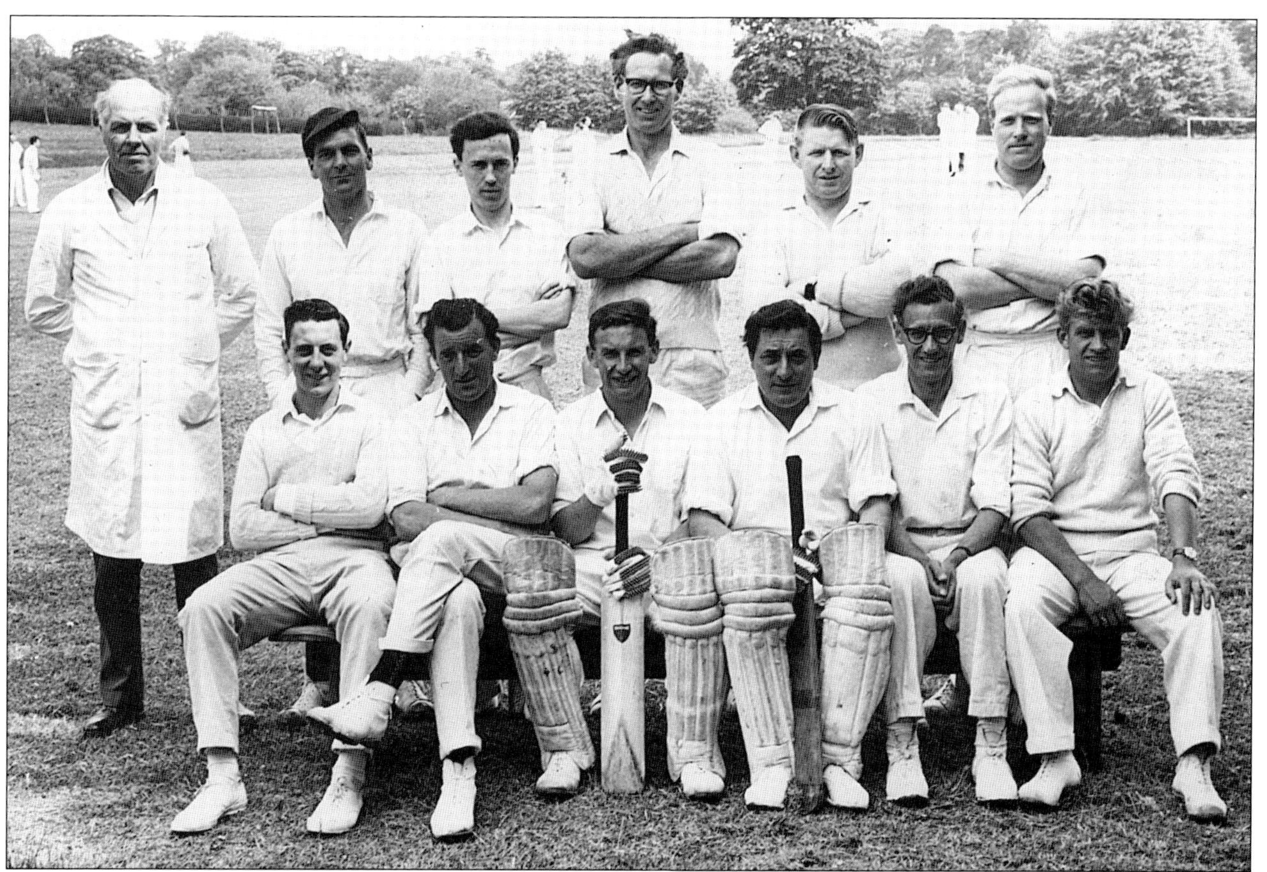

Frensham in 1964, the year they thought they should have won the I'Anson Cup. Standing, from the left: C. Badland (umpire), C. Plant, G. Pelling, G. Pither, G. Iliffe, G. Colbran. Seated: Michael Fathers, E. Jones, R. Dibdin (captain), G. Jones, H. Skeet, M. Hill. Picture courtesy of George Pither.

points from three of the first four games, which were all won, taken away because one of the players had been found to be ineligible. This was a bitter blow, because before the season started, and unable to bring the matter before the stewards, Dibdin had personally sought clearance for the player from opposition captains, without objection. Frensham thought the league had 'stabbed them in the back', recounted Chuter, whose family have been connected with the competitions from the outset. His great uncle Tom played for the club when they joined the I'Anson Cup in the second season; Bill Chuter, the first centurion and, with Doug Wells, holder of the all-time I'Anson Cup eighth-wicket partnership record, was his uncle; his father John, still chairman of the parish council, played until 1962; and brother Richard, who made his senior debut, aged 15, in 1978, was captain when the old trophy was won in each of the last two seasons. Peter, himself, made his I'Anson debut against Grayshott in the final match of 1964. He was bowled by Peter Clapham, and in turn dismissed the Grayshott player. Chuter was to say much later that he had to wait eight years before being asked to bowl again in an I'Anson match. Twenty-seven years on from his debut, on 11 May 1991, Clapham again bowled him with a wicked inswinging yorker, when Chuter was playing for Thursley II against Grayshott II, having joined his new club in 1989. He went to The Bourne in 1999, where he helped the newly established Third XI become the inaugural winners of Division Five, and returned home in 2001 to captain Frensham's Third XI – and have the dubious distinction of not only leading them to relegation to Division Four but denying promotion to John Storey's fourths, as champions of Division Five.

Hollowdene, with its short boundary, has always been a batsman's ground but for too many years it was known as the place where Headley's Bob White set a new I'Anson record of 151 not out in May 1957. So, there was jubilation when, on 11 May 1974, John Bennington scored 126 not out at home to Thursley, then only the third century by a Frensham player in the competitions. He hit nine sixes and 12 fours in a knock lasting 90 minutes, and put on 126 for the third wicket with Ray Clarke (46). It was by far Frensham's best season since 1932 and they finished one point behind champions Whitehill. In fact, skipper Mike Fathers and his team, having beaten Churt in the last game, thought they had won the cup, and were already celebrating when news came through that Whitehill had won at Headley in what many still hold was darkness. Bennington scored 476 runs in 23 innings that year, but it was the player who headed the batting averages who was to make the lasting impression. The previous August the *Herald* had referred to the player as a 'promising newcomer' when reporting that he had scored 27 in a partnership of 48 with David Bone for the sixth wicket against Headley, and now, a year later, Sheoghan Dickinson had scored 213 runs in eight innings to head Frensham's batting. Dickinson, whose record-breaking 1984 season is recorded elsewhere, scored his first century for the club, 102 not out, on 16 August 1975, and he again topped the averages. But part-way through the 1976 season his teaching commitments took him away and it was not until early in the next decade that this outstanding batsman/wicketkeeper returned.

THE TEAM TO BEAT

Frensham began to work up a head of steam before Rowledge left the competitions at the end of 1985. Two second places and a third in four seasons to the six-times winners made them the heirs apparent, and since 1986 they have won the cup on ten occasions. The standard of cricket at Hollowdene lifted perceptively with the arrival of John Storey and Mick Knowles from Farnham in 1983, and although Knowles did not stay long, Frensham also secured the services of Dave Gooda, a stylish opening batsman, who had played with Storey for the Civil Service, and Roger 'Rusty' Moorcroft, a mercurial all-rounder and another seasoned Farnham player. The experience these players brought to the club was immense, and the young home-grown talent grew in stature as the seasons progressed. There was another plus-point, Sheoghan Dickinson had returned after a few seasons away. Throughout this transformation, three players in particular remained as the core of old Frensham: Ray Clarke, Peter Chuter and Trevor Jeffery.

John Storey (right) and 'Rusty' Moorcroft brought great experience with them from Farnham.

Clarke was skipper in Storey's first season, in which he took 82 wickets with his at times unfathomable leg-spin, and they finished second. There were two milestones: Jeffery, who first played for Frensham in 1961, took his 750th I'Anson wicket. He had taken 50 wickets in a season seven times, and his best return was 9-21 against Thursley in 1980. And Chuter clocked up his 5,000th I'Anson run when making 69 not out in a first-wicket stand of 128 with Jeffery against Headley.

The run-machine took over the captaincy the following year, when they were again runners-up, and Dickinson scored his record-breaking 1,020 runs while Storey took 76 wickets. Chuter, as Robin Dibdin had been in the 1960s, was an unlucky skipper, for a dropped catch in the penultimate match of the season that allowed the 15-year-old Graham Thorpe to go on and make a century prevented Frensham from beating Wrecclesham, and possibly stopping the mighty Rowledge from winning for a fifth successive time.

Clarke was back in charge in 1985 when Storey's son, John junior, was also in the team. They finished fourth, but Storey senior took 100 wickets and brought his total in the league in his first three seasons with Frensham to 258 (plus any officially unrecorded in second innings where there was not a result).

The Northerner was now ready to take over the reins and, with his old club Rowledge out of the way, it was soon a question of who were going to be the runners-up. Needless to say there were great celebrations as the I'Anson Cup came back to Frensham for the first time since 1932, and old-timers from that team who witnessed the presentation were Bert Holdaway, 'Driver' Swan, Cliff Jarrett, Jack Farr and 'Sammy' Veale. The present squad was invincible again the following season, but there was a collective sigh of relief away from Hollowdene when Grayshott stopped the hat-trick. However, the seconds ensured there was silverware to display in the Holly Bush by winning the Miller Cup for the first time. Mike Fathers received the cup from John Chuter, a former Frensham captain, who remarked: 'It's been a long time coming. I can well remember a time when it was our ambition not to finish bottom.' How times had changed. Paul Thayer, whose sudden death two years later, at the age of 28, stunned his friends and colleagues, scored the runs that clinched the Miller Cup. Paul was a member of a large family from Frensham and Dockenfield, and, as a professional groundsman, the club had benefited from his work at Hollowdene.

By August 1988 Storey had taken more than 500 I'Anson wickets since returning to the league, but it was his son, with a century, and club secretary John Turbard, who set a club record opening stand of 144 as Frensham set a new I'Anson record total of 320-6 declared in 44 overs at Thursley, who had ten men. It beat the 300-5 by Blackmoor against Frensham as long ago as 1903. Turbard was another player whose sudden death, on the eve of his 47th birthday, shocked the club.

In 1989 it was the turn of Dickinson to be the captain and by the end of the season Frensham had done the double. The *Herald* said it was the high point of the club's re-emergence as a force in the 1980s; Dickinson had

Ray Clarke receives the I'Anson Cup from Keith Mayson in 1997.

Richard Chuter holds the cup in the competitions' centenary year.

brought a very different, but no less effective, leadership. It was a year when Storey junior went into the army and did not play for the club until the end of July; Peter Chuter made his I'Anson debut for Thursley and scored his 6,500th cup run; and Peter Slinger joined the club. The second XI retained the Miller Cup with an emphasis on youth, more than half of the players coming from the strongest under-17 side ever put out by the club.

Frensham entered the nineties by retaining both trophies. Storey took back the captaincy while Mike Fathers led the seconds to a hat-trick of successes. In May, he and Paul Hammond put on 222 for the second wicket against Churt II, the biggest partnership in the Miller Cup, and Hammond's record 151 included nine sixes and 17 fours in a display of uninhibited strokeplay. The match was completed when Matt Page took an all-bowled hat-trick. Gooda became the first Frensham player to hit two I'Anson centuries in a season; the evergreen Chuter scored his 7,000th I'Anson run; Storey junior struck a 69-minute century against Churt, receiving 59 balls and hitting five sixes and 15 fours, and two days later he was stumped when on 98 for the Army v Sussex II at Arundel.

In a season of riches, Dickinson, aged 33, broke Bob White's 1957 scoring record with 182 v Headley at Hollowdene on 1 September. He received only 66 balls in an innings lasting 81 minutes against White's old team, who had only ten players. Dickinson, who included 15 sixes and 16 fours in his innings, shared a first wicket stand of 149 with Dave Gooda, who made 35, and was caught by Roger Vernier off Randall Leonard's bowling to the only chance he gave. It was such a one-sided match that saw Frensham make 276-3 declared (Peter Slinger 50no) in 23.4 overs, and then dismiss the visitors for 60 (Dickinson two catches behind the stumps), Danny Coldicott taking 8-22 and ending it with a hat-trick.

So Frensham became only the second club to do the I'Anson/Miller double two years running, The Bourne having achieved the feat in 1927-28 and 1950-51. What a way in which to end the history of the original I'Anson Cup Competition. Fittingly, Clarke was called up to receive the trophy from Norman Disney, and a decade later, as the competitions' centenary was being celebrated, and Frensham were lifting the cup yet again, he and his colleagues, including another veteran, Graham Senior, who was enjoying a second career after many years at The Bourne, could bask in the glory of 16 outstanding seasons.

During that time Bob Campbell and Ken Bone, presidents past and present, have driven the club forward, and have been given wonderful support by the membership. Although the boundaries are short, the ground lends itself to great occasions, and Frensham have staged matches for county beneficiaries and, in the centenary year of the I'Anson Cup, a fixture against Lord's Taverners, when Hollowdene, adorned by two large hospitality marquees, looked a picture.

GRAYSHOTT

THE club whose inspired secretary Albert Kent was the brains behind the I'Anson Cup, won the trophy twice in the first four decades of the second half of the century – in 1969 when they also won the first Stevens KO Cup final, Geoff Tribe and Harold ('Spud') Murphy were the respective captains, and again in 1988 when Neil Elisha received the cup from Percy ('Snowy') Hicks, a fine wicketkeeper in his time who was the only surviving member of the club's successful 1929 side. Club president Brian Spencer said that winning the cup had been a victory for the club. The success of the youth policy had been demonstrated by the fact that five of the side had received Miller Cup medals in 1983. 'The combination of experience and youth has worked well. This is a happy club,' he said. It was very much a family affair, too, for 15-year-old Gary Clapham had become the third member to bear that surname into a side wearing the green and red cap, while his cousin Richard Baker had several years earlier joined father Gerald in the team. Gary, who went to Farnham and became captain, made his I'Anson debut against Frensham, after a series of good innings in the Miller, scoring 36 and taking 4-27, including the wickets of both Storeys. Gary's father Peter and Gerald

Double winners in 1969. Geoff Tribe captained the league side to the I'Anson Cup and Harold ('Spud') Murphy led the midweek team to become the first winners of the Stevens KO Cup. Standing, from the left: J. Sanders (scorer), D. White, W. Oakford, E. Gulliver, G. Baker, P. Clapham, G. Nixson. Seated: B. Lillis, D. Harris, P. Jones, G. Tribe, H. Murphy, H. Williams, C. Dodge.

Baker, both of whom continue to play, married sisters Betty and Joan Langrish, whose father had skippered the Second XI to the Miller Cup in 1925, and their long service to the club is the very essence of the competitions.

The sisters' father could recall the Oxford University and Somerset player, R.C. Robertson-Glasgow, when he taught at St Edmund's School, Hindhead, and played for Grayshott. In his autobiography, *46 Not Out*, published in 1948, he observed: 'The village cricket club played its matches on a pitch which had a fair enough appearance but was, in fact, little more than a whited sepulchre. Our opening bowlers were Mr Messenger, the village policeman, and Mr Percy Burrage, painter and decorator. The policeman, at slow-medium pace, was yet the more artistic attacker of the two. He had some subtlety of flight and a persuasive way with different umpires. Like Yorkshire's Wilfred Rhodes, when he hit the batsman's leg and knew it was not quite out, he would do much peering down the pitch and taking of angles, as if unwilling to let the umpire commit himself to a false decision. Then, when the moment came, he would turn round and say: "But how's that?" When the umpire failed to accept the bait, Mr Messenger would shake his head sadly, as at a sick child refusing a cream bun.

Percy Burrage and A.H. Messenger: immortalised by R.C. Robertson-Glasgow.

'But Mr Burrage used no arts. He bowled round the wicket, at a very brisk and threatening pace, with lowish arm, and he grunted at delivery. He was short and stiff-built, with short, stiff grey hair. He didn't care about angles and flights, blasting his way at the stumps, and appealing without apology or doubt when the ball hit the batsman on any part soever. When decisions were good, for him, he allowed himself a bleak smile. When otherwise, he cursed, loud and openly, and, retiring to a fielding position of his own invention, a sort of deep fourth slip, continued to rumble away like a frustrated volcano. Rest his soul; he was a proper enemy at cricket and, in his season, a very prominent poacher.'

TWO WEST INDIANS

Over the years Grayshott have had the services of many outstanding players, and this is why they have been close to winning the main prize on several occasions. Players such as the two Jamaicans, Gladstone ('Ken') Bullock, a tall opening batsman and wicketkeeper, and the all-rounder Sid Hibbert. They came to this country during World War Two, having played cricket in their native Caribbean, and after military service at Longmoor they remained in the area and became popular and competitive members of the local cricket scene. Bullock, who died in 1997, aged 76, first played for Grayshott while still serving in the Royal Engineers. He rarely crouched when keeping wicket, and seldom stood back to fast bowlers. His taking of the ball on either side of the wicket was of a class seldom seen in local cricket, reported the *Herald*, after a representative fixture against Haslemere in 1952. Bullock, who attended Grayshott's centenary functions in 1996, was proud of his roots and returned to the Caribbean every Christmas. He liked to tell the story of how, when keeping wicket in a benefit match for Jim Laker in Farnham Park in 1956, the summer of Laker's amazing 19 wickets against Australia at Old Trafford, the off-spinner told him that he had heard of an up-and-coming compatriot by the name of Garfield Sobers. Hibbert's best score was probably the 76 not out against Headley in 1955 – a match in which there was an all-run four plus four overthrows off one shot.

Standing up with the slips well back. Wicketkeeper 'Ken' Bullock at Tilford in the 1950s. Jack Warner is the batsman; Walter Loader is at first slip.

Eddie Gulliver was an opening batsman who punished bowlers for many seasons from the late 1970s, and among his record-breaking seven centuries in the I'Anson Cup is a memorable 139 not out at holders Rowledge in May 1984. Geoff Tribe, now the president, took hundreds of wickets in two spells with the club, and his 9-11 against Wrecclesham in 1964, when he took four wickets in as many deliveries and extended it to six in eight balls, was bettered by only eight players in the history of the I'Anson Cup. Colin Dodge, who also played briefly for Lindford, toiled long and hard and effectively with the ball, and has the distinction of taking the last hat-trick in the old I'Anson Cup competition, ironically against Lindford, on 15 September 1990. Dodge, who remains a loyal supporter of Grayshott and of the competitions, was also a handy middle-order batsman and twice appears in partnership records. In fact his stand of more than 130 with Richard Lake at Tilford in 1984 will remain as the best for the fifth wicket. Tim Wheatley was a product of the youth policy, who caught the eye of Liphook in 1989 and has proved to be a good wicket-taker over the years. And then there was Walter Loader, who started with the club before the war, and wrote himself into the record books on 26 May 1956, when he became the second player to take all ten wickets in an innings in the competition. His 10-33 against Frensham stands as the third best I'Anson return, and the details are given elsewhere.

Ken Williams, former Grayshott secretary, and hard-working member of our centenary committee, with Phil Bates (right), managing director of Grayshott Pottery, who is a great supporter of the club, and whose assistance during the competitions' centenary year was invaluable. Ken Williams was a member of The Bourne in the early 1950s and appears in the club's 1953 cup-winning picture.

Grayshott's time will come again. Richard Baker continues the unbroken link of his extended family's involvement in the senior team, and has been joined in recent years by brother-in-law Andy Wheble, whose explosive batting style is guaranteed to quicken the tempo of a game while not always lengthening its duration. On the opening day of the 1993 season the then Loughborough student scored 100 not out off 73 balls (10 sixes and six fours) at Tilford. driving with enormous power and conviction and executing the pull shot with a fair degree of ferocity. Two years later, using a bat that he designed, Wheble raised his century in under 50 minutes as he and fellow opener Mike Absolom needed only 82 deliveries to reach the 147 required to beat Badshot Lea. Paul Osborn is a relative newcomer but has already captained the side to evening knockout success. Mark Sobey, whose bowling has slowed considerably as the years catch up, can still produce match-winning performances. Grayshott have also invested heavily in a youth policy, and this is already paying off with a number of players taking their places in the first team, among them batsman James Tomlinson and bowlers Alastair Lindsey Clark and Daniel Schwick. It was therefore a smart move to have a Third XI elected to Division Five in our centenary year, with old hand Gerald Baker at the tiller. And while on the subject of centenaries, Ken Williams, opening batsman for The Bourne in the early 1950s and associated with Grayshott for several decades, masterminded the club's celebrations in 1996, and subsequently utilised his knowledge of organising such events as a member of the competitions' centenary committee.

HEADLEY

A TOTAL of three I'Anson Cup titles are lean pickings indeed for one of the founder members of the competition. Of the four other clubs in 1901, Grayshott and Churt each have their name engraved on the cup five times, Lynchmere, who withdrew at the end of the 1910 season, won the original trophy three times, and Blackmoor had two wins before disappearing during World War One. So Headley, with the I'Anson Cup's acknowledged best all-rounder, Frank Kenward, associated with all three championships, in 1938, 1962 and 1979, and four unsuccessful play-offs in 1940, 1948, 1950 and 1963, have been something of a sleeping giant.

The 1938 season is recorded in *A Cup for Cricket*, whose author, Theo Pope, was an opening batsman for the Hampshire club, and so, too, is the career of Kenward. But at the halfway point in the story of the I'Anson Cup, he was still only 36 and, like the competition through which he walked so tall, was only midway through his career. Apart from the 1951 season spent with Grayshott, for whom he topped both batting and bowling averages (469 runs in 16 innings for an average of 31.26; 68 wickets at 4.47), Kenward spent his entire career with the club in the village where he was born in 1914.

Norman Disney (right) with Frank Kenward and former players Bill Hodgson, Tom Lemon and Fred Courtnage when Headley won the Miller Cup in 1972. Picture courtesy of Norman Disney.

There were so many outstanding all-round performances in a long career and some have been recounted by Theo Pope. Another was at Churt in 1957 when he made 90 of Headley's 141-7 declared (he shared a first wicket stand of 64 with Peter Lee, who made two) and then returned 8-6 in 7.2 overs and 6-20 as the home side were dismissed for 19 and 52. Just how good he would have been on the pitches of today can only be speculated, but the expectation is that he would have ruled as he did in his heyday. Even in older age he was still a mighty performer, and in 1972, when he was 58, he made a massive contribution towards the second XI's first Miller Cup title since 1936. When Norman Disney, who is still the club's president as well as being the life president of the competitions, presented the cup he was accompanied by Bill Hodgson, captain when Headley first won the Miller Cup in 1929, who was able to recall that a teenager named Kenward was a member of that side. Frank was not prepared to rest on his laurels after that Miller Cup success in Headley's centenary year, and the following year he appeared often in the first team and took his 100th wicket of the season in a Miller Cup match against Kingsley in August on his way to figures of 9-33. By the end of the summer he had more than 100 wickets to his name in the Miller Cup alone. That nine-wicket haul was the last of five in the competitions by the master, his 9-19 against Elstead in 1964 being his best return. He continued to play until he was well past 75, and had enjoyed Headley's third I'Anson Cup title in 1979 when Barry Woodger was the captain. (Woodger, incidentally, after a considerable break, is back in the I'Anson fold with Wood Street, one of the new intake of clubs.)

Kenward did not know when to stop playing. In 1981, when he was 67, he opened the season with 8-79 against Frensham II. He took 98 wickets for the seconds in the next three years, and, aged 71, finished 1985 in the first team. When Frank died in 1995, aged 81, Norman Disney paid this tribute to his old friend and colleague: 'I kept wicket to

Headley, winners in 1962. Standing, from the left: C. Nichols (scorer), R. Woods, N. Harris, J. Burton, B. Berry, E. Chesham, D. Bradley, A.S.C. Courtnage (umpire). Seated: R.C.B. Thackeray (president), R. Cowie, R. White (captain), F. Kenward, N. Disney, B. Courtnage. Picture courtesy of Norman Disney.

him from 1948, and he was still the quickest around. As a batsman he had the ability to put bowlers all over the ground – he had all the strokes. Players who didn't know him might not have been impressed when he came on to the ground. He often turned up wearing flannels held up with string or a tie. He never paced out his run-up; he would wander back, shuffle a bit, and put the ball on a dinner plate. At the end of an over he would wander back to the slips and then nonchalantly pluck a catch out of the air.' Until almost the end, he was the club's groundsman, and Norman added: 'He was a chap who would do anything on behalf of the club. If we asked a favour of him, he would always say the same thing: "That'll be all right".'

OUT OF THE SHADOW

Kenward's name was often linked to that of Bob White, who was no mean all-rounder in his own right but who, apart from one Saturday in 1957, was usually overshadowed. That day was when White smashed the record for the highest individual score in the I'Anson Cup, which had stood since 1947, with an undefeated 151 at Frensham, and covered elsewhere in this history. Hollowdene was a happy hunting ground for White, who scored 103 not out there in 1965, and 113 in 1976. He and Kenward operated in tandem throughout the 1950s and 1960s, and in 1956 they both did the hat-trick in the first innings at Churt. All six batsmen were bowled, and White finished with 5-15 (8-31 in the match) and Kenward 4-8 (9-38 in the match). White also made 50 not out in a total of 71 which saw Headley home by one wicket, but the fuller story gives a perfect illustration of the nature of I'Anson Cup cricket at that time, for, in spite of Churt's batting frailties, their score of 59 was almost good enough when Frank Covey took the eighth and ninth wickets with successive deliveries and four runs were still required. The hat-trick was prevented and Headley's last pair scored the necessary runs and secured a lead of 12. They then dismissed Churt again for 74, and were 41-8 at the close, some way off their target of 63.

Links with the past are an important ingredient of the competitions, and at Headley in July 1952 Percy Snow, who had played before World War One and was in Grayshott's championship team in 1920, took 4-17 at a critical period of Headley's second team fixture with Tilford. In the same match, George Barlow, who had been umpiring for the First

Headley now have a clubhouse for the 21st century, but when the Thackeray pavilion was opened in 1954 it was considered to be most modern in the district. It was presented to the village by Mr and Mrs R.C.B. Thackeray, Reg Thackeray being the club president. The clock was erected in memory of Ernest Turner, for many years the club secretary.

XI, made his first appearance of the year and scored 29. Both are mentioned in *A Cup for Cricket*, Snow being described as an evergreen veteran and a swerve bowler of more than ordinary ability, and Barlow as a stylish batsman and most useful all-rounder in his heyday. There was never a keener player or student of the game, said Theo Pope, and his undefeated century against Thursley in 1930 was the first in the I'Anson Cup by a Headley player.

Another whose skill was recalled in Theo Pope's book was Fred Dopson, who served Headley for nearly a quarter of a century and took a crop of wickets every year, including 89 when they won the cup in 1938. His medium pacers off a couple of steps had a remarkable fizz from the pitch and were coupled with immaculate length. His even temperament, ready smile and good sportsmanship marked him out as a good colleague and opponent, and therefore it was a huge loss to the competitions when he died, aged 43, in 1953. Collections and donations from clubs amounted to £21 6s (£21.30), and £11 6d (£11.03) was raised at a special match between Headley and Lindford.

SPLIT DOWN THE MIDDLE

There was a unique outcome to a Second XI match against Tilford at the start of the 1956 season. A talented teenager named Jim Wade took 8-0 in 5.5 overs with his off-breaks as the visitors were dismissed for 11 in reply to 31. Headley made 66 in their second knock, and at stumps Tilford were 86-7, leaving the aggregate scores level. For some reason it was believed to be a win for Headley on the first innings as Tilford's second knock had not been completed, and a ruling was sought from the MCC. The word from Lord's was that the match was drawn and the stewards simply divided equally the five points awarded for a win over two innings. Wade later went to live in Australia, and on a visit back in 1983 he turned out for the second XI and made 32, sharing a fifth-wicket stand of 52 with Peter Lee, whose son Trevor has enjoyed his cricket with Headley and now Lindford.

Apart from the play-off defeat in 1963, and second place in 1970 and 1978, the first team were also-rans until their third title in 1979, when they won the cup by the biggest margin to date thanks to the introduction of a new, but subsequently discredited, form of bonus points, which rewarded good batting and bowling but often required defeated sides to remain in the field while their vanquishers piled on still more runs. However, in that spell from the mid-1960s, several young players were given their first taste of the competitions, notably Bob Shergold, who announced himself, at the age of 15, with a knock of 92 for the seconds against Frensham II in July 1965. He quickly established himself in the first team, and his partnership of 128 with Kenward, then aged 53, against Thursley in 1967 remains as the second best in the I'Anson Cup for the fifth wicket. Shergold moved on to Farnham in 1974 and scored more than 1,000 runs in his first season in the Park. Thereafter he scored copious amounts of runs, and was the captain when the club celebrated its bicentenary in 1982. Now Farnham's president, he still has a soft spot for his village club and occasionally shows why he was such a class player.

Headley have always produced some good home-grown players, among them Dick Holden, now retired, who gave great service in a long career, and Richard Lewis, whose all-round talent eventually took him to Liphook. The Cook brothers, Ashley and David, Andy Clarke, Roger Vernier, Kevin Williams, Graham Badland, Ashley Canning and Randall Leonard have all given sterling service in recent years, but above them all stands Alan Rooney, who started at Whitehill, then moved to Headley, on to Farnham and back to Headley via Whitehill in 1992, in which season he headed the Division One batting averages with 60.7 (668 runs from 16 innings), with team-mate Gavin May second with 50.2 (502 from 14). Rooney, who continues to play a large part in every first team fixture, became only the second player in the I'Anson Cup to score successive centuries, in June 1978, and to date he leads the list of century-makers in the senior grade with ten. His partnerships with John 'Jock' Burton, also once of Whitehill and subsequently with Rowledge, and, more latterly, with Ashley Cook and Gavin May, grandson of Norman Disney, are a matter of record.

Headley's presentation at the centenary exhibition in Farnham Maltings was adjudged to be the best by the Herald's *editorial manager, Peter Thompson, who is pictured making his assessment of the entry.*

OVER AND OUT

Back in 1971, after 26 drawn matches in the I'Anson Cup, there was a move to generate support for limited overs cricket. Charlie Kemp, chairman of Headley and now a vice-president of the competitions, led the campaign and said he wanted to force the issue at the annual delegates' meeting. He said his players were fed up with what they saw as a weekly stalemate and had inquired about joining a proposed league in the Petersfield area, which would offer cricket where there was no draw. He was sure there was support within the I'Anson Cup for a change, although the *Herald* quoted Mike Poulter, of The Bourne, and Geoff Tribe, of Grayshott, as saying their clubs were against such a move. In the next week's issue, John Covey, who had played for Churt before they left the competition for the first time, supported Kemp and added that he thought I'Anson matches should be played on Sundays when there were fewer demands on players' time. At the annual meeting that year, the matter of limited overs cricket did not arise. The secretary, Alan Staves, alluded to it in his report, when he said: 'The season was notable for the number of drawn games; possibly a more attacking approach is called for with the will to win more prominent than the theme of not losing.' Mr Staves was a member of the victorious Thursley team that retained the I'Anson Cup after losing the first three games of the season. The subject of ridding the competitions of 'boring draws' is still discussed, but there has never been a majority of clubs in favour of adopting limited overs in the league.

KINGSLEY

THE honours have been few, but Kingsley should never be underestimated. They are seasoned campaigners and are back in Division One for the first time since 1996. *A Cup for Cricket* records the fascinating history of the club, and reveals why their first and second appearances in the I'Anson Cup were separated by more than half a century. In between they were runners-up in the Miller Cup in 1950 and well placed in 1951, when Arthur Yeomans took all ten wickets for just three runs against Frensham II, who made 28, on 4 August. This will probably stand for ever as the best return in the history of the competitions. Yeomans then took his match figures to 15-13 in the second innings, but Kingsley lost the game on their new ground at Lode Farm because they were twice dismissed for under 20! Then came some bad news: the club were not re-elected in 1952 because of the condition of their ground. The *Herald* reported that talks of a merger with Oakhanger had been held, but had come to nothing. Kingsley's ground was above the village pond but the outfield surrounding the concrete wicket had become unplayable. John Haydon, a former chairman, said there was still talent in the village, and it was thought possible in time that the ground would heal itself to some extent, and that work in the autumn would put it right. Oakhanger had played in the Miller Cup in the last three seasons and in the I'Anson before the war; the club was still in being and it continued to own the ground, although it was not tended. T.H.B. Boyson, the Oakhanger secretary, said the main problem was that most of the players worked at weekends during the summer. Cricket did restart in 1953 when Kingsley were among the first clubs to play in the new league for the Stevens Cup, and Fred Edwards immediately wrote himself into the record books when he took 9-9 against Thursley, who won the league. However, in the following year they withdrew in mid-season, citing a familiar problem in the more rural areas where so many players were agricultural workers and were required to work on summer weekends.

They did not appear again in the Miller Cup until 1968, and, in spite of many attempts, were unable to gain admission to the I'Anson Cup until 1986, when they secured the place vacated by Rowledge. They, and neighbours Lindford before them, were always the losers in the closed shop that was the competitions up until the format was changed at the start of the 1990s.

Kingsley's only title in the competitions is the Miller Cup victory in 1982. Standing, from the left: Mr Kirby (president), Margaret Turner (scorer), M. Neill, D. Emery, M. Jones, B. Francis, A. Cull, T. Turner (umpire). Seated: M. Ansell, R. Yeomans, N. Orbell, M. Heat (captain), M. Couzens, R. Anderson. Picture courtesy of club secretary Brian Francis.

When the club at last got their chance to play again in the I'Anson Cup, few realised that 53 years earlier they had finished runners-up to Tilford. Still fresh in the mind, though, was the 1982 season when Mick Heat, a free-scoring opening batsman, led them to the Miller Cup title. Heat and all-rounder Bob Anderson, who took a stack of wickets, were often in a different class that season, which ended with a one-point lead over Wrecclesham, the teams having tied in one of their meetings. Kingsley had built up to this successful year by finishing runners-up in the two previous seasons, and winning the title convinced them that they were ready for entry into the I'Anson Cup, but their application was again rejected. However, unlike in the previous two seasons, when their submission was defeated by a show of hands, this time there was a secret ballot.

At the annual delegates' meeting in 1981, Kingsley had asked that the stewards form a sub-committee to look at the format of the competitions, but one year on nothing had changed. Meetings had been held with many of the clubs in attendance, but no way could be found to accommodate more than a dozen teams in either league. The stewards, therefore, recommended that election be by ballot, and at the annual delegates' meeting in 1982 this course of action was proposed by Frensham, and seconded by Wrecclesham. In a somewhat charged atmosphere the delegates, one from each of the 13 clubs, made their decision. The result was awaited with bated breath, but when the tellers were called it was to announce that there would be no change. Kingsley's application had been voted down by six clubs. Lindford had received three crosses and, perhaps predictably, Rowledge, by then not everyone's favourites, two. A further two clubs abstained, but the result was clear-cut: Kingsley were still outsiders.

Mick Heat was unable to continue as captain in 1983, because over the winter he had moved to Yorkshire, and Robin Yeomans took over. They finished second in the table, and again applied for entry into the I'Anson Cup. Another secret ballot was held, this time on the proposition of Wrecclesham, seconded by Elstead, although three clubs indicated they did not want to go down this route again. Kingsley were once more disappointed, ten clubs voting against them. Lindford and Elstead each received one negative vote, and one club declined to express an opinion. The third secret ballot took place in 1984 and the result was another resounding reverse for Kingsley, 11 clubs failing to support their bid with the other two wanting Rowledge out. Meanwhile, in the ballot for the Miller Cup composition, Lindford were again unsuccessful in their bid to have their second team elected, and Frank Lunt reminded delegates that his club's annual application was made 'in the spirit of rule two', which stated that the 'I'Anson Cup is basically for First XIs and the Miller Cup for Second XIs'.

Mick Heat receives the Miller Cup from the then president of the competitions, Jack Warner, in 1982. To Jack's left is Robin Yeomans, whose father Arthur holds the record for the best bowling figures in the history of the competitions – 10-3 for Kingsley against Frensham II in the Miller Cup in August 1951. Picture courtesy of club secretary Brian Francis.

Then came the breakthrough. In 1985, Kingsley were again runners-up in the Miller Cup, albeit a massive 35 points behind Churt, but there was good news at the ADM held in Frensham RBL on Thursday, 28 November: the club's application to join the I'Anson Cup, and to bring their Second XI into the Miller from the Farnham League, was approved. Rowledge's withdrawal had created the space, and Lindford could bring their seconds in as well. Kingsley's delegate that night was Brian Francis, who, with his wife Janette (they are secretary and treasurer), has been the backbone of the club for many years.

So the agonies of constant rejection were over, but Kingsley's fortunes on the field took a nosedive. While the first team were strong enough to be front-runners in the Miller Cup, they were putty in the hands of most I'Anson sides. Equally, the second XI found it difficult to step up a gear from the Farnham League. However, the club did not give up heart and have always been known for their sportsmanship and camaraderie. Occasionally, they have sparkled on the field. Denis Emery, a police officer, produced good performances with bat and ball, and Roger Gingell, who was in the RAF at Oakhanger and had played for Glamorgan II, scored 116 against The Bourne in 1989. Ron Woodward, an old hand at I'Anson and Miller cricket in East Hampshire, has taken hundreds of wickets, and his son Glen captured all ten in a Division Two match against The Bourne II in 1998. Mick Jones has been an honest and dependable toiler through thick and thin, and Nick Randall has carried the club's batting and bowling responsibilities on his shoulders for many years. Twice the league Player of the Year, he is one of several Kingsley players who have the ability to perform well in Division One. The 2002 season will be only their eighth in the top flight and, discounting 1933, their record has been abysmal: second to last once and last four times in the I'Anson Cup (when there was no threat of relegation), and second to last and relegated in Division One in 1996. It is time for the tide to turn. One thing that has not changed, though, is the geology. Kingsley sits on a bed of clay, and their current ground is liable to be unplayable after heavy rain. Hopefully, they will never face de-selection again.

LINDFORD

THE present Lindford club was formed in 1971 and came into the Miller Cup the following year, playing its home matches at Alexandra Park, Bordon. Its predecessor had its base at the old Royal Exchange ground in the village, long since built over but retaining a link with the past through the name Cricket Lea, and first appeared in the Miller Cup before the war. In 1953 the club switched to become founder members of the Stevens Cup, and C. Butcher scored the first century, against Whitehill, on 4 July, while putting on 127 for the first wicket with his skipper, Archie Cooper. They won the league the following year, and its donor, the president of the competitions, A.J. Stevens, presented the cup. The team photograph is interesting because, seated next to Mr Stevens, is the Lindford wicketkeeper, Norman Disney, the current president. It was the first trophy the club had won, and in the evening they celebrated in the Working Men's Club where the players received small shields from Col. J.D'A. Champney. When the Stevens Cup league was halted at the end of the 1955 season, during which Ted Rooney, father of master batsman Alan, took five wickets in an over against Rowledge II, Lindford reverted to the Miller Cup for three years, after which they withdrew from the competitions.

One of the five residents who met to discuss the formation of a new club in 1971 was Frank Lunt, and for the last 30 years he has given outstanding and selfless service to cricket in both Lindford and the competitions. He continues to be the club secretary, and in 2001 may well have been the oldest player in the league. Frank first attended a meeting of the stewards in May 1976, and has been an ever-present member of the management committee since it first met in 1993, as well as one of the seven people on the centenary committee. The other co-founders of the club were Clive Hudson, Ken Jones, George Mansfield and George Wilson.

Lindford's return to the Miller Cup in 1972 was followed by admission to the I'Anson Cup the following year, while the Second XI continued to play in the Farnham and District League. They were frustrated in their attempts to bring their seconds into the competitions by the will of the majority to restrict each league to a maximum of 12 teams. This meant that Kingsley, who were in the Miller Cup, were similarly frustrated, and it was only when Rowledge departed at the end of 1985 that Kingsley were able to move up and both their and Lindford Second XIs could be admitted.

Frank Lunt and his colleagues, among them Ken Jones, a non-cricketer who ran the village shop until he retired, and who died in 2001, former player and village bobby Mike Pike, who, in 1981, scored Lindford's first I'Anson century since they rejoined the competitions, and John Gray, a leading umpire in the competitions, were determined that the club should have its own ground, and in 1983 a self-build project on Broxhead Common became a reality and is a tribute to the hard-work of the members. The sward of green contrasts with the purple of the heather and the yellow blossom of the gorse at the boundary's edge, and is certainly one of the more attractive grounds in the league. The first I'Anson match on the new ground took place on 30 April 1983, and the Lindford team was P. Williams (captain), K. Mansell, W. Scott, D. Thorne, M. Pike, S. Giles, J. Thorne, J. Shaw, M. Smith, B. Othen, P. Collins. Gordon Filmer, who worked hard for the club and on behalf of the competitions as the umpires' convenor, said the facilities would eventually become 'the best in the competition' and paid tribute to the members, especially Ken Jones and Fred Knight. The pavilion was opened officially on Sunday, 5 June, by Peter Whitfield, the president and owner of the farm on which that part of Broxhead Common is situated. Former Lindford player Colin Dodge, then with Grayshott, led an I'Anson XII in a match against the club to mark the opening, and in the side were M. Pryce (Tilford), M. Absolom (Elstead), K. Tilson (Thursley), J. Burton (Rowledge), M. Neill (Kingsley), M. Poulter (The Bourne), T. Jeffery (Frensham), M. Warner (Churt), D. Mann (Whitehill), A. Hughes (Wrecclesham) and D. Lambert (Headley). The following Saturday Bill Scott's unbeaten 100 against Tilford was the first I'Anson century scored at

A delightful watercolour of cricket at Lindford's Broxhead Common ground by local artist Wendy Bennett, who kindly gave her permission for its reproduction here.

Broxhead. (The first player to score a century for Lindford had been A. Ness, who made 108 not out against Headley II on 4 August 1951, including four sixes in one 26-run over.)

GRAHAM THORPE STUMPED TWICE

Ken Mansell, the senior wicketkeeper for many years, was a popular figure on and off the field, and remains so to this day as a member of the umpires' panel. Among his dismissals were two stumpings at the beginning and end of the future England star Graham Thorpe's career in the competitions. It was on 8 August 1981, one week past his twelfth birthday, that Thorpe made his debut for Wrecclesham in the I'Anson Cup against Lindford, and when he had reached five he played and missed at a delivery from Don Tailford and Mansell did the rest. Just over three years later, on 22 September 1984, Thorpe, with a century against Frensham the previous week, reached his half-century against Lindford when Mansell struck again. Not only was it Thorpe's final game before moving on to Farnham, but it was also Ken Mansell's farewell appearance and he was applauded all the way back to the pavilion when stumps were drawn.

Ken Mansell, once a leading wicketkeeper, now a respected umpire, in relaxed mood at a centenary year function. With him is Herald *sports editor Carl Obert, a former Frensham player, who has reported the competitions' matches and activities since the 1970s.*

Neither Lindford team has enjoyed great success, but they are doughty fighters and popular members of the league, and some of their players' names appear in the records of the competitions. Only a year before his death, and in the corresponding fixture at Frensham, Mick Hill made an unbeaten 56 and was assisted by Michael Henderson in an unbroken partnership of 76 that stands as the fifth best for the eighth wicket in the I'Anson Cup. In 1984, Don Tailford and Darren Collins, whose appearances were limited by football, shared a stand of 80 against Elstead, that remains as fourth best for the ninth wicket, and four years earlier, at Thursley, two Lindford tailenders, whose names went unrecorded in the *Herald*, added 62 for the tenth wicket, a total beaten only twice in the I'Anson Cup and eighth highest in the history of all of the divisions. Jeremy 'Jingles' Hall is a whole-hearted all-rounder who has done much to keep the club competitive in the last decade and, fittingly, with Gavin Rose, he holds the record for a fourth wicket stand in Division One with 170 made as he scored an unbeaten century at Fernhurst in 2001.

In the all-time Miller Cup bowling records Jack Burton's name appears twice. At Tilford in August 1956, he took 9-23 to cause an upset against the second-placed team, who needed only 64 to win a two-innings game. Burton, who had taken 3-27 in the first innings, could do nothing wrong and Tilford were dismissed for 38 when he took the last two wickets in as many balls in the final over. The following season, Burton, whose son John ended his career with Rowledge, improved on his figures when taking 9-15 as Lindford went to Rowledge II and beat the leaders by four runs in steady rain. It was a typical Miller Cup match of the time, Lindford being dismissed for 50, with Norman Disney making 18, and the veteran 'Driver' Swan opening with 11 maidens on his way to 8-11. Rowledge collapsed to 46 all out with eight players failing to score, and Doug Tanner and Arthur Peach made all but nine of the total. Earlier in the season Burton had had a match haul of 16-18 against Wrecclesham II.

DEATH HALTS A MATCH

Tragedy struck at the very heart of the club on 23 April 1977, when the first team captain, Mick Hill, collapsed and died during the opening match of the season at Frensham, for whom he had played from 1957-68, skippering the first team in the last three seasons. Mick, who was 41, collapsed at the non-striker's end as Lindford closed in for victory, having already bowled his side into a commanding position by taking 5-29 in 13 overs with his well flighted slow-medium deliveries which he had perfected. Jim Sinclair and Frank Lunt applied mouth to mouth resuscitation and cardiac massage, and Mick was taken to Frimley Park Hospital. He was a driving instructor at SEME Bordon, and had joined Lindford three years earlier after a spell with Headley. Tributes paid included those from Frank Lunt – 'Mick took a tremendously active part in everything. He was the life and soul of every party, and I cannot remember a bad time with him.' – and close friend Trevor Jeffery, who was prevented by injury from playing for Frensham that day, and who was also to die at a young age – 'There was not a better chap you could wish to meet.' The match, of course, was abandoned as a draw, and shortly afterwards a thunderstorm left the ground under water. Mick Hill was 16 not out and, with Ron Miles, had steered Lindford from 36-5 to 77-5 in reply to Frensham's 86. In May, the annual match between Frensham and Dockenfield raised £205 for the Mick Hill Benevolent Fund, and this was doubled by one of the Frensham club's great supporters, George Jackson. Alec and Eric Bedser attended the match and signed autographs at 5p a time. A second fixture was held between a combined Headley and Frensham XI and Lindford at Alexandra Park. Hill died leaving his wife, daughter Kay and son Raymond, who was to follow his father into the Lindford side and who also died in tragic circumstances, in a work-related accident, in2000.

Mick Hill.

ROWLEDGE

WHEN Peter Prior received the cup in 1959 it confirmed what few needed to know: Rowledge were at last a sustainable force. In 1956 and 1957, Geoff Hebden, a former Hampshire and Dorset player who scored 13,000 runs in his 20 seasons with Farnham, had occasionally appeared for Rowledge, but the side was not yet equipped to take the mantle of top team from The Bourne. However, when they welcomed back all-rounder Les Crumplin, son of the 1949 winning captain, in 1959, things changed. He topped the batting averages, although Cyril Watkins, who had known success at Wrecclesham three years earlier, scored most runs, but above all Rowledge had D.J. ('Joe') Piper, fast left-armer, back in the fold and taking a monumental haul of 147 wickets at 4.67 in all matches. His full analysis was 335.1 overs, 117 maidens, 687 runs, 147 wickets. During the presentation ceremony, the new secretary of the competitions, Peter Warman, was introduced to the spectators, whose number included this writer's grandfather, William ('Jock') Thomson, a 'sprightly octogenarian', said the *Herald*, who had kept wicket for Rowledge before the war and had also seen the club lift the trophy in 1947 and 1949.

Prior and his men retained the cup in 1960, but when Piper dropped out the following year they let it slip. However, that diamond jubilee year of 1961 was significant because Rowledge introduced a young fast bowler from the North who was to rock opposing sides to their foundations. John Storey was arguably the quickest bowler ever to play I'Anson cricket, and for three seasons he ripped the heart out of established batting line-ups. His best match return in his first season was 7-8 and 5-13 at Elstead, and in 1963, when Rowledge beat Headley in a play-off at Thursley and Storey lifted the cup in the absence of the injured Piper, he took 9-11 against Tilford. When he, Piper and Crumplin operated at full bore there was not a better attack in the league, and between them they got a hatful of wickets. But Crumplin's 10-19 against Wrecclesham in 1962 has pride of place. Forty years on it remains the best senior haul in the history of the competitions, and is followed by team-mate Tony Peach's 10-21 against Frensham recorded a year earlier.

Storey left Rowledge for Farnham in 1964 and did not return to the I'Anson Cup until almost 19 years later when Frensham gained his services. There were many who said he might have made a county player, and when, in 1971, aged 32, he was selected to play for Surrey II against Hampshire II at Basingstoke, he said: 'It's come much too late in life to give me any ideas about county cricket. Perhaps six years ago I might have seriously considered a career in cricket if the opportunity had presented itself.' Storey described himself as an all-rounder with a preference for batting. 'Bowling is really my strong point, but like many bowlers, I enjoy batting.' Born on Teesside, he had moved south when his father took up a military post in Aldershot. He had played for the army while in Singapore, and then for Bishop Auckland in the North Yorkshire/South Durham League. A generation later John Storey junior, who also played for the army, teamed up with his father in some successful years at Frensham but went into the record book as the scorer of the highest individual total, 211 not out for Wrecclesham against The Bourne II in Division Two in 1995.

THE BEST CAPTAIN?

Rowledge, who were to win the cup six years in succession in the 1980s before removing their senior sides, were also the dominant side of the 1960s, with Piper, whose brother Roy was a good batsman, leading them to a hat-trick in 1965-67, a period that saw Alan Prior emerge from his elder brother's shadow and chart a career that was to make him arguably the best captain in the history of the competitions. Alan, like so many of his age, had come up through the Two Counties Youth Competition which had been restarted in 1964, and in the 1967 season he took 91 wickets at 4.83, with another youngster, John Kersley, claiming 54.

The second XI were part of a Rowledge league and cup treble in 1975. Standing, from the left: D. Havenhand, J. Stonard, K. Maddocks, R. Jessop, J. Wood, D. Shaw, P. Maidment. Seated: D. Radley, T. Pritchard, A. Peach (captain), R. Piper, D. Tanner. Picture courtesy of Mrs June Tanner.

With the accent on youth, Rowledge took time to regroup and it was to be 1975 before they again won the cup, this time with 'Algy' Prior at the helm. But more than that, the club became the first to do the treble in one year because Prior also lifted the Stevens Cup and Tony Peach, who made a 380-mile round trip from his home in Kingsbridge, South Devon, each week, led the seconds to the Miller Cup. At a joint end-of-season presentation, J.G. Caesar handed the senior trophy to Prior, and also a miniature silver cup to mark his captaining both league and knockout sides to victory. Peach received the Miller Cup from the widow of Bill Lee, who had captained Rowledge in 1938, the only other occasion they had won the trophy, and was handed the ball, mounted and inscribed, with which he had taken 9-40 against Frensham II earlier in the season. He had also had a match haul of 15-31 (8-15 and 7-16) against Whitehill II in that great year.

Two seasons earlier Peach had taken 9-19 against Grayshott II, and in 1978 he had come up with a 9-30 against Whitehill II. A demon bowler indeed, but the Miller Cup records show other Rowledge players who were capable of running through opposing sides: Mick Cane took 10-17 v Elstead II in 1966, Peter Crow 10-24 against Frensham II in 1959, Barry Guest 9-2 v Grayshott II and 9-26 v Wrecclesham II, both in 1962, E.R. ('Chick') Parratt 9-8 v Lindford in 1951, spinner Brian Silver 9-18 v Frensham II in 1967 (16-26 in the match), John Dunbar, another spinner, 9-20 against Elstead II in 1981, and A.F. ('Driver') Swan, who had played for Frensham when they had first won the I'Anson Cup in 1932, 9-32 v Shottermill II in 1959. Mention here of 'Chick' Parratt recalls an interesting match on Sunday, 14 September 1952, when Rowledge played a team of Parratts, all members of one of the largest families in the district. There was CL, Harry, R, Arthur, Alfred, C, ER, D, Harold, L and Frank, while two others, T and F, were playing for the Rest against Miller Cup winners Wrecclesham. In the match at Rowledge, Tony Millard made 102 not out, which was only the second century to be

An I'Anson and Pope double in 1981 for Rowledge. Standing, from the left: P. Cooper, J. Burton, P. Prior, J. Yates, R. Simpson, S. Huckle, Jo Copeland (scorer). Seated: P. Maidment, N. Dunbar, A. Prior (captain), A. Field, B. Silver. Picture courtesy of Mrs June Tanner.

scored on the recreation ground, the first being by 'Toddy' Parratt earlier in the year.

CHAMPIONS OF ENGLAND

Rowledge swept all before them in seasons 1980 to 1985, winning the I'Anson Cup six years in succession and playing at Lord's in the final of the National Village Cup. It was a golden era for the club, but it also signalled their departure from the competitions. The move into the Hampshire League came as no surprise, because over the years Rowledge had expressed their dissatisfaction with certain aspects of the league that had been their home since 1932, their frustration showing through most notably over the subject of limited overs cricket. They had proved themselves to be adept at this form of the game in the evening knockout cups, and more recently in the National Village Cup in which some adrenalin-charged performances culminated in the day out at Lord's in 1985 where, unfortunately, the occasion got the better of them and they allowed the Scottish side Freuchie to win by the narrowest of margins, fewer wickets lost with the scores level.

When Rowledge did the treble in 1975 it signalled the emergence of Alan Prior as a master tactician. He had learnt well under brother Peter and 'Joe' Piper in the 1960s, and took over the reins in the 1970s when the club hauled in three successive Stevens Cup titles and then a Pope Cup championship, in addition to the I'Anson and Miller Cups in 1975. No other club could sustain a challenge as Prior and Chris Yates walked tall as the best all-rounders in the competitions. And just to underline his class, Prior took a year out from Rowledge in 1973 and assisted Tilford to I'Anson Cup supremacy.

Tactically astute, Prior was the first captain to forfeit an innings in pursuit of extra points. It occurred at Grayshott in July 1985 after rain had delayed the start. He elected to bat first and Rowledge declared at 152-3 after 38 overs. Then the left-armer Yates, on a drying pitch and aided by some sharp catching, took 7-4 in six overs while spinner Brian Silver picked up 3-20 at the other end and Grayshott, without Eddie Gulliver, were all out for 29. Ten minutes plus 20 overs were left and Prior informed opposing captain Richard Lake and umpires Bob Burchett and Reg Parratt that he was going to forfeit the second innings. So Grayshott had a minimum of 20 overs to score 124 to win and they went for the runs, but after losing some wickets they abandoned the chase and ended at 63-6. The *Herald* thoughtfully printed Law 14 to assist readers to understand this new development in I'Anson cricket. Subsequently, other captains used the ploy and The Bourne were the first team to win a game in which an innings was forfeited, while Frensham were the first team to forfeit an innings and win.

Successful clubs are never wholly popular, and Rowledge, and Prior in particular, came in for criticism as the playing strength increased. There were accusations made in respect of the manner in which Rowledge secured their players, but no one was able to level anything against the signing of the admirable Tony Field, a fast bowler who had played for Warwickshire II. His career in the Birmingham League pitted him against such legends as Tom Graveney and Basil d'Oliveira. He had in fact hung up his boots when he moved into the village, but was persuaded to have another go when his son Anthony joined the club. Bowling straight and quick, Field was at times simply too good for the opposition and his contribution to the six straight championships must never be understated. He made an already good team so much better and encouraged his team-mates to raise their games just that little bit more.

Paul Offord, after profitable seasons with Whitehill and Grayshott, where he formed strong opening partnerships with Alan Rooney and Eddie Gulliver respectively, was one of Rowledge's controversial signings, but the move was legal. Offord, who could hit the ball as far as any rival, played some spectacular innings, but could just as soon be out without scoring. He was also a leading wicketkeeper for a number of seasons, always standing up to the stumps to the pace of Tony Field, but his career was ended prematurely, and abruptly, by a serious road accident that left him wheelchair-bound.

THEIR LAST SUMMER

Only the uncharitable refused to share in the club's appearance at Lord's in 1985. They were the first I'Anson club to compete in the National Village Cup, and in 1985 there were some memorable performances among the eight games played on the way to the meeting with Freuchie, who were led through the Grace Gates and into Lord's by a piper.

Rowledge at Lord's for the final of the National Village Cup in 1985. Standing, from the left: C. Yates, N. Dunbar, P. Offord, P. Cooper, J. Dunbar, A. Hook, A. Field, A. Field jnr. Seated: B. Silver, A. Prior (captain), J. Reffold, R. Simpson.

Rowledge under-performed on that Sunday and no magic that Alan Prior could conjure up was good enough to overcome the Scots. Rowledge were dismissed for 134 with three balls of their allotted 40 overs remaining (Neil Dunbar 33, Tony Hook 28) and Freuchie finished their innings on 134-8 (Tony Field 2-14, Brian Silver 2-18).

Earlier in the summer, Rowledge had beaten Blackheath by seven wickets (Hook 48), Woldingham by 79 runs (Bob Simpson 58), Outwood by five wickets (Hook 85), West Ilsley by 75 runs (Hook 49, Silver 43 not out, Chris Yates 41, Paul Offord 39) and Crockham Hill by 83 runs (Yates 91) before a thrilling seventh round tie at home to Winchmore Hill in which Prior used all his cunning and know-how to outwit a useful opposition on a ground left saturated by heavy overnight rain. Rowledge were asked to bat first and scored 169-7 (Simpson 41, Prior 35, Yates 33) and restricted the visitors to 144-9 (Yates 4-29, Prior 2-31 and four catches, Silver 2-32). This sent them to Hertfordshire and a potentially tricky quarter-final against Langleybury, but after Rowledge had made 164-7 (Yates 86) the bowlers, led by Jimmy Reffold (4-13), put Langleybury out for 103. There was more travelling in the semi-final, and although Kilve, on the Somerset coast near Minehead, had obviously to be treated with care, they presented no obstacle whatsoever to Prior and his men as Lord's beckoned. Prior won the toss and was a happy skipper when his batsmen posted 242-6, with the in-form Hook making 72, Yates 38, Prior himself 37 not out and Neil Dunbar 33, and then the home side shouldered arms for 75 in the face of Prior (3-6), Field (3-16) and Reffold (3-33).

After the elation and disappointment surrounding the match at Lord's, came the parting. The club had announced at the end of the 1984 season that they could be playing in a different league in two years; they had applied to both the Three Counties League and the Hampshire League. 'Things are only exploratory at the moment,' Alan Prior said. 'We are investigating various possibilities, but we have thought for some time that it would be nice to play against different sides on different grounds.' They had informed the competitions some weeks ago. The *Herald* reported that the club had decided in 1983 that continuing success was likely to create problems. A majority view, although by no means a very great majority, had decided that the healthy future of the club was at stake. They argued that many of the players would want a tougher standard of opposition week by week or they would drift away from Rowledge. While a hard core of players were outstanding in the senior side, there was not the depth of top talent through the club. The Three Counties League rejected the club's application, but, in the summer of 1985, the Hampshire League made an offer, with strings attached – the invitation was to join the lower reaches of the county's regional set-up. Club chairman John Birch called two emergency meetings, and at the second members heard that Hampshire would not negotiate on Rowledge's application. They would have to enter North Hants Division Two, which was the bottom rung of the ladder. A heavy vote in favour showed that most members were prepared to take a backward step in order to move forward. They would also be playing limited overs cricket. The county league was informed the following day. Twenty-two members were in favour, with veteran John Stonard against and two abstentions. Alan Prior, who previously had misgivings about moving into the bottom division, said he had been persuaded to think otherwise by fellow first XI players. Four regular players had said they would not be prepared to play in the I'Anson Cup again. A second vote also ended 22-1 in favour of the second team leaving the Miller Cup and seeking to join the Farnham and District League, Hampshire having said that the seconds could join at the earliest opportunity. At the annual delegates' meeting in 1985, John Birch thanked clubs for 'enjoyable cricket and valuable friendships' in more than 50 years of membership of the competitions.

To their credit, Rowledge rose to the challenge and climbed through the divisions to reach the top in Hampshire. It cannot be denied that they left a hole in the I'Anson competitions, and with Churt also talking of moving away there began a process of thought and discussion, which led to the decisions taken at Tilford in 1989. In time, Rowledge entered a third and, later, a fourth XI into the competitions, but the club's glory days in their local league are now but a memory.

THURSLEY

'JOE' Piper switched his allegiance from Rowledge to Thursley and the fortunes of the latter club looked up, with the I'Anson Cup being won in three consecutive years, 1970-72, under Bryan Karn's captaincy. Karn was one of several players who had moved from neighbouring Elstead when Thursley had re-entered the I'Anson Cup in 1957, and was one of the finest batsmen to play in the competitions. Indeed, when called upon he will still pad up and show players one-quarter his age how to play straight and true. When the cup was held aloft in 1970 some memories extended back 46 years to the day when the club had first won the I'Anson Cup. The 1924 captain, Lionel Rapley, was on the ground, along with team-mates Henry Rushbrooke, Henry Swallow, the wicketkeeper and village schoolmaster, and Fred Howard. It was a joyous occasion for these old-timers, and in particular Rapley, who, with members of his extended family, which has been synonymous with the club for many decades, played in the Thursley team that won the Stevens Cup when it was first put up for competition in 1953, the skipper, Albert Rapley,

Albert Rapley and the Thursley team with the Stevens Cup after becoming the first winners of the new trophy in 1953.

taking four wickets in as many deliveries, and 8-5 in the innings, in the match against Binsted that confirmed their position as champions.

Karn, with 495 runs, and Piper, with 70 wickets at 6.2, were the key figures in Thursley's 1970 success, which was clinched in the final game of the season at Frensham when Karn scored an undefeated 72 and Piper claimed 6-37. Behind these two was a workmanlike side, and the skipper was able to keep them together for two more years. In fact, in 1972, when they pipped Tilford by a single point, only 14 players appeared in the first team. Phil Baldwin, who is the current chairman of the club and whose brother was a young hero in Elstead's 1952 play-off success, Don Hardy, Jimmy Reffold, who was to go on to Rowledge and play at Lord's, and whose father Charlie had been a key member of Elstead teams since the war, before having a spell at Tilford, Alan Staves, outstanding all-rounder, previously with Wrecclesham, who was the secretary of the competitions at the time, Peter Pietrusiewicz, one of the most feared fast bowlers of his day, George Pilbeam and Robert Linegar had been regulars in all three championship-winning sides. Another was David Williams, who had taken hundreds of wickets since joining the team in 1947. His father Bert first played for the club in 1925 and continued until 1949 after which he became the groundsman. He also umpired between 1949 and 1970. His wife Nellie had prepared the teas since 1938, and daughter Mary married Ron Rapley. Among others who helped to keep Thursley at the top of

Thursley, winners in 1970. Standing, from the left: J. Reffold, P. Balwin, D. Hardy, P. Pietrusiewicz, A. Tilson, A. Davidson. Seated: A. Staves, D.J. Piper, B. Karn (captain), G. Pilbeam, R. Linegar, D. Williams. Picture courtesy of the late Eddie Gale.

the tree for three years was Tony Tilson, batsman/wicketkeeper, whose son Keith has accumulated a vast number of runs in two spells at Thursley, interrupted by a few seasons at Farnham.

More than two decades after Thursley's domination, two of the stars appeared again. George Pilbeam played his first league game for 14 years in June 1994, taking a smart slip catch before making a duck batting at 10, one of Graham Badland's eight wickets for 12 runs as Thursley were dismissed by Headley for 60. A month later Peter Pietrusiewicz played several times, including at Tilford where he bowled 12 'tight' overs and, said the *Herald*, 'if the old searing pace was missing, he was lively enough to beat the bat on more than one occasion'. He may well have chosen to play in that match for sentimental reasons, for this was the ground where 'Petro' had played the part of the fast bowler and blacksmith in the film version of *England, Their England* in 1973. After his first spell with Thursley, Pietrusiewicz, who grew up in Elstead and first played cricket in that village's youth team with this writer, enjoyed success with Dorking.

Thursley were runners-up to Tilford in 1973, but since then the club's fortunes have ebbed and flowed, with the main prize always out of reach. There was success for the seconds in 1976 when Roy Walker's side won the Miller Cup, only four years after re-entering the competition. The ever-present skipper took 111 wickets at 7.3, and Bryan Karn, dropping down a notch, scored 953 runs at 52.9, probably the highest aggregate in the Miller Cup. During the season Karn's brother Aubrey, also prominent with Elstead in their infancy in the competitions, reappeared for Thursley II after an absence of seven years, scoring eight not out at number four in a win over, needless to say, Elstead II. Brother Bryan took 3-32 and made 68 to rub salt into the wound.

FIRST WINNERS OF DIVISION TWO

Keith Tilson, aged 20, scored his maiden I'Anson century in 1981 at Grayshott. The Thursley skipper had tapped a rich vein of form, having scored a midweek century against Waverley (Farnham) and then getting another, all undefeated, for Thursley on the Sunday. Three years later the runs were still flowing, 1,093 in the I'Anson and Stevens Cups alone, including unbeaten league centuries against Tilford and Lindford, plus a ton for the I'Anson representative XI at Godalming, another on tour in Torquay and four on Sundays. To underline his all-round capabilities, Tilson also took 22 league wickets. Nine years on, in 1993, having returned from a short spell with Farnham, he was still the team's main run-getter with 859 in 19 league outings for an average of 53.7. That was in Division One after Thursley had become the first winners of the Herald Shield, the Division Two trophy donated by the local newspaper. This was the period when there were signs of rebuilding under the captaincy of John Stressing, a batsman who had played a higher grade of cricket. In his short time with the club he introduced many boys to the sport at coaching sessions on the club's ground on Monday evenings, A colts section was started after a break of ten years, and Stressing said: 'On the first Monday around a dozen turned up, but now the word has spread and every week one or two more youngsters arrive, and currently we have 24 registered. Parents in the village are delighted with the venture, the kids are having great fun, and it's proving to be a great success.' Children aged five to 14 attended and Waverley council, the National Cricket Association and Lord's Taverners helped to finance it. Mike Edwards, cricket development officer at The Oval, gave support, and Chris Bullen, Dave Armstrong and Rod Berkeley held coaching sessions. The results were instantaneous, with three youngsters selected for the senior sides, but after Stressing left the club the impetus was lost and Thursley resorted to type until, with an injection of new players, they again claimed the Division Two title in our centenary year.

Through so many of those barren years Barry Rapley has upheld the name of one of the most celebrated families in I'Anson history, following his father Ron, grandfather 'VC',

Family affair. Tony Cheeseman, now an umpire and league management committee member, played for Elstead and then Thursley, where he was joined by sons Peter (left) and Robin. Peter, a fast bowler who later played for Guildford, took 51 wickets to help Thursley become the initial winners of Division Two in 1991, and was the first player from outside of the top flight to be selected for the I'Anson Cup representative XI. Robin now plays for The Bourne after a spell at Wrecclesham. Picture courtesy of Tony and Sandra Cheeseman.

great grandfather 'MC' and assorted uncles and cousins, both direct and through marriage, and often captaining the side as his forbears did. In 1984 he found himself batting with a cousin, Julian Watt, grandson of Lionel Rapley, a brother of VC, when Julian scored his maiden half-century in the competitions. And also playing a part has been John Pilbeam, son of George, who was a pacy bowler and long-handled batsman for Elstead before gaining some rewards at Thursley, and nephew of Don, who enjoyed his cricket with Thursley and Elstead, and during one season took more than 100 Miller Cup wickets for Wrecclesham. John's wife Anita is now the club secretary, a position often held by a Rapley in the past, and also by Tony Cheeseman, whose sons Robin and Peter have played for the club. The president is Pat Hastings, management committee member and chairman of the working party that burnt the midnight oil in transforming the I'Anson Cup from a moribund league into the healthy competition it is today.

TILFORD

IF The Bourne were the team of the 1950s, Tilford were never far behind them and won the I'Anson Cup three times to their rivals' four. After a second place and two thirds came the title in 1954, by seven points from The Bourne. Jack Warner, a Tilford institution, received the cup on the steps of Tilford Institute, the traditional place for presenting trophies over the last century. Some of the players from the victorious 1910 side were present, and the original I'Anson Cup, which the club had won outright in that year, was brought out from its resting place in the snug of the Barley Mow and shown to the large crowd.

A.J. Stevens, the president of the competitions, in handing over the trophy, said Warner was 'small but audacious, always trying to sever point's hand or perforate short leg if he came too close'. And when the club celebrated their first championship in 21 years, with a dinner in the Institute, Meyrick Payne, the four times Cambridge Blue and Middlesex player who had last appeared for Tilford in the season of 1933, said 'Jack Warner and Jim Eddey won the cup that year for us, as they have done so much to win it again this year'. Warner and Eddey were Tilford for season after season either side of the war, but after 1954 Eddey dropped down to the second team and the firsts slumped to sixth out of nine in the senior league. Meanwhile, the seconds lost the Miller Cup in a play-off with Elstead in 1955, the season when Eddey, the captain, and Robin Collins, aged 17, put on 118 for the eighth wicket against Wrecclesham II. Collins, who lives in the old school house overlooking the Green, made 83 (four sixes and seven fours), and in the same match Ron Miles returned the quite extraordinary figures of 9-5 in nine overs, six of them maidens. The next year Eddey, aged 52, set a Miller Cup

Tilford, winners after a play-off in 1958. Standing, from the left: J. Miles (umpire), D. Wells, C. Johns, J. Warner, Col. G.A. Campbell (president), M. Warner, P. Alderton, H. Jarrett (scorer). Seated: J. Eddey jnr, R. Miles, A. Farnfield (captain), R. Bridger, D. Chester, K. Young.

record that will never be broken of 156 wickets in the season at 5.66 apiece. He was still a force to be reckoned with, and in 1957 he was back in the first team and helping to win the I'Anson Cup again. By this time Alf Farnfield, a doughty competitor from Hale, had taken over as the captain, and he led the run-scoring while Eddey and Miles took almost 150 wickets between them. For Eddey, whose son, 'Young Jim', also played for Tilford, it was the end of an illustrious career, which he had begun with his native Headley and then Grayshott before settling with Tilford. In the words of A.J. Stevens, he was the 'perenniel bowler', whose total wicket haul was in the region of 20,000. He became an umpire, but died, aged 60, in 1964, a couple of months after another veteran, Jim Kneller, aged 48, of Alexandra Park, had taken 147 Miller Cup wickets in the season at an incredible average of just over two runs each.

Tilford's third win in five years came in 1961, when the first team had been boosted by the inclusion of Elstead's Robin Pryce and Charlie Reffold, and Peter Taylor, a fast bowler from Churt. Standing, from the left: J. Eddey (umpire), A. North, P. Mitchell, S. Goolding, K. Young, H. Jarrett (scorer). Seated: Col. G.A. Campbell (president), D. Robinson, P. Taylor, R. Miles, R. Bridger (captain), A. Farnfield, C. Reffold, R. Pryce.

STALWART IS THE HERO

It took a play-off against Rowledge to retain the cup in 1958 when Farnfield was forced to take on the role of wicketkeeper after a football injury sustained by regular stumper Ken Bicknell kept him out for the season. The sudden death game took place at Headley and it was Ray 'Patsy' Bridger, great stalwart of I'Anson cricket over the years, who emerged the hero, bowling unchanged in tandem with Miles, whose father Jim was the team's umpire, and taking 7-28 in 17.4 overs, and then making a hard-hit 24 in a match-winning partnership with Jack Warner. Farnfield received the cup from The Bourne's pre-war star, Lew Goodchild, now in a wheelchair after a wartime accident had robbed him of a leg.

These were good times for Tilford, with players like Bridger, Miles, who pushed the ball through with some pace off a short run, and quick bowler David Robinson, then the headmaster of the village school, and who continues to live just off the Green, providing a balanced attack, while Farnfield, Jack Warner and his son Mick, and the veteran Cuth Johns kept the scoreboard moving. And not to be outdone, the seconds, captained by 'Cody' Goolding, a well-known year-round sportsman and administrator in Farnham and district, won the Miller Cup for the first time in 1959. Bridger, like Jim Eddey before him, stepped down into the seconds and scored 213 runs in six innings, including a maiden century, seven wickets for five runs and a hat-trick in one match against Frensham. He became a first teamer again the following year when he took over as captain from Farnfield, and Tilford finished third, but in 1961, with Robin Pryce having moved from Elstead, where he had captained that club to victory in a play-off on Tilford Green in 1952, the I'Anson Cup was won for the third time in five seasons. Pryce made a vast difference to the side, but Farnfield and the equally hard-hitting Sid Goolding scored more runs, while Miles, with 82, Bridger and the fiery Peter Taylor, who had played for Churt, captured more than 160 wickets.

Jack Warner's long career, which had begun in the 1920s, came to a climax in 1963 when, aged 50, he captained the Second XI to another Miller Cup title. His family's connection with Tilford cricket stretched back to before the present club was founded in 1885, and his service to both club and the competitions continued until his death in 1988, when he was president of both organisations.

BAND OF BROTHERS

In an era when centuries were still hard to come by, John Gould scored 120 at home against Whitehill in July 1970. It was the first ton by a Tilford player in the cup since 1940 when Miles Merrett made 103 against Grayshott. Gould was one of a number of talented younger players in the 1960s and 1970s, and was a member of Paul Dance's team that won the I'Anson Cup in 1973. Dance, a police officer, had the services of Alan Prior, on a year's sabbatical from Rowledge, while Robin Pryce took part in his third title-winning season. Five years later, it was Tilford's turn again, and skipper Chris Aust was able to call on three sets of brothers, the Coopers, Humes and Turners, and they probably secured the championship in July when they beat Headley and Rowledge on successive weekends. Paul 'Nobby' Cooper, who later played for Rowledge, and Martin Pryce, son of Robin and a backbone of Tilford cricket since the late 1970s, scored 606 and 556 runs respectively, and Brian Turner, who returned to I'Anson cricket with Farncombe Wanderers as the league expanded, was an excellent all-rounder with 657 runs and 52 wickets.

In the *Herald* in June 1977, a heading read 'Martyn the wrecker' over a report of a match played by Farnham College in which a student named Nigel Martyn took 7-11,

Alan Prior's single season with Tilford in 1973 saw the cup come to the Green again. Standing, from the left: M. Landry (scorer), P. Covey, A. Prior, P. Cooper, P. Moran, R. Newman, J. Warner (president). Seated: J. Gould, R. Pryce, P. Dance (captain), M. Warner, K. Bicknell, D. Pike.

including an all-bowled hat-trick. It was an early warning of the impending arrival of a fast bowler who was to be the scourge of batsmen throughout the last two decades of the first century of the competitions. Martyn was in the next generation of Tilford players, as was Nick Cowell, whose pace had troubled all teams in 1982, when he had a first-season haul of 41 wickets, and had played a large part in the one-run win over Churt in the final of the Pope Cup. Sadly, Tilford and the competitions lost Cowell, who was fatally injured in a road accident while returning from an I'Anson match at Churt in August 1983.

IN TOUCH BY MOBILE PHONE

A leg broken playing football forced Martyn to sit out the 1992 season when Tilford next won the I'Anson Cup, clinching the title on the last day of the season with a winning draw at Headley who, with Frensham, could also have won the trophy going into the match. Tilford required three points and Headley could only win the cup if they picked up a minimum of five points. A winning draw would have handed the championship to Tilford but would have interested Frensham who were confident of taking maximum points at lowly Whitehill. The scene was set for a thrilling climax to the season with scouts and mobile phones keeping tabs on the action at both grounds. As the afternoon progressed, and with Frensham having accounted for Whitehill not long after the tea interval to leave them one point ahead of their two rivals, the spotlight turned fully to the match at Headley, where Tilford had been put in by Dick Holden and had been restricted to 175-8, David Jervis (60) and Martin Pryce (45) in fine form. Headley's strong batting line-up had this target well within its sights with positive contributions from Alan Rooney and Bob Shergold (35 each), Roger Vernier (23) and Gavin May (20), and then a sixth-wicket partnership of 44 between Shergold and Dave Cook (17) brought them to within 21 of victory with four overs left and the I'Anson Cup for the first time since 1979. But Tilford skipper Hamish Macdonald did not lose his nerve, and persevered with brother Alistair's mixture of the unplayable and the erratic and Russ White's left-arm spin. They were to prove the right ingredients and Headley's challenge petered out at 162-9. The *Herald* reported: 'Few will begrudge Tilford their success. They have had several near misses in recent years and, at the start of the season, they would have given themselves little chance without the services of Nigel Martyn.' The newspaper added that Tilford had turned the tables on Frensham who had won two more games. Two years earlier,

Frensham had won fewer games but pushed Tilford into second place on bonus points picked up in games, which, under the old rules, went to two innings.

One of many former juniors at Farnham to have found their way to Tilford, Martyn has enjoyed a rich harvest over the years and was proud to lead the side to the cup in 1998. However, Tilford, with a nucleus of players who have grown up together, have so often lost their way when riches have beckoned. Their two senior titles since 1978, plus the Miller Cup in 1986 and 1987, is scant reward for a club that, because of its location, has never had any difficulty in attracting players.

Notable in more recent times have been the brothers Slinger, Peter and Paul, sons of former player Ted and his wife Mollie, who ran the Barley Mow for many years. As youngsters the boys went to Churt where there was youth cricket. Peter, a big-hitter, also appeared for Frensham during some of their glory years, before returning to the Green, while Paul has played some major innings for Tilford and pulled off some spectacular catches. Hamish and Alistair Macdonald have also been influential, as have David Jervis and Roger Grogut, who were a dependable opening partnership with Pryce, Chris Cobbett and Hamish Macdonald to follow. Now they have Matt Barnes, who was the first player to score more than 200 in an innings when he made 206 not out for Badshot Lea in 1995. While Martyn has tended to take many of the recent bowling plaudits, the contributions of the much improved Geoff Coombe, all-rounder Steve Crawte and spinner Mick Gorman should not be overlooked.

Jim Eddey's 10-38 in 1949 stands as Tilford's best in the league, but there were nines for 'Patsy' Bridger (1952 and 1955), Ron Miles (1958), Tim Laskey (1965), Noel Hume (1976), Brian Turner (1979) and Martyn (1990), before, in the last four seasons, Martyn (2000), Matt Barnes's brother Ashley, on his debut in 2001, and Coombe (1998) had similar hauls to lead the Division One best bowling list.

The days of Eddey and Warner are long gone, but one man whose family connections can bridge the gap is Michael Landry, gardener, bellringer and club scorer, whose grandfather, Harry Jarrett, was in charge of the pencil and scorebook from the 1920s to the 1960s, and was pictured with the teams and the I'Anson Cup in 1933, 1957, 1958 and 1961. Harry was a familiar figure sitting at the scoring table in front of the Institute on match days, and grandson Michael has continued the tradition.

ON THE TELEVISION

The location of the village green at Tilford acts as a magnet to film-makers, and in August 1973 there was excitement when the *Herald* announced that BBC TV was seeking 'extras' for the filming of *England, Their England* by A.G. Macdonell at Tilford in September. Cricketers and spectators aged from five to 65, who would receive £7.50 a day, were sought for the production of this classic tale, the book of which was first produced in 1926 and depicted the Barley Mow on the dust jacket. More than 500 people turned up at the Green in the hope of being chosen for a part, among them Peter Pietrusiewicz, a policeman, who was cast as a blacksmith and the demon fast bowler of the local team, a role for which he was adequately equipped since he had been terrorising batsmen throughout the league in recent times as a member of Thursley's victorious treble side. Alan Prior, who had spent the summer of 1973 helping Tilford win the I'Anson Cup, also had a part in the hour-long film, and there were shots of many other familiar faces when it was broadcast.

WHITEHILL

IN 1974 Whitehill did the double; less than two decades later they quit the competitions on their way to extinction. It proved to be an inglorious end to the club, which had grown out of the old Blackmoor side, one of the five founder members, after World War One. In 1974 the first team headed off Frensham by one point in a title race that went to the final weekend. It was their first success since 1931 and when J.G. Caesar presented the cup to Les Parkins he remarked that in 1932 Frensham had won the cup for the first time, and they had also enjoyed their best season since. Alan Chalkley, with 88 wickets, and Alan King, with 80, shared the bulk of the bowling. Alan Rooney, who had followed his father Ted and uncles Jake and Tommy into the Whitehill side, scored 317 runs and headed the batting. It was a sign of things to come by a player who was destined to become one of the most commanding batsmen in the competitions. Ten years earlier King, always a great competitor, took 10-24 for the Second XI against Wrecclesham II to join Fred Courtnage (10-34 v Headley II in 1932) as the second player from the club to take the lot in a Miller Cup match. And in 1966 King was captain when Whitehill's only team in the competitions won the Miller Cup for the first time since 1924 – he received the trophy from E.C. Ashford, a pre-war Miller captain at the club. The following year Whitehill entered both leagues, while neighbours Alexandra Park dropped down to the Miller after one season in the I'Anson. The seconds won the cup in 1969, lost a play-off against Elstead in 1971 and then struck gold again three years later.

Mick Greathurst, whose premature death in 1986 was mourned throughout the competitions, captained them in 1974. Eleven years later Mick's son Ian, aged 28, who had played youth cricket for Grayshott and Frensham, and for Lindford in the I'Anson Cup, died as a result of a road accident at Frith End. They were popular members of the

Whitehill twice won the Miller Cup in the 1960s. Above, Alan King was the captain of the club's only team in the competitions in 1966. Standing, from the left: A. Lock (groundsman), C. Hawkins, I. Ridley, R. Jones, H. Hawkins, K. Burt, C. Kingswood (umpire), F. Norris (secretary). Seated: Mrs J. King (scorer), L. Austin, R. King, A. King, Pat Finch, A. Chalkley, L. Parkins. Below, when Whitehill had two sides competing, Harry Hawkins led the seconds to the Miller Cup. However, he was on his honeymoon when L.T. Pope presented the trophy, and vice-captain Ray Jones stepped up during the tea interval of the Winners v The Rest match. Standing, from the left: A. Lock (groundsman), N. Parkins, M. Herzke, A. Chalkley, K. Burt, J. Kneller, D. Burton, F. Norris (secretary). Seated: Peter Finch, R. Woodward, R. Jones, R. Othen, Pat Finch. Whitehill clinched the title in the last game of the season when Ron Woodward took 6-16 and 8-22 as Grayshott II were beaten by an innings.

local cricket fraternity, and it was typical of Mick, when presented with the Miller Cup, to immediately hand it to secretary Fred Norris, who had done so much work for the club. Whitehill's success was a fitting climax to a season in which they had used their new pavilion for the first time. The work had been carried out by members at no cost to the club. Much of the material had come from the old club building, and the working parties had been led by Les Parkins, who had skippered the first team since the club re-entered the I'Anson Cup in 1967. On 7 June 1975, Brian Dewey hit a century in 76 minutes at home to Lindford, Whitehill's first since returning to the cup. He scored 110 before going the way of so many in those days, st Mansell b Dodge.

There was a curious incident at the start of a Miller Cup match on 7 June 1980, when the toss had to be made a second time against The Bourne II. The reason? A Jack Russell raced off with the coin as it landed at the first attempt!

WHAT WOULD 'WW' THINK?

Sadly, those days are but a memory and the club, whose pedigree stemmed from W.W. Stratford's great Blackmoor club when the I'Anson Cup was launched, capitulated after one match of the 1993 season and withdrew from the competitions. They had requested they be allowed to retain one side in Division Three, but an emergency meeting of the management committee ruled this to be unacceptable. 'We hope that the club will be able to rebuild, and be in a position to re-apply to join the league in the near future,' the competitions secretary said, but at the annual delegates' meeting that year Graham Collyer's words left no one in any doubt as to the feelings of the administration. Whitehill, he said, were 'a shambles who had let the competitions down badly'. Almost ten years on, the Whitehill ground is a forlorn sight next to a clubhouse that has been destroyed by fire. What would WW, so often referred to as the 'father of the competition', think of it all? He died in February 1953, aged 87, and for more than 30 years until his retirement in 1926 he was headmaster of Blackmoor school and, said the *Herald*, a man of sterling character, with the ability to bring out the best in those with whom he came into contact.

WRECCLESHAM

BILL Poulter moved across from The Bourne for four seasons, and Wrecclesham won the I'Anson Cup in 1956. Ironically, they clinched victory on August 18 when, without a game, they watched The Bourne, who were the holders, lose by three wickets to Elstead in damp, dark conditions. The mathematics were such that The Bourne would have had to have beaten Elstead over two innings and also taken five points against Wrecclesham the following Saturday (which in the event was rained off) to have had any chance of retaining the trophy. Wrecclesham, runners-up the previous year, had led the table from the start and showed their worth when they beat The Bourne by 18 runs in June. Without skipper Poulter they made 78, John Stonard taking 6-33, and dismissed The Bourne, on their own ground, for 60 after they had been 21-0, Johnny King taking 6-30 and George Williamson 4-27, and Phil Burchett snapping up three fine catches.

Theo Pope presented the cup to Poulter and made a special mention of Williamson who had taken nearly 250 wickets in the I'Anson Cup in the last four seasons. The club president, the Revd C.F. Leverton, hoisted the championship pennant on a newly-erected flagstaff. Towards the end of the year the Bedser twins, Alec and Eric, joined club members in the parish hall to celebrate the victory, and H.C. 'Mickey' Bicknell, the secretary of The Bourne, paid tribute to his old ally Poulter who, he thought, was the most astute captain in the district and a good sport, but a player who never gave an inch. Former secretary Norman Bailey recalled the days when the club was reformed after World War Two when the team travelled to matches on a sand wagon. There was very little equipment, and players turned out in a variety of clothes that made one member look very conspicuous when he appeared for the first game of the season in whites.

Bill Poulter's captaincy, during a three-year sabbatical from The Bourne, led Wrecclesham to the I'Anson in 1956. Standing, from the left: C. Marlow (scorer), M. Foster, D. Wells, M. Poulter, F. Drake, P. Burchett, M. Sercombe, B. Waterman. Front: H.J. Knight (competitions secretary), J. King, P. Clark, W. Poulter, G. Williamson, B. Jarman, F. Hole (secretary). Picture courtesy of Peter Clark.

Wrecclesham had finished fifth in their first I'Anson season in 1953, T.A. (Tim) Dimes topping the batting with 247 runs at 15.44, followed by C.A. (Cyril) Watkins, 239 at 14.06. G.O. Williamson took 78 wickets at 5.65. Poulter and Phil Barlow, from Headley, joined the club in 1954 when a quick bowler, W. Shaw, took their first hat-trick in the competitions as he reduced Tilford to 13-9 in reply to 77, and claimed 8-19 in seven overs. They again came fifth, then climbed to second before that great summer of 1956.

Wrecclesham had joined the competitions in 1951 when they finished third in the Miller Cup. The following season they won the trophy and Doug ('Jock') Heron received it from Mr H. Sanders, a well-known Farnham and Surrey councillor and Tilford's umpire when they won the I'Anson Cup outright in 1910, at the conclusion of the Winners v The Rest match on Sunday, 14 September. The match had been postponed after wet weather had prevented play the previous Sunday, and there was a good crowd, in spite of a counter-attraction in Farnham of the arrival of circus elephants. Mr Sanders said Wrecclesham sportsmen had had two successes in the year, the footballers having won the Surrey Intermediate Cup. Referring to the efforts of Farnham UDC in regard to the recreation ground, he said he knew the facilities were not ideal. There were many other grounds that required attention but he felt

The first of Wrecclesham's two trophies since they joined the competitions half a century ago. Doug ('Jock') Heron was the captain when the club's only team won the Miller Cup in 1952. Making the presentation is Mr H. Sanders, well-known in local government circles in Farnham and Tilford's umpire in 1910 when they won the original I'Anson Cup outright. Picture courtesy of Wrecclesham CC.

the work already done was now bringing forth fruit. (It was to be another 13 years before Wrecclesham's new £3,000 pavilion was opened, and as recently as 1990 groundsman Tony Hughes turned the square through 90 degrees in an attempt to overcome drainage difficulties.) Heron, who also played for Rowledge, said he looked forward to a time when the club could compete in a higher sphere, and they hoped to be able to run two teams in 1953. George Williamson's 94 wickets at 3.53 was a mammoth effort, and he was to play a huge part in the growth of the club.

GRAHAM THORPE

In 1977, with Wrecclesham having been in the doldrums for some time, the award for first team batting went to Geoff Thorpe. A few years later that surname was to ring around the district as the youngest of Geoff's three sons made his way through school, youth and adult cricket to become the finest batsman in England. With the advantage of having been born into an enthusiastic cricketing family – parents Geoff and Toni and older brothers Ian and Alan – Graham could not wait to join in. Steve Pinn, who was Wrecclesham's youth manager in the 1970s, recalls that he finally got his chance in 1978, making his debut for the under-13s on a breezy Sunday morning at Odiham & Greywell, aged just eight! For three seasons, Wrecclesham were unbeaten at this age level, and Graham's contribution to that success became increasingly important – a fact that was only too obvious to seasoned cricket observers. He played in three winning cup sides for the under-13s. Young Graham, though, was every bit as good at football, and it is well known that he could have followed that route. In fact, it was in the winter game that his name first appeared in the sports pages of the *Herald*, on October 21, 1977, for he scored four times as Farnham Town under-11s beat Farncombe 6-1.

By 1980 it was cricket that was to the fore and in July he was selected to play for the county schools XI in the first of five games. Demonstrating that he was very much an all-rounder in those early days, he took 7-10 in his first appearance and then captained the team to further wins against Wales and Essex. Later that summer, Graham and Alan joined Ian and the rest of the Wrecclesham under-15 side as Ian received the Surrey cup from county captain Roger Knight in front of 10,000 people during a Sunday league match at The Oval.

From the age of eight Graham watched his dad and brothers play for Wrecclesham, and probably first appeared in the competitions, aged 12 and one week, on August 8, 1981, when, batting at eight, he made five against Lindford before being stumped by Ken Mansell off the bowling of Don Tailford. The following week he went in at ten against Elstead and had made nine before falling leg before to Roger Elgie. His first full season was 1983 when, aged 13, he scored 486 runs in 16 innings (74 and 63 against Tilford) for an average of 30.4, which put him seventh in the overall Miller Cup averages, and just ahead of that great veteran, John Tanner, who scored 446 runs for The Bourne. Graham also took 29 wickets, and Wrecclesham, second earlier in the season, finished in fourth place. Some of the bowlers who can say they dismissed Graham Thorpe are Tony Cheeseman (Thursley), Peter Clapham (Grayshott), Ron Skilton (Elstead), the late Alec Liddicott (Frensham), Andy Hall (Churt), Mick Hicks (Thursley), Chris Emblow (Elstead), Peter Lee (Headley), George Pither (Frensham), Dave Searle (The Bourne) and Alistair Macdonald (Tilford). Another player who has cause to remember that season is *Herald* sports editor Carl Obert, who gave the young Thorpe a return catch when six short of a century – his highest score.

Graham Thorpe: started when he was eight and rose to be England's premier batsman. Inset: Tim Laskey, fitness guru and former I'Anson player with Tilford and Thursley.

The following year saw him in the first team at Wrecclesham, and his talent had further developed. It was the year Sheoghan Dickinson scored 1,020 runs in the season for Frensham, and Thorpe, with an unbeaten 100 against Frensham in his penultimate game and 50 against Lindford in the final fixture, totalled 522 runs in 17 knocks for an average of 34.8, which put him in seventh place in the I'Anson Cup averages behind Dickinson, Keith Tilson (Thursley), Eddie Gulliver (Grayshott), Bob Simpson (Rowledge), Richard Lewis (Headley) and Martyn Gowar (Elstead). Bowlers who claimed his wicket included Russell Mayhew (The Bourne), Ray Smith (Whitehill), John Watson (Churt), Chris Yates (Rowledge), with figures of 9-16 in 13.5 overs, Pat Murphy (Elstead), twice, John Storey (Frensham) and Keith Tilson (Thursley).

The following season, 1985, Graham joined his brothers at Farnham (they had gone up to the Park two years earlier) and in 1987 was offered a contract by Surrey. He made his first-class debut the following year and scored a century against Australia at Trent Bridge when he made his Test debut in 1993.

NEW RECORD SCORE

On 1 July 1995, John Storey junior broke the record for the highest overall individual score in the competitions when he made 211 not out for Wrecclesham away to The Bourne II in Division Two. Nine weeks earlier, Matt Barnes had set a new best of 206 not out for Badshot Lea in a Division One fixture on the same ground. Storey, who had already played for Frensham and Grayshott in previous seasons, needed only 36 overs and hit 14 sixes and 20 fours. He was dropped off an easy chance at 125 and survived two difficult ones. Wrecclesham elected to bat first and it was suggested that this was because a record attempt was to be made. They declared at 304-4, and The Bourne replied with 180 (Storey 3-58) after openers John Moore (44) and Barry Croucher (60) had put on 105. Three weeks earlier the left-hander had scored 160 (10 sixes and 18 fours) in 25 overs in a powerful display against Headley, and he followed his record score with knocks of 92 and then 77 against Frensham II, skippered by his father, J.H. Storey. After nine innings with Wrecclesham, Storey went off to join Normandy, having scored 801 runs for an average of 114.4.

Since 1959, Cyril Crawte, a member of the competitions' management committee and the umpires' secretary, has been a prime mover at Wrecclesham, and he has watched the ups and downs of a club whose ground is but a six-hit from the cottage in which the great 'Silver Billy' Beldham was born in 1766. He saw the early promise of Graham Thorpe, and took delight in the successes of the youth sides in which the three brothers played. He was heartened, too, when Nick Morant, who played for the seconds, was the leading wicket-taker on Surrey under-15s' northern tour in 1998. And he was delighted when the first team won Division Three in 2001. Dave Rook, a cousin of Graham Thorpe's mother Toni, used his years of I'Anson know-how to keep a talented side focussed and the reward was the return to the club of the Miller Cup after an absence of 49 years. For Rook's able vice-captain, David Harfield, it was also a nice feeling to get his hands on the trophy after years of endeavour, including a 10-23 return against Kingsley II in 1986, the third best analysis in the original Miller Cup competition.

Wrecclesham, perhaps, are entering their second half-century in the competitions with an eye on a place in the top flight again.

Team of the century

THE secretary was asked to put his head on the block at the centenary exhibition held in Farnham Maltings, and came up with the following: Bryan Karn (Elstead and Thursley), Alan Rooney (Whitehill and Headley), John Tanner (The Bourne), Sheoghan Dickinson (Frensham), wicketkeeper, Bill Poulter (The Bourne and Wrecclesham), Alan Prior (Rowledge and Tilford), captain, Chris Yates (Rowledge), Frank Kenward (Headley and Grayshott), John Storey sen (Rowledge and Frensham), D.J. ('Joe') Piper (Rowledge and Thursley), Nigel Martyn (Tilford). Twelfth man: Peter Pietrusiewicz (Elstead and Thursley).

An era of change

IT was in a traditional and familiar setting that a new dawn began. The delegates who gathered in Tilford Institute on Friday, 10 March 1989, for an extraordinary meeting of the competitions, made a number of radical decisions that, in time, would result in fundamental changes to local village cricket.

The *Herald* reported: 'In keeping with the past, delegates were reluctant to take on board too radical a package. Better go for "stage one" on the road to reform, as Grayshott's Ken Williams put it. He worried that important decisions might be made under pressure on the night. The majority of delegates agreed.'

At the end of the meeting, the delegates had agreed to:

- Increase the catchment area for clubs from eight to 12 miles (approximately) from Grayshott Village Hall (delegates voted 9-2 to keep Grayshott as the central point.)
- Change the eligibility law, allowing clubs to select players living within eight miles of their ground (the previous limit was five miles).
- Form a rules committee and a working party. The committee would formulate proposals to change the rules, to be presented to the annual meeting, and the working party, which was to comprise one member from each of the 12 clubs, would decide upon future strategy and the direction the competition was to take.
- Increase the number of registered players per club from three to five.
- Remove the word 'village' from Rule 1 in anticipation that in time strong town Second or Third XIs, constitutional clubs or service teams might be admitted to membership.

Headley's proposal that the radius for clubs be scrapped altogether had only two votes in favour, the *Herald* reported. 'This was despite support from Churt whose two articulate representatives, Rod Berkeley and Chris Barnes, maintained that all such restrictions were negative and would not help the quality of cricket as the league attempted to improve its standard and enlarge.

The newspaper report continued: 'The current restructuring of cricket in Surrey might cause problems for a league with such restrictions, Mr Barnes added. (Mr Berkeley reminded the meeting that Churt were attempting to gain admission to the Three Counties League but stressed that the club would remain loyal to the competition while it was a member.)

'However, Andrew Fry (the competitions treasurer) argued that a radius helped keep a character to the league, and Ken Williams agreed. "It's important for a competition to identify with an area," he said.

'Andy Clarke (Headley) thought it was unfair on clubs just outside the area which might like to enter, and delegates agreed to Tony Cheeseman's suggestion that the word "approximately" be added to the rule, giving stewards some flexibility when considering applications in the future. Grayshott's proposal was approved, with nine votes in favour.

'The new 12-mile radius, as illustrated on a map circulated at the meeting, dramatically increases the scope of the competition. On opposite points of the compass, Farnborough, Chawton, Cocking and Cranleigh are all inside the limit.

'While Tilford favoured keeping the (existing) radius, they also put forward an amendment that abolished the rule on eligibility of players and opened the competition to anyone who might like to play. This was where caution prevailed although, in fact, the proposal was only defeated by five votes to four with three abstentions.

'Thursley's proposal that the eligibility law be replaced by one that called for a club to merely register all its players met with a curiously indecisive vote of 3 3 with six abstentions. Instead, delegates approved (seven in favour) the less adventurous amendment proposed by both Grayshott and Lindford that made players eligible if they lived within eight miles of the club's ground,' the newspaper continued.

The *Herald* stated that the rest of the eligibility rule remained unchanged, which meant that a player, not conforming to the distance radius, but who was born in the parish of the club, or who had had long family residence in the parish, or who had previously played for the club under the same qualifications, would be eligible.

It was also agreed, on Lindford's proposal, that the number of players who could be specially registered by a club be increased from three to five, and that two of these registrations could be service personnel, provided they lived within eight miles of the club.

The idea of a working party was put forward by Grayshott, and was greeted with enthusiasm by the delegates. The newspaper report said: 'This think-tank might well hold the key to the future well-being of the competition. Its members, one from each of the 12 clubs, will discuss the direction the I'Anson/Miller is to take over the next few crucial years, with a particular view to expansion, taking in other clubs, including Second and

Aldershot West Indians made an impression in their short stay in the competitions. Here, Norman Disney congratulates Danny Stephenson and his team on being runners-up in Division Two, and gaining promotion, in 1992. They also reached the final of the Stevens Cup in that season.

Third XIs, and forming divisions. Members will have a brief to approach other leagues and compare problems.'

On the matter of a rules committee, the *Herald* reported that it would comprise an I'Anson umpire, two seasoned players and a steward under the chairmanship of the president, Norman Disney. Andrew Fry said: 'We get in an awful tangle with the rules (at the annual meeting). It's not easy for 12 delegates to get agreement. But a rules committee, composed of knowledgeable men, could meet as necessary and present their ideas for the ADM to consider.'

Following that meeting, the work was largely achieved behind the scenes and perhaps the first sign of progress came with an announcement in the *Herald* on 8 September 1989, stating that the competitions invited new clubs to apply to play in 1991, and that non-village sides were welcome to show an interest. At the annual meeting that year Badshot Lea and Farncombe Wanderers were the first newcomers to be elected. They were members of the Farnham League and Wey Valley League respectively.

So the 1990 season became the last to be played to the traditional league formats for the I'Anson Cup and the Miller Cup. The working party was investigating ways of restructuring the competitions for 1991, and the implication of two I'Anson Cup divisions, with promotion and relegation, was not lost on clubs. Final league positions could well decide in which division a club started the 1991 season.

Three more clubs applied to join in the early months of 1990 and an extraordinary meeting was held at Lindford on 12 July. As a result, Tongham, Dogmersfield 2nd XI and Rowledge 3rd XI, who had all been members of the Farnham League, were elected and approval was given to make two divisions in the I'Anson Cup. The top eight finishers in 1990 would go into Division One, and the bottom four plus the five newcomers into Division Two, with a trophy donated by Herald Newspapers. A subsidiary knockout competition would be introduced to make up the fixtures deficit.

Pat Hastings (Thursley), the chairman of the working party, reporting on behalf of a committee comprising Ken Williams (Grayshott), Chris Barnes (Churt), Roger Vernier (Headley), Pat Murphy (Elstead) and John Stuttaford (Frensham), urged delegates to hear the arguments and vote without preconceived ideas. 'There is no way back now – we've already accepted the need for major change,' he said. The likely strength of the newcomers might disappoint some member clubs who wanted to see the standard improved sooner rather than later, he said, but there was a general feeling that 'we have got to start somewhere'. The voting for each of the applicants was: Rowledge 9-1 (Headley opposed), Dogmersfield 11-0 and Tongham 8-0.

Chris Barnes voiced what was perhaps a general fear, reported the *Herald*, when he said that club second or third teams might demean the competition. Ian Webster (Tilford) had similar reservations. However, most delegates seemed pleased that Rowledge were returning after four years, and Alan Prior said that with the pending demise of the Farnham League the club were looking for a respectable competition for their third team. Matches would be played at Alexandra Park, Bordon.

The Farnham League situation had also persuaded Dogmersfield and Tongham to apply for membership, but Dogmersfield's delegate, Giles Smeath, revealed that the club's two sides were selected on travel considerations and the First XI would remain in the Hampshire League. However, there was a strong youth policy and the club required a better standard locally for the second team. Robert Evans said Tongham did not have the use of their own ground, which needed major restorative work, and had been using army pitches at Aldershot, but planned to move to Frimley.

All this was entirely new territory for the competitions, and there was a requirement for cool heads among the older brigade as the important annual meeting of 1990 approached. The *Herald* called it an historic meeting for the 90-year-old competitions. 'Not only were the final touches put to the new two-division I'Anson Cup format, but a 40 overs a side knockout tournament was also announced, to be sponsored by Hollands Sports of Farnham,' it reported.

The article continued: 'The other main business concerned a new set of I'Anson rules, presented as a fait accompli by the joint working party/rules committee, set up last year to investigate ways of extending and improving the competition.

'Norman Disney, the president, told a packed meeting in blunt terms that he expected the rules to be approved without too much discussion. Only small amendments could be made on the night. Suggestions for major amendments would have to be made at the next ADM.

'There was some criticism, but delegates recognised the need to accept the findings of their appointed working party who have worked tirelessly over several months to come up with the best format,' the newspaper reported.

The new rules limited I'Anson Cup matches to one innings per side. The start time was brought forward to 2pm and games would be of a maximum of 90 overs, with the side batting first having a maximum of 45 overs. Teams would no longer be able to gain 10 points for a second innings win, and Pat Hastings said this would prevent a team winning the cup having won fewer games than the second placed team (champions Frensham had won fewer games than Tilford in 1990). John Storey (Frensham) regretted this, saying that it was not unusual for village games to finish early. Frensham also regretted there was not more incentive for a team to bat first, with only one point available to a beaten team which had batted out its 45 overs.

Miller Cup matches would also be of 90 overs but there continued to be provision for second innings points.

The *Herald* went on: 'It was a significant ADM and members will perhaps now be aware of the enormous amount of work behind the radical shake-up that has produced two divisions and a supplementary knockout competition. The fixture list, when complete, will have left more than a few grey hairs.'

In his report, secretary Graham Collyer mentioned the work of working party chairman Pat Hastings and also Roger Vernier, who had negotiated the sponsorship deal with Hollands Sports, which was to last for three years. David Hollands, who traded at the Ridgway crossroads in Farnham, told the meeting that the 18 I'Anson Cup teams would play in four groups throughout the season. The group winners would meet for the Hollands Sports Cup, and the runners-up for the Hollands Sports Shield. All matches would be 40 overs a side with bowlers limited to nine overs each. The sponsorship provided match balls, trophies, medals, pennants and man of the match awards.

Graham Collyer said: 'The success of the new-look competition is in your hands. We need to make the new clubs feel welcome and wanted. With one exception (Rowledge), they have much to learn about us. We are taking a big step – much bigger than any we have taken in the 90 years of our existence – and we should all remember that what we are doing is with the full backing of the membership, for it was a unanimous decision of all 12 clubs at a SDM that gave the go-ahead to reorganisation.

'May I urge everyone to give the new format a fair go next year and, if problems arise, as I expect they will, to keep your steward informed so that modifications for 1992 can be considered by the rules committee.'

Five new clubs had already been admitted, and Aldershot West Indians, runners-up in the Farnham League the previous season, brought the membership to 18, having won a ballot against Farnham 4th XI.

At this stage, Chris Barnes, a member of the working party, questioned the strategy behind the recruitment of new clubs. He said that Churt were disappointed with the way clubs had been approached and suggested that new teams should have been of the same standard as the stronger I'Anson members. He found little support, however.

Point made!

IN general, the new format in 1991 caused few problems, but there was an amusing incident in a match between Frensham and Elstead well into the season. Elstead batted first and, reported the *Herald*, 'abandoned the run chase and played out John Storey's last over for a maiden. Puzzled spectators were informed of the new law, but it was obvious that Elstead had given up any hope of winning at that stage'.

Elstead ended their 45 overs on 115-9, thereby guaranteeing one point in the event of them losing, which duly happened in the 32nd over of Frensham's reply.

The report drew a response from the Elstead captain, John Moore, in the following week's sports pages. He said: 'Elstead had been restricted by very tight bowling and some nondescript batting to just 115 runs after 44 overs – hardly a massive target on a ground the size of Frensham's. With nine wickets down, the only sensible option to a captain who knew the rules was to put one point in the bank. The "puzzled spectator" was, in fact, the captain of Frensham who admitted to not knowing the rule in question.' He added: 'I might also point out that Frensham, batting first at Elstead on 27 April, also batted out their full 45 overs to finish at 112-9, thereby securing one point!'

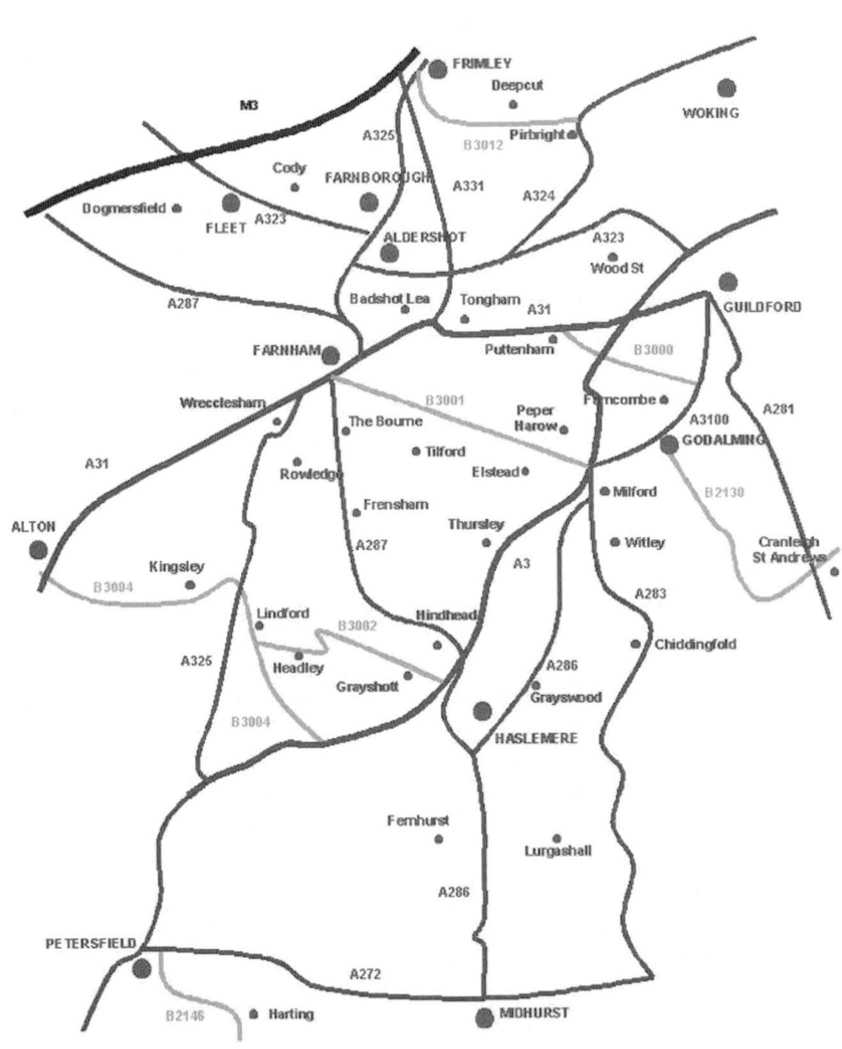

Breaking with tradition

THE thirst for change was unquenchable and at the annual meeting in 1991 it was agreed to launch a third division by 15 votes to the three of The Bourne, Tilford and Churt. Thus, the Miller Cup, which had been donated in 1922 to foster Second XI and junior cricket, became the trophy for the third division. It was a significant move, and a huge break with what had come to be regarded as untouchable territory.

However, in this period of change, there had to be some unpalatable decisions and so the teams which finished first and second in the last season of the traditional Miller Cup competition, The Bourne II and Tilford II, were promoted to Division Two, whose top two sides, Thursley and Wrecclesham, were elevated to Division One, with only Lindford being relegated from the top flight, thereby making 10 teams in each division.

Pat Hastings said: 'We have first to get the right structure to attract new clubs. Twelve teams in each I'Anson division made it difficult to add new clubs – the season is long enough as it is.' Ideally, he said, the working party wanted two divisions for the Miller Cup and if, in the near future, a new club wanted to enter two teams, the competition would have to accommodate them. Ken Williams said the proposal was 'a stepping stone towards four divisions'. They were responding to criticism by Chris Barnes who, said the *Herald*, had the unanimous backing of his club's annual meeting in saying the proposal was not the right way forward. 'The only way is to attract new clubs, and the only way to do that is to open your borders. The I'Anson Cup should go out and sell itself, and sell its history. We feel it is a great pity to abolish the Miller Cup.'

The accompanying amendment, that a club could not have two teams in the same division, brought more impassioned protests from Churt, with strong support from other delegates. Donald Limon urged delegates to 'throw this rule out. It is most unfair to division three teams who cannot win promotion and others who have nothing to play for'. Ian Webster said that for 70 years Second XIs had had no prospect of promotion, and he assured the audience that Tilford seconds would be going all out to win Division Two. Frank Lunt suggested that the amendment be put back until the next annual meeting, but president Norman Disney, who, said the *Herald*, 'chaired the meeting with stern authority', ruled that clubs were entitled to submit different proposals to the rules committee as the change would only take effect from 1993. The vote in favour of the amendment was 12-6.

The ultimate aim of having four divisions came another step nearer when eight new teams were accepted at the annual meeting in 1992. The working party set up in March 1989 would continue its five-year programme and a fourth division was anticipated for the 1994 season. This was also the time for administrative change with a management committee replacing the traditional body of stewards.

Graham Collyer said: 'The few critics have continued to snipe, but the officers who work so hard for the competitions have stuck to their guns and have the overwhelming support of the majority of clubs and their members. The proof of the pudding is in the fact that we are attracting new clubs – three are here tonight. The word must continue to be spread that we can offer a more than decent standard of cricket without the need to spend time and money in excess in travelling to away games. This, in my judgment, is a very strong selling point as we face up to yet another year of economic difficulties.'

The new clubs, Crown Taverners (based at Minley), Frimchett (from Frimley Green) and Witley, the latter two with two teams each, had grown weary of the travel involved in their leagues. Crown brought only their Second XI and left their firsts in the Hampshire League, a decision that was never entirely accepted by the majority of the league membership. (Crown eventually went back to the Hampshire League at the end of the 2000 season.) Dogmersfield, on the other hand, moved their first team from the Hampshire League to join their seconds, and Aldershot West Indians and Frensham entered their Second and Third XIs respectively.

The *Herald* said the applications of Frimchett and Witley were a boost to the working party after the disappointment of losing Churt to the Fullers Surrey League in 1993. Frimchett competed in Hampshire Division Three in 1992, Dogmersfield were in Hampshire Division Five and Witley were in Division One of the Wey Valley League.

The defection of Churt concerned Tilford, whose chairman, Clive Thursby, said following a committee meeting: 'The local character of the I'Anson and Miller leagues is important to a club such as ours. We value the long-standing and generally good-natured rivalry with neighbouring villages. Although we voted against this year's change in the structure of the competition, we hope there will be further attempts to enhance the appeal of these leagues.'

The new clubs for 1993 meant that Wrecclesham and Whitehill were spared relegation from Division One, and Lindford, Aldershot West Indians and Farncombe Wanderers were promoted from Division Two.

By September 1993 there were two more new clubs and four extra teams. Tongham had their second team elected at a SDM, along with the cricketing section of Guildford and Godalming Rugby Football Club, and DERA (formerly RAE Farnborough and now known as Cody in recognition of the pioneer aviator Samuel Cody) and The Bourne Third XI joined at the annual meeting. There was also a change to the points system with none now awarded for a defeat but two extra for teams which batted first and won and one for a team which batted first and secured the faster scoring rate in a draw.

Norman Disney, who had overseen so many changes in a short time, was called upon to make a casting vote after delegates had voted 9-9 on the rules committee's motion that the side batting first had the option of continuing for 48 of the 90 overs, instead of the 45 as previously. He came down in favour. 'It will encourage teams to bat first and open the way for a side batting second to gain a winning draw,' said Pat Hastings. 'It will give a captain who wins the toss a decision to make,' added Pat Murphy.

Graham Collyer said the new management committee had been a success. Attendance had been excellent and the committee had shown its teeth by issuing fines when breaches of the rules had been proved.

Two more divisions

THE next move came on 22 August 1994, when the working party agreed to recommend to the annual meeting that a fourth division be formed for 1995. This was made necessary by the mid-year election of Milford (two teams) and Badshot Lea's wish to enter a Second XI. At least one other club was expected to apply before the deadline.

And on 1 October, the annual meeting approved unanimously a fourth division with Badshot Lea II and Chiddingfold being elected. It was agreed that the top two divisions would each be of 12 teams, Division Three would comprise 10 (including Milford), with each playing the other twice and four teams meeting for a third time, and Division Four would have eight teams playing each other three times (there was an aggravation when Aldershot West Indians withdrew their Second XI after the fixtures had been published). The Farnham branch of the Association of Cricket Umpires and Statisticians donated a shield to be known as the Bob Burchett Trophy, in recognition of the former Elstead player, steward and umpire who was a vice-president until his death in 1999.

At the same meeting Wood Street's two teams were elected for the 1996 season, once they had left the Wey Valley League.

Graham Collyer said: 'I can foresee many more clubs coming in, but problems tend to increase the bigger you get.' The management committee would continue to take a stern line on matters of indiscipline, he added. 'The image of the competitions can be tarnished when members step out of line. The clubs must take charge themselves when individuals behave badly, and not always leave it to us.'

Hindhead returned to the competitions after an absence of 65 years, and Robert Dobson (kneeling third from the left) led them to the Division Three title in 1997.

The rule governing eligibility was tightened so that applications by players who had played in another league in the same year could not be considered after 1 August. Peter Chuter (Thursley) attempted unsuccessfully to persuade delegates to vote out the rule that offered bonus points to sides batting first and winning. Clubs were not fully in favour of a fourth point for a faster scoring draw, if batting first, because it left little distinction between it and a six-point win, he argued.

Hindhead, Peper Harow, Chiddingfold II and DERA II were admitted at the 1995 annual meeting. Hindhead, from the Wey Valley League, had been I'Anson Cup members from 1913-31, when their ground was behind the Royal Huts Hotel on the A3. Peper Harow, with one of the oldest grounds in the country, were making their first venture into league cricket. But there was disappointment when Aldershot West Indians, who had brought a new dimension to the competitions, dropped out.

In 1996, Fernhurst were admitted at a mid-year meeting, and Grayswood came in at the annual meeting, having beaten Whitehill, who wished to return three years after withdrawing, 23-1 in a ballot. The current Grayswood club is at least the third to operate in the village, the first was in the competitions between the wars, and the second inquired about membership in 1972 but did not proceed.

This was the year in which the management committee asked all clubs to complete a questionnaire in an attempt to discover the likes and dislikes of the membership. All but three of the then 27 clubs took part in the survey and the results helped to shape the thinking of the administrators. Two points came across loud and clear: that there was unanimous accord with what had been achieved, and that there was practically no support for limited overs cricket.

The competitions had grown beyond the wildest dreams of anyone connected with them and, as the secretary had warned, they presented some difficult problems. In September 1997, the management committee issued clubs with a threat of expulsion if fees for 1998 remained unpaid at the annual meeting. The committee had voted to take this action in view of the fact that many clubs had not conformed to the rules and kept to the deadline for entries. Whereas in the past a blind eye was turned on defaulting clubs, it was now decided that this practice could not be allowed to continue. The management committee was prepared to make an example of clubs that continued to ignore the rules.

Peper Harow play on one of the oldest grounds in the country but were new to league cricket when they joined the competitions in 1996. Steve Bradley's team won Division Four in 1999, the shield being presented by Cyril Crawte.

The 1997 meeting was at times difficult and prickly, with procedure for rule amendments called into question. That old thorn in the side, the substantive amendment proposed on the night, came under particular scrutiny, and Peter Chuter (Thursley) told officers they were in a 'state of confusion' as they considered alterations to one agenda item. The main debate concerned the management committee's proposal for a new set of points. Norman Disney agreed to an amendment increasing the proposed eight points for a win to 12, but this proved to be the final straw for Mr Chuter, who was already annoyed that the committee had failed to meet during the year to discuss procedure on these matters. 'You can't put this to the meeting,' he told Mr Disney. 'This is not a little amendment, it is a big one and delegates haven't had the chance to go back to their club members to discuss it. This meeting should only vote on agenda items.' He had the support of most delegates and the chairman was forced to revert to the original proposal, which offered winning sides batting first an extra two points on the existing eight, and a maximum five for a draw. It was passed 18-8.

A management committee proposal to limit promotion to the top two teams, if eligible, was carried. This followed an absurd situation in 1997 when Lindford II, who finished fourth in Division Three 35 points behind the winners, went up because two of the sides above them were ineligible.

On the composition front, there were some downs. In 1997, DERA withdrew their Second XI after the fixtures had been compiled, and Guildford and Godalming resigned at the end of the season. However, there were still clubs waiting to come in. For 1998, Cranleigh St Andrews, of the Arun Valley League, took G&G's place in Division Three, having been attracted by the prospect of promotion and relegation spicing up their cricket. They also brought their Second XI in, as did Hindhead, and Pirbright made a leap into league cricket for the first time.

This was now beginning to make the management committee think a fifth division was necessary, and the next moves confirmed it. Puttenham's two sides were elected in mid-1998, although the move to admit the Fullers League club was not unanimous. Perhaps clubs were beginning to be nervous about the rapid growth of the competitions. Puttenham came in on a 21-2 vote, with five abstentions,

The story behind this photograph epitomises, perhaps, the spirit of the I'Anson Cup – most definitely when it was competed for in its traditional format. It is a reflection of a different, less frenetic age. Taken in 1961, it shows two Tilford stalwarts celebrating another championship for the club on the Green. Col. G.A. Campbell was Tilford's president and Bob Morris the oldest living former player. At Col. Campbell's funeral service in 1965, the vicar of Tilford, the Revd A.E. Jaggs, said there was a copy of the photograph on the president's writing table. 'It is the I'Anson Cup, and it is full of champagne,' the vicar said. 'There he is enjoying himself to the full. It is a great victory the cricket club has just accomplished. It is a great cup, a magnificent vintage in the cup, and he is with his friends.' Bob Morris, who first played for Tilford in the 19th century, died at Christmas 1965, and the Herald *reported: 'His old world courtesy and gentle manner made him a welcome figure wherever he went. Whenever Tilford won the cup no one was more pleased, and he never missed an important match.' At his funeral service, the vicar said: 'Some people don't trouble to make friends; some try hard to do so. Bob didn't seem to worry much either way. By some extraordinary ability he seemed always to have plenty. He was as much part of the Tilford scene as the Barley Mow, the Oak, the river with its bridge, or the cricket that he loved so well.'*

but this was a clear enough mandate not to concern the management committee unduly. The club's first team went into in Division Three.

The fifth division was introduced at the annual meeting in 1998 and life president Norman Disney donated a trophy. Peper Harow introduced their second XI and Rowledge their fourth team. The latter's admission was opposed by Tilford, whose delegate said: 'They turned their back on the competitions and now they seem to be asking the I'Anson to act as a nursery for their senior sides.' The sentiment found no public support, and Rowledge assured the meeting that the club remained fully committed to the competitions and would field a balance of youth and senior players in their I'Anson teams.

One year later, Fernhurst and Frensham brought their Second and Fourth XIs into the competitions, and in 2000, as Crown Taverners II and Rowledge III left for Hampshire, Grayshott, the village where the league had started 100 years earlier, introduced a third team. Finally, in our centenary year, Harting and Lurgashall, both new to league cricket, were admitted and brought the number of West Sussex clubs to three.

These additions clearly indicate the success of the enlarged league, which is enabling more players to enjoy the cut and thrust of competitive cricket, something that had been the preserve of too few only a decade earlier.

So, the story of how the oldest continuous village cricket league in the country was born again is complete. Those who had faith in what they were trying to achieve in 1989 have been rewarded with a vibrant competition. There are clubs within the catchment area still to commit themselves to league cricket; still more competing in other leagues. There is no reason why the I'Anson Cup Competitions should not continue to expand, but perhaps it would be wise to slow the rate of growth for a year or two.

The final decision, as always, will be taken by the membership. This wonderful competition belongs to the clubs. They, as always, will decide who will join them.

Records section

The following records have been compiled from reports submitted by clubs to the *Herald* over the last 50 years. Where appropriate, statistics from the first 50 years of the competitions have been included in these lists.

I'Anson Cup

The century-makers

There were 138 centuries scored in the I'Anson Cup from 1901-90, after which the competition was replaced by the divisional format. Eddie Gulliver (Grayshott) recorded seven between 1982-86, and Bill Poulter hit six for The Bourne between 1935-51.

Leading individual scores (*denotes home team):

182 S. Dickinson, *Frensham v Headley, 1 Sept 1990
151 no R. White, Headley v *Frensham, 11 May 1957
144 P. Offord, *Whitehill v The Bourne, 16 July 1983
142 no K. Brown, *Churt v Thursley, 8 June 1974
141 no J. Voller, *The Bourne v Shottermill, 29 June 1947
139 no N. Higgins, Churt v *Elstead, 5 June 1982
139 no E. Gulliver, Grayshott v *Rowledge, 5 May 1984
136 F. Kenward, Headley v *Tilford, 20 May 1950
135 no N. Randall, Kingsley v *The Bourne, 1 Sept 1990
133 no P. Kingshott, Grayshott v Whitehill, 1935
130 no J.G. Storey, Frensham v *The Bourne, 21 May 1988
131 no B. Harms, *Headley v The Bourne, 27 Aug 1983
129 J.H. Storey, *Frensham v Churt, 16 Sept 1989
127 no F. Kenward, Headley v *Tilford, 23 July 1938
127 W. Poulter, The Bourne v Grayshott, 1940
126 no J. Bennington, *Frensham v Thursley, 11 May 1974
126 no B. Karn, *Thursley v Elstead, 6 Sept 1975
126 no P.A. Slinger, *Tilford v Churt, 25 July 1987
126 E. Gulliver, Grayshott v *Frensham, 10 Aug 1985
123 no J.H. Storey, *Frensham v Whitehill, 9 Aug 1986
123 E. Johnson, Grayshott v Headley, 1908
123 J.H. Storey, *Frensham v The Bourne, 18 June 1983
121 D. Gooda, *Frensham v Grayshott, 17 Sept 1988
120 no A. Christmas, *Thursley v Lindford, 18 Sept 1982
120 no K. Tilson, Thursley v *Lindford, 19 May 1984
120 J. Gould, *Tilford v Whitehill, 18 July 1970

A.H. Hartwright of Lynchmere scored centuries in three successive league matches in 1907 – 108 not out v Grayshott (when he also took 8-39), 102 v The Bourne, and 116 not out v Shottermill. In that season he scored more than 500 runs in nine innings for an average of 73.85 (a figure believed to have been beaten only once, when Sheoghan Dickinson, like Hartwright, a headmaster, averaged 78.5 in his record-breaking 1984 season when he scored 1,020 runs in 22 innings). Hartwright also took 63 wickets at under four runs each in 1907. Remarkably, the century against The Bourne in 1907 was the only one scored against that club in the I'Anson Cup until Alan Rooney's 107 not out for Headley in 1978. Rooney is the only other player to have scored successive I'Anson Cup centuries (two in 1978).

Record partnerships

(* denotes home team)

First wicket

200 K. Tilson (86) and M. Taylor (101no), *Thursley v Lindford, 5 Sept 1981
197 R. Simpson (102no) and N. Dunbar (92), *Rowledge v Thursley, 7 July 1984
186 no R. Woods (81no) and G. Phipps (100no), *Thursley v Frensham, 20 Sept 1975
175 E. Gulliver (97) and G. Baker (76), Grayshott v *Thursley, 11 June 1983
174 no L. Knight (85no) and A. Young (69no), *The Bourne v Tilford, 11 July 1970
173 L. Knight (96) and C. Fry (66no), The Bourne v *Elstead, 22 May 1982
172 no K. Brown (142no) and P. Allatt (26no), *Churt v Thursley, 8 June 1974
158 no H.C. Bicknell (104no) and J. Voller (50no), *The Bourne v Headley, 17 Aug 1947
157 no L. Knight (90no) and J. Tanner (62no) *The Bourne v Wrecclesham, 8 May 1965
156 no P. Offord (105no) and E. Gulliver (46no), Grayshott v *Wrecclesham, 21 June 1980
152 no E. Gulliver (101no) and B. Gainey (38no), Grayshott v *Elstead, 19 June 1982
150 D. Gooda (121no) and J.G. Storey (70), *Frensham v Grayshott, 17 Sept 1988

Second wicket

176 A. Rooney (89) and J. Burton (76), *Headley v Tilford, 22 July 1978
174 E. Gulliver (126) and R. Lake (62no), Grayshott v *Frensham, 10 Aug 1985

171 no J. Burton (106no) and A. Rooney (61no), *Headley v Grayshott, 18 Aug 1979
166 B. Turner (103no) and M. Pryce (76), Tilford v *Thursley, 17 June 1978
165 G. Bullock (80) and P. Clapham (84), *Grayshott v Frensham, 29 Aug 1964
164 P. Chuter (76) and S. Dickinson (90no), Frensham v *Whitehill, 11 May 1985
164 C. Cobbett (93) and R. Grogut (69), *Tilford v Wrecclesham, 24 June 1989
163 C. Bayman (109no) and A. Pride (78), Elstead v *Whitehill, 27 April 1985
156 A. Hook (95) and N. Dunbar (63), Rowledge v *Grayshott, 21 July 1984
154 M. Absolom (81) and G. Baker (64), *Grayshott v Lindford, 9 July 1988
150 K. Tilson (120no) and M. Sterio (54), Thursley v *Lindford, 19 May 1984

Third wicket

145 no R. Lewis (70no) and M. Bond (82no), *Headley v Thursley, 5 May 1984
143 no C. Cobbett (67no) and P.A. Slinger (67no) *Tilford v The Bourne, 25 Aug 1990
139 A. Davidson (100ret) and A. Karn (44), Elstead v *Rowledge, 5 July 1952
137 M. Pryce (86no) and R. Grogut (55), *Tilford v Headley, 9 Aug 1980
134 M. Hoy (72) and M. Farnfield (67), The Bourne v *Frensham, 5 June 1982
131no S. Dickinson (72no) and D. Gooda (52no), *Frensham v Kingsley, 19 Sept 1987
131 M. Taylor (80) and W. Brown (54), Thursley v *Elstead, 16 Sept 1978

Fourth wicket

157 R. White (151no) and F. Kenward (52), Headley v *Frensham, 11 May 1957
155 P.J. Slinger (98) and W. Hill (56no), *Churt v Thursley, 2 May 1981
147 no D.B. Whittaker (102no) and A. Karn (39no), Elstead v *Whitehill, 31 May 1952
137 A. Rooney (87) and A. Shipton (66no), *Headley v Lindford, 10 Sept 1977
139 P.J. Slinger (117no) and P. Allatt (60), Churt v *Rowledge, 8 May 1982
132 J. Yates (100) and A. Prior (61), Rowledge v *Elstead, 23 Sept 1978
130 no J.G. Storey (104no) and S. Dickinson (37no), Frensham v *The Bourne, 21 May 1988

Fifth wicket

130+ R. Lake (66) and C. Dodge (78no), Grayshott v *Tilford, 7 July 1984
128 R.Shergold (60) and F. Kenward (77no), *Headley v Thursley, 8 July 1967
125 J.H. Storey (65no) and S. Dickinson (54), *Frensham v Headley, 12 Aug 1989
125 J. Daddo (90) and S. Gooding (50), Churt v *The Bourne, 4 Aug 1990
115 J. Yates (79no) and A. Prior (50), *Rowledge v Churt, 22 July 1978
110 P. Clapham (56) and C. Dodge (59no), *Grayshott v Elstead, 8 Aug 1964 (Clapham also 6-3)

Sixth wicket

150no J. Turbard (100no) and R. Poulter (52no), *Frensham v Lindford, 22 May 1982
130no C. Yates (103no) and A. Prior (39no), Rowledge v *Frensham, 21 June 1980
129 F. Kenward (90) and J. Burton (36no), Headley v *Rowledge, 12 Aug 1961
120 no J. Warner (58no) and M. Merrett (53no), Tilford v *The Bourne, 8 Sept 1951
111 no J. West (65no) and R. Goff (52no), *Whitehill v Binsted, 23 June 1951 (West also 8-4)
111 D. Wells (58) and J. Ramsey (53), *Frensham v Headley, 18 Aug 1956
c110no B. Dewey (114no) and B. Oakley (28no), *Whitehill v Grayshott, 24 June 1978

Seventh wicket

122 no W. Dale (62no) and F. Bargery (45no), Shottermill v Hindhead, July 1920
114 R. Gabriel (50no) and J. Eames (32), *Churt v Frensham, 11 Aug 1961
105 D. Rook (75) and J. Girling (44), *Wrecclesham v Thursley, 11 Aug 1984
103 P. Clapham (40) and G. Tribe (51no), *Grayshott v Thursley, 17 Sept 1977
99 no N. Heaton (42no) and R. McSorley (52no), Churt v *The Bourne, 30 Aug 1980
97 no A. Phipps (44no) and D. Bevan (55no), Thursley v *Lindford, 23 Aug 1986
94 F. Kenward (73no) and M. Bate (48), Headley v *Thursley, 24 Aug 1968
91 D. Longman (41no) and D. Cooper (50), *Whitehill v The Bourne, 18 Aug 1973

Eighth wicket

106 W. Chuter (71) and D. Wells (55), *Frensham v Tilford, 6 August 1955

98 D. Harris (74) and D. Limon (19), Churt v *Frensham, 31 July 1965

90 no J. Brookes (60no) and P. Copplestone (36no), Elstead v *Whitehill, 15 Sept 1990

83 D. Cooper (78) and N. Smith (35), Whitehill v *The Bourne, 19 May 1984

76 no M. Hill (56no) and M. Henderson (17), Lindford v *Frensham, 31 July 1976

67 R. Clarke (49) and J. Turbard (21no), *Frensham v Elstead, 15 June 1985

63 G. Baker (78) and H. Williams, Grayshott v *Thursley, 24 May 1969

62 no D. Yeomans (30no) and D. Rust (21no), *Kingsley v Frensham, 4 July 1987

Ninth wicket

106 no D. Wells (78no) and G. Harris (37no), The Bourne v Thursley, 29 August 1959 (in 37 minutes)

91 A. Young (69no) and C. LeClercq (38), *The Bourne v Rowledge, 27 July 1963

86 G. Pither (51) and C. Plant (40), *Frensham v Churt, 31 July 1965

80 D. Tailford (45) and D. Collins (46), *Lindford v Elstead, 18 Aug 1984

63 no W. Poulter (24no) and D. Wells (38no), *The Bourne v Wrecclesham, 17 Aug 1963

61 R. Birch (31no) and J. Watson (8no), Churt v *Whitehill, 26 May 1990 (plus 21 extras)

60 no R. Piper (51no) and J. Peach (30no), *Rowledge v Elstead, 15 June 1957

Tenth wicket

84 L. Goodchild (47) and W. Wells (31no), The Bourne v Headley, 1937

70 B. Francis (63) and W. Thomson (7no), *Kingsley v Churt, May 28, 1988

62 Unknown and Unknown, Lindford v *Thursley, Aug 23, 1980

61 B. Druce (34) and C. Grant (24no), *Elstead v Rowledge, Sept 23, 1978

60 W. Spooner (25) and B. Rapley (34no), Thursley v *The Bourne, Sept 19, 1987

51 S. Connor (36no) and C. Grant (15), *Elstead v Headley, June 24, 1978

Best bowling

10-19 L. Crumplin, Rowledge v Wrecclesham, 14 July 1962
10-21 A. Peach, Rowledge v Frensham, 5 Aug 1961
10-33 W. Loader, Grayshott v Frensham, 26 May 1956
10-38 J. Eddey, Tilford v Shottermill, 13 Aug 1949
10-48 D. Knight, The Bourne v Whitehill, 30 April 1983

9-6 E. Parratt, Rowledge v Headley, 1947
9-8 C. Reffold, Elstead v The Bourne, 21 May 1955
9-9 D. Piper, Rowledge v Wrecclesham, 5 June 1965
9-11 J.H. Storey, Rowledge v Tilford, 17 Aug 1963
9-11 G. Tribe, Grayshott v Wrecclesham, 1 Aug 1964
9-14 W.W. Stratford, Blackmoor v Grayshott, 1906
9-15 J. Stonard, The Bourne v Rowledge, 2 May 1953
9-16 R. Miles, Tilford v Headley, 16 Aug 1958
9-16 D. Williams, Thursley v Tilford, 2 Sept 1978
9-16 C. Yates, Rowledge v Wrecclesham, 9 June 1984
9-19 F. Kenward, Headley v Elstead, 24 May 1964
9-20 N. Hume, Tilford v Whitehill, 21 Aug 1976
9-20 M. Sobey, Grayshott v The Bourne, 29 July 1989
9-21 R. Bridger, Tilford v Rowledge, 4 June 1955
9-21 D. Piper, Rowledge v Frensham, 24 Aug 1963
9-21 T. Jeffery, Frensham v Thursley, 16 Aug 1980
9-22 D. Piper, Rowledge v Elstead, 15 Aug 1959
9-23 W. Chuter, Frensham v Headley, 27 June 1953
9-24 D. Harris, Churt v Wrecclesham, 8 Aug 1964
9-25 F. Kenward, Headley v Churt, 11 June 1949
9-25 L. Crumplin, Rowledge v Binsted, 18 Aug 1951
9-26 M. Smith, Lindford v Elstead, 8 May 1982
9-27 M. Ricketts, The Bourne v Frensham, 1 June 1963
9-28 J. Partridge, The Bourne v Headley, 21 July 1962
9-28 G. Iliffe, Frensham v Tilford, 8 Aug 1964
9-29 D. Harris, Grayshott v Frensham, 15 June 1968
9-31 F. Kenward, Headley v Tilford, 7 May 1949
9-31 M. Harris, Churt v Elstead, 4 Sept 1976 (4 in 4 to clinch title)
9-32 M. Cane, Wrecclesham v Churt, 27 July 1963
9-32 J. Pilbeam, Thursley v Whitehill, 30 April 1988
9-33 D. Piper, Rowledge v Wrecclesham, 15 Aug 1964
9-34 H. Hubbard, Shottermill v Elstead, 27 Aug 1960
9-35 J.H. Storey, Frensham v Kingsley, 13 May 1989
9-37 L. Crumplin, Rowledge v Grayshott, 7 July 1951
9-37 R. Bridger, Tilford v Whitehill, 5 July 1952
9-39 F. Kenward, Headley v Rowledge, 30 June 1962
9-39 T. Laskey, Tilford v The Bourne, 28 Aug 1965
9-40 D. Harris, Churt v Grayshott, 5 June 1965
9-40 D. Piper, Rowledge v Thursley, 2 Sept 1967
9-41 D. Edgar, Churt v The Bourne, 19 June 1965
9-45 J. Peach, Rowledge v Thursley, 29 June 1957
9-45 N. Martyn, Tilford v Wrecclesham, 2 June 1990
9-47 G. Williamson, Wrecclesham v The Bourne, 13 June 1953
9-49 G. Pither, Frensham v Churt, 7 July 1973
9-49 J.H. Storey, Frensham v Headley, 20 Sept 1986
9-53 B. Turner, Tilford v Headley, 14 July 1979
9-55 T. Jeffery, Frensham v Thursley, 29 July 1972
9-75 A. Chalkley, Whitehill v Churt, 7 July 1979

Best aggregates

17-39 D. Piper (8-18 and 9-21), Rowledge v Frensham, 24 Aug 1963

15-51 D. Harris (9-29 and 6-22), Grayshott v Frensham, 15 June 1968

15-62 N. Martyn (6-17 and 9-45), Tilford v Wrecclesham, 2 June 1990

15-81 J.H. Storey (6-32 and 9-49), Frensham v Headley, 20 Sept 1986

Hat-tricks

The number of times the hat-trick was achieved in the I'Anson Cup is unknown, but the double hat-trick – six wickets in six consecutive deliveries – was recorded only once. Walter Dale, long-time skipper of Shottermill, brought a Churt innings in 1937 to a spectacular close when he dismissed the last six batsmen in quick succession.

A list of hat-tricks in the first 50 years of the competition is not included in *A Cup for Cricket* and, apart from Dale's achievement, only those of Tom Wisdom, of Thursley, Hector Chappell (Binsted), who took two in an innings, and Jim Eddey, of Tilford, are recorded. Wisdom took the first five Headley second innings wickets with as many deliveries in 1925, and Headley lost another four wickets in getting the 17 runs needed to win. Eddey took three in a row in 1938 when Churt were dismissed for five.

In the period 1951-90, after which the I'Anson Cup league was replaced by divisions, there were 92 hat-tricks recorded. The competitions' greatest all-rounder, Frank Kenward, claimed six from 1951-75 (plus one in the Miller Cup in 1973), Churt's paceman Mike Harris had four from 1960-76 (and two in the Miller Cup in 1956 and 1986), and there were three each for Cliff Parratt (Rowledge), 1954-59, George Pilbeam (Elstead and Thursley), 1964-70, and Geoff Tribe (Grayshott), 1963-78 (plus one in the Miller Cup in 1957).

From 1951-90, there were five occasions when a bowler took four wickets in four balls: Fred Aldred, for Frensham v Elstead in 1966; Ron Cowie, for Headley v Wrecclesham in 1961; Mike Harris, for Churt v Thursley in 1974 (and five in six deliveries) and v Elstead in 1976 (which clinched the title); and Geoff Tribe, for Grayshott v Wrecclesham in 1964 (and six in eight deliveries). Tim Laskey took four wickets in five balls for Thursley v Tilford (his former club) in 1970.

On only one occasion between 1951-90 did two bowlers both take a hat-trick in the same innings: Bob White and Frank Kenward, for Headley v Churt in 1956. The only other time in that period when there were two hat-tricks in an I'Anson Cup match was in 1952: Don Wells for Frensham and John Stonard for The Bourne.

Miller Cup

The century-makers

There were 55 centuries recorded in the Miller Cup from 1950-91, after which the competition was replaced. One was noted in *A Cup of Cricket*. Paul Hammond (Frensham II) and Russ White (Tilford II) both hit three in 1990-91. Paddy Connor (Elstead II) and Mike Thompson (Tilford II) scored two successive centuries in 1981 and 1986 respectively.

Leading individual scores (* denotes home team):

151 P. Hammond, *Frensham II v Churt II, 5 May 1990

149 A. Gardner, *Wrecclesham II v Kingsley II, 25 Aug 1990

127 no P. Whiddett, *Rowledge II v Frensham II, 27 May 1967

127 no R. White, *Tilford II v Whitehill II, 8 June 1991

121 no P. Hammond, *Frensham II v Churt II, 22 June 1991

118 no P. Smith, *Thursley II v Tilford II, 7 June 1975

116 N. Thorne, *Churt II and Tilford II, 8 Sept 1979

115 M. Thompson, *Tilford II v Lindford II, 6 Sept 1986

113 no P. Connor, Elstead II v Rowledge II, 5 Sept 1981

113 M. Norris, *Churt II v Kingsley II, 10 June 1989

111 no D. Harfield, Wrecclesham II v *Headley II, 21 Sept 1985

110 no M. Jordan, *Shottermill v Headley II, 12 July 1958

110 no D. Piper, *Thursley II v Elstead II, 7 July 1973

110 no M. Harris, Elstead II v *Wrecclesham II, 12 July 1986

110 P. Hubbard, Elstead II v *Thursley II, 7 Sept 1991

Record partnerships

(* denotes home team)

First wicket

168 no D. Hounsham (109no) and M. Thompson (52no), Tilford II v *Thursley II, 30 June 1990

165 B. Karn (82no) and R. Linegar (93), *Thursley II v Headley II, 17 July 1976

158 K. White (61) and P. Connor (81), Elstead II v *The Bourne II, 29 Aug 1981

153 no M. Thompson (100no) and T. Fry (47no), Tilford II v *Frensham II, 30 Aug 1986

153 no M. Norris (103no) and A. Mayson (45no), Churt II v *Headley II, 15 Aug 1987

143 R. Hooker (73) and H. Ford (61 no), *Tilford II v Alexandra Park II, 7 May 1955

143 M. Harris (110no) and M. Stock (53), Elstead II v *Wrecclesham II, 12 July 1986

Second wicket

222 P. Hammond (151) and Mi Fathers (79no), *Frensham II v Churt II, 5 May 1990

159 no R. Blain (56no) and H. Edmunds (84no), *Elstead II v Headley II, 16 July 1988

151 no C. Jenkins (88no) and C. Watkins (50no), *Wrecclesham v Whitehill II, 23 June 1951

150 no I. Whalley (70no) and R. Berkeley (70no), *Churt II v Elstead II, 18 June 1983

146 L. Knight (73) and R. Pharo (97no), *The Bourne II v Rowledge II, 15 May 1971

143 R. Bowden (78) and G. Poulter (70), *The Bourne II v Wrecclesham II, 13 May 1987

131 no M. White (68no) and A. Coates (60no), *Tilford II v Kingsley II, 16 Sept 1989

120 A. Hockey (85) and R. Morant (51no), *Wrecclesham II v Thursley II, 11 May 1985

105 no R. Ward (99no) and N. May (34no), The Bourne II v *Elstead II, 19 July 1986

103 P. Grout (60) and D. Read (46), Grayshott II v *Frensham II, 18 Sept 1982

Third wicket

156 J. Crutcher (109no) and R. Elgie (60), *Elstead II v Lindford II, 3 August 1991

147 M. Thompson (115) and M. Russell (62), *Tilford II v Lindford II, 6 Sept 1986

141 D. Fry (66) and R. White (95), *Tilford II v Lindford II, 14 Sept 1991

136 no S. Huckle (76no) and M. Farnfield (69no), The Bourne II v *Churt II, 2 July 1977

134 A. Thomas (73no) and C. McIntosh (66), The Bourne II v Churt II, 30 June 1979

132 R. Vaughan (93) and C. Cooper (39), Tilford II v *Thursley II, 4 May 1985

130 A. Cheeseman (84) and D. Hardy (50), Thursley II v *The Bourne II, 19 July 1975

128 no B. Karn (84no) and A. Tilson (40no), *Thursley v The Bourne II, 23 June 1956

c125 N. Higgins (74) and T. Hill (72), Churt II v *Frensham II, 22 Aug 1981

125 A. Ralph (63no) and N. May (50), *The Bourne II v Grayshott II, 12 May 1984

Ken Warner: 16-year-old bowler took 78 wickets for The Bourne's victoriou[s] Miller Cup team in 1954. He enjoyed a successful career with the club.

Fourth wicket

146 no M. Jones (70no) and A. Liddicott (86no), *Frensham II v Tilford II, 14 June 1980

131 R. Vaughan (59) and D. Wilkinson (85), Tilford II v *Frensham II, 11 Aug 1990

124 no R. Bridger (87no) and D. Robinson (46no), *Tilford II v Rowledge II, 4 July 1959

121 D. Briggs (52no) and M. Poulter (66), *The Bourne II v Elstead II, 21 Aug 1976

Fifth wicket

138 no D. Mattock (109no) and D. Whillians (50no), Headley II v *Whitehill II, 18 June 1983

100 K. Warner (70) and J. Voller (45), The Bourne II v *Headley II, 10 July 1954 (Ken Warner, aged 16, also took 8-8 in 7.4 overs)

Sixth wicket

111 no J. Tanner (79no) and S. Cooper (34no), *The Bourne II v Churt II, 24 April 1982

101 no A. Gardner (98no) and I. Ferguson (39no), *Wrecclesham II v Whitehill II, 25 June 1982

93 J. Turbard (41no) and A. Newman (55), *Frensham II v Tilford II, 22 July 1989

89 R. Gray (86) and J. Stonard (29), *Rowledge II v The Bourne II, 7 July 1979

89 R. Elgie (61) and G. Crutcher (43), Elstead II v *Thursley II, 28 April 1990

71 D. Dean (82no) and T. Ricketts (25), *Whitehill II v Wrecclesham II, 29 Aug 1981

70 R. Baverstock (65no) and L. Attwood (38), *Rowledge II v Churt II, 27 May 1961

70 A. Messenger (77) and G. Banks (23), Thursley II v *Wrecclesham II, 24 April 1982

Seventh wicket

120 no P. Whiddett (127no) and P. Sturgess (30no), *Rowledge II v Frensham II, 27 May 1967

110 no R. Kemp (57no) and J. Thorne (68no), Churt II v *Rowledge II, 24 July 1982

100 no A. Chalkley and M. Herzke, Whitehill II v *Headley, 14 June 1969

85 no W. Hill (31no) and A. Hall (49no), Churt II v *Whitehill II, 18 Aug 1984

83 A. Liddicott (74no) and C. Obert (24), Frensham II v *Rowledge II, 11 Aug 1984

75 G. Poulter (49no) and C. LeClercq (27), The Bourne II v *Whitehill II, 30 April 1983

74 D. Knight (54) and J. Smithee (22no), *The Bourne II v Tilford II, 25 August 1990

70 no P. Cornwell (46no) and S. King (24no), *Whitehill II v Kingsley, 18 May 1985

Eighth wicket

126 no R. Moorcroft (66no) and A. Gardiner (67no), *Frensham II v Elstead II, 27 April 1991

118 R. Collins (83) and J. Eddey (29), *Tilford II v Wrecclesham II, 2 July 1955

91 C. Crawte (37no) and N. Crawley (58), *Wrecclesham II v Tilford II, 28 Aug 1976

89 J. Arnold (60) and G. Knight (33), *The Bourne II v Frensham II, 26 May 1962

72 J. Thorne (37no) and J. Watson (41), Churt II v *Rowledge II, 28 Aug 1976

Ninth wicket

107 J. Greenough (78) and F. Osgood (42), Oakhanger v *Binsted II, 23 June 1951

69 no R. Burberry (53no) and A. Lang (24no), *Churt II v Rowledge II, 14 July 1979

60 A. Messenger (44no) and G. Reffold (11), *Thursley II v Rowledge II, 26 July 1975

56 R. Taphouse (44) and L. Robins (50), *Frensham II v Elstead II, 2 May 1970

55 C. Crawley (31no) and I. Thorpe (11), *Wrecclesham II v The Bourne II, 28 July 1979 (Ian Thorpe, aged 14, also took 8-24)

52 M. Foster (40no) and P. Moran (27), *Tilford II v Churt II, 27 May 1978

51 J. Yeomans (25) and M. Stoker (26), *Tilford II v Elstead II, 22 April 1989

Tenth wicket

93 no M. Hudson and A. Lang, Churt II v *Rowledge II, 8 Aug 1981

87 J. Ingrams (55) and J. Sanders (33no), Grayshott II v *Rowledge II, 15 Sept 1979

55 no P. Gladstone (50no) and S. Warner (6no), Churt II v *Whitehill II, 17 July 1982

54 C. Thursby (33) and P. Withers (18no), Tilford II v *Frensham II, 22 July 1989

c50 T. Elliott (48no) and L. Hunter-Jones (23), Tilford II v *Whitehill II, 22 May 1982

50 J. Stuttaford (59no) and R. Bridger (30), *Frensham II v Tilford II, 27 June 1981

49 A. Ralph (30no) and S. Golding (18), *The Bourne II v Tilford II, 3 Aug 1957

47 H. Williams (39no) and A. Partridge (16), Wrecclesham II v *Tilford II, 11 July 1981

47 A. Cheeseman (42no) and L. Bonsey (6), *Thursley II v The Bourne II, 1 May 1982

44 F. Swan (28no) and A.F. Swan (14), *Rowledge II v Frensham II, 3 Aug 1957

43 R. Riddett (27no) and R. Kemp (23no), *Churt II v Thursley II, 18 July 1981

40 no J. Arnold (50no) and F. Cordier (3no), The Bourne II v *Grayshott II, 22 June 1963

Best bowling

10-3 A. Yeomans, Kingsley v Frensham II, 4 Aug 1951

10-17 M. Cane, Rowledge II v Elstead II, 9 July 1966

10-23 D. Harfield, Wrecclesham II v Kingsley II, 5 July 1986

10-24 P. Crow, Rowledge II v Frensham II, 1 Aug 1959

10-24 A. King, Whitehill II v Wrecclesham II, 21 June 1964

10-25 K. Huckle, The Bourne II v Headley II, 1963

10-30 S.J. Coombes, Headley II v Shottermill II, 13 Aug 1938

10-34 F. Courtnage, Whitehill II v Headley II, 30 July 1932

10-50 A. Liddicott, Frensham II v Rowledge II, 31 July 1982

9-2 B. Guest, Rowledge II v Grayshott II, 19 May 1962

9-4 R. Petter, Grayshott II v Frensham II, 15 August 1959

9-4 E. Hammond, Tilford II v Elstead II, 1 June 1963

9-5 R. Miles, Tilford II v Wrecclesham II, 2 July 1955

9-7 M. Jeffery, Elstead II v Frensham II, 10 July 1961

9-8 E.R. Parratt, Rowledge II v Lindford, 14 July 1951

9-8 D. Winchester, Grayshott II v Frensham II, 11 July 1953

9-8 M. Jeffery, Frensham II v Shottermill II, 23 July 1960

9-9 F. Parratt, The Bourne II v Elstead II, 30 Aug 1952

9-9 R. Bailey, Grayshott II v Whitehill II, 11 Aug 1973
9-10 S. Butcher, Whitehill II v Tilford II, Aug 1931
9-10 A. Liddicott, Frensham II v Whitehill II, 2 Aug 1980
9-11 G. Williamson, Wrecclesham v Oakhanger, 28 July 1951
9-12 S. Butcher, Whitehill II v Tilford II, Aug 1931
9-13 D. Pilbeam, Elstead II v Kingsley, 3 Aug 1968
9-14 G. Iliffe, Frensham II v Rowledge II, 4 June 1966
9-14 A. Partridge, Wrecclesham II v Grayshott II, 4 July 1981
9-14 A. Lang, Churt II v Thursley II, 20 Sept 1986
9-15 J. Burton, Lindford v Rowledge II, 22 June 1957
9-16 F. Drake, Wrecclesham II v Elstead II, 3 June 1961
9-17 P. Taylor, Churt II v Grayshott II, 17 May 1952
9-17 D. Paine, Tilford II v Elstead II, 27 April 1968
9-18 H. Clark, Wrecclesham II v Frensham II, 1 Aug 1953
9-18 B. Silver, Rowledge II v Frensham II, 27 May 1967
9-18 A. Gardner, Wrecclesham II v Headley II, 8 Sept 1990
9-19 A. Peach, Rowledge II v Grayshott II, 9 June 1973
9-20 R. Anderson, Whitehill II v Elstead II, 28 April 1979
9-20 J. Dunbar, Rowledge II v Elstead II, 20 June 1981
9-21 R. Walker, Thursley II v Kingsley, 27 April 1985
9-23 J. Burton, Lindford v Tilford II, 11 Aug 1956
9-23 R. Lawry, Grayshott II v The Bourne II, 19 June 1971
9-24 A. King, Whitehill II v Kingsley, 10 Aug 1968
9-25 N. Martyn, Tilford II v Whitehill II, 25 July 1981
9-26 B. Guest, Rowledge II v Wrecclesham II, 26 May 1962
9-26 R. Frommholz, The Bourne II v Wrecclesham II, 20 May 1972
9-27 R. Burchett, Elstead II v The Bourne II, 18 July 1953
9-27 A. Lang, Churt II v Rowledge II, 27 April 1985
9-28 R. Skilton, Elstead II v Kingsley, 2 July 1977
9-29 R. Earle, Alexandra Park v Frensham II, 22 July 1967
9-29 R. Frommholz, The Bourne II v Rowledge II, 16 May 1970
9-30 A.Peach, Rowledge II v Whitehill II, 15 July 1978
9-31 R. Stevens, Kingsley II v Headley II, 27 June 1987
9-32 A.F. Swan, Rowledge II v Shottermill II, 27 June 1959
9-32 D. Robinson, Tilford II v Thursley II, 15 June 1974
9-33 F. Kenward, Headley II v Kingsley, 23 Aug 1973
9-35 J. Eddey, Tilford II v Headley II, 13 August 1955
9-37 P. Taylor, Tilford II v Frensham II, 15 July 1972
9-40 A. Peach, Rowledge II v Frensham II, 6 Sept 1975
9-40 J. Girling, Wrecclesham II v Tilford II, 2 June 1984
9-44 M. Sheldon, Whitehill II v Wrecclesham II, 25 May 1985
9-58 S. Lomas, Tilford II v Frensham II, 27 June 1981
9-59 E. Dolton, Elstead II v Whitehill, 11 June 1965
9-59 C. Cobbold, Whitehill II v Churt II, 21 June 1986

Best aggregates

18-22 (9-10 and 9-12) S. Butcher, Whitehill II v Tilford II, Aug 1931 (hat-trick in both innings)
17-36 (9-25 and 8-11) N. Martyn, Tilford II v Whitehill II, 25 July 1981
16-26 (7-8 and 9-18) B. Silver, Rowledge II v Frensham II, 27 May 1967
16-18 (8-5 and 8-3) J. Burton, Lindford v Wrecclesham II, 8 June 1957
15-13 (10-3 and 5-10) A. Yeomans, Kingsley v Frensham II, 4 Aug 1951
15-31 (8-15 and 7-16) A. Peach, Rowledge II v Whitehill II, 31 May 1975
15-47 (9-26 and 6-21) R. Frommholz, The Bourne II v Wrecclesham II, 20 May 1972
15-26 (8-8 and 7-19) C. Hudson, Kingsley v Elstead II, 14 June 1975

Most wickets in season

156 J. Eddey (Tilford II) in 1956 (322.4 overs 72 maidens 884 runs)
147 J. Kneller (Alexandra Park) in 1964

Near misses

R. Earle took 9-29 for Alexandra Park v Frensham II on 22 July 1967, including a hat-trick, and he dropped a return catch that would have given him all 10.

R. Frommholz also took 9-29 for The Bourne II v Rowledge II on 16 May 1970, and he held the catch that secured the tenth wicket.

Hat-tricks

There were 118 recorded hat-tricks in the Miller Cup between 1951 and 1991, after which the format of the competition, first started in 1922, was changed. A list does not exist for the period up to and including 1950, and the only reference to Miller Cup hat-tricks in *A Cup for Cricket* concerns the match at Tilford in 1931 when there were three, including one in each innings by S. Butcher, aged 17, of Whitehill II. His match details are included in the Miller Cup bowling records in this section.

There is only one instance of a bowler taking two Miller Cup hat-tricks in an innings: Basil Payne bowled all his victims in his pair of triple strikes and finished with figures of 8-3 for Elstead II against Headley II in 1954. Payne was a fast right-arm bowler who normally appeared for the first team, and later played for Headley.

Two bowlers took five wickets in six successive deliveries:

David Williams, for Thursley II v Elstead II in 1984, and Mike Harris, for Elstead II v Lindford II in 1986.

Denis Emery included five wickets in seven balls when taking 6-6 for Kingsley against Frensham II in 1983.

The following took four wickets in as many deliveries: Robin Frommholz, for The Bourne II v Frensham II in 1974; Martin Herzke, for Whitehill II v Rowledge II in 1975; Nick Cowell, for Tilford II v The Bourne II in 1981; Alan Lang, for Churt II v Grayshott II in 1984; and Ron Woodward, for Whitehill II v Lindford II in 1990.

The youngest player to take a Miller Cup hat-trick was P. Stock, aged 14, for Frensham II v Grayshott II in 1965. Derek Winchester was 16 when he took wickets with his first three deliveries for Grayshott II v Tilford II in 1953.

Ray ('Patsy') Bridger included a hat-trick in his 7-5 for Tilford II v Frensham II in 1959 and went on to claim 10-15 in the match, in which he also scored his maiden century.

Division One

The century-makers

There have been 103 scores of 100 or more recorded in Division One, including the 206no by Matt Barnes for Badshot Lea at The Bourne in 1995, the second highest individual score in the history of the competitions. Alan Rooney (Headley) has scored eight centuries, Neil Mansbridge (Witley) and Andy Wheble (Grayshott) seven, and Gavin May (Headley) six.

Rooney's two I'Anson Cup centuries in 1978 put him on top of the all-time list of centurions with 10, ahead of the nine of Michael Allen (Fernhurst), all scored in Divisions Two, Three and Four, and the eight of Wheble (who scored one ton in Division Three), Frensham's Paul Hammond, scored in Divisions Two, Three and Four plus the Miller Cup, and John Morrison (Wood Street), all in Division Two.

Leading individual scores (* denotes home team):

206 no M. Barnes, Badshot Lea v *The Bourne, 22 April 1995
164 A. Wheble, Grayshott v *Witley, 25 July 1998
153 N. Mansbridge, *Witley v Frimchett, 12 June 1999
151 no N. Mansbridge, *Witley v Headley, 22 Aug 1998
132 no S. Hobson, Witley v *Frensham, 15 Aug 1998
130 no M. Barnes, Tilford v *Frensham, 18 Aug 2001
127 A. White, *Witley v Tilford, 18 Sept 1999
126 no D. Gooda, *Frensham v Farncombe W, 30 April 1994
125 K. Tilson, Thursley v *Dogmersfield, 18 May 1996
124 S. Dickinson, *Frensham v Thursley, 20 Aug 1994
122 F. Iqbal, Aldershot West Indians v *Frimchett, 24 June 1995
123 no A. Rooney, *Headley v Wrecclesham, 25 July 1992
123 no A. Cook, *Headley v Lindford, 8 July 1995
123 A. Sale, *The Bourne v Elstead, 30 July 1994
120 no R. Baker, Grayshott v *Frimchett, 16 July 1994
120 no M. Barnes, *Tilford v Dogmersfield, 30 June 2001
120 A. White, Witley v *Chiddingfold, 15 May 1999

Record partnerships

(* denotes home team)

First wicket

200 no Gav May (106no) and A. Rooney (92no), *Headley v Elstead, 15 Aug 1992
195 A. Cook (117) and A. Rooney (89no), *Headley v Milford, 26 June 1999
176 no J. Wright (92no) and W. Jones (64no), Chiddingfold v *Lindford, 10 July 1999
173 A. Wheble (164) and A. Lang (54), Grayshott v *Witley, 25 July 1998
165 A. Rooney (74) and Gav May (83), *Headley v AWI, 20 May 1995
163 M. Allen (83) and D. Foster (64), *Fernhurst v Dogmersfield, 2 Sept 2000
159 M. Absolom (46) and R. Baker (120no), Grayshott v *Frimchett, 16 July 1994
158 A. Rooney (108) and A. Cook (58), Headley v *Farncombe W, 4 Sept 1993
157 D. Jervis (95no) and J. Hunt (76), Tilford v *Dogmersfield, 22 July 2000
156 G. Boardman (96) and S. Cosier (83), *Lindford v Kingsley, 29 June 1996
156 N. Mansbridge (153) and M. White (47), *Witley v Frimchett, 12 June 1999
154 no M. Potter (102no) and R. Chuter (36no), *Frensham v Lindford, 27 May 1995
151 no D. Gooda (91no) and R. Chuter (36no), *Frensham v Lindford, 23 July 1994
c150 N. Smith (112) and A. Rooney (53no), Whitehill v *Headley, 27 April 1991
148 no A. Wheble (108no) and M. Absolom (32no), *Grayshott v Badshot Lea, 29 April 1995
146 K. Tilson (125) and P. Chuter (58), Thursley v *Dogmersfield, 18 May 1996
145 R. Chuter (63) and B. Maxwell (84), *Frensham v Headley, 6 Sept 1997
144 A. Cook (123no) and J. Huntley (63), *Headley v Lindford, 8 July 1995

142 Gav May (89) and A. Cook (64), Headley v *Thursley, 15 June 1996

c140 A. White (120) and N. Mansbridge (63), Witley v *Chiddingfold, 15 May 1999

139 T. Robinson (89) and T. Champneys (42), Puttenham v *Frensham, 21 July 2001

138 N. Hales (105no) and A. Sale (68), *The Bourne v Dogmersfield, 21 July 2001

137 B. Maxwell (102) and R. Chuter (51), Frensham v *Badshot Lea, 30 Aug 1997

132 A. Rooney (77) and A. Cook (72no), *Headley v Witley, 4 Sept 1999

130 M. Murphy (58) and D. Hindle (80), Dogmersfield v *Elstead, 30 April 1994

130 G. Gwilliam (40) and K. Goodship (70), *Milford v Tilford, 15 May 1999

Second wicket

193 Gav May (114) and A. Clarke (65), *Headley v The Bourne, 29 April 1995

184 M. Barnes (206no) and P. Hillman (43), Badshot Lea v *The Bourne, 22 April 1995

180 A. Rooney (110no) and Gav May (69no), Headley v *Thursley, 24 April 1993

170 A. White (71) and S. Hobson (103), *Witley v Frimchett, 18 July 1998

168 no J. Hall (48no) and K. Waller (105no), *Lindford v Milford, 27 June 1998

153 A. Cook (104no) and R. Vernier (63) *Headley v Whitehill, 27 April 1991

153 M. Barnes (101) and D. Pover (75), *Badshot Lea v Lindford, 10 June 1995

152 A. White (127) and M. White (43), *Witley v Tilford, 18 Sept 1999

151 D. Hounsham (86) and M. Pryce (72), *Tilford v AWI, 31 July 1993

c150no M. Gilbert (76no) and N. Phipps (72no), Thursley v *Headley, 13 June 1992

145 no D. Gooda (85no) and J. Willson (80no), *Frensham v Dogmersfield, 18 June 1994

141 A. Wheble (88) and R. Baker (66no), Grayshott v *Wrecclesham, 14 Aug 1993

Third wicket

165no P.Marden (109no) and I. Spicer (75no), Chiddingfold v *Frensham, 9 June 2001

158 T. Robinson (64) and J. Crouch (81), *Puttenham v Elstead, 22 Sept 2001

155 A. Reid (97) and A. Hicks (72), *Frimchett v Headley, 17 May 1997

c150no G. Gwilliam (111no) and S. Rowe (76no), *Milford v Frimchett, 8 Aug 1998

153 Gav May (102no) and A. Clarke, Headley v *Witley, 24 June 1995

152 no R. Baker (92no) and R. Lake (80no), *Grayshott v Farncombe W, 23 July 1994

149 A. Reid (102) and R. Garfoot (52), *Frimchett v The Bourne, 3 Sept 1994

c140no R. Baker (79no) and S. Whitley (76no), Grayshott v *Headley, 27 June 1992

c140no N. Mansbridge (151no) and I. Munday (49no), *Witley v Headley, 22 Aug 1998

c140 N. Poulter (76) and G. Poulter (95), *The Bourne v Milford, 8 May 1999

c140 A. White (81no) and N. Mansbridge (97), Witley v *Frimchett, 24 July 1999

131 Gav May (64) and A. Clarke (65), *Headley v AWI, 11 Sept 1993

Fourth wicket

170 J. Hall (100no) and G. Rose (77), Lindford v *Fernhurst, 9 June 2001

149 I. Munday (91) and A. White (52), *Witley v Frensham, 20 May 1995

131 N. Mansbridge (115no) and A. White (29), *Witley v Dogmersfield, 17 May 1997

129 F. Iqbal (87) and N. Chaudry (68), AWI v *Headley, 18 June 1994

126 M. Potter (97) and P. Harrison (66), *Frensham v Puttenham, 21 July 2001

123 A. White (114) and D. Penny (53), *Witley v Frimchett, 7 Sept 1996

Fifth wicket

143 M. West (86) and N. Ralph (71), *Fernhurst v Elstead, 28 July 2001

133 S. Crawte (67) and H. Macdonald (57), *Tilford v Frensham, 2 June 2001

130 no P. Harrison (71no) and L. Pattison (58no), Frensham v *Headley, 20 June 1998

119 no S. Dickinson (68no) and T. Falkiner (62no), *Frensham v Tilford, 2 July 1994

117 J. Willson (90no) and J. Kohler (41), Frensham v *Elstead, 15 Sept 2001

114 T. Caston (109) and J. Kohler (68), Frensham v *Witley, 13 July 1996

109 H. Macdonald (109no) and P.A. Slinger (53), *Tilford v Kingsley, 11 May 1996

108 no N. Mansbridge (91no) and M. Rawlinson (38no), *Witley v The Bourne, 13 May 1995

107 S. Crawte (68) and D. Jervis (46), *Tilford v Headley, 19 July 1997

103 no J.Willson (51no) and J. Kohler (70no), *Frensham v The Bourne, 27 July 1996

100+ G. Poulter (97) and A. Culham (29), The Bourne v *Frensham, 1 July 1995

c100no S. Dickinson (105no) and N. Thayer (17no), *Frensham v AWI, 6 Aug 1994

100 no J. Stressing (55no) and D. Kelley (40no), *Thursley v AWI, 8 May 1993

100 P.A. Slinger (47) and C. Cobbett (48), *Tilford v Witley, 17 Aug 1996

Sixth wicket

117 no S. Lewis-Jones (58no) and G. Badland (58no), *Headley v Milford, 15 Aug 1998

108 A. Culham (55) and P. Watson (61), The Bourne v *Grayshott, 2 July 1994

100+ G. Poulter (63) and J De Vlieg (50), The Bourne v *Witley, 3 July 1999

100 D. Banner (97no) and C. Gamble (47), Badshot Lea v *Tilford, 10 Aug 1996

100 J. Taylor (102) and P. Hillman (24), *Badshot Lea v Dogmersfield, 24 May 1997

86 T. Falkiner (71) and M. Potter (27), *Frensham v Grayshott, 1 Sept 2001

Seventh wicket

100+ M. Carson (55) and L. Duemke (65), *Frimchett v Lindford, 17 July 1999

88 J. Ingrams (67) and R. Eastment (42), *Fernhurst v Headley, 4 Aug 2001

86 no M. Barnes (52no) and J. Commerford (35no), *Tilford v Milford, 17 July 1999

c85 S. Crawte (58) and C. Purdie (46no), Tilford v *Witley, 3 May 1997

82 no O. Caston (38no) and R. Chuter (38no), *Frensham v Tongham, 18 Sept 1999

79 no N. Thayer (67no) and S. Hopper (43no), Frensham v *Headley, 30 July 1994

79 no J. Evans (66no) and S. Meyer (20no), *Tongham v Milford, 22 Aug 1998

79 G. Badland (65no) and G. Downham (19), *Headley v The Bourne, 28 July 2001

77 T. Falkiner (58) and R. Doran (43), *Frensham v Elstead, 5 July 1997

74 A. Culham (83no) and R. Ward (25), The Bourne v *Tilford, 4 Sept 1993

74 P.A. Slinger (51) and M. White (21), Tilford v *Frensham, 2 July 1994

63 no R. Holden (21no) and G. Badland (41no), *Headley v AWI, 18 June 1994

62 M. Pike (28) and J. Hall (27), Lindford v *Elstead, 15 June 1991

61 no I. Munday (39no) and K. Ritchie (32no), Witley v *Lindford, 30 Aug 1997

Eighth wicket

114 M. Cartwright (100no) and I. Hyland (49), *Dogmersfield v Farncombe W, 11 June 1994

93 A. Page (63) and O. Caston (41), Frensham v *Witley, 8 July 2000

86 M. Sobey (60) and D. Schwick (25no), *Grayshott v Tilford, 8 July 2000

82 no P. Harrison (56no) and N. Thayer (24no), *Frensham v Lindford, 29 April 2000

77 A. Jones (39) and J. Fawkes (28no), Witley v *Fernhurst, 8 Sept 2001

72 G. Badland (42no) and M. Hughes (24), *Headley v Milford, 21 Aug 1999

62 M. Sobey (42) and M. Stephens (35), *Grayshott v Milford, 3 July 1999

Ninth wicket

100 M. Slater (75no) and M. Carson (65), Frimchett v *The Bourne, 21 Sept 1996

74 M. Sobey (62no) and L. Conway (33), *Grayshott v Frensham, 2 Aug 1997

64 A. Kelly (67) and L. Watson (22), Witley v *Grayshott, 27 May 1995

63 no R. Cunningham (51no) and A. Potter (26no), Puttenham v *Chiddingfold, 15 Sept 2001

59 no J. Hall (46no) and T. Lee (16no), *Lindford v Headley, 30 May 1998

50 P. Dolan (20no) and A. Stuart (20), Farncombe W v *Grayshott, 28 Aug 1993

47 R. Clarke (50) and R. Moorcroft (18), *Frensham v Lindford, 19 June 1993

Tenth wicket

74 M. Sobey (57) and P. Clapham (25no), Grayshott v *Frensham, 12 June 1999

61 M. Spencer (22) and G. Clarke (27no), Grayshott v *Badshot Lea, 2 Sept 1995

51 no J. Evans (51no) and N. Topliss (6no), *Tongham v Witley, 20 June 1998

c50 D. Hindle (48no) and M. Coleman (41no), *Dogmersfield v Elstead, 16 July 1994

47 no T. Lee (21no) and R. Leonard (15no), *Headley v Lindford, 3 July 1993

47 no P. Bransby (41no) and R. Hindle (15no), Dogmersfield v *Lindford, 1 June 1996

47 no N. Martyn (48no) and R. David (7no), Tilford v *Frensham, 13 Sept 1997

c40 no N. Morris (33no) and S. Emmins (15no), Frimchett v *Frensham, 1 June 1996

Best bowling

Nigel Martyn: three nine-wicket hauls in his league career and Tilford's winning captain in 1998.

9-18 N. Martyn, Tilford v Headley, 23 Sept 2000
9-24 A. Barnes, Tilford v Fernhurst, 1 Sept 2001 (debut)
9-32 G. Coombe, Tilford v Frimchett, 29 Aug 1998
9-33 N. Harman, Chiddingfold v Headley, 13 May 2000
9-44 D. Kelley, Thursley v Frimchett, 31 Aug 1996
8-12 G. Badland, Headley v Thursley, 25 June 1994
8-18 M. Sobey, Grayshott v Lindford, 11 Aug 2001
8-21 A. Rooke, The Bourne v Witley, 6 May 2000
8-25 N. Ayling, Chiddingfold v Dogmersfield, 28 Aug 1999
8-26 N. Martyn, Tilford v Frimchett, 11 Sept 1999
8-26 G. Badland, Headley v Chiddingfold, 22 Sept 2001
8-29 I. Hyland, Dogmersfield v Cranleigh SA, 15 July 2000
8-30 A. Wheble, Grayshott v Wrecclesham, 14 Aug 1993
8-32 D. Coldicott, Frensham v Grayshott, 23 Sept 2000 (title decider)
8-39 R. Moorcroft, Frensham v AWI, 10 June 1995
8-39 S. Meyer, Tongham v Milford, 28 Aug 1999
8-42 P. Bransby, Dogmersfield v Frimchett, 20 Aug 1994
8-46 C. Thomas, Headley v Badshot Lea, 3 May 1997
8-51 R. Clarke, Frensham v Grayshott, 15 Aug 1992
8-66 M. Cartwright, Badshot Lea v The Bourne, 16 Aug 1997
8-72 D. Coldicott, Frensham v Tilford, 9 Sept 2000

Division One hat-tricks: Eight have been recorded, including two by Matt Siebert (The Bourne) in 1991 and 1997. Others have been taken by G. Burt (Lindford), N. Mansbridge (Witley), T. Carrington (Tongham), J. Mitchinson (Chiddingfold), A. Rooke (The Bourne) and N. Martyn (Tilford).

Division Two

The century-makers

There have been 113 scores of 100 or more recorded in Division Two, including the highest score in the history of the competitions, 211no, by John Storey junior for Wrecclesham away to The Bourne II in 1995. In 2001, Jack Harris (Hindhead) scored 203 away to Tilford II and 103 the following Saturday against Wood Street. John Morrison (Wood Street) has scored eight centuries, including three in four innings in 1999. Nick Randall (Kingsley) has scored seven, including two in successive matches in 1994. Mike Eddleston (Tongham) scored two successive tons in 1995.

Leading individual scores (* denotes home team):

211no J.G. Storey, Wrecclesham v *The Bourne II, 1 July 1995
203 J. Harris, Hindhead v *Tilford II, 28 July 2001
160 J.G. Storey, Wrecclesham v *Headley II, 10 June 1995
156 B. Turner, Farncombe W v *Thursley, 16 Aug 1997
144 J. Morrison, Wood Street v *Tilford II, 19 June 1999
140 P. Hammond, *Frensham II v Elstead, 12 Aug 2000
137 T. Hughes, Frensham II v *The Bourne II, 31 Aug 1996
136 no T. Caston, *Frensham II v Kingsley, 14 July 2001
136 M. Allen, *Fernhurst v Thursley, 29 May 1999
131 R. Doran, *Frensham II v Wrecclesham, 21 Sept 1996
130 no A. Wisbey, DERA v *Witley II, 9 Aug 1997
130 no J. Heyworth, *Thursley v Tilford II, 6 June 1998
127 no M. Cartwright, Dogmersfield v *The Bourne II, 1 May 1993
126 no D. Gooda, *Frensham II v Headley II, 20 July 1996
126 N. Diacon, *Elstead v Tilford II, 15 Aug 1998 (and 5-59)

124 no S. Hopper, *Frensham II v Wrecclesham, 3 May 1997
124 no M. Allen, *Fernhurst v Cranleigh SA, 10 July 1999
124 no R. Garfoot, *Badshot Lea v Farncombe W, 3 June 2000
123 J. Morrison, *Wood Street v Hindhead, 3 July 1999
122 no J. Carpenter, Witley II v *Headley II, 22 July 1995 (36 balls)
121 R. White, *Tilford II v Witley II, 3 May 1997
120 R. Doran, *Frensham II v The Bourne II, 25 May 1996

Record partnerships

(* denotes home team)

First wicket

233 R. Doran (126) and D. Gooda (115no), *Frensham II v The Bourne II, 25 May 1996
219 C. Fry (115) and B. Croucher (101no), The Bourne II v *Grayshott II, 16 July 1994
218 J. Hunt (91) and R. White (121), *Tilford II v Witley II, 3 May 1997
202 M. White (117) and A. White (88), Witley v *Frensham II, 9 July 1994
198 J. Harris (203) and M. Shirley-Price (60), Hindhead v *Tilford II, 28 July 2001
175 R. De Caires (112) and A. Baiden (82), Thursley v *Frensham II, 2 June 2001
165 M. Allen (136) and M. West (47), *Fernhurst v Thursley, 29 May 1999
162 G. Gwilliam (87) and B. Green (52), *Milford v Frimchett, 9 Sept 2000
161 J. Heyworth (95) and J. Watts (58), Thursley v *Hindhead, 17 July 1999
153 Y. Senior (67) and R. Samways (84), *Cranleigh SA v Farncombe W, 28 Aug 1999
151 A. White (93) and M. White (84), *Witley v The Bourne II, 3 Sept 1994
151 K. Tilson (52) and J. Heyworth (130no), *Thursley v Tilford II, 6 June 1998
142 R. Garfoot (124no) and P. Hillman (50), *Badshot Lea v Farncombe W, 3 June 2000
149 T. Cartwright (92) and M. Pryce (66), Tilford II v *Thursley, 6 June 1998
138 W. Jones (80no) and J. Webster (79), *Chiddingfold v The Bourne II, 2 Aug 1997
137 J. Goodeve (95no) and M. Jones (41), Kingsley v *Wrecclesham, 23 Aug 1997
135 no R. Samways (57no) and Y. Senior (72no), *Cranleigh SA v Grayswood, 30 June 2001
134 J.H. Storey (67) and K. Bone (83no), *Frensham II v Lindford II, 22 July 1995
134 B. Smithers (95) and J. Pusey (39no), *Witley II v Wrecclesham, 3 Aug 1996
132 K. Bone (73) and A. Page (68), *Frensham II v Tilford II, 17 July 1993
131 M. Pryce (65) and R. Vaughan (65), *Tilford II v Hindhead, 29 Aug 1998
131 R. De Caires (68) and A. Baiden (65), *Thursley v Badshot Lea, 1 Sept 2001
127 no C. Fry (75no) and C. Ray (38no), *The Bourne II v Crown Tavs II, 19 Aug 1995
124 K. Tilson (78) and P. Chuter (48), *Thursley v Kingsley, 8 July 1995

Second wicket

c200no R. Chuter (100no) and S. Hopper (124no), *Frensham II v Wrecclesham 3 May 1997
190+ K. Williams (101) and R. Vernier (96), Headley II v *Tongham, 29 July 1995
190+ R. Vernier (109no) and D. Cook (71), Headley II v *Kingsley, 19 August 1995
164 M. Murphy (45) and M. Cartwright (112), *Dogmersfield v Rowledge III, 17 July 1993
162 D. Vasey (113) and I. Carter (40), Rowledge III v *The Bourne II, 15 May 1993
152 M. Murphy (74) and J. Crutcher (71), *Elstead v Kingsley, 17 July 1999
151 J. Harris (79) and A. Butcher (67), *Hindhead v Badshot Lea, 16 June 2001
c150 D. Richardson (89no) and G. Gwilliam (96), Milford v *Headley II, 7 Sept 1996
149 no C. Cobbett (89no) and T. Cartwright (54no), Tilford II v *DERA, 12 July 1997
146 R. Bowden (64) and B. Croucher (70), The Bourne II v *Tongham, 8 Aug 1992
140 L. Duemke (71) and G. Carson (82), Frimchett v *Kingsley, 29 May 1993
c140 M. Howard (92) and K. Tidey (84), Farncombe W v *Frensham II, 23 Sept 2000
138 K. White (57) and M. Druce (77), Elstead v *The Bourne II, 21 Sept 1996
136 K. White (51) and M. Druce (83), *Elstead v Lindford II, 20 July 1996
135 A. Wisbey (84) and D. Whitehead (68), *DERA v Thursley, 23 Aug 1997
133 L. Duemke (43) and A. Reid (67no), *Frimchett v Rowledge III, 26 June 1993
130 M. Murphy (109no) and K. White (63), Elstead v *Witley II, 15 June 1996

Third wicket

223 no S. Hopper (111no) and R. Doran (101no), *Frensham II v Kingsley, 26 June 1993

186 no N. Randall (100no) and S. Parrott (73no), Kingsley v *Lindford II, 2 Sept 1995
186 G. Howard (69) and J. Morrison (94), Wood Street v *Fernhurst, 31 July 1999
173 N. Randall (113) and M. Jones (90), *Kingsley v Crown Tavs II, 5 August 1995
172 no C. Pay (108no) and S. Kyte (64no), *Hindhead v Frimchett, 15 July 2000
165 J. Morrison (123) and E. Harding (73), *Wood Street v Hindhead, 3 July 1999
162 no M. Pryce (89no) and P. Knight (80no), *Tilford II v Wood Street, 30 May 1998
155 J. Morrison (86) and E. Harding (75), Wood Street v *Kingsley, 17 May 1997
149 C. Pay (89) and G. Harmer (73), *Hindhead v Thursley, 9 Sept 2000
c145 M. Druce (75) and C. Druce (114), Elstead v *The Bourne II, 20 June 1998
142 A. Bowden (41) and J. Renders (88), *Wrecclesham v Kingsley, 6 Aug 1994

Fourth wicket

188 C. Howard (108) and M. Sulley (75no), *Frensham II v Wood Street, 23 Aug 1997
153 R. Gray (81no) and R. Doran (118), *Frensham II v Farncombe W, 4 July 1998
150 no R. Emmerson (74no) and M. Wright (71no), *Crown Tavs II v Hindhead, 29 July 2000
144 J.G. Storey (211no) and G. Collier (28), Wrecclesham v *The Bourne II, 1 July 1995
141 G. Cox (96no) and N. Lyons (58), *Lindford II v Kingsley, 23 May 1998
c130 M. Jones (66) and J. Renders (101no), *Wrecclesham v Crown Tavs II, 18 June 1994
129 R. Cummins (66) and J. Birch (51), Rowledge III v *Frensham II, 29 May 1993
125 no D. Lee (74no) and A. Hockey (51no) *Wrecclesham v Rowledge III, 13 July 1991
125 I. Munday (87) and D. Penny (41), Witley v *Grayshott II, 27 Aug 1994

Fifth wicket

162 no C. Williamson (80no) and I. Mason (69no), *Frensham II v Hindhead, 16 May 1998
156 N. Randall (99) and D. Rust (42), Kingsley v *Frensham II, 26 June 1993
144 no S. Cook (55no) and D. Penny (86no), Witley v *Badshot Lea, 8 May 1993
135 no D. Foster (54no) and N. Ralph (88no), *Fernhurst v Wood Street, 31 July 1999
132 no R. White (88no) and P. Miles (54no), Farncombe W v *Fernhurst, 17 July 1999

Sixth wicket

224 no M. Thompson (106no) and N. Fletcher (103no), *Tilford II v Frensham II, 31 May 1997
c135 C. Howard (84) and T. Falkiner (76), Frensham II v *Milford, 20 July 1996
133 no C. Druce (84no) and M. Murphy (61no), Elstead v *Lindford II, 6 June 1998
128 G. Sampson (75) and D. Sharpling (29), Grayshott II v *Lindford II, 27 May 1995
104 N. Wood (45) and S. Neil (68), *The Bourne II v Kingsley, 30 May 1992
101 J. Morrison (85) and K. Haymon (40), *Wood Street v Cranleigh SA, 23 June 2001

Seventh wicket

104 M. Bailey (95) and S. Bidwell (60), *Farncombe W v Thursley, 19 August 1995
96 no P. Robinson (85no) and P. Butcher (25no), *Badshot Lea v Crown Tavs II, 23 July 1994
71 A. Sale (56) and C. Ray (24), The Bourne II v *Kingsley, 24 April 1993
70 D. Hopkins (39) and M. Pearse (42), *Elstead v Kingsley, 22 Aug 1998
59 no P. Hammond (48no) and R. Sherman (36no), Frensham II v *Cranleigh SA, 4 Aug 2001

Eighth wicket

90 E. Robinson (53) and P. Fathers (31), *Frensham II v Headley II, 24 Sept 1994
86 P.A. Slinger (83no) and J. Newbould (32), *Tilford II v Rowledge III, 7 Aug 1993
81 K. Williams (24no) and K. Ellis (57), *Headley II v Dogmersfield, 18 Sept 1993
80 no A. Partridge (29no) and M. Richardson (51no), *Wrecclesham v Lindford II, 8 July 1995
77 no J. Barnard (62no) and K. Greenslade (18no), Hindhead v *Frensham II, 17 June 2000
c75 M. Bailey (39) and S. Bidwell (44no), Farncombe W v *Tilford II, 27 July 1996
75 P. Francis (38) and C. Jarvis (29), *Lindford v AWI, July 25 1992
66 P. Wood (46no) and D. Hopkinson (41), Witley II v *Frensham II, 13 May 1995
60 R. Gray (24) and A. Gardiner (38), *Frensham II v Chiddingfold, 30 Aug 1997
59 T. Carrington (84no) and J. Wilkinson (16), Tongham v *Badshot Lea, 30 May 1992
59 W. Archer-Burton (51) and D. Knight (18), The Bourne II v *Badshot Lea, 9 July 1994
55 C. Shedd (22) and G. Woodward (28), Kingsley v *Dogmersfield, 5 June 1993

53 G. Woodward (20no) and B. Francis (33), Kingsley v *Fernhurst, 21 Aug 1999
52 C. Andrews (27) and J. Wilkinson (35no), *Tongham v Kingsley, 27 June 1992

Ninth wicket

83 no B. Turner (96no) and B. Dawkins (5no), *Farncombe W v Wrecclesham, 20 Sept 1997
77 M. Stock (75no) and S. Gaylard (18), *Elstead v Wood Street, 26 June 1999
71 M. Handcock (55) and T. Knott (17), *Badshot Lea v Lindford II, 17 July 1993
65 no T. Carrington (84no) and M. Gaines (23no), Tongham v *Badshot Lea, 30 May 1992
52 K. Nutt (25) and C. Grant (26), Elstead v *Milford, 13 July 1996
c50 D. Piper (36) and P. Meek (35no), Rowledge III v *Tilford II, 25 July 1992
47 no G. Woodward (30no) and B. Francis (19no), *Kingsley v Frensham II, 11 Sept 1993
47 C. Andrews (24no) and S. Day (29no), Tongham v *Grayshott II, 5 Aug 1995
45 S. Cooper (23) and B. Francis (18no), *Kingsley v Grayswood, 21 July 2001

Tenth wicket

65 L. Duemke (50) and E. Bacon (11no), *Frimchett v Elstead, 29 July 2000
61 no M. Davis (54no) and F. Lunt (10no), *Lindford II v Thursley, 19 Sept 1998
59 M. Jones (13) and M. Richardson (38no), *Wrecclesham v Tongham, 14 Sept 1996
45 F. Lunt (11) and D. Hudson (25no), *Lindford II v Frensham II, 23 Sept 1995
39 no R. Goldsmith (22no) and C. Boucher (15no), *Cranleigh SA v Milford, 9 June 2001
36 no S. Day (33no) and G.J. Littlefield (3no), Tongham v *Kingsley, 20 May 1995
35 J. Sanders (13no) and B. Cope (24), *Grayshott II v Witley II, 24 June 1995
c35 no G. Hirst (14no) and D. Crane (24no), Lindford II v *The Bourne II, 15 Aug 1998
32 R. Morant (30) and M. Cane (4no), Wrecclesham v *The Bourne II, 6 July 1996

Best bowling

10-21 G. Woodward, Kingsley v The Bourne II, 27 June 1998
9-16 E. Harding, Wood Street v Thursley, 10 June 2000
9-30 D. Stephenson, Aldershot West Indians v Wrecclesham, 11 May 1991
9-42 S. Cooper, Kingsley v Frimchett, 11 Aug 2001
8-14 A. Thomas, Milford v Wood Street, 1 July 2000
8-15 G. Burt, Lindford v Rowledge III, 18 July 1992
8-15 P. Murphy snr, Elstead v Cranleigh SA, 31 July 1999
8-21 J. Hall, Lindford v Badshot Lea, 12 Sept 1992
8-22 D. Stephenson, AWI v Dogmersfield, 15 Aug 1992
8-22 B. Turner, Farncombe W v Elstead, 1 May 1999 (incl hat-trick)
8-24 J. Puttock, Farncombe W v Rowledge III, 11 May 1991
8-26 S. Mitchell, Tilford II v Chiddingfold, 17 May 1997
8-27 D. Knight, The Bourne II v Kingsley, 26 July 1997
8-29 T. Carrington, Tongham v Rowledge III, 9 July 1994
8-29 C. McNally, Kingsley v Puttenham, 17 June 2000
8-30 S. Hook, Cranleigh SA v Kingsley, 25 Aug 2001
8-31 R. Leonard, Headley II v Tilford II, 26 June 1993
8-35 E. Harding, Wood Street v Wrecclesham, 6 Sept 1997
8-35 P. Crouch, Puttenham v Badshot Lea, 1 July 2000 (incl hat-trick)
8-36 S. Barham, DERA v Wrecclesham, 15 June 1996
8-36 J. Mitchinson, Chiddingfold v Wood Street, 20 Sept 1997
8-43 N. Randall, Kingsley v Grayshott II, 25 June 1994
8-43 S. Curran, Lindford II v Farncombe W, 8 May 1999
8-45 A. Barnes, Badshot Lea v Grayshott II, 28 May 1994
8-45 T. Carrington, Tongham v Milford, 31 Aug 1996
8-45 N. Randall, Kingsley v Frensham II, 29 May 1999
8-49 M. Edge, Badshot Lea v Frensham II, 22 May 1999
8-51 J. Etherton, Farncombe W v Dogmersfield, 22 June 1991
8-70 S. Bidwell, Farncombe W v Grayshott II, 12 Aug 1995

Division Two hat-tricks: Fifteen were recorded in seasons 1991-2001. Two were by the Murphy brothers, Patrick and Matthew, playing for Elstead in 1996 and 2000 respectively. In order not to be upstaged, their father, Pat, achieved a hat-trick for Elstead II in Division Four in 1999.

Division Three

The century-makers

There have been 69 centuries scored in Division Three. Several players have scored two, including Graham Sampson (Grayshott II), who recorded tons in successive matches in 1997, and Eddie Smith, aged 16, who hit two consecutively in 2001.

Leading individual scores (* denotes home team):

162 P. Hammond, *Frensham III v Badshot Lea II, 20 Sept 1997
159 D. Osgood, Wrecclesham v *Badshot Lea II, 30 May 1998
155 no M. Netterfield, *Cranleigh SA v Kingsley II, 23 May 1998
154 K. Haymon, *G&G v Frimchett II, 17 June 1995
151 no G. Chapman, *Thursley II v Headley II, 9 May 1998
150 no J. Aubrey, *Headley II v Farncombe W, 26 May 2001
140 no A. Wheble, *Grayshott II v Whitehill II, 23 May 1992
140 no I. White, Wrecclesham v *Kingsley, 30 July 1994
140 N. Grimes, Hindhead v *Milford II, 14 June 1997
140 R. Goddard, Kingsley II v *Frensham III, 14 June 1997
140 K. Smith, Puttenham v *Wrecclesham, 19 June 1999
139 no M. Allen, *Fernhurst v Crown Tavs II, 30 May 1998
139 no E. Smith, Dogmersfield II v *Wrecclesham, 23 June 2001
135 no D. Whitehead, *DERA v Dogmersfield II, 2 Sept 1995
132 R. Young, *Crown Tavs II v Wrecclesham, 4 Sept 1999
129 no A. Champneys, *Puttenham v DERA, 17 July 1999
127 P. Marden, *Chiddingfold II v Crown Tavs II, 8 Aug 1998
125 M. Allen, *Fernhurst v Badshot Lea II, 29 Aug 1998
121 J. Crouch, *Puttenham v Kingsley II, 28 Aug 1999

Record partnerships

(* denotes home team)

First wicket

184 G. Gwilliam (104no) and K. Goodship (101), *Milford v DERA, 19 Aug 1995
183 M. Allen (125) and S. Melrose (81no), *Fernhurst v Badshot Lea II, 29 Aug 1998
174 W. Jones (92) and J. Wright (82), Chiddingfold v *Dogmersfield II, 15 June 1996
174 N. Overend (111) and F. Richards (63), *Crown Tavs II v Chiddingfold II, 20 June 1998
163 J. Tomlinson (114) and T. Fry (34), *Grayshott II v Frimchett II, 7 Sept 1996
160 J. Webster (93) and W. Jones (72), *Chiddingfold v Frimchett II, 13 July 1996
151 no E. Smith (106no) and P. Millerick (38no), *Dogmersfield II v Peper Harow, 30 June 2001
150 D. Stovold (119no) and S. Bradley (51), *Peper Harow v Chiddingfold II, 1 July 2000
148 P. Wood (95) and A. Jones (60), *Witley II v Grayshott II, 5 Sept 1998
146 no G. Beynon (70no) and C. Alder (62no), *G&G v Thursley II, 2 Aug 1997
143 no M. Allen (82no) and M. West (50no), Fernhurst v *Grayshott II, 20 June 1998
139 R. Eynon (101) and A. Lewis (45), Dogmersfield II v *Milford, 17 June 1995
138 P. Bennett (79) and H. Wylie (46), Churt II v *Thursley II, 27 June 1992
133 M. Hoban (106) and D. Sharpe (61), *Lindford II v Kingsley II, 27 Sept 1997
132 A. Thomas (86no) and R. Bowden (59), The Bourne III v *Lindford II, 2 July 1994

Second wicket

252 P. Hammond (162) and I. Mason (113no), *Frensham III v Badshot Lea II, 20 Sept 1997
c175 I. White (140no) and P. Bridger (67), Wrecclesham v *Kingsley, 30 July 1994
168 K.Haymon (154) and C. Mercer (50), *G&G v Frimchett II, 1 June 1995
160 no C. Obert (73no) and M. Whitford (75no), *Frensham III v Wrecclesham II, 14 Aug 1993
145 R. White (100no) and P. Knight (87), *Tilford II v Frimchett II, 13 May 1995
140 no J. Yates (72no) and I. Carter (59no), *Rowledge III v Frensham III, 8 July 1995
135 no P. Wood (61no) and A. Jones (78no), *Witley II v DERA, 17 Sept 1994
134 A. Thomas (89) and S. Barkla (72), Grayswood v *Wrecclesham, 17 June 2000
133 R. Croucher (102no) and J. De Vlieg (67), *The Bourne II v Dogmersfield II, 5 Aug 2000
131 M. Hale (59no) and J. Wright (83), *Chiddingfold v Badshot Lea II, 20 July 1996
130 M. Thompson (117no) and M. Pryce (44), *Tilford II v Frensham III, 17 June 2000

Third wicket

169 R. Young (96no) and M. Wright (47no), *Crown Tavs II v Puttenham, 11 Sept 1999
163 M. Whitford (76) and M. Hooper (83), *Frensham III v The Bourne III, 27 Aug 1994
157 R. Dobson (69) and T. Harrison (67), Hindhead v *Chiddingfold II, 17 May 1997
c150 B. Wood (95) and A. Gardner (78), *Wrecclesham v Frensham III, 9 June 2001
148 B. Fisher (77) and G. Sampson (72no), *Grayshott II v Dogmersfield II, 29 June 1996
133 no W. Jones (63no) and M. Hale (57no), Chiddingfold v *Thursley II, 3 Aug 1996

126 B. Karn (59) and A. Tumber (66no), *Thursley II v AWI II, 24 July 1993
122 D. Hubbard (40) and J. Huntley (91), Headley II v *Frensham III, 2 Aug 1997
120 no P. Hannam (53no) and G. Sampson (56no), Grayshott II v *Lindford II, 1 July 2000
120 J.H. Storey (60) and P. Hammond (93), *Frensham II v Lindford II, 25 July 1992

Fourth wicket
156 A. Grant (79) and S. Rowe (107no), *Milford v DERA, 22 July 1995
147 no G. Sampson (106no) and P. Hannam (52no), Grayshott II v *Kingsley II, 2 Aug 1997
137 A. Johnson (72) and J. Savage (64no), The Bourne II v *Lindford II, 9 Sept 2000
131 no D. Whitehead (135no) and A. Johnson (27no), *DERA v Dogmersfield II, 2 Sept 1995
116 G. Sampson (76no) and A. Lindsey Clark (54), Grayshott II v *Headley II, 3 May 1997

Fifth wicket
136no N. Elisha (90no) and M. Spencer (54no), *Grayshott II v AWI II, 21 Aug 1993
134 no M. Lear (87no) and J. Heyworth (51no), *Thursley II v Dogmersfield II, 14 June 1997
116 B. Karn (56) and B. Harms (68), *Thursley II v Dogmersfield II, 28 Aug 1993
100+ M. Davey (70) and S. Bell (50), Chiddingfold II v *Grayshott II, 7 June 1997
100 T. Hill (50) and W. Wilson (50), Frensham III v *Tongham II, 11 June 1994
c100 J. Ingrams snr (89no) and I. Eden (37no), Fernhurst v *Crown Tavs II, 1 Aug 1998

Sixth wicket
118 C. Andrews (76) and L. Voyce (43), Dogmersfield II v *Farncombe W, 9 June 2001
112 no S. Barkla (83no) and A. Gloak (45no), *Grayswood v Grayshott II, 16 Sept 2000
109 M. Hawtin (50no) and J. Hall (62no), *Lindford II v G&G, 20 Aug 1994
100 P. Marden (64) and S. Thorpe (45), Chiddingfold II v *Wrecclesham, 22 Aug 1998
c85 A. Taylor (58) and M. Patterson (54no), Churt II v *Elstead II, 25 July 1992
84 M. Champion (40) and P. Senior (38), The Bourne III v *Witley II, 25 June 1994
84 I. Spicer (68) and N. Ayling (27no), Chiddingfold v *Grayshott II, 8 June 1996
80 J. Robertson (51no) and T. Hughes (31), *Frensham III v Dogmersfield II, 22 July 1995

Seventh wicket
94 no C. Standeven (41no) and I. McLean (43no), Frensham III v *DERA, 17 June 1995
87 A. Dakeyne (46) and D. Snowden (47), *Hindhead v Chiddingfold, 4 May 1996
86 no K. Backenburg (52no) and C. Ray (32no), *The Bourne II v Headley II, 28 July 2001
82 no M. Herzke (46no) and K. Ellis (36no), *Headley II v Peper Harow, 1 Sept 2001
80 no G. Sampson (62no) and G. Baker (12no), *Grayshott II v G&G, 24 May 1997
75 no D. Snowden (48no) and P. Carter (38no), *Hindhead v Dogmersfield II, 30 Aug 1997
73 no G. Sampson (37no) and A. Shrubb (32no), *Grayshott II v Elstead II, 1 Aug 1992
70 no A. Dakeyne (85no) and D. Snowden (40no), Hindhead v *Frensham III, 29 June 1996

Eighth wicket
120 R. Bawden (78) and R. Ashworth (36), G&G v *Crown Tavs II, 8 June 1996
89 B. Carew (47) and M. Hannaway (40), *Crown Tavs II v Grayswood, 15 May 1999
60+ G. Hirst (67no) and R. Cahn (44), Kingsley II v *Elstead II, 20 Aug 1994
58 A. Carder (37) and B. Plant (28), *The Bourne III v Witley, 16 July 1994
53 no E. Power (48no) and M. Gaines (26no), *Tongham II v Elstead II, 7 June 1997

Ninth wicket
62 I. Heap (21no) and S. Dyer (45), Milford II v *Lindford II, 7 June 1997
50 no A. Grogut (44no) and C. Lee (19no), *Badshot Lea II v Kingsley II, 1 June 1996
49 no J. Karki (20no) and M. Chandler (24no), AWI II v *Witley II, 25 Sept 1993
46 D. Clarke (32) and C. Ray (9), *The Bourne II v Cody, 8 Sept 2001
45 J. Bone (18) and S. Naylor (17), *Frensham III v Thursley II, 5 July 1997
40 M. Gubby (19) and R. Walker (18), *Thursley II v Wrecclesham II, 5 June 1993

Tenth wicket
84 C. Obert (25no) and G. Spittles (62), Frensham III v *G&G, 9 Sept 1995
54 J.H. Storey (50) and M. Kensett (1no), Frensham III v *Dogmersfield, 11 Sept 1999
40 no J. Reynolds (39no) and G. Wycherley (16no), *Elstead II v Frimchett II, 4 Sept 1993
40 D. Brook (23) and C. Neighbour (21no), Rowledge III v *Dogmersfield II, 27 May 1995

Best bowling

9-17 N. Gill, Cranleigh SA v Headley II, 4 July 1998 (incl hat-trick)
9-25 T. Lewis, Frimchett II v Dogmersfield II, 20 July 1996
9-26 J. Sanders, Grayshott II v Frimchett II, 3 July 1993
9-26 M. Selley, Dogmersfield II v Thursley II, 20 Aug 1994
9-56 J. Bone, Frensham III v Chiddingfold II, 23 Aug 1997
9-83 D. Shepherd, DERA v Frensham III, 12 June 1999
8-11 D. Snowden, Hindhead v Chiddingfold II, 17 May 1997
8-12 D. Sharpling, Grayshott II v G&G, 12 July 1997
8-16 D. Snowden, Hindhead v Frimchett II, 8 June 1996
8-30 P. Stone, Frensham III v DERA, 25 June 1994
8-31 P. Wilson, Witley II v Frensham III, 19 June 1993
8-31 M. Hannaway, Crown Tavs II v Grayshott II, 29 May 1999
8-42 D. Williams, Headley II v Hindhead, 28 June 1997
8-45 J. White, Cranleigh SA v Grayshott II, 19 Sept 1998
8-47 D. Williams, Headley II v Whitehill II, 20 June 1992
8-48 P. Burke, Peper Harow v The Bourne II, 12 Aug 2000
8-50 K. Haymon, G&G v Thursley II, 2 Aug 1997
8-52 G. Badland Headley II v Churt II, 18 July 1992
8-53 D. Morgan, Tongham II v DERA, 2 July 1994
8-58 G. Hughes, Kingsley II v Witley II, 29 May 1993
8-70 J. Sanders, Grayshott II v Wood Street, 21 Sept 1996

Division Three hat-tricks: There have been 14 recorded, including one by the future England rugby star Jonny Wilkinson, for Frensham III against Elstead II on 13 August 1994.

Division Four

The century-makers

There have been 43 scores of more than 100 in Division Four, including 200no by Michael Allen (Fernhurst) in 1997, the fourth highest individual score in the competitions.

Leading individual scores (* denotes home team):

200 no M. Allen, Fernhurst v *Crown Tavs II, 23 Aug 1997
193 no P. Hammond, Frensham III v *Peper Harow, 15 Aug 1998
170 no P. Marden, *Chiddingfold v Milford II, 19 Aug 1995
164 M. Allen, *Fernhurst v Peper Harow, 9 Aug 1997
158 no C. Ford, Rowledge III v *Elstead II, 31 May 1997
153 no P. Hammond, *Frensham III v *Cranleigh SA II, 6 June 1998
150 no P. Marden, Chiddingfold v *Tongham II, 20 May 1995
149 A. West, *Chiddingfold II v The Bourne III, 28 July 2001
147 no A. Woods, *Chiddingfold II v Elstead II, 3 Aug 1996
147 no R. Cheeseman, The Bourne III v *Chiddingfold II, 28 July 2001
139 C. Ford, *Rowledge III v Milford II, 20 July 1996
132 D. Cole, *Milford II v Hindhead II, 27 June 1998
131 no M. Allen, *Fernhurst v Tongham II, 12 July 1997
131 no B. Plant, The Bourne III v *Hindhead II, 20 June 1998

Record partnerships

First wicket

224 no P. Williams (108no) and P. Jackson (105no), *Grayswood v Wood Street II, 18 July 1998
194 D. Turner (110) and F. Holland (81), *Tongham II v DERA II, 21 Sept 1996
175 R. Morant (92) and P. Bridger (68), *Wrecclesham II v Tongham II, 13 Sept 1997
172 P. Marden (170no) and W. Jones (81), *Chiddingfold v Milford II, 19 Aug 1995
169 M. Allen (200no) and M. West (53), Fernhurst v *Crown Tavs II, 23 Aug 1997
169 A. Connor (87) and C. Ford (71), *Rowledge III v Milford II, 31 July 1999
141 W. Carpenter (63) and D. Connery (58no), *Pirbright v Peper Harow, 3 July 1999

Second wicket

208no C. Watts (110no) and S. Griffiths (101no), *Chiddingfold II v Tongham II, 7 Sept 1996
160 M. Allen (131no) and S. Melrose (48), *Fernhurst v Tongham II, 12 July 1997
c150 P. Williams (75no) and J. Chapman (87no), *Grayswood v Tongham II, 31 May 1997
c140no P. Williams (42no) and J. Chapman (119no), *Grayswood v Frimchett II, 13 Sept 1997
c140no J. Chapman (112no) and P. Jackson (42no), *Grayswood v Hindhead II, 9 May 1998

Third wicket

164 no S. Moulden (82no) and D. Ralf (72no), *Milford II v Rowledge III, 22 June 1996
150 no T. Knight (95no) and R. Elliot (48no), *DERA v Puttenham II, 13 May 2000

100 no T. Wainhouse (61no) and T. Midgley (43no), Wood Street II v *The Bourne III, 17 Aug 1996
100 T. Ames (73) and G. Wycherley (33), *Elstead II v Tongham II, 3 May 1997
91 M. Slater (63) and M. Carson (43), Frimchett II v *Tongham II, 26 July 1997
90 D. Boniface (57) and N. Morant (37no), *Wrecclesham II v Grayswood, 12 Sept 1998

Fourth wicket

192 no A. Woods (147no) and M. Taylor-Lord (46no), *Chiddingfold II v Elstead II, 3 Aug 1996
124 B. Karn (77) and A. Wells (46), *Thursley II v Milford II, 24 June 1995
72 T. Ames (83no) and M. Egan (22), *Elstead II v Wood Street II, 27 July 1996
64 D. Atkins (60no) and P. Murphy (19), Elstead II v *Rowledge III, 5 Sept 1998

Fifth wicket

102 M. Bartlett (81no) and B. Bannatyne (45), *Chiddingfold II v Wrecclesham II, 29 June 1996
97 no J. Chapman (53no) and J. Orr (50no), *Grayswood v Wood Street II, 26 April 1997
51 B. Bridger (42) and N. Morant (19), Wrecclesham II v *Peper Harow, 12 July 1997
50 M. Pearse (28) and D. Munden (36), *Elstead II v Tongham II, 29 June 1996

Sixth wicket

72 no S. Moulden (51no) and D. Ralf (17no), *Milford II v Tongham II, 25 May 1996
60 no J. Andrews (33no) and G. Lofting (16no), *Tongham II v Badshot Lea II, 13 May 1995
54 J. Eaton (79no) and I. Moore (24), *Rowledge III v Elstead II, 5 Sept 1998

Seventh wicket

146 G. Bailey (97) and J. Moore (57no), *Rowledge III v Grayswood, 19 Sept 1998
94 C. Enticknap (65) and M. Enticknap (35no), *Milford II v DERA II, 7 Sept 1996
70 M. Champion (33no) and D. Briggs (27no), *The Bourne III v Wood Street II, 17 Aug 1996

Eighth wicket

c30 D. Boniface (18) and J. Boniface (15), Wrecclesham II v *Cranleigh SA II, 1 Aug 1998

Ninth wicket

42 G. Spittles (22) and G. Lofting (21), *Tongham II v Wrecclesham, 22 June 1996

Tenth wicket

72 M. Payne (24) and R. Lissenborough (18no), plus many extras, Milford II v *Tongham II, 31 Aug 1996
44 J.H. Storey (24no) and S. Naylor (20), Frensham III v *The Bourne III (Binsted), 12 Sept 1998
31 K. Dunstone (24no) and S. Fincham (14), Peper Harow v *Crown Tavs II, 26 July 1997

Best bowling

9-7 P. Collyer, The Bourne III v Tongham II, 9 Aug 1997
9-14 P. Gubby, Thursley II v Elstead II, 10 June 1995
9-28 G. Larby, Wrecclesham II v Frimchett II, 25 July 1998
9-42 G. Eden, Fernhurst II v Puttenham II, 4 Aug 2001
8-14 J. Hopper, Elstead II v Wood Street II, 22 June 1996
8-21 J.H. Storey, Frensham III v Wrecclesham II, 11 July 1998
8-22 W. Tremlett, Cranleigh SA II v Fernhurst, 7 July 2001
8-27 C. Phelps, Wood Street II v Rowledge III, 8 June 1996
8-27 G. Larby, Wrecclesham II v Chiddingfold II, 10 Aug 1996
8-27 D. Clarke, The Bourne III v Elstead II, 8 July 2000
8-28 J. Andrews, Tongham II v Rowledge III, 20 July 1996
8-37 M. Hunt, Rowledge III v Thursley II, 5 June 1999
8-43 M. Hunt, Rowledge III v Tongham II, 30 May 1998
8-49 G. Larby, Wrecclesham II v Wood Street II, 31 Aug 1996
8-53 J. Andrews, Tongham II v Wrecclesham II, 12 Aug 1995
8-66 T. Gray, Badshot Lea II v Puttenham II, 22 July 2000

Division 4 hat-tricks: Three have been recorded.

Division Five

The century-makers

The following players have scored centuries in Division Five (* denotes home team):

151no A. Gardner, *Wrecclesham II v Peper Harow II, 10 July 1999
146 A. Stone, Cranleigh SA II v *Wood Street II, 31 July 1999
117 M. Gaines, *Tongham II v Peper Harow II, 5 June 1999
114 no C. Howard, *Frensham IV v Tongham II, 12 Aug 2000

105 no I. Eden, *Fernhurst II v Peper Harow II, 1 July 2000
105 J.H. Storey, *Frensham IV v Thursley II, 21 July 2001
104 R. Insall, *Puttenham II v Cranleigh SA II, 29 May 1999
104 ret J.H. Storey, *Frensham IV v Hindhead II, 7 July 2001
103 no M. Shotter, *Fernhurst II v Peper Harow II, 1 July 2000
100 no J. Lay, Puttenham II v *Peper Harow II, 17 July 1999
100 ret J.H. Storey, *Frensham IV v Tongham II, 12 Aug 2000

John Storey, with Norman Disney, at the end of the 2001 season, after he had received the Division Five trophy donated by the life president. It was just one more triumph for the old warrior, aged 62, as he neared the completion of his second decade with Frensham.

The record partnership in Division Five is 230no for the second wicket by I. Eden (105no) and M. Shotter (103no) for Fernhurst II at home to Peper Harow II on 1 July 2000.

Best bowling

8-4 C. Boucher, Cranleigh SA II v Frensham IV, 5 Aug 2000
8-10 G. Larby, Wrecclesham II v Peper Harow II, 8 May 1999
8-42 W. Pearse, Hindhead II v Rowledge IV, 19 June 1999

Stevens & Pope Cups

The century-makers

There have been seven centuries scored in the Stevens Cup, six of them in the evening knockout competition. Matt Barnes (Badshot Lea, then Tilford) and Will Gear (Tilford) have each scored two, Gear's coming in 1996. Barnes has also scored a century in the Pope Cup. The following is the list of hundreds (Stevens Cup unless indicated):

136 M. Barnes, Badshot Lea v Kingsley, 1995 (Pope Cup)
126 no M. Absolom, Grayshott v Whitehill, 1988
119 M. Barnes, Badshot Lea v Tongham, 1994
106 C. Butcher, Lindford v Whitehill, 4 July 1953
106 W. Gear, Tilford v Wood Street, 1996
100 J. Huntley, Headley v Badshot Lea, 1995
100 W. Gear, Tilford v G&G RFC, 1996
100 M. Barnes, Tilford v Grayshott, 1998 (final)

Century partnerships

217 no M. Absolom (126no) and N. Elisha (73no), first wicket, Grayshott v Whitehill, 1988
151 no J. Taylor (81no) and M. Barnes (54no), first wicket, Badshot Lea v Tongham, 1997
144 no K. Brown (94no) and P. Allatt (34no), first wicket, Churt v Thursley, 1978
144 no S. Rowe (81no) and D. Richardson (64no), second wicket, Milford v The Bourne, 1998
134 S. Dickinson (99) and J.G. Storey (54), second wicket, Frensham v Elstead, 1986 (Pope Cup final)
131 no M. Pryce (73no) and N. Hume (69no), second wicket, Tilford v Churt, 1984
127 C. Butcher (106) and A. Cooper (40), first wicket, Lindford v Whitehill, 4 July 1953
115 J. Voller (57no) and J. Rivers (49), first wicket, The Bourne II v Alexandra Park, 27 Aug 1955
107 P. Hammond (89) and Unknown, Frensham v Tongham, 1993

Best bowling

9-9 F. Edwards, Kingsley v Thursley, 2 May 1953
8-5 A. Rapley, Thursley v Binsted, 22 August 1953
8-6 J. Burton, Lindford v Whitehill, 3 July 1954
8-26 A. Rapley, Thursley v Whitehill, 10 July 1954
8-43 A. Bicknell, Shottermill v The Bourne II, 13 Aug 1955

Hat-tricks

A. Rapley, four in four, Thursley v Binsted, 22 August 1953
B. Woods, Kingsley v Binsted, 4 July 1953
W. Rapley, Thursley v Whitehill, 25 July 1953
J. Kneller, Alexandra Park v Lindford, 14 August 1954 (five in five deliveries)
E. Rooney, Lindford v Rowledge II, 25 June 1955 (five in six deliveries)
A. Rapley, Thursley v Lindford, 23 July 1955
A. Rapley, Thursley v The Bourne II, 30 July 1955
C. LeClercq, The Bourne v Rowledge, 1971 (final)
R. Moorcroft, Frensham v Tilford, 1992
S. Meyer, Tongham v Witley, 1996
P. Collyer, The Bourne v Milford, 1997

Representative matches

THE history of matches between teams representing the competitions and those from other leagues or clubs goes back to 1909. The details of many of the early matches are recorded in *A Cup for Cricket.* The following is a record of representative fixtures played in the last 50 years (matches played on opponents' grounds unless stated):

13 May 1951: (Whit Sunday): I'Anson 103 (J. Warner 38, F. Kenward 21, R. Goff 21; D. Bowden 7-29) lost to Farnham 186-6 (G. Dawkins 47, R. Watson 37, F. Foley 33) by 6wkts.

10 June 1951: I'Anson 149 (W. Poulter 83) drew with Armament and Electrical Trades School (Bordon) 90-2.

5 Aug 1951: Hampshire clubs 158 (W. Loader 32no, R. White 31, J. Remnant 30, R. Woods 24, J. Miller 20; W. Crebbin 3-34) bt Surrey clubs 134 (J. Warner 38, W. Poulter 25, A. Karn 23; L. Crumplin 7-46) by 1wkt at Whitehill.

Sunday, 12 August 1951: There were 4,000 spectators in Farnham Park for Jack Parker's benefit match. More than £280 was raised, the largest sum collected at any such match in Surrey. Much of the money came from a competition for four autographed bats, and £83 8s 3d (£83.41) was collected on the ground. The popular Surrey all-rounder included five Test players in his side – Frank Worrell, Alec Bedser, Laurie Fishlock, Peter May and Jim Laker – plus Tony Lock, who was to become the next capped player. Arthur McIntyre, another England player, and Stuart Surridge dropped out of the published side. Worrell travelled down from Radcliffe where he was playing in the Central Lancashire League, while May, aged 21, was then a Cambridge University star. Rain restricted play. Scorecard:

District XV

W. Poulter (The Bourne) c and b Worrell	5
J. Warner (Tilford) run out	1
E.D. Milburn (Farnham) st Constable b E.A. Bedser	19
F. Kenward (Grayshott) b Worrell	0
G. Dawkins (Farnham) b A.V. Bedser	5
R. Goff (Whitehill) not out	25
K.S. Trollop (Farnham) b Lock	15
F.F. Foley (Farnham) st Constable b Lock	0
J. Tanner (The Bourne) b Laker	4
A.J. Hillyer (Farnham) not out	2
Extras	8
Total (8 wkts dec)	84

Did not bat: R. Piper (Rowledge), B. Karn (Elstead), C. Fry (Tilford), R. Cross (Farnham), F. Cordier (The Bourne).
Bowling: Worrell 2-11, Lock 2-13, A.V. Bedser 1-12, Laker 1-14, E.A. Bedser 1-16.

J.F. Parker's XI

F.M. Worrell not out	54
E.A. Bedser c Dawkins b Cordier	25
P.B.H. May not out	15
Extras	0
Total (1 wkt)	94

Did not bat: J.F. Parker, L.B. Fishlock, B. Constable, J.C. Laker, A.V. Bedser, J.W. McMahon, T. Young, G.A.R. Lock.
Bowling: Cordier 1-25.

Alec Bedser had a close affinity with the competitions and, with twin brother Eric, appeared in benefit matches and spoke at numerous dinners. Here he signs autographs in Farnham Park in 1956 when a District XV played Jim Laker's XI in aid of the Surrey and England off-spinner's benefit. It was the year in which Laker took 19 wickets against Australia at Old Trafford.

The bats were won by Mr A. Skerritt, of Brington, Alfred Road, Farnham, Mr G. Clarke, of 28 Old Park Close, Farnham, Mr A. Boxall, of Elstead, and Mr A.V. Wilkinson, of Woodlands, Runfold. Parker gave a boy's bat autographed by famous players to Terry Knight, son of H.J. Knight, the I'Anson secretary, who answered correctly that Alec Bedser had taken 157 Test wickets. The Surrey players were anxious to hear the names of the players selected for the forthcoming final Test at The Oval, and a wireless set was brought to the pavilion in time for the 6pm news. Alec Bedser, Laker and May were named. Before returning to London most of the visitors joined the local players at the Nelson Arms.

19 Aug 1951: I'Anson 160 (J. Stonard 38, W. Burchett 26, J. Seddon 21) bt AETS 96 (R. White 3-39, F. Cordier 2-2, J. Stonard 2-14) by 64 runs at Bordon.

22 June 1952: I'Anson 207-4dec (F. Kenward 49, J. Kingshott 48, D. Whittaker 39no, J. Seddon 35) bt Haslemere 159 (J.

Dunlop 50, R. Glover 44; B. Payne 6-59, F. Kenward 3-42) by 48 runs.

7 July 1952: Surrey clubs 202 (J. Seddon 57, J. Warner 45, D. Whittaker 40; A.F. Swan 4-37, D. Piper 3-32) bt Hampshire clubs 92 (R. White 23; B. Payne 5-41, J. Batchelor 3-14) by 110 runs at Rowledge.

4 Aug 1952: I'Anson 175 (D. Whittaker 48, J. Kingshott 24, J. Warner 20; E.D. Milburn 5-47, R. Cross 3-45) drew with Farnham 131-8 (R. Watson 29, K. Trollop 25; F. Kenward 4-46, B. Payne 4-48).

6 Aug 1952: Playing for Surrey Association of Cricket Clubs, J. Tanner (5-60) and W. Crebbin (4-39 in 22.1 overs) dismissed Farnham for 168, but I. Lindsay (5-25) and R. Cross (3-26) put the visitors out for 82.

24 Aug 1952: Hampshire Miller clubs 142 (J. Miller 51; G. Williamson 5-17, R. Hole 3-45) bt Surrey Miller clubs 97 (Williamson 22; J. Lee 3-15) by 45 runs at Churt.

31 May 1953: I'Anson 175 (J. Seddon 94, D. Whittaker 28) drew with Alton 147-6.

21 June 1953: I'Anson 140 (J. Warner 30, A. Hodgkinson 23, W. Crebbin 21) drew with Haslemere 47-2 (rain).

28 June 1953: Hampshire clubs 90 (R. White 17, R. Piper 14no, J. Kingshott 14, W. Loader 14; G. Williamson 3-26, J. Stonard 3-28, R. Reffold 2-8) and 113 (F. Kenward 46; Stonard 4-17, Williamson 2-23) bt Surrey clubs 55 (Loader 6-18, White 3-8) at The Bourne. Surrey were 9-3 at tea and 13-5 against the hostile Loader, who, reported the *Herald*, gets 'lift in any circumstances and exploited a worn spot'.

5 July 1953: 4th (Armnt) Trg Bn REME 129 (J. Stonard 4-35, D. Whittaker 3-16) and 62-1 bt I'Anson 52 (W. Burchett 18; Malley 7-31) and 130-7dec (A. Hodgkinson 34, J. Warner 31) by 9wkts at Bordon.

Sunday, 2 August 1953: There was a crowd of 10,000 in Farnham Park for Alec Bedser's benefit match. Takings amounted to £777, and a cheque for £727 4s 10d (£727.24) was sent to the Bedser benefit fund. Among the visitors were the former Australian Test player Syd Barnes, who had promised Bedser in 1946 that he would appear in his benefit programme, and the Portsmouth and England footballer Jimmy Dickinson, a much respected local sportsman. Boris Karloff, the horror movie star and cricket buff, was one of the umpires. Scorecard:

Farnham and District XV

A.J. Hillyer (Farnham) b Laker 58
A.R. Hodgkinson (Grayshott) c McIntyre b A.V. Bedser..8
J. Seddon (The Bourne) c McIntyre b A.V. Bedser..........0
E.D. Milburn (Farnham) c Lock b Laker 3
J. Warner (Tilford) c Surridge b Laker 0
J. Tanner (The Bourne) b Lock 4
K.S. Trollop (Farnham) b Laker 0
G.H.A. Hewes (Farnham) b Barnes 3
R. Piper (Rowledge) b Laker 26
F.F. Foley (Farnham) b A.V. Bedser 3
G. Williamson (Wrecclesham) b Clark 18
J. King (Nelsonian) c Surridge b Lock 5
A.H. Wellby (Farnham) not out 16
C.A. Watkins (Wrecclesham) not out 8
Extras 11
Total (12 wkts dec) 163
J.D. Munday (Farnham) did not bat.
Bowling: Laker 5-20, A.V. Bedser 3-19, Lock 2-36, Clark 1-8, Barnes 1-34.

Alec Bedser's XI

S.G. Barnes c King b Williamson....................10
P.B.H. May b King 45
T.H. Clark lbw b Piper 26
B. Constable hit wkt b Milburn....................50
E.A. Bedser c Wellby b Piper 37
J. Dickinson not out 49
A.V. Bedser not out 19
W.S. Surridge b King 4
R. Subba Row not out 2
Extras 4
Total (7wkts) 246
Did not bat: G. A.R. Lock, J.C. Laker
Bowling: Piper 2-39, King 2-50, Milburn 1-20, Williamson 1-40, Munday 1-48.

3 Aug 1953: Farnham 151 (J. Broatch 30, J. Banks 23; W. Loader 5-47, F. Kenward 4-49) bt I'Anson 142 (W. Burchett 40, A. Hodgkinson 26, F. Kenward 20; E.D. Milburn 8-51) by 9 runs. I'Anson went from 71-0 to 100-3 at tea and then lost their last five wickets for eight runs.

20 June 1954: I'Anson 147 (D. Whittaker 40, J. Seddon 30; B. Woods 5-70, including hat-trick) lost to Haslemere 151-6 (C. Pye 68, N. Lock 41; R. White 4-27) by 4wkts.

27 June 1954: Surrey clubs 166 (D. Whittaker 35, R. Bridger 26, H. Bicknell 23, J. Stonard 19; L. Crumplin 3-40, R. White 3-43) bt Hants clubs 68 (F. Kenward 26; Bridger 4-29, Bicknell 3-21, Stonard 2-6) by 98 runs at Rowledge.

18 July 1954: I'Anson bt Alton by 58 runs at The Bourne, in spite of D.J. ('Joe') Piper taking 10-39 in 19.1 overs (six maidens). Piper, who subsequently starred for both Rowledge and Thursley, varied his flight cleverly. A heavy shower made the wicket lively when Alton replied and two run outs did not help. Kenward took 2-10 in 11 overs and held a brilliant one-handed catch.

I'Anson XI

J. Warner (Tilford) b Piper 9
G. Bullock (Grayshott) b Piper 0
J. Seddon (The Bourne) lbw b Piper 5
F. Kenward (Headley) b Piper 44
B. Karn (Elstead) b Piper 30
H. Bicknell (The Bourne) c Browning b Piper 23
R. Bridger (Tilford) b Piper 0
J. Stonard (The Bourne) b Piper 8
R. White (Headley) c Browning b Piper 0
L. Crumplin (Rowledge) c Phillips b Piper 12
W. Crebbin (Churt) not out 13
Extras 1
Total 145
Bowling: Piper 10-39.

Alton 87 (White 3-20, Kenward 2-10, Bridger 2-16).

Monday, 2 August 1954: I'Anson's first win, by eight wickets, over Farnham. Farnham were all out for 34 in 90 minutes with Wrecclesham's W. Shaw (who was not in the selected XI) taking 5-12 to add to his 8-20 and 4-51 v Headley two days earlier. Scorecard:

Farnham

A.J. Hillyer b Shaw 8
J.A. Broatch c Crebbin b Shaw 4
L.G. Cooper b Crumplin 0
K.S. Trollop c Whittaker b Crumplin 3
A. Wellby c Bridger b Shaw 0
G. Dawkins b Crumplin 2
G. Phillips c Crebbin b Kenward 1
R. Hewes b Bridger 6
G. Hewes c Seddon b Shaw 1
J.D. Banks c Kenward b Shaw 3
J. Goolding not out 2
Extras 4
Total 34
Bowling: Shaw 5-12, Crumplin 3-6.
Second innings: 87-7.

I'Anson XI

G. Bullock (Grayshott) c R. Hewes b Wellby 26
D. Wells (Frensham) c Hillyer b Banks 10
J. Tanner (The Bourne) b R. Hewes 0
J. Seddon (The Bourne) c Dawkins b R. Hewes 51
F. Kenward (Headley) c Trollop b Goolding 16
D. Whittaker (Elstead) b Banks....54
L. Crumplin (Rowledge) c Cooper b Banks....0
R. Bridger (Tilford) c and b R. Hewes 8
W. Crebbin (Churt) not out 19
J. Warner (Tilford) not out 3
Extras 13
Total (8 wkts) 200
Did not bat: W. Shaw (Wrecclesham).
Bowling: R. Hewes 3-28, Banks 3-55.

Sunday, 1 Aug 1954: A Farnham and District XV lost to Surrey by four wickets and Alec Bedser said thank you for his benefit match of the previous year. A crowd of around 4,000 watched in the Park and gross receipts were £485 10s 8d (£485.53). Farnham CC and the 15 clubs in the competitions each received £15 10s 7d (£15.53), and Woodlarks at The Bourne was given a donation of £27 12s 1d (£27.60) plus £8 3s (£8.15) from a street collection by the Leadswingers' Jazz Band. The winning run was scored by Peter Eyles, a New Zealand friend of Jim Laker, who acted as 12th man and was then included in a 12-man batting line-up. Scoreboard:

Farnham and District XV

A.J. Hillyer (Farnham) run out 43
T.H. Whittaker (Farnham) b Lock 13
J. Tanner (The Bourne) b E. Bedser 13
L. Cooper (Farnham) c A. Bedser b Subba Row 24
F. Kenward (Headley) b E. Bedser 0
D. Whittaker (Elstead) c and b E. Bedser....0
K.S. Trollop (Farnham) c Laker b Constable....0
J. Warner (Tilford) st Willett b Subba Row 5
A.H. Wellby (Farnham) c and b Lock 27
D. Wells (Frensham) st Willett b Subba Row 1
R. Bridger (Tilford) st Willett b Lock....0
R. White (Headley) b Lock 15
J.D. Banks (Farnham) c Subba Row b E. Bedser 2
G. Bullock (Grayshott) not out 1
J. Goolding (Farnham) b E. Bedser 0
Extras 10
Total 154
Bowling: E.A. Bedser 5-3, Lock 4-34, Subba Row 3-29.

Surrey

T.H. Clark b Bridger 63
M.J. Stewart b Kenward....9
J.C. Laker c Hillyer b Goolding....6
K.F. Barrington c Wellby b Bridger....28
P. Eyles c Cooper b Bridger....25
B. Constable c Bullock b Bridger 31

M. Willett c T. Whittaker b Bridger 13
E.A. Bedser not out 1
R. Subba Row b Kenward 5
Extras 5
Total (8 wkts) 186
Did not bat: W.S. Surridge, G.A.R. Lock, A.V. Bedser.
Bowling: Bridger 5-43, Kenward 2-41, Goolding 1-25.

15 Aug 1954: Hampshire Miller clubs 63 (H. Courtnage 24; R. Parratt 3-15, K. Warner 3-16, G. Pilbeam 2-5, D. Paine 2-9) and 48-5 (R. Petter 24no) lost to Surrey Miller clubs 106-4dec (F. Drake 41no, G. Harris 20) at Headley.

22 May 1955: I'Anson 194 (G. Bullock 55, S. Hibbert 35, R. Pryce 26, J. Warner 23, W. Poulter 18) bt Old Paulines 145 (F. Kenward 4-41, L. Crumplin 2-21, G. Williamson 2-49) by 49 runs at Thames Ditton, victory coming in the last over when Bill Poulter could not hold a hard chance at point but recovered to run out the batsman.

5 Sept 1954: I'Anson 124 (D. Whittaker 44, L. Crumplin 29, D. Wells 23; F. Kenward 3-9) bt Lindford and District 78 (N. Disney 21; B. Karn 3-6, D. Whittaker 3-20).

24 July 1955: I'Anson 173 (S. Hibbert 49, F. Kenward 32, G. Williamson 27; D. Mackley 5-65) bt Haslemere 82 (F. Kenward 4-20, R. White 3-28, W. Shaw 2-12) by 91 runs.

Sunday, 31 July 1955: Hampshire clubs 212-7 (F. Kenward 66, R. White 25no, J. Cheeseman 24, G. Bullock 21; W. Shaw 3-44) bt Surrey clubs 94 (R. Bridger 21; B. Penny 6-18, C. Parratt 2-5) by 118 runs at Tilford.

Monday, 1 Aug 1955: I'Anson 58 (R. Pryce 22; J. Banks 8-28, Wellby 2-10) and 107 (G. Williamson 28no, R. Bridger 22, J. Banks 7-37, J. Goolding 2-36) lost to Farnham 143 (K.S. Trollop 75; F. Kenward 3-35, W. Crebbin 2-11, G. Knight 2-20, W. Shaw 2-24) and 25-0 by 10wkts.

28 Aug 1955: Surrey Stevens/Miller clubs 105 (M. Ricketts 24, S. Golding 19, R. Miles 18, M. Poulter 17; E. Rooney 4-25, J. Kneller 3-24, A. Gandy 2-15) and 37-6 bt Hampshire Stevens/Miller clubs 42 (G. Whiddett 13; E. Winter 6-20, Miles 4-12) by 63 runs at Rowledge.

Sunday, 27 May 1956: Old Paulines 257-2dec (G. Nolan 112no, J. Murray 107 – 211 partnership for 2nd wkt) bt I'Anson 178-8 (W. Poulter 51no, F. Kenward 37, R. White 26) at Thames Ditton.

10 June 1956: Surrey clubs 89 (F. Agar 35, J. Stonard 34; L. Crumplin 5-17, W. Loader 3-32, R. White 2-21) lost to Hampshire clubs 90-8 (C. Watkins 26, F. Kenward 14, G. Bullock 14; Stonard 2-18, A. Karn 2-22, Agar 2-28) by 2wkts at Grayshott.

10 June 1956: Hindhead 97 (C. Smith 25no, D. Grinstead 23; G. Whiddett 5-20, A. Rapley 2-23, W. Rapley 2-41) bt Miller 58 (A. Rapley 22; J. Owen 7-18) by 39 runs.

Sunday, 17 June 1956: One thousand people saw what the Herald describe as 'gay Surrey batting' when a Farnham and District XV entertained Jim Laker's XI on a wet and cold day in the Park. A total of about £350 was raised for Laker's benefit. The local side declared at 94-4 (A.J. Hillyer 44) to allow the crowd to see the visitors bat. They made 198 with Bernard Constable (50) and Chelsea footballer and Surrey 2nd XI player Ron Tindall (48) top-scoring. Micky Stewart, who was playing instead of Hampshire's West Indian opener Roy Marshall, scored 24, and Peter May, the England captain who arrived from a Test selection meeting in London, made 21. Eric Bedser (20), Ken Barrington (15) and county captain Stuart Surridge (12) also got into double figures. P.A. Whitcombe, the former Oxford University and Middlesex fast bowler, then playing for Frensham, took 4-18 in six overs and dismissed Tindall and Laker in successive balls, but Surridge stopped the hat-trick.

Sunday, 15 July 1956: Alton 102 (G. Stratford 30; J. Stonard 4-28, M. Ricketts 3-10, F. Kenward 2-23) lost to I'Anson 177-6 (R. White 54, W. Poulter 20no) at Rowledge.

Aug 1956: I'Anson v Farnham (rain, no play).

26 May 1957: I'Anson 70 (F. Agar 31) and 79-3 (R. Pryce 21, Agar 20) lost to Old Paulines 184-5dec (J.I.C. Murray 60ret, G. Nolan 53ret) by 10wkts at Headley. I'Anson were 29-9 when Frank Agar, at nine, was joined by last man Albert Rapley (3no) in a stand of 41 in 31 minutes .

9 June 1957: Hampshire clubs 142 (R. Hole 36no, R. White 28; R. Miles 6-47, C. Reffold 3-28) drew with Surrey clubs 27-2 (J. Tanner 18no) at Churt (rsp). Ron Hole was one of three players from The Bourne II drafted in to play for Hampshire at short notice.

23 June 1957: I'Anson 142 (J. Tanner 29, R. Pryce 22, E. Warner 20; R.R. Glover 6-41) lost to Haslemere 146-5 (N. Lock 39no, P. Madgwick 30no; R. White 2-43, F. Kenward 1-30 in 21 overs) by 5wkts.

14 July 1957: I'Anson beat Alton by three wickets with two balls to spare at Rowledge. With 30 minutes left, they still needed 60, having been left a little under two hours to reach

Leading cricketers and footballers were at Tilford in May 1958 for Eric Bedser's benefit match against an I'Anson Cup XI. Standing, from the left: Ben Barnett (former Australian wicketkeeper), P.G.H. Fender (former Surrey captain and England batsman), Harry Jarrett (Tilford scorer), G.W. Porter, Chelsea footballers Peter Brabrook, Jimmy Greaves and Ron Tindall (the latter also played cricket for Surrey), David Sydenham (Surrey), Chelsea players John Mortimore and Peter Sillett, Jimmy Dickinson (Portsmouth and England), Eric Bedser, Robin Pryce (Elstead), John Tanner (The Bourne), L.C. Elmer (Farnham, umpire), Bryan Karn (Thursley), Peter Prior (Rowledge), George Williamson (Wrecclesham), Reg Glastonbury (Rowledge, umpire). Kneeling: John Edrich (Surrey and England), Frank Kenward (Headley), Jim Eddey (Tilford), 'Ken' Bullock (Grayshott), Ron Miles, Alf Farnfield, 'Patsy' Bridger (all Tilford).

the target of 163. Bryan Karn batted almost throughout and his 85 not out included eight fours. Earlier, Frank Kenward had taken 8-34 in 28 overs (13 maidens).

21 July 1957: Hindhead 221-5dec (J. Mattock 108no, J. Hopwood 74 – 138 for 2nd wkt) drew with I'Anson 123-2 (B. Karn 42no, G. Bullock 37). A heavy storm during the tea interval led to a new pitch being cut, but a target of 200 runs in 90 minutes was beyond the league side.

28 July 1957: Hampshire clubs 107 (A. Gandy 30, J. Wade 24; R. Reffold 5-39, F. Cordier 4-20) bt Surrey clubs 79 (A. Howard 27; A.F. Swan 5-27, Gandy 2-7) by 28 runs at The Bourne.

5 Aug 1957: I'Anson 207-7dec (G. Williamson 49, R. Bridger 34no, R. White 33, J. Tanner 30, E. Warner 28no) drew with Farnham 122-7 (G. Hebden 35; F. Kenward 3-30).

18 May 1958: Hindhead 82 (G. Williamson 4-14, R. White 3-21, F. Kenward 2-14) and 65-4 lost to I'Anson 175-8dec (Williamson 53no, Kenward 50, G. Bullock 27) by 8wkts.

25 May 1958: I'Anson 177 (G. Williamson 54, J. Tanner 28, F. Kenward 25, R. Pryce 21) bt Eric Bedser's XI 161 (P.G.H. Fender 37, J. Greaves 24, J. Dickinson 23, R. Tindall 23, J. Edrich 21; R. Miles 5-40, Williamson 2-31) by 16 runs at Tilford.

1 June 1958: Alton 103 (M. Harris 3-9, G. Williamson 3-21, R. Miles 2-28) bt I'Anson 100 (F. Agar 20) by 3 runs at The Bourne.

8 June 1958: Old Paulines 233-7dec (F. Kenward 2-49, R. White 2-50) bt I'Anson 167 (G. Bullock 39, R. Miles 33no, E. Warner 26, B. Karn 21) by 66 runs at Thames Ditton.

The pre-war Surrey and England player P.G.H. Fender dominates this picture taken at Tilford during the match in aid of Eric Bedser's benefit year in 1958. Fender, who is wearing his England blazer, was aged 65 and made the top score for Bedser's team against an I'Anson Cup XI. Others pictured are, from the left, John Tanner (The Bourne), Ben Barnett, former Australian wicketkeeper who captained the visiting side, Jimmy Dickinson, the Portsmouth and England footballer who lived at Alton and was a good club cricketer, and Alec Bedser.

Peter May, the Surrey and England captain, and Jimmy Dickinson, the Portsmouth and England footballer, go out to bat at Farnham Park in Eric Bedser's benefit match against a District XV in August 1958. To the left of May is Roy Swetman, the Surrey wicketkeeper.

22 June 1958: Haslemere 138-8dec (R. Haynes 58, T. Bryant sen 51; J. Tanner 6-40, R. White 2-34) drew with I'Anson 56-4 (M. Warner 20no), rsp.

---

3 Aug 1958: Farnham and District XV 92 (A. Young 18, J. Tanner 14, M. Warner 14; K. Barrington 5-22, R. Tindall 4-18, J. Laker 3-14, P. Loader 1-4, G.A.R. Lock 1-14) lost to Surrey 297-7 (P.B.H. May 78, J. Laker 65, R. Swetman 50, J. Dickinson 34; G. Williamson 2-24, M. Harris 2-50, V. Ireson 2-66, R. Bridger 1-24). Surrey were the county champions and the match was in aid of Eric Bedser's benefit.

---

4 Aug 1958: I'Anson 75 (J. Banks 4-32) lost to Farnham 76-5 (A.J. Hillyer 34; R. Miles 5-29 in 22 overs) by 5wkts.

---

17 May 1959: Farnham and District XV lost to a Hampshire XI by 72 runs in Farnham Park, in a benefit match for the Hampshire opening bowler Vic Cannings, who had started his career with Farnham. Scorecard:

Hampshire

J.R. Gray c Whittaker b Bowtell	22
H. Horton st Bullock b Ricketts	65
D.O. Baldrey c Banks b Bowtell	1
P.J. Sainsbury c Bullock b Burchett	28
D. White c Saul b Burchett	2
R.E. Marshall c Ireson b Ricketts	4
A.C.D. Ingleby-Mackenzie c and b Burchett	7
V.H.D. Cannings not out	23
M. Heath c Pryce b Burchett	6
D. Shackleton c Bullock b Ireson	14
M. Burden b Ireson	0
Extras	14
Total	186

Bowling: M. Ricketts 2-19, V. Ireson 2-20, R. Bowtell 2-27, P. Burchett 2-45.

Farnham and District XV

T.H. Whittaker (Farnham) b White	12
A.J. Hillyer (Farnham) c Gray b Heath	15
A. Farnfield (Tilford) c and b Sainsbury	5
G.G.L. Hebden (Farnham) b White	1
A.N. Groom (Farnham) c Burden b Cannings	0
M. Ricketts (The Bourne) st Baldrey b Sainsbury	0
A. Saul (Farnham) st Baldrey b Sainsbury	1
J. Tanner (The Bourne) st Baldrey b Sainsbury	4
R. Pryce (Elstead) c Horton b Sainsbury	23
G. Bullock (Grayshott) b Ingleby-Mackenzie	14
J.D. Banks (Farnham) c Shackleton b Sainsbury	13
V. Ireson (Farnham) c Horton b Sainsbury	2
P. Burchett (Wrecclesham) c White b Sainsbury	5
B. Payne (Headley) b Burden	11
R. Bowtell (Farnham) not out	2
Extras	6
Total	114

Bowling: D. Shackleton 4-0-6-0, M. Heath 5-1-18-1, D

Vic Cannings, who partnered Derek Shackleton in Hampshire's opening attack for many years, began his career at Farnham, and on Whit Sunday in 1959 he led a county side against a District XV in Farnham Park. Standing, from the left: F. Hollyer (umpire), Peter Sainsbury, Jimmy Gray, David ('Butch') White, Robin Pryce (Elstead), Vic Ireson (Farnham), Tom Whittaker (Farnham), 'Ken' Bullock (Grayshott), Jim Banks (Farnham), Mervyn Burden, John Hillyer (Farnham), L.C. Elmer (umpire). Seated: Malcolm Heath, Henry Horton, Michael Ricketts (The Bourne), Basil Payne (Headley), Vic Cannings, R.C. ('Bob') Radford (Farnham president), Geoff Hebden (Farnham), Colin Ingleby-Mackenzie, Ray Bowtell (Farnham), Roy Marshall, Derek Shackleton. On ground: Tony Groom (Farnham), John Tanner (The Bourne), Denis Baldrey, Phil Burchett (Wrecclesham), Alf Farnfield (Tilford), Tony Saul (Farnham).

White 4-1-5-2, V. Cannings 3-3-0-1, P. Sainsbury 10-4-27-8, M. Burden 5.4-1-9-1, C. Ingleby-Mackenzie 4-0-21-1, R. Marshall 4-1-16-0.

---

31 May 1959: Alton 92 (M. Doyle 3-22, R. Miles 3-23, M. Ricketts 3-40) lost to I'Anson 93-3 (R. Pryce 31no, F. Collier 23) by 7wkts at The Bourne

---

7 June 1959: Old Paulines 65 (D. Piper 18-4-28-7, incl hat-trick) and 85 (F. Kenward 3-12) lost to I'Anson 166-5dec (F. Collier 100, R.Piper 25, G. Bullock 16no) at Rowledge.

---

21 June 1959: Haslemere 177 bt I'Anson 150 (B. Karn 55) by 27 runs.

---

3 August 1959: Farnham 196 (R.I. Clark 40) bt I'Anson 149 (Clark 8-59) by 47 runs.

---

5 June 1960: Old Paulines 188 (D. Robinson 4-62, M. Harris 3-53, F. Kenward 2-40) bt I'Anson 87 (Kenward 29no) by 101 runs.

---

19 June 1960: I'Anson 187 (G. Bullock 84, F. Kenward 25, M. Harris 20no, E. Warner 20) bt Haslemere 91 (C. Pye 34; G. Pilbeam 4-6, Kenward 4-17, Harris 2-21) by 96 runs.

Aug 1960: I'Anson bt Farnham by four wickets in the last over of a rain-affected match. The start was delayed and Farnham were 60-3 when an early tea was taken. Another pitch was cut and Farnham went on to 98-9dcc off 61 overs (T.H. Whittaker 33, G.G.L. Hebden 21; F. Kenward 22-9-33-5, R. Bridger 3-23), leaving the visitors 90 minutes' batting. Elstead's George Pilbeam and Frank Collier went cheaply, but 'Ken' Bullock (Grayshott) and John Tanner (The Bourne) added 64 for the third wicket before Hebden slowed the chase by bowling Bullock for 48, and having Tanner (31) and Robin Pryce (Elstead) both stumped. With three runs needed off the last over, skipper Frank Kenward (Headley) took charge and won the game with a single off the penultimate ball.

---

25 June 1961: Haslemere 181-7dec (M. Cane 3-35) bt I'Anson 52 (R. Glover 6-21, incl hat-trick) by 129 runs.

---

6 Aug 1961: Farnham 249-3dec (T.H. Whittaker 101, V. Ireson 58, A. Saul 54no) bt I'Anson 51 (T. Job 7-22, J. Banks 3-27) by 198 runs.

---

1 July 1962: Haslemere 124 (R. Glover 50; J.H. Storey 4-27, G. Tribe 3-13, D. Robinson 2-27) lost to I'Anson 128-6 (D. Robinson 43, R. Dibdin 22; R. Glover 4-26) by 4wkts

---

Aug 1962: Farnham v I'Anson (no play, rain).

30 June 1963: Haslemere 147-5 drew with I'Anson 107-9.

5 Aug 1963: Farnham 135 (G. Hebden 32; J. Storey 25-9-43-5, D. Piper 5-55 in 19.5 overs) lost to I'Anson 138-6 (B. Karn 62no; J. Banks 3-32) by 4wkts. Farnham were put in by Robin Pryce and John Storey and 'Joe' Piper exploited a damp pitch.

22 June 1964: I'Anson 112 (M. Ricketts 39) lost to Haslemere 113-6 (D. Piper 5-28) by 4wkts.

3 Aug 1964: I'Anson 198-8dec (A. Staves 48, G. Bullock 44, F. Kenward 23no, P. Hounsome 21no, D. Wells 21; J. Banks 4-39, J. Storey 3-48) lost to Farnham 199-3 (N. Wilson 107, D. Banks 52 – stand of 170) by 7wkts. Neil Wilson had scored 163 v Stoner the day before.

4 July 1965: Haslemere 132 (A. Macauley 52; R. Chambers 3-21, A. Peach 2-18, A. Staves 2-20, F. Kenward 2-42) bt I'Anson (only 10 men and nine finished, R. White injuring a leg while bowling) 81 (M. Harris 22no, J. Tanner 22, F. Kenward 21) by 51 runs.

30 Aug 1965: Farnham 260-5dec (M. Knowles 82, G. Hebden 77) drew with I'Anson 193-6 (R. Pryce 66, M. Ricketts 56, A. Staves 26, J. Tanner 21; J. Storey 3-50). Pryce and Ricketts put on 117 for 3rd wkt.

3 July 1966: I'Anson 195-5dec (D. Piper 60no, G. Bullock 44, J. Burton 42) drew with Haslemere 137-7 (J. Kneller 3-35, D. Piper 2-28)

29 Aug 1966: I'Anson 146-9dec (R. Pryce 44, D.J. Piper 40) v Farnham 1-1 (rsp).

2 July 1967: Haslemere 58 (J. Kersley 5-16, J. Partridge 3-15, incl hat-trick, A. Prior 2-9) lost to I'Anson 61-6 (R. Pryce 20) by 4wkts.

28 August 1967: I'Anson beat Farnham by one wicket off the penultimate ball. Scorecard:

Farnham

J. Tanner b Knight 30
G. Hebden c Moss b Kersley 0
R. Chambers c Moss b Prior 31
R. Brown c King b Piper 51
A. Kieft c Piper b Prior 7
J. Storey lbw b Piper 26
J. Banks b Knight 12
A. Wellby c Bullock b Piper 1
R. Hewes c Kersley b Piper 27
V. Ireson not out 9
G. Southgate lbw b Piper 4
Extras 25
Total 223
Bowling: D. Piper 5-36, A. Prior 2-33, D. Knight 2-48, J. Kersley 1-40.

I'Anson

G. Bullock c Wellby b Chambers 47
R. Shergold c Tanner b Storey 2
R. Pryce c Tanner b Chambers 22
J. Burton c Storey b Ireson 11
R. Moss c Storey b Hewes 16
A. King c Kieft b Hewes 9
D. Piper c Tanner b Storey 29
A. Prior not out 40
D. Knight b Storey 28
J. Partridge c Brown b Chambers 9
J. Kersley not out 2
Extras 11
Total (9 wkts) 226
Bowling: Chambers 3-54, Storey 3-78, Hewes 2-42, Ireson 1-26.

30 July 1968: Haslemere 204-7dec (R. Haynes 54) bt I'Anson 58 (T. Bryant 6-24) by 146 runs.

2 Sept 1968: I'Anson 85 (L. Knight 29; J.H. Storey 6-26, A. Kieft 4-7) lost to Farnham 86-6 (G. Hebden 31, M. Knowles 26; D. Harris 3-14, D. Piper 2-24) by 4wkts.

29 July 1969: I'Anson 38 lost to Haslemere 41-6 by 4wkts.

1 Sept 1969: I'Anson 221-8dec (A. Young 117, J. Burton 25, P. Clapham 24; J.H. Storey 4-73, C. Stedman 2-60) bt Farnham 161 (M. Knowles 43, N. Wilson 31, G. Hebden 27, A. Prior 5-29, G. Tribe 2-31) by 60 runs. Alan Young, who hit 18 fours, was dropped off a difficult chance at 95. Farnham were 139-3 when Alan Prior caused a collapse. John Storey and Chic Stedman held out for almost 30 minutes until 'Joe' Piper induced Stedman to put up a catch.

28 June 1970: I'Anson 154 (R. Shergold 58, R. Chambers 32, A. Young 26; A. Whitcher 5-54) drew with Haslemere 84-8 (D. Piper 5-37, G. Tribe 2-21).

30 Aug 1970: Farnham 230-8dec (N. Wilson 80, R. Brown 46; D. Piper 3-57, P. Clapham 2-16) drew with I'Anson 123-9 (R. Shergold 30, G. Tribe 29, L. Knight 20; J.H. Storey 26-12-47-7).

26 June 1971: Haslemere v I'Anson (no play, rain).

28 Aug 1971: Farnham lost to I'Anson by three wickets. Scorecard:

Farnham

N. Wilson c Terrill b Tribe 2
M. Knowles c Shergold b Chambers 89
R. Brown c Terrill b Tribe....................3
K. Robson c Young b Tribe....................8
A. Broadrick c Terrill b Tribe 5
A. Wallis lbw b Jeffery....................21
J. Storey not out 68
R. Simpson c and b Jeffery 2
A. Kieft c Terrill b Jeffery 22
J. Banks not out....................6
Extras 5
Total (8 wkts dec) 231
G. Southgate did not bat
Bowling: G. Tribe 4-32, T. Jeffery 3-40.

I'Anson

R. Shergold c Robson b Knowles 41
A. Young b Storey 11
A. Staves c Simpson b Knowles 48
R. Chambers st Wallis b Knowles....................14
J. Burton c Kieft b Storey 46
A. Prior run out 7
T. Jeffery run out....................50
P. Clapham not out....................7
D. Harris not out....................0
Extras 9
Total (7 wkts) 233
J. Terrill and G. Tribe did not bat
Bowling: M. Knowles 3-59, J. Storey 2-67.

---

11 June 1972: I'Anson 106-8dec (J. Terrill 29; F. Kenward 3-28) drew with Headley 102-5 (J. Burton 52, B. Lewis 22) in Headley's centenary year.

---

25 June 1972: Haslemere 133 (E. Gee 61; G. Tribe 5-56, R. Chambers 2-18, T. Jeffery 2-27) lost to I'Anson 135-3 (P. Jones 51, R. Chambers 41, R. Shergold 20) by 7wkts.

---

2 July 1972: I'Anson 151-8dec (B. Silver 36no, R. Shergold 30, A. Rooney 28; T. Cooper 4-40) v Tilford 69-2 (P. Cooper 45no), aban, rain. This was a charity match in aid of a local swimming pool appeal.

---

27 Aug 1972: Farnham lost to I'Anson by six wickets. Scorecard:

Farnham

J. Tanner c Staves b Prior 22
M. Knowles b Jeffery....................15
D. Banks b Prior 7
C Burchett b Prior 0
A. Kieft c Clapham b Tribe....................32
R. Brown c Terrill b Chambers 21
G. Southgate lbw b Chambers 7
D. Bishop b Chambers 0
J. Storey c Burton b Chambers....................1
C. Gordon c Chambers b Tribe 0
C. Stedman not out....................1
Extras 15
Total 121
Bowling: R. Chambers 4-5, A. Prior 3-38, G. Tribe 2-26

I'Anson

R. Shergold lbw b Southgate 16
P. Jones b Stedman 6
R. Chambers c Bishop b Storey 22
J. Burton not out....................50
A. Rooney st Tanner b Storey....................3
A. Staves not out 13
Extras 12
Total (4 wkts) 122
Did not bat: A. Prior, P. Clapham, J. Terrill, T. Jeffery, G. Tribe.
Bowling: J. Storey 2-34

---

24 June 1973: Haslemere 207-7dec (H. Best 81; D. Rook 2-43, A. Chalkley 2-46, P. Pietrusiewicz 2-54) drew with I'Anson 150-8 (J. Walker 39, P. Chuter 34, D. Rook 26).
On the same day, Roy Marshall brought a team of Hampshire and West Indian players to Grayshott. West Indies skipper Rohan Kanhai, who had scored a century v Hampshire at Southampton the previous day, watched the match. Marshall's XI 211 (R. Lewis 99; G. Tribe 4-46, C. Yates 4-60, R. Chambers 2-35) drew with I'Anson 183-9 (C. Yates 66no, B. Burberry 39, A. Prior 30).

---

26 Aug 1973: Farnham 233-9dec (C. Burchett 126; P. Pietrusiewicz 4-42, A. Prior 3-39) v I'Anson 93-6 (C. Stedman 3-16, J. Storey 2-22), aban, rain.

---

23 June 1974: I'Anson 83 (J. Burton 21; B. Windebank 5-25) lost to Haslemere 84-7 (N. Woods 34no; P. Dance 5-34) by 3wkts.

---

11 Aug 1974: Miller 115 (D. Pilbeam 26, J. Stonard 22; A. Talman 4-34) drew with TCYC 96-9 (A. Pippett 22, R. Polley 22; D. Pilbeam 6-45, J.Stonard 2-30).

---

4 Aug 1975: Farnham v I'Anson (no play, rain).

---

22 June 1975: Haslemere 176 (T. Bryant 75; T. Jeffery 6-30, A. Prior 2-59) lost to I'Anson 178-5 (M. Warner 55, C. Yates 48, B. Dewey 24).

3 Aug 1975: Farnham 248-8dec (C. Burchett 55, R. Shergold 52; T. Jeffery 4-82) bt I'Anson 100 (J. Burton 25; C. Stedman 4-18, J. Storey 3-29) by 148 runs.

10 Aug 1975: TCYC 90 (J. Stonard 5-20) lost to Miller 93-7 (A. Tumber 31) by 3wkts at Whitehill.

20 June 1976: Haslemere v I'Anson (no play, rain).

11 July 1976: TCYC 208-8dec (C. Cobbett 117no; J. Stonard 3-26) bt Miller 185 (C. Crawte 43, A. Tumber 29; N. Crawley 4-69) by 23 runs.

25 July 1976: Farnham 241-7dec (R. Shergold 64, C. Burchett 43; N. Hume 3-49) bt I'Anson 157 (T. Jeffery 36; J. Storey 7-81) by 84 runs.

26 June 1977: I'Anson 144 (G. Baker 51, K. Brown 31, C. Yates 25) lost to Haslemere 145-8 (G. Tribe 4-48) by 2wkts.

7 Aug 1977: I'Anson 201-7dec (A. Rooney 50, R. Chambers 39no, A. Prior 31, C. Yates 30) lost to Farnham 202-3 (R. Shergold 56no, M. Wilkes 51, J.H. Storey 50no; R. Chambers 3-47) by 7wkts.

18 June 1978: Miller 182-4dec (D. Elson 77, D. Read 51, R. Woodward 30) bt TCYC 78 (D. Croucher 6-27, J. Stonard 3-13) by 104 runs.

25 June 1978: I'Anson 221-9dec (B. Turner 74, K. Brown 50, J. Burton 25, N. Hume 20no) bt Haslemere 75 (N. Hume 7-28, incl hat-trick) by 146 runs.

6 Aug 1978: I'Anson 100 (A. Rooney 23, A. Prior 22; J.H. Storey 7-30) lost to Farnham 101-3 (Storey 30no, R. Shergold 24) by 7wkts. The match was played at Grayshott at short notice because the Farnham pitch was unfit.

24 June 1979: Haslemere 198 (J. Bennington 82; A. Prior 3-22) lost to I'Anson 199-7 (A. Rooney 58, J. Burton 37, C. Yates 25, A. Prior 23no) by 3wkts.

1 July 1979: TCYC 148 (G. May 31) bt Miller 62 (P. Storer 3-4, S. Charter 3-5, P. Sharratt 3-28) by 86 runs.

5 Aug 1979: Farnham 122 (R. Shergold 43, M. Knowles 31; C. Yates 3-45, A. Prior 3-45, P. Pietrusiewicz 2-5, B. Turner 2-18) lost to I'Anson 123-9 (A. Prior 33no, C. Yates 21; C. Stedman 5-43, J.H. Storey 3-36) by 1wkt.

9 Sept 1979: Haslemere II 239-5dec drew with Miller 193-5 (A. Peacock 88no, P. Connor 36) at Whitehill.

July 1980: I'Anson beat Haslemere.

3 Aug 1980: Farnham 224-8dec (R. Shergold 74, S. Finzel 63; B. Turner 3-52) drew with I'Anson 190-7 (J. Burton 45 A. Rooney 29 A. Prior 27no, R. Clarke 27; R. Moorcroft 4-71).

13 July 1980: Miller 125-7dec (A. Tumber 44no, A. Liddicott 29; G. Larby 2-30, S. Rowe 2-41) drew with TCYC 119-8 (T. Powell 38, P. Davey 25, A. Gardner 21; T. Lee 4-41, R. Anderson 2-16).

13 Sept 1980: Haslemere II 65 (D. Williams 5-19) lost to Miller 67-3 (D. Mann 24no, A. Tumber 23no) by 7wkts.

21 June 1981: I'Anson 249-2dec (J. Burton 101no, E. Gulliver 63, P. Offord 55, N. Dunbar 22no) drew with Haslemere 118-6 (H. Best 40; R. Birch 4-36). Offord and Gulliver put on 70 for the first wicket; Gulliver and Burton 92 for the second; Burton and Dunbar 87 undefeated for the third.

5 July 1981: TCYC 111-9dec (I. Thorpe 35no, A. White 20; A. Lang 2-26, S. Jones 2-32) bt Miller 91 (P. Clapham 20no; R. Jenkinson 6-39) by 20 runs at Witley.

1 Aug 1981: Farnham 149 (R. Shergold 31, A. Rooney 24, C. Gordon 24, C. Cobbett 22; C. Yates 21-8-59-7, R. Holden 2-29) bt I'Anson 128 (Yates 49no; C. Stedman 18-4-51-6, N. James 2-20, J.H. Storey 2-33) by 21 runs. Yates, at times unplayable as the ball moved off the seam, dismissed both Storey and Knowles first ball. A last-wicket stand of 40 by skipper Charles Gordon and Nick James boosted Farnham. The visitors were 29-6 against Chic Stedman, but Yates, skipper Alan Prior and Dick Holden staged a recovery before Storey's leg-spin accounted for the latter two. Yates kept the strike but Stedman claimed the last two wickets.

20 June 1982: I'Anson 222-3dec (P. Offord 110no, P.A. Slinger 35, R. Simpson 29, A. Prior 25no) drew with Haslemere 169-7 (J. Bayston 86; R. Holden 5-50). Offord batted 143 minutes, hitting 16 fours.

4 July 1982: TCYC 101 (T. Munday 25, H. Macdonald 24; J. Stonard 4-10, R. Anderson 3-30, R. Frommholz 2-45) lost to Miller 102-3 (M. Heat 28) by 7wkts at Thursley.

1 Aug 1982: I'Anson 225-7 dec (P.A. Slinger 51, P. Offord 40, A. Field 28 E. Gulliver 25, C. Yates 21; J.H. Storey 3-33) bt Farnham 103 (C. Stedman 51no; N. Martyn 4-23, A. Field 3-24) by 122 runs in the town club's bicentenary. Farnham were 10-4 at tea against Nigel Martyn (three wickets) and Tony Field.

12 Sept 1982: Haslemere II 149 (M. Butterfield 4-30, D. Pope 3-30, R. Woodward 2-38) drew with Miller 127-6 (R. Woodward 36, M. Heat 30, M. Butterfield 22no).

19 June 1983: Haslemere 159 (C. Rose 51; J. Storey 4-27 in 17 overs of leg-spin, M. Sterio 2-10, N. Martyn 2-24) lost to I'Anson 165-4 (E. Gulliver 67no, N. Higgins 38, K. Tilson 27) by 6wkts.

3 July 1983: Miller 159-8dec (P. Clapham 34, R. Kemp 25, M. Neill 21) bt TCYC 118 (J. Bishop 47, G. Boxall 26; A. Liddicott 4-31, Clapham 3-31, G. Larby 3-26).

31 July 1983: Farnham 160-9dec (S. Bentley 28, P. Green 24, C. Cobbett 22; N. Hume 5-39 in 20 overs, J. Storey 2-32) drew with I'Anson 158-7 (P. Offord 56, J. Storey 27, R. Lake 24, M. Knowles 21; S. Perry 3-36, T. Jermyn 2-44). I'Anson failed to score the three needed off the last ball from Steve Perry, the highly-rated 17-year-old pace bowler.

11 Sept 1983: Miller 159-7dec (T. Fry 57, J. Birch 28) drew with Haslemere II 91-5 (J. Stonard 2-21).

1 July 1984: TCYC 221-5 (R. Woods 49, C. Druce 43, J. Chapman 40, T. Wheatley 32no, A. Hockey 29) lost to Miller 224-7 (A. Cunningham 80, N. Higgins 54, D. Emery 24no, D. Whillians 21no; R. Lewis 3-68) by 3wkts at Lindford.

22 July 1984: I'Anson 247-8dec (K. Tilson 101, R. Lewis 48, E. Gulliver 37, C. Bayman 22) drew with Godalming 149-8 (N. Martyn 3-53, R. Lewis 2-17, B. Silver 2-39).

5 Aug 1984: I'Anson bt Farnham by 26 runs, thanks to five-wicket hauls by leg-spinner John Storey and paceman Nigel Martyn.

I'Anson

E. Gulliver c Jermyn b Stedman	37
S. Dickinson c Warriner b Perry	1
K. Tilson c Stedman b Perry	0
R. Lewis c Stedman b Perry	9
C. Bayman c and b Stedman	37
H. Macdonald c I. Thorpe b Perry	30
J.H. Storey c I. Thorpe b Stedman	19
B. Silver c Warriner b Jermyn	7
A. Prior not out	0
A. Field c Cobbett b Perry	1
N. Martyn c Cobbett b Perry	0
Extras	9
Total	150

Bowling: S. Perry 6-18 in 10.4 overs, C. Stedman 3-66.

Farnham

I. Thorpe c Dickinson b Storey	29
P. Green c Storey b Martyn	13
R. Warriner b Martyn	14
A. Rooney c Silver b Storey	5
C. Cobbett b Storey	1
R. Vernier c Prior b Storey	4
T. Jermyn st Dickinson b Storey	5
J.G. Storey c J.H. Storey b Martyn	2
C. Stedman b Martyn	32
A. Macdonald b Martyn	9
S. Perry not out	0
Extras	10
Total	124

Bowling: J.H. Storey 5-44, N. Martyn 5-58.

9 Sept 1984: Farnham League 227-6 (P. Hillman 82, C. Myles 45; R. Anderson 3-54, R. White 2-41) bt Miller 114 (D. Emery 22, N. Higgins 20; S. Clarke 3-33). This was the Farnham League's first representative match for more than 60 years. In a rain-affected fixture at Lindford, the umpires reduced the overs from 40 to 25 a side which meant the Miller lost by 20 runs on a revised target. Frank Lunt presented the Representative Challenge Trophy to Farnham League skipper Chris Myles (Belle Vue), who had shared an opening stand of 106 with Paul Hillman (Badshot Lea).

23 June 1985: I'Anson 211-3dec (S. Dickinson 101no, E. Gulliver 62, P.A. Slinger 21no) drew with Godalming 147-6.

1985: Matches v Farnham and Liphook, no play, rain.

30 June 1985: Miller 200-6 (R. Berkeley 52, R. Yeomans 41, D. Lee 30, M. Jones 22; S. Long 3-44) bt TCYC 55 (A. Coates and T. Brown four wickets each) by 145 runs.

18 Aug 1985: Miller 59 (A. Hockey 22; S. Clarke 4-7) lost to Farnham League 60-1 (P. Hillman 46) by 9wkts.

18 Aug 1985: Tilford 130-9dec (R. Grogut 34, C. Wilson 29; R. Birch 3-25, R. Lewis 3-29) bt I'Anson 73 (E. Gulliver 18; A. Macdonald 3-9, R. Pike 2-2, N. Martyn 2-20, N. Hume 2-23) by 57 runs in the club's centenary year.

22 June 1986: Miller 81 (A. Lang 29; S. Oakey 6-29, G.P. Thorpe 4-24) lost to TCYC 82-3 (G.P. Thorpe 35no, A. Lang 30) by 7wkts at Wrecclesham.

29 June 1986: I'Anson 142-9 (A. Hunter 58no; C. Yates 4-29) bt Rowledge 140-9 (A. Christmas 40, A. Prior 30; J. Shaw 3-21, R. Birch 3-39) by 2 runs.

1986: I'Anson v Farnham, no play, rain.

5 July 1987: Rowledge 133-8 (C. Yates 47; N. Martyn 3-18) lost to I'Anson 134-5 (J.G. Storey 38no R. Baker 24, P.J. Slinger 22no, M. Pryce 21) by 5wkts in Rowledge's centenary season.

5 July 1987: Miller 140-9 (G. Chapple 36, T. Fry 31) bt TCYC 135 (A. Lang 3-23, A. Gardiner 3-36) by 5 runs.

2 Aug 1987: Farnham 186-9dec (A. Thorpe 53, G. Thorpe 38, S. Bentley 22; J.H. Storey 3-20, N. Martyn 3-50) drew with I'Anson 128-8 (S. Dickinson 36no, J.H. Storey 25; M. Kirkland 5-25).

2 May 1988: Frensham/Farnham XII 195-10 (C. Burchett 37, R. Clarke 30, P. Chuter 29, R. Shergold 21, R. Poulter 21) lost to I'Anson XII 196-6 (M. Gowar 50, J.H. Storey 34, A. Gardner 31, R. Cheeseman 22) by 5wkts. This fixture was in aid of the sons of the late Trevor Jeffery, of Frensham.

12 June 1988: Farnham II 181-7dec (A. Kieft 45no; A. Lang 3-40, A. Coates 2-39) drew with Miller 165-5 (A. Tumber 46, W. Hill 41, L. Edwards 36no, R. Yeomans 25no) at Lindford.

31 July 1988: Farnham 209 (I. Thorpe 68, R. Norman 44; T. Wheatley 4-58, J.G. Storey 2-47) drew with I'Anson 141-9 (M. Absolom 41, D. Jervis 29; C. Stedman 7-50). I'Anson were 46-5 to father and son Chic and Andrew Stedman, but rain intervened, and Farnham had only 13 overs left to get the remaining wickets. Mike Absolom and David Jervis put together a seventh wicket partnership of 55, before Chic Stedman dismissed both and then had J.H. Storey caught in the gully. Nick Randall negotiated the last five balls for a draw.

21 Aug 1988: I'Anson 65 (A. Cook 20; R. Simpson 4-10, L. Rogers 2-8, M. Richardson 2-25) lost to Rowledge 70-4 (P. Offord 35no; J. Mace 3-24) by 6wkts.

2 July 1989: I'Anson 220-7 (N. Smith 79, D. Gooda 62 – 128 opening stand, S. Dickinson 24; S. Rowe 2-21, B. Turner 2-37) beat Wey Valley League 182-8 (M.Brunwin 51, S. Garner 37; J.H. Storey 3-34, M. Sobey 2-31, P. Murphy 2-34) by 38 runs at Milford.

6 Aug 1989: Farnham 235-9dec (A. Thorpe 46, J. Barrow 45no, R. Warriner 36, I. Thorpe 30; I. Watkins 5-68) bt I'Anson 153 (P.J. Slinger 54, C. Cobbett 27; C. Stedman 3-4, S. Perry 2-15, J. Barrow 2-18) by 82 runs.

20 Aug 1989: I'Anson 194-4 (A. Cook 62, R. Grogut 43 – 126 for 1st wicket, J.G. Storey 25, P.J. Slinger 24no; C. Yates 3-42) bt Rowledge 181-6 (C. Yates 46, B. Silver 44, N. Dunbar 26; P. Murphy 3-24) by 13 runs.

1 July 1990: Wey Valley League 125-9 (W. Scott 4-12, N. Martyn 2-4) bt I'Anson 86 (N. Smith 33, Martyn 17; A. Chater 4-16) by 39 runs at Whitehill.

5 August 1990: I'Anson beat Farnham by six wickets with skipper Chris Cobbett and Sean Dickinson putting on a match-winning undefeated 124 for the fifth wicket. Scorecard:

Farnham

A. Thorpe c Dickinson b Martyn	13
A. Jenner b Murphy	70
S. Bentley c Whitley b Macdonald	2
I. Thorpe b Murphy	17
R. Norman lbw b Martyn	26
S. Robson b Storey	32
J. Barrow c Smith b Whitley	1
A. Stedman b Martyn	6
C. Stedman c Macdonald b Martyn	12
R. Warriner c Baker b Whitley	0
J. Hobdell not out	3
Extras	20
Total	202

Bowling: N. Martyn 4-35, S. Whitley 2-18, P. Murphy 2-35, A. Macdonald 1-17, J.G. Storey 1-46.

I'Anson

N. Smith (Whitehill) c A. Thorpe b Robson	29
M. Absolom (Grayshott) lbw b Hobdell	20
J.G. Storey (Frensham) b Hobdell	0
R. Baker (Grayshott) c Norman b Robson	8
C. Cobbett (Tilford) not out	55
S. Dickinson (Frensham) not out	61
Extras	31
Total (4 wkts)	204

Did not bat: S. Whitley (Grayshott), P. Murphy (Elstead), A. Macdonald, N. Martyn (both Tilford), D. Coldicott (Frensham).

Bowling: Hobdell 2-14, Robson 2-52.

19 Aug 1990: Rowledge v I'Anson, cancelled, rain.

3 Aug 1991: Farnham 181-7dec (S. Bentley 59, R. Brown 41; P. Murphy 2-30, J.H. Storey 2-51) bt I'Anson 120 (C. Cobbett 19, M. Pryce 18; N. Marsh 3-17) by 61 runs.

18 Aug 1991: I'Anson 138-9 (S. Whitley 38, R. Baker 27, C. Cobbett 21; L. Rogers 4-27) lost to Rowledge 140-4 (J Harland 43, J. Humphreys 35no, P. Offord 33) by 6wkts.

10 July 1992: I'Anson 226-7 dec (P. Murphy 50no, M. Pryce 41, J. Daddo 37, I. White 29, J. Puttock 21) drew with Godalming 223-9 (B. Rapley 5-52, D. Stephenson 2-37) to mark the 225th anniversary of cricket first having been played in Godalming district.

---

2 Aug 1992: Farnham 258-4 dec (M. Cooper 59, I. Thorpe 56no, S. Bentley 52, A. Thorpe 52; A. Gardiner 2-63) bt I'Anson 222 (D. Jervis 82, S. Dickinson 38, M. Pryce 30; C. Stedman 5-41, S. Robson 4-65) by 36 runs.

---

16 Aug 1992: I'Anson 144-6 (M. Pryce 57, D. Fry 28; S. Armstrong 5-28) lost to Rowledge 145-3 (P. Tanner 74, N. Dunbar 23) by 7wkts.

---

1 August 1993: I'Anson drew with Farnham. Alan Thorpe and Mike Cooper reached 202 off 35 overs at lunch and both then completed their centuries. The declaration came after 51 overs, which left I'Anson ample time. Martin Pryce and Keith Tilson went after Andrew Stedman, but Chic Stedman got in the groove immediately. Tilson went at 49, then Pryce and John Stressing added 136, with the former falling just short of a deserved century, having shown a resilience and shot selection not seen by an I'Anson player in the Park in recent years. I'Anson needed 95 off the last 20 overs, but Chic Stedman and Ben Maxwell bowled tightly and restricted the run flow.

Farnham

A. Thorpe b Garfoot	104
M. Cooper b Kelly	102
S. Bentley st Potter b Kelly	36
R. Norman not out	30
I. Thorpe not out	7
Extras	9
Total (3 wkts dec)	288

Bowling: A. Kelly 2-77, R. Garfoot 1-55.

I'Anson

M. Pryce (Tilford) lbw b Maxwell	94
K. Tilson (Thursley) lbw b Stedman	20
J. Stressing (Thursley) b Stedman	54
A. Reid (Frimchett) c Robson b Maxwell	30
G. Poulter (The Bourne) c Norman b Maxwell	4
M. Potter (Frensham) c Cooper b Stedman	10
R. Garfoot (Badshot Lea) not out	36
A. Kelly (Witley) c Ray b Maxwell	3
N. Martyn (Tilford) not out	1
Total (7 wkts)	252

Did not bat: A. Gardiner (Frensham), A. Canning (Headley).
Bowling: B. Maxwell 4-66, C. Stedman 3-29.

5 Sept 1993: Haslemere 190-4dec (J. Howard 76) drew with I'Anson 177-8 (R. Baker 64no, T. Caston 33, G. Poulter 24; G. Boxall 4-41).

---

19 June 1994: I'Anson 206-4dec (A. Reid 63no, R. Baker 55, H. Macdonald 28, G. Poulter 24) drew with Haslemere 197-7 (G. Boxall 62; R. Mayhew 4-70, R. Clarke 3-95).

---

15 July 1994: Witley 155-7 dec (M. Barrow 46, A. White 27, A. Kelly 21; P. Murphy jnr 5-24) lost to I'Anson 156-5 (J. Willson 47, R. Scarth 35, B. Rapley 33; P. Wilson 3-34) by 5wkts in the Witley club's 125th year.

---

17 July 1994: I'Anson 252-6dec (M. Barnes 126no, D. Jervis 33no, M. Pryce 21) lost to Liphook 254-7 (D. Murphy 85; M. Cartwright 3-59, R. Clarke 2-60) by 3wkts. Former Grayshott player Tim Wheatley (18no) saw Liphook home in the last over. Matt Barnes, batting at eight, scored his runs in 19 overs after the I'Anson had been 65-5.

---

31 July 1994: I'Anson 208 (A. Reid 45, A. Culham 38, M. Barnes 28, M. Cartwright 26, D. Jervis 25, A. Sale 20; D. Kirkland 5-61) drew with Farnham 206-7 (R. Norman 59, M. Cooper 39, S. Bentley 31, M. Potter 29; R. Clarke 3-53, G. Clarke 2-52, T. Falkiner 2-58). Skipper Ray Clarke caught Rod Warriner off the last ball of the match after Warriner had hit Toby Falkiner's previous delivery into the Castle moat.

---

3 Aug 1994: I'Anson 232-1 dec (Q. Woods, a guest from Churt, 120no, A. Sale 57, G. Poulter 43no) v Alton 82-0, aban, rain.

---

14 Aug 1994: I'Anson 155-8 (R. Baker 83, R. Scarth 28) lost to Rowledge 156-2 (P. Offord 62, J. Harland 60no; R. Newnes-Smith 2-56) by 8wkts.

---

25 June 1995: I'Anson 219-7 dec (N. Mansbridge 39no, S. Whitley 35, R. Baker 34, G. May 28, J.G. Storey 25, A. Rooney 21no) drew with Haslemere 178-7 (I. Futcher 55, A. Tull 39, G. Swan 31; Whitley 3-34).

---

6 August 1995: Farnham 193-7 dec (P. Dickinson 55no, A. Thorpe 52, T. Caston 32; R. Clarke 3-58, A. Wheble 2-7) drew with I'Anson 189-9 (A. Reid 47, H. Macdonald 23, M. Potter 22, A. Wheble 21; Harpreet 5-77). Ray Clarke needed to hit Chic Stedman for six off the last ball. Farnham had nine men on the boundary, but Clarke, facing his only delivery, could only strike the ball into the covers.

---

20 Aug 1995: I'Anson 189-9 (M. Barnes 40, A. Culham 36, N. Mansbridge 25, M. Potter 22) bt Rowledge 177-7 (C.

Yates 62, D. Mitchell 28, S. Armstrong 27; R. Clarke 2-8) by 12 runs.

3 Sept 1995: I'Anson 213 (A. Page 70, A. Wheble 38, D. Jervis 28no, A. Reid 28) drew with Normandy 210-6 (R. Moorcroft 2-38, J.H. Storey 2-55) in Normandy's centenary season.

21 July 1996: Liphook 287-6 (C. Nevin 88; D. Whitehead 2-19, B. Maxwell 2-41, A. Culham 2-65) bt I'Anson 245 (B. Maxwell 66, A. Sale 33 – 112 for the 1st wicket, N. Mansbridge 32, D. Whitehead 29) by 42 runs. New Zealand Test player Chris Nevin and Graham Durtanovich (37) put on 126 for the third wicket.

28 July 1996: I'Anson 230-8 dec (G. Boardman 70, K. Waller 70, B. Maxwell 31, D. Jervis 22; E. Gulliver 4-40) drew with Grayshott 172-9 (E. Gulliver 66, D. Clarke 40; C. Fry 2-1, D. Clarke 2-47) in Grayshott's centenary season.

4 Aug 1996: I'Anson 259-8 dec(A. Reid 50, J. Kohler 38, A. Wheble 38, M. Potter 34, D. Coldicott 30no, R. Clarke 25no; Harpreet 6-96) lost to Farnham 263-4 (G. Clapham 129, R. Norman 62, A. Thorpe 45; A. Wheble 2-26) by 6wkts. Farnham were left 160 minutes and won in the last over. Gary Clapham and Richard Norman put on 114, and then Clapham and Alan Thorpe added a further 100.

13 July 1997: I'Anson 208 (H. Macdonald 102, N. Poulter 20; T. Shirley 3-18) bt Dogmersfield 104 (N. Shirley 31; P. Murphy jnr 6-21, N. Martyn 2-14, N. Mansbridge 2-20) by 104 runs in Dogmersfield's 50th anniversary cricket week.

20 July 1997: I'Anson 203-8 dec (A. Reid 83, H. Macdonald 31; R. Glaysher 5-49) lost to Liphook 207-2 (S. Riley 119no, G. Durtanovich 47, C. Nevin 32; B. Maxwell 2-53) by 8wkts.

3 Aug 1997: I'Anson 123-2 v Farnham, aban, rain.

19 July 1998: I'Anson 236-7dec (D. Jervis 85, J. Kohler 31, A. Wheble 29, R. Baker 27, N. Mansbridge 25; N. Thayer 3-29) lost to Liphook 238-5 (S. Riley 108, R. Hindley 68 – second-wicket stand of 200; A. Wheble 3-37) by 5wkts. I'Anson lost Sean Hopkinson, having made a duck on his debut, with a dislocated finger.

2 Aug 1998: Farnham 178-9 dec (I. Thorpe 78, M. Potter 46, G. Clapham 24; N. Thayer 4-61, A. Culham 2-36) bt I'Anson 161 (J. Kohler 49, S. Hopkinson 48, A. Page 22; P. Dickinson 7-42) by 17 runs. A damp pitch after overnight rain, but the game changed when Gary Clapham recalled Peter Dickinson and he took four wickets in an over, including a hat-trick.

9 Aug 1998: I'Anson 209 (R. Chuter 44, L. Pattison 36, A. Thomas 32, D. Jervis 29, S. Hopkinson 22; G. Senior 3-38, R. Pearce 3-46, A. Culham 2-30) bt The Bourne 157 (M. Siebert 31, A. Carder 22, S. Clark 22, W. Archer-Burton 22; N. Ayling 4-32, B. Croucher 2-26) by 52 runs in The Bourne's centenary season.

11 July 1999: Frensham 213 (J. Willson 35, S. Hopper 31, Ja Roberston 29; N. Martyn 2-2, N. Randall 2-26, A. Sale 2-29) lost to I'Anson 218-4 (R. Champneys 57no, N. Randall 55, H. Macdonald 37, M. Barnes 25, A. Sale 22no) by 6wkts in Frensham's centenary season.

Also 11 July 1999: I'Anson 275-7 (M. Allen 89, S. Hopkinson 44, B. Maxwell 38) bt Liphook 257 (C. Nevin 68; N. Mansbridge 5-38) by 18 runs.

1 Aug 1999: Farnham 239-6dec (A. Thorpe 99, P. Dickinson 45; A. Culham 4-50) bt I'Anson 203 (A. Cook 51, O. Harker-Smith 30, D. Foster 28, J. Webster 23; P. Dickinson 5-39, P. Murphy jnr 2-31) by 36 runs.

20 Aug 1999: Tongham 173-7 (M. Henderson 41, S. Reynolds 25, M. Eddleston 24; S. Ketley 4-28) bt I'Anson 126 (J. Crutcher 26, J. James 21no; T. Carrington 4-41, M. Henderson 3-43, M. Eddleston 2-19) by 47 runs in club's cricket week.

16 July 2000: Liphook 235 (M. Pasupati 68, J. Bulled 54; R. Garfoot 4-28, K. Haymon 4-49) bt I'Anson 173-8 (A. Cook 37, D. Foster 24) by 62 runs.

6 Aug 2000: Farnham 273-7dec (G. Hicks 72, A. Thorpe 56; R. Garfoot 4-56, A. Culham 2-51) bt I'Anson 234 (A. Culham 48, G. Badland 41no, A. Cook 40, O. Harker-Smith 27; P. Dickinson 3-54) by 39 runs.

Centenary year

22 July 2001: I'Anson 185 (A. Cook 75, K. Ritchie 20, N. Thayer 20) bt Liphook 146 (D. Elliott 51; A. Rooke 4-17) by 39 runs at Witley.

5 Aug 2001: I'Anson 133 (T. Robinson 33, A. Cook 26, J. Kohler 20; N. Whitworth 4-20, P. Murphy jnr 3-19) lost to Farnham 136-2 (N. Whitworth 76no, G. Hicks 30no) by 8wkts at Dogmersfield.

7 Aug 2001: Old England 210-4 (G. Humpage 56, P. Parker

The I'Anson Cup XI that played Farnham at Dogmersfield at the start of the centenary year cricket week in 2001. Standing, from the left: David Havenhand (umpire), Nick Thayer (Frensham), Kevin Goodship (Milford), John Kohler (Frensham), Travis Robinson (Puttenham), Len Smith (captain, Dogmersfield), Andy Rooke (The Bourne), Andy Sale (The Bourne), Ashley Cook (Headley), Tony Stillwell (umpire). Seated: Graham Badland (Headley), Alastair Lindsey Clark (Grayshott), Eddie Smith (Dogmersfield).

45, R. Tolchard 44no, R. Parks 34; G. Sylvester 3-50) drew with I'Anson 110-8 (M. Barnes 22, J. Crutcher 20; T. Pigott 3-29, D. Underwood 2-11) at The Bourne.

---

8 Aug 2001: MCC 211-3dec (J. Butler 159no) bt I'Anson 188 (P. Osborn 71, A. Cook 51, N. Ayling 36; A. Stedman 3-17, V. Sethi 3-39) by 23 runs at Grayshott.

Test players of the past made up the Old England XI against an I'Anson representative XI at The Bourne in the centenary year cricket week. In front, David Allen (left), the captain, and Jim Parks, the manager. Behind, from the left: Roger Tolchard, Paul Parker, Derek Underwood, Richard Ellison, Geoff Humpage, Tom Cartwright, Tony Pigott, David Ward, Peter Lever, Clive Radley, Bobby Parks. Picture courtesy of the Herald.

Paul Bedford, MCC captain, presents Ken Williams with a plaque to commemorate the centenary cricket week match against an I'Anson XI at Grayshott. Norman Disney and Keith Mayson make up the quartet.

10 Aug 2001: I'Anson 288-5 (A. Cook 70, A. Sale 52, J. Kohler 51, S. Whitley 45, M. Druce 29; B. Daniels 3-35) bt Lord's Taverners 211 (B. Daniels 78, D. Capel 35, M. Denness 25, C. Tavare 22; B. Rapley 4-47) by 77 runs at Frensham.

Festival cricket at Frensham for our centenary year match with Lord's Taverners. The batsman is Simon Whitley of Grayshott. Picture courtesy of the Herald.

Tindle Newspapers, publishers of the Herald, *were the main sponsors in our centenary year. Here, managing director Bob West receives a plaque from actor John Alderton, on behalf of Lord's Taverners, during the cricket week match at Frensham. Also pictured, from the left, are Graham Collyer, Norman Disney, John Price, the former Middlesex and England fast bowler who is the Taverners' director of cricket, John Snow, the former Sussex and England opening bowler, Keith Mayson and Peter Thompson, editorial manager of the* Herald. *Picture courtesy of the* Herald.

12 Aug 2001: I'Anson 170-9 (R. Baker 51, A. Wheble 46; H. Tiffen 3-14) bt England Ladies 106 (D. Holden 39, C. Atkins 22; P. Murphy 4-7, M. Eddleston 4-22) by 64 runs at Hindhead.

23 Sept 2001: Bat and Ball (Hambledon) 172-9 (K. Wheatley 62; J. Fairall 7-60) bt I'Anson 135-6 (A. Champneys 71, A. Rooney 40; J. Balmer 4-10) by 37 runs at Headley.

Man of the match! Barbara Daniels, of England Ladies, was adjudged the player of the match when she appeared for Lord's Taverners against an I'Anson XI at Frensham in the centenary year cricket week. She is pictured with Ken Bone, the Frensham president.

Former England captain Mike Denness, who skippered Lord's Taverners, presents a bag of youth cricket equipment to Frensham president Ken Bone, to mark the club's hosting of the centenary year match. Also pictured are Barry Rapley (Thursley), Ray Clarke (Frensham), Nigel Martyn (Tilford), Neil Poulter (The Bourne) and former England batsman Chris Tavare.

I'Anson and Lord's Taverners teams and officials line up at Frensham. Picture courtesy of the Herald.

England Ladies captain Clare Connor receives a memento of the match against an I'Anson XI from Hindhead chairman Stephen Marshall. The match marked the 50th anniversary of England Ladies' first appearance at Hindhead.

They were mostly veterans who turned out for the I'Anson and Bat and Ball (Hambledon) teams at Headley in September 2001, the final representative fixture in centenary year.

How they finished

1951

I'Anson Cup

	P	W	D	L	Pts
The Bourne	22	15	5	2	35
Tilford	22	15	3	4	33
Elstead	22	14	3	5	31
Grayshott	22	13	5	4	31
Headley	22	10	5	7	25
Rowledge	22	8	7	7	23
Binsted	22	6	6	10	18
Shottermill	22	6	4	12	16
Frensham	22	5	4	13	14
Whitehill	22	5	4	13	14
Thursley	22	5	3	14	13
Churt	22	4	3	15	11

Miller Cup

	P	W	D	L	Pts
The Bourne	20	16	3	1	35
Elstead	20	16	2	2	34
Wrecclesham	20	14	4	2	32
Rowledge	20	11	3	6	25
Tilford	20	9	5	6	23
Frensham	20	9	4	7	22
Grayshott	20	10	2	8	22
Kingsley	20	9	3	8	21
Headley	20	7	5	8	19
Oakhanger	20	6	4	10	16
Shottermill	20	6	3	11	15
Lindford	20	3	4	13	10
Whitehill	20	3	4	13	10
Binsted	20	3	2	15	8
Churt	20	3	2	15	8

1952

I'Anson Cup

	P	W	D	L	Pts
Elstead	18	15	0	3	30
The Bourne	18	14	2	2	30
Tilford	18	12	2	4	26
Headley	18	10	2	6	22
Rowledge	18	10	1	7	21
Grayshott	18	9	2	7	20
Churt	18	5	2	11	12
Frensham	18	4	2	12	10
Whitehill	18	2	1	15	5
Shottermill	18	1	2	15	4

Elstead beat The Bourne in a play-off

Miller Cup

	P	W	D	L	Pts
Wrecclesham	16	14	0	2	28
The Bourne	16	12	1	3	25
Binsted	16	11	2	3	24
Elstead	16	10	3	3	23
Lindford	16	9	0	7	18
Thursley	16	8	2	6	12
Tilford	16	8	1	7	17
Rowledge	16	7	2	7	16
Shottermill	16	5	2	9	12
Grayshott	16	5	1	10	11
Churt	16	5	0	11	10
Headley	16	1	1	14	3
Frensham	16	1	1	14	3

1953

I'Anson Cup

	P	W	D	L	Pts
The Bourne	16	15	0	1	30
Elstead	16	12	1	3	25
Tilford	16	12	1	3	25
Grayshott	16	9	0	7	18
Wrecclesham	16	8	0	8	16
Rowledge	16	5	0	11	10
Headley	16	4	0	12	8
Churt	16	3	0	13	6
Frensham	16	3	0	13	6

Stevens Cup

	P	W	D	L	Pts
Thursley	16	14	0	2	28
Binsted	16	9	0	7	18
Lindford	16	9	0	7	18
Kingsley	16	5	1	10	11
Whitehill	16	2	1	13	5

Miller Cup

	P	W	D	L	Pts
The Bourne	16	15	0	1	30
Rowledge	16	15	0	1	30
Elstead	16	11	0	5	22
Tilford	16	8	0	8	16
Grayshott	16	7	0	9	14
Wrecclesham	16	7	0	9	14
Frensham	16	5	0	11	10
Churt	16	3	0	13	6
Headley	16	1	0	15	2

The Bourne beat Rowledge in a play-off

1954

I'Anson Cup

	P	W	D	L	Pts
Tilford	16	11	3	2	53
The Bourne	16	9	4	3	46
Elstead	16	8	3	5	40
Headley	16	8	2	6	39
Wrecclesham	16	9	0	7	37
Rowledge	16	7	3	6	35
Grayshott	16	4	4	8	25
Frensham	16	5	2	9	24
Churt	16	0	1	15	2

Stevens Cup

	P	W	D	L	Pts
Lindford	10	8	1	1	35
Alexandra Pk	10	5	2	3	24
Thursley	10	4	2	4	21
Shottermill	10	3	2	5	17
Whitehill	10	3	1	6	14
Binsted	10	2	2	6	12

Miller Cup

	P	W	D	L	Pts
The Bourne	16	16	0	0	71
Rowledge	16	11	1	4	49
Grayshott	16	10	0	6	45
Wrecclesham	16	10	1	5	44
Elstead	16	7	2	7	35
Tilford	16	5	3	8	27
Churt	16	4	1	11	19
Frensham	16	4	1	11	18
Headley	16	0	1	15	2

1955

I'Anson Cup

	P	W	D	L	Pts
The Bourne	16	13	1	2	56
Wrecclesham	16	11	1	4	49
Grayshott	16	9	1	6	39
Headley	16	8	0	8	36
Elstead	16	8	1	7	35
Tilford	16	7	2	7	35
Rowledge	16	7	1	8	32
Frensham	16	3	2	11	20
Churt	16	1	1	14	6

Stevens Cup

	P	W	D	L	Pts
The Bourne II	10	7	1	2	31
Thursley	10	7	0	3	29
Shottermill	10	4	2	4	21
Lindford	10	4	1	5	19
Rowledge II	10	4	0	6	16
Alexandra Pk	10	2	0	8	8

Miller Cup

	P	W	D	L	Pts
Elstead	14	13	0	1	64
Tilford	14	13	0	1	64
Frensham	14	7	0	7	32
Grayshott	14	6	0	8	29
Wrecclesham	14	6	0	8	29
Churt	14	5	0	9	22
Headley	14	3	0	11	14
Alexandra Pk	14	3	0	11	13

Elstead beat Tilford in a play-off

1956

I'Anson Cup

	P	W	D	L	Pts
Wrecclesham	16	13	2	1	60
The Bourne	16	10	2	4	48
Tilford	16	10	2	4	45
Rowledge	16	7	3	6	38
Elstead	16	8	2	6	37
Grayshott	16	8	1	7	36
Headley	16	4	2	10	22
Frensham	16	4	1	11	19
Churt	16	0	1	15	2

Miller Cup

	P	W	D	L	Pts
The Bourne	22	16	2	4	79
Thursley	22	15	3	4	70
Tilford	22	14	1	7	66.5
Rowledge	22	13	3	6	66
Lindford	22	10	5	7	57
Shottermill	22	9	3	10	47
Grayshott	22	10	1	11	45
Elstead	22	8	3	11	41
Wrecclesham	22	7	2	13	36
Frensham	22	7	2	13	35
Churt	22	5	2	15	25
Headley	22	3	3	16	20.5

1957

I'Anson Cup

	P	W	D	L	Pts
Tilford	18	14	2	2	64
The Bourne	18	11	3	4	52
Rowledge	18	10	4	4	50
Headley	18	10	2	6	46
Elstead	18	9	1	8	43
Wrecclesham	18	9	3	6	40
Thursley	18	7	2	9	33
Grayshott	18	5	4	9	30
Churt	18	1	3	14	11
Frensham	18	1	2	15	8

Miller Cup

	P	W	D	L	Pts
Shottermill	20	17	1	2	77
The Bourne	20	16	0	4	70
Rowledge	20	12	1	7	61
Headley	20	9	3	8	45
Lindford	20	9	2	9	43
Elstead	20	9	0	11	39
Tilford	20	7	2	11	36
Grayshott	20	8	1	11	35
Wrecclesham	20	7	1	12	33
Frensham	20	5	2	13	25
Churt	20	4	1	15	18

1958

I'Anson Cup

	P	W	D	L	Pts
Tilford	18	13	2	3	60
Rowledge	18	12	3	3	60
The Bourne	18	12	1	5	52
Elstead	18	9	2	7	44
Thursley	18	9	2	7	42
Wrecclesham	18	8	2	8	41
Headley	18	9	1	8	38
Grayshott	18	6	1	11	29
Churt	18	3	0	15	17
Frensham	18	1	2	15	8

Tilford beat Rowledge in a play-off

Miller Cup

	P	W	D	L	Pts
The Bourne	20	17	0	3	79
Shottermill	20	17	0	3	79
Rowledge	20	15	0	5	67
Tilford	20	14	0	6	59
Headley	20	8	1	11	36
Wrecclesham	20	7	2	11	33
Lindford	20	7	2	11	32
Elstead	20	7	1	12	30
Frensham	20	6	1	13	28
Grayshott	20	4	1	15	19
Churt	20	4	0	16	16

The Bourne beat Shottermill in a play-off

1959

I'Anson Cup

	P	W	D	L	Pts
Rowledge	20	16	1	3	72
The Bourne	20	15	2	3	65
Tilford	20	12	5	3	62
Headley	20	11	3	6	54
Elstead	20	11	3	6	52
Thursley	20	7	6	7	42
Wrecclesham	20	8	3	9	36
Shottermill	20	2	4	14	20
Grayshott	20	3	4	13	20
Churt	20	4	2	14	20
Frensham	20	3	3	14	18

Miller Cup

	P	W	D	L	Pts
Tilford	18	17	0	1	75
The Bourne	18	15	0	3	66
Rowledge	18	13	1	4	62
Elstead	18	10	0	8	41
Shottermill	18	6	1	11	29
Wrecclesham	18	7	0	11	29
Grayshott	18	6	0	12	27
Churt	18	6	1	11	26
Frensham	18	5	0	13	21
Headley	18	3	1	14	16

V.O. ('Cody') Goolding, who was a well-known sportsman and official in Farnham and district, and in particular Farnham Town FC, was Tilford II's captain when they won the Miller Cup in 1959. Making the presentation is Maj. Anthony Knight, of Thursley, who was a key figure in the early days of the Two Counties Youth Competition. 'Cody' Goolding was Tilford's president when he died in 1994.

1960

I'Anson Cup

	P	W	D	L	Pts
Rowledge	20	18	0	2	76
Headley	20	14	2	4	63
Tilford	20	13	2	5	62
The Bourne	20	13	3	4	60
Elstead	20	9	3	8	43
Wrecclesham	20	8	3	9	40
Grayshott	20	5	5	10	30
Thursley	20	5	1	14	23
Frensham	20	4	3	13	22
Churt	20	3	4	13	20
Shottermill	20	4	2	14	20

Miller Cup

	P	W	D	L	Pts
The Bourne	18	16	1	1	75
Tilford	18	16	1	1	74
Rowledge	18	10	0	8	45
Elstead	18	9	2	7	43
Grayshott	18	7	2	9	35
Churt	18	8	0	10	34
Wrecclesham	18	7	0	11	31
Frensham	18	7	0	11	30
Headley	18	5	0	13	22
Shottermill	18	2	0	16	9

1961

I'Anson Cup

	P	W	D	L	Pts
Tilford	18	13	3	2	60
The Bourne	18	11	3	4	53
Rowledge	18	11	2	5	53
Thursley	18	9	4	5	44
Wrecclesham	18	8	3	7	38
Headley	18	8	2	8	38
Grayshott	18	8	1	9	34
Frensham	18	3	4	11	20
Churt	18	3	3	12	18
Elstead	18	2	3	13	15

Miller Cup

	P	W	D	L	Pts
The Bourne	16	11	3	2	54
Tilford	16	11	2	3	51
Frensham	16	10	1	5	44
Wrecclesham	16	9	0	7	37
Elstead	16	7	1	8	33
Rowledge	16	6	1	9	27
Headley	16	6	1	9	27
Grayshott	16	4	0	12	18
Churt	16	3	1	12	15

1962

I'Anson Cup

	P	W	D	L	Pts
Headley	18	15	1	2	65
The Bourne	18	12	2	4	54
Tilford	18	10	3	5	50
Frensham	18	9	1	8	43
Grayshott	18	9	2	7	41
Rowledge	18	8	1	9	39
Thursley	18	7	2	9	32
Churt	18	5	1	12	23
Elstead	18	4	2	12	21
Wrecclesham	18	3	1	14	14

Miller Cup

	P	W	D	L	Pts
The Bourne	14	12	1	1	56
Tilford	14	12	1	1	56
Frensham	14	10	0	4	47
Rowledge	14	9	0	5	44
Wrecclesham	14	5	1	8	25
Grayshott	14	2	1	11	12
Elstead	14	2	0	12	10
Headley	14	2	0	12	9

The Bourne beat Tilford in a play-off

The time-honoured place for presentations at Tilford – the steps of the Institute. Here, Jack Warner makes his speech after receiving the Miller Cup in 1963. In the foreground is Lt-Col. Jim Cornwell, the club secretary who was shortly to become the competitions treasurer and subsequently the secretary. From the left, the other players are Peter Taylor, Pat Alderton, Robin Collins, John Fullbrook, Charlie Reffold, Don Paine and Ted Hammond.

1963

I'Anson Cup

	P	W	D	L	Pts
Rowledge	18	13	2	3	64
Headley	18	13	4	1	64
The Bourne	18	10	5	3	51
Thursley	18	8	4	6	40
Grayshott	18	7	4	7	37
Tilford	18	7	3	8	33
Frensham	18	6	3	9	33
Elstead	18	6	3	9	32
Churt	18	2	4	12	17
Wrecclesham	18	1	3	14	10

Rowledge beat Headley in a play-off

Miller Cup

	P	W	D	L	Pts
Tilford	14	10	3	1	53
Rowledge	14	9	3	2	47
The Bourne	14	8	5	1	44
Headley	14	5	4	5	28
Wrecclesham	14	5	2	7	24
Frensham	14	4	3	7	24
Grayshott	14	2	3	9	15
Elstead	14	1	1	12	6

1964
I'Anson Cup

	P	W	D	L	Pts
The Bourne	18	13	2	3	60
Rowledge	18	12	2	4	57
Headley	18	12	1	5	51
Tilford	18	10	2	6	44
Grayshott	18	9	2	7	41
Elstead	18	6	1	11	28
Wrecclesham	18	6	1	11	27
Frensham	18	4	2	12	23
Churt	18	5	1	12	23
Thursley	18	4	2	12	20

Miller Cup

	P	W	D	L	Pts
The Bourne	18	17	1	0	80
Alexandra Pk	18	15	0	3	68
Rowledge	18	11	1	6	51
Frensham	18	10	1	7	44
Tilford	18	9	1	8	41
Whitehill	18	9	1	8	41
Wrecclesham	18	9	1	8	41
Headley	18	4	3	11	25
Grayshott	18	3	1	14	15
Elstead	18	0	0	18	0

1965
I'Anson Cup

	P	W	D	L	Pts
Rowledge	18	14	3	1	68
The Bourne	18	12	3	3	55
Tilford	18	11	4	3	54
Headley	18	10	3	5	47
Thursley	18	8	6	4	46
Grayshott	18	8	1	9	35
Frensham	18	5	3	10	26
Elstead	18	4	0	14	18
Churt	18	2	4	12	17
Wrecclesham	18	2	2	14	12

Miller Cup

	P	W	D	L	Pts
The Bourne	18	15	1	2	66
Rowledge	18	13	1	4	62
Alexandra Pk	18	12	3	3	57
Tilford	18	11	1	6	53
Whitehill	18	9	0	9	41
Wrecclesham	18	9	1	8	40
Frensham	18	6	3	9	33
Headley	18	4	1	13	19
Grayshott	18	4	2	12	17
Elstead	18	1	1	16	6

1966
I'Anson Cup

	P	W	D	L	Pts
Rowledge	18	12	3	2	56
Tilford	18	10	5	3	52
Thursley	18	9	6	3	48
The Bourne	18	9	4	5	46
Frensham	18	9	1	8	38
Grayshott	18	8	2	8	36
Headley	18	8	2	8	36
Alexandra Pk	18	4	5	8	27
Elstead	18	4	1	13	21
Wrecclesham	18	1	2	15	9

Tie: Rowledge v Alexandra Park

Miller Cup

	P	W	D	L	Pts
Whitehill	16	12	1	3	56
Frensham	16	11	1	4	50
Tilford	16	8	4	4	43
Wrecclesham	16	8	3	5	40
Rowledge	16	7	2	7	35
Headley	16	6	1	9	30
The Bourne	16	6	2	8	30
Grayshott	16	3	3	10	20
Elstead	16	2	1	13	10

1967
I'Anson Cup

	P	W	D	L	Pts
Rowledge	18	12	6	0	62
Thursley	18	8	7	3	47
Grayshott	18	8	4	6	43
The Bourne	18	9	3	6	42
Tilford	18	6	8	4	41
Headley	18	8	4	6	40
Wrecclesham	18	8	2	8	38
Whitehill	18	4	3	11	22
Frensham	18	4	2	12	20
Elstead	18	2	4	12	17

Miller Cup

	P	W	D	L	Pts
Alexandra Pk	18	13	2	3	59
Rowledge	18	12	1	5	53
Tilford	18	9	3	6	44
Wrecclesham	18	9	4	5	44
Headley	18	9	2	7	41
The Bourne	18	8	3	7	39
Whitehill	18	6	3	9	32
Frensham	18	5	3	10	28
Grayshott	18	5	4	9	28
Elstead	18	2	2	14	13

1968
I'Anson Cup

	P	W	D	L	Pts
The Bourne	18	9	7	2	52
Grayshott	18	9	5	4	47
Rowledge	18	7	8	3	46
Wrecclesham	18	8	6	4	44
Thursley	18	6	9	3	43
Tilford	18	5	7	6	34
Whitehill	18	5	5	8	31
Headley	18	5	5	8	31
Elstead	18	4	6	8	28
Frensham	18	2	2	14	12

Miller Cup

	P	W	D	L	Pts
The Bourne	20	13	5	2	66
Alexandra Pk	20	9	5	6	47
Grayshott	20	10	3	7	47
Kingsley	20	9	3	8	42
Rowledge	20	7	6	7	41
Wrecclesham	20	7	6	7	40
Whitehill	20	7	4	9	38
Frensham	20	6	6	8	37
Headley	20	6	4	10	34
Elstead	20	6	4	10	34
Tilford	20	4	7	9	30

1969
I'Anson Cup

	P	W	D	L	Pts
Grayshott	18	9	8	1	56
Thursley	18	10	6	2	54
The Bourne	18	9	7	2	52
Headley	18	6	10	2	42
Whitehill	18	6	7	5	38
Tilford	18	6	5	7	34
Wrecclesham	18	4	6	8	28
Frensham	18	5	2	11	26
Rowledge	18	2	8	8	24
Elstead	18	2	3	13	14

Miller Cup

	P	W	D	L	Pts
Whitehill	18	13	3	2	64
The Bourne	18	12	5	1	58
Wrecclesham	18	10	2	6	46
Kingsley	18	8	3	7	40
Elstead	18	8	1	9	40
Grayshott	18	8	4	6	40
Headley	18	5	4	9	28
Rowledge	18	4	4	10	24
Frensham	18	3	3	12	20
Tilford	18	3	3	12	18

1970

I'Anson Cup

	P	W	D	L	Pts
Thursley	18	13	3	2	62
Headley	18	13	3	2	60
The Bourne	18	9	5	4	48
Grayshott	18	9	4	5	46
Rowledge	18	8	3	7	40
Whitehill	18	6	5	7	36
Frensham	18	5	3	10	28
Tilford	18	3	5	10	24
Elstead	18	3	3	12	18
Wrecclesham	18	2	4	12	16

Miller Cup

	P	W	D	L	Pts
The Bourne	18	13	4	1	68
Grayshott	18	13	3	2	62
Headley	18	12	1	5	54
Kingsley	18	10	3	5	46
Whitehill	18	10	1	7	46
Tilford	18	6	1	11	28
Wrecclesham	18	6	1	11	28
Rowledge	18	3	3	12	20
Elstead	18	4	1	13	18
Frensham	18	2	2	14	15

1971

I'Anson Cup

	P	W	D	L	Pts
Thursley	18	11	3	4	58
Rowledge	18	9	7	2	50
The Bourne	18	7	7	4	42
Grayshott	18	6	7	5	40
Headley	18	5	10	3	40
Tilford	18	5	8	5	36
Whitehill	18	5	7	6	34
Wrecclesham	18	4	5	9	26
Elstead	18	4	3	11	24
Frensham	18	3	5	10	22

Miller Cup

	P	W	D	L	Pts
Elstead	18	12	2	4	58
Whitehill	18	11	1	6	58
The Bourne	18	13	0	5	56
Grayshott	18	8	4	6	40
Wrecclesham	18	8	2	8	40
Rowledge	18	5	8	5	38
Kingsley	18	7	3	8	34
Tilford	18	4	4	10	24
Frensham	18	3	5	10	22
Headley	18	4	1	13	18

Elstead beat Whitehill in a play-off

1972

I'Anson Cup

	P	W	D	L	Pts
Thursley	20	12	7	1	55
Tilford	20	11	4	4	54
Rowledge	20	9	8	2	52
Headley	20	8	6	6	40
The Bourne	20	7	9	4	39
Frensham	20	7	6	7	36
Whitehill	20	7	4	9	34
Churt	20	4	8	8	24
Grayshott	20	3	11	6	23
Elstead	20	2	5	13	13
Wrecclesham	20	1	8	11	12

Tie: Tilford v Rowledge

Miller Cup

	P	W	D	L	Pts
Headley	22	14	6	2	62
Frensham	22	12	4	6	54
Tilford	22	10	6	6	46
The Bourne	22	8	9	5	45
Lindford	22	10	4	8	44
Wrecclesham	22	8	6	8	41
Churt	22	8	5	9	37
Kingsley	22	8	3	11	37
Grayshott	22	7	8	7	36
Whitehill	22	6	5	11	31
Rowledge	22	4	7	11	23
Elstead	22	3	5	14	9

1973

I'Anson Cup

	P	W	D	L	Pts
Tilford	22	14	6	2	64
Thursley	22	13	6	3	58
Headley	22	11	8	3	54
Whitehill	22	10	7	5	47
The Bourne	22	10	6	6	46
Grayshott	22	8	9	5	38
Churt	22	7	7	7	37
Rowledge	22	7	7	8	37
Wrecclesham	22	3	10	8	24
Frensham	22	3	6	13	18
Lindford	22	2	7	13	17
Elstead	22	1	6	15	10

Tie: Churt v Wrecclesham

Miller Cup

	P	W	D	L	Pts
Churt	22	15	3	4	71
Headley	22	15	2	5	70
Tilford	22	14	3	5	59
The Bourne	22	13	3	6	59
Thursley	22	12	1	9	57
Kingsley	22	12	2	8	50
Grayshott	22	11	3	8	49
Rowledge	22	9	4	9	42
Whitehill	22	6	3	13	27
Frensham	22	4	4	14	20
Wrecclesham	22	3	2	17	14
Elstead	22	2	2	18	10

1974

I'Anson Cup

	P	W	D	L	Pts
Whitehill	22	13	6	3	60
Frensham	22	13	5	4	59
Rowledge	22	12	5	5	55
Tilford	22	11	8	3	54
Churt	22	10	7	5	47
The Bourne	22	10	7	5	47
Headley	22	10	6	6	46
Elstead	22	6	5	11	29
Grayshott	22	4	6	12	27
Wrecclesham	22	4	3	15	19
Thursley	22	4	2	16	18
Lindford	22	3	5	14	17

Miller Cup

	P	W	D	L	Pts
Whitehill	22	17	0	5	72
Churt	22	13	6	3	60
Kingsley	22	11	4	7	56
Thursley	22	12	2	8	56
Grayshott	22	9	5	7	45
The Bourne	22	7	8	7	36
Headley	22	7	7	8	35
Elstead	22	7	3	12	34
Tilford	22	7	5	10	33
Rowledge	22	5	6	10	30
Wrecclesham	22	3	8	11	20
Frensham	22	3	6	13	20

Tie: Grayshott v Rowledge

1975

I'Anson Cup

	P	W	D	L	Pts
Rowledge	22	12	9	1	59
Churt	22	11	9	2	53
The Bourne	22	11	6	5	52
Thursley	22	10	7	5	47
Whitehill	22	8	8	6	44
Frensham	22	7	6	9	36
Headley	22	6	12	4	36
Tilford	22	6	9	7	33
Grayshott	22	4	11	7	27
Lindford	22	5	6	11	26
Elstead	22	2	8	12	16
Wrecclesham	22	2	5	15	13

Miller Cup

	P	W	D	L	Pts
Rowledge	22	15	5	2	67
Thursley	22	13	2	7	58
Kingsley	22	11	6	4	56
Whitehill	22	11	4	7	52
Churt	22	10	5	7	47
Headley	22	10	4	8	44
The Bourne	22	8	4	9	40
Tilford	22	7	7	8	35
Elstead	22	6	4	12	28
Frensham	22	5	6	11	26
Grayshott	22	5	2	15	22
Wrecclesham	22	4	3	15	19

Tie: Kingsley v The Bourne

1976

I'Anson Cup

	P	W	D	L	Pts
Churt	22	19	1	2	81
The Bourne	22	15	2	5	62
Rowledge	22	12	4	5	60
Frensham	22	12	2	8	50
Tilford	22	9	4	7	48
Grayshott	22	9	6	7	42
Headley	22	9	2	10	40
Whitehill	22	8	3	11	37
Thursley	22	8	1	13	33
Elstead	22	5	2	15	22
Lindford	22	5	1	16	21
Wrecclesham	22	4	2	16	18

Ties: Rowledge v Tilford; Tilford v Headley

Miller Cup

	P	W	D	L	Pts
Thursley	22	16	1	5	77
Kingsley	22	16	1	5	75
Churt	22	13	2	6	56
Frensham	22	11	2	9	48
Rowledge	22	10	3	9	43
Headley	22	8	2	12	43
Tilford	22	9	2	10	42
Wrecclesham	22	8	2	12	38
Whitehill	22	8	0	13	37
Grayshott	22	8	2	12	36
The Bourne	22	6	4	12	28
Elstead	22	5	3	14	23

Tie: Churt v Whitehill

1977

I'Anson Cup

	P	W	D	L	Pts
Churt	22	13	6	3	60
The Bourne	22	11	9	2	55
Grayshott	22	10	10	2	50
Headley	22	10	7	5	49
Tilford	22	10	7	5	47
Rowledge	22	9	9	4	45
Whitehill	22	7	7	8	39
Thursley	22	6	7	9	31
Frensham	22	6	6	10	30
Elstead	22	5	4	13	24
Lindford	22	3	5	14	17
Wrecclesham	22	0	7	15	7

Miller Cup

	P	W	D	L	Pts
Churt	22	14	5	2	69
Kingsley	22	12	8	2	60
Tilford	22	10	7	5	49
Grayshott	22	10	5	7	45
Thursley	22	9	4	9	44
Headley	22	9	5	8	43
Whitehill	22	7	4	10	38
The Bourne	22	7	5	10	35
Frensham	22	7	5	10	35
Elstead	22	6	5	11	31
Wrecclesham	22	4	7	11	23
Rowledge	22	4	4	14	20

Tie: Churt v Whitehill

1978

I'Anson Cup

	P	W	D	L	Pts
Tilford	22	16	4	2	70
Headley	22	14	4	4	62
Rowledge	22	13	4	5	56
The Bourne	22	12	4	6	54
Churt	22	11	7	4	51
Grayshott	22	9	7	6	43
Frensham	22	8	3	11	37
Whitehill	22	7	6	9	34
Wrecclesham	22	4	10	8	26
Lindford	22	4	6	12	22
Thursley	22	1	5	16	9
Elstead	22	0	6	16	6

Miller Cup

	P	W	D	L	Pts
The Bourne	22	16	4	2	74
Churt	22	14	3	4	65
Kingsley	22	12	6	4	54
Rowledge	22	10	5	6	49
Grayshott	22	10	4	7	48
Thursley	22	9	4	9	42
Tilford	22	9	3	10	41
Wrecclesham	22	7	4	10	36
Frensham	22	7	3	12	31
Elstead	22	6	6	10	30
Headley	22	4	2	16	18
Whitehill	22	3	2	17	14

Ties: Churt v Rowledge; Grayshott v Wrecclesham

1979

I'Anson Cup

	P	W	D	L	BP	Pts
Headley	22	16	5	1	93	169
Rowledge	22	13	7	2	88	153
Churt	22	9	8	4	95	141
Thursley	22	9	9	3	86	133
The Bourne	22	8	5	8	90	129
Tilford	22	7	9	6	80	117
Whitehill	22	6	10	6	82	116
Grayshott	22	6	9	7	80	113
Frensham	22	7	4	11	80	112
Elstead	22	5	6	10	64	92
Wrecclesham	22	2	8	12	66	82
Lindford	22	0	4	18	48	52

Ties: Churt v The Bourne, Thursley v Elstead

Miller Cup

	P	W	D	L	BP	Pts
Churt	22	12	9	1	98	159
The Bourne	22	13	6	3	90	154
Kingsley	22	14	4	4	84	152
Grayshott	22	13	8	1	86	152
Headley	22	9	5	8	83	124
Rowledge	22	7	6	9	83	117
Whitehill	22	6	5	11	76	105
Thursley	22	6	3	13	69	96
Elstead	22	5	6	11	70	96
Frensham	22	5	4	13	69	93
Wrecclesham	22	4	9	9	65	90
Tilford	22	2	7	13	61	76

1980

I'Anson Cup

	P	W	D	L	BP	Pts
Rowledge	22	16	5	1	127	202
Churt	22	12	10	0	109	171
Grayshott	22	12	7	3	109	168
The Bourne	22	8	9	5	100	141
Tilford	22	9	5	8	93	134
Headley	22	7	6	9	90	124
Whitehill	22	7	5	10	89	122
Frensham	22	6	6	10	90	122
Wrecclesham	22	6	8	8	85	117
Thursley	22	6	6	10	81	113
Lindford	22	4	1	17	67	84
Elstead	22	3	5	15	63	80

Miller Cup

	P	W	D	L	BP	Pts
Churt	22	13	5	4	126	189
Kingsley	22	15	4	3	107	177
Frensham	22	14	2	6	105	171
Headley	22	13	3	5	105	168
Rowledge	22	10	9	3	94	143
The Bourne	22	9	5	8	93	134
Wrecclesham	22	8	4	10	92	128
Thursley	22	6	4	12	89	117
Elstead	22	6	6	9	79	111
Grayshott	22	5	6	11	74	100
Tilford	22	5	3	14	69	92
Whitehill	22	0	4	18	54	58

Tie: Headley v Elstead

1981

I'Anson Cup

	P	W	D	L	BP	Pts
Rowledge	22	15	5	2	101	187
Tilford	22	12	6	4	88	160
Frensham	22	9	8	5	92	148
Churt	22	9	10	3	82	146
The Bourne	22	8	9	5	87	139
Grayshott	22	9	7	6	74	135
Headley	22	5	9	8	79	119
Thursley	22	6	7	9	74	117
Lindford	22	6	8	8	65	109
Wrecclesham	22	5	7	10	61	102
Elstead	22	2	8	12	64	91
Whitehill	22	1	6	15	56	76

Miller Cup

	P	W	D	L	BP	Pts
Churt	22	16	3	3	94	185
Kingsley	22	14	5	3	86	180
Frensham	22	11	6	5	83	160
Rowledge	22	10	6	6	82	144
Elstead	22	11	4	7	74	144
Wrecclesham	22	11	3	7	70	141
The Bourne	22	9	4	9	74	131
Thursley	22	7	4	11	66	114
Grayshott	22	6	3	12	60	106
Tilford	22	5	5	11	60	103
Headley	22	5	2	14	55	90
Whitehill	22	2	1	19	40	54

Ties: Wrecclesham v Grayshott, Tilford v Headley

1982

I'Anson Cup

	P	W	D	L	BP	Pts
Rowledge	22	14	6	2	99	178
Whitehill	22	13	3	6	104	175
Tilford	22	11	8	3	94	160
Churt	22	10	5	7	94	152
Grayshott	22	9	8	5	92	150
Frensham	22	8	6	8	88	137
Wrecclesham	22	7	6	9	82	123
The Bourne	22	5	9	8	80	117
Headley	22	7	5	10	72	115
Thursley	22	3	7	12	65	93
Elstead	22	3	10	9	51	82
Lindford	22	3	5	14	52	78

Miller Cup

	P	W	D	L	BP	Pts
Kingsley	22	15	4	2	113	199
Wrecclesham	22	15	4	2	112	198
Churt	22	11	6	5	94	155
The Bourne	22	11	2	9	85	142
Rowledge	22	8	5	9	92	136
Thursley	22	10	3	9	78	134
Whitehill	22	8	7	6	85	134
Frensham	22	7	5	10	84	130
Grayshott	22	5	8	8	72	113
Tilford	22	5	3	14	67	98
Headley	22	5	5	12	58	94
Elstead	22	2	4	16	58	75

Ties: Kingsley v Wrecclesham; Whitehill v Grayshott

1983

I'Anson Cup

	P	W	D	L	BP	Pts
Rowledge	22	16	4	2	109	196
Frensham	22	13	5	4	98	183
Tilford	22	12	3	7	87	153
Whitehill	22	9	5	8	77	133
Grayshott	22	9	6	7	73	130
Churt	22	8	9	5	72	127
Headley	22	7	7	8	79	127
Thursley	22	7	5	10	62	111
Wrecclesham	22	5	9	8	67	107
Lindford	22	5	6	11	70	107
The Bourne	22	5	5	12	70	103
Elstead	22	2	4	16	51	71

Miller Cup

	P	W	D	L	BP	Pts
Grayshott	22	15	5	2	90	184
Kingsley	22	12	6	4	88	170
Frensham	22	11	7	4	86	154
Wrecclesham	22	9	8	5	81	145
Churt	22	7	6	9	78	128
Thursley	22	9	5	8	66	122
Rowledge	22	6	7	9	75	121
Headley	22	6	7	9	77	120
The Bourne	22	7	5	9	68	116
Elstead	22	6	2	13	62	102
Tilford	22	5	7	10	55	96
Whitehill	22	3	5	14	56	88

Tie: The Bourne v Elstead

1984

I'Anson Cup

	P	W	D	L	Pts
Rowledge	22	17	4	1	108
Frensham	22	15	2	5	96
Headley	22	13	4	5	89
Grayshott	22	11	4	7	77
Elstead	22	11	3	8	70
Churt	22	10	3	9	63
Tilford	22	8	4	10	54
Whitehill	22	8	2	12	51
Wrecclesham	22	5	5	12	42
The Bourne	22	5	4	13	35
Lindford	22	3	6	13	26
Thursley	22	2	7	13	20

Miller Cup

	P	W	D	L	Pts
Churt	22	13	6	3	94
Kingsley	22	14	4	4	90
Frensham	22	12	6	4	82
Headley	22	12	6	4	79
Tilford	22	9	3	10	62
Elstead	22	9	4	9	58
Thursley	22	9	3	10	58
Rowledge	22	6	6	10	45
Whitehill	22	6	5	11	44
The Bourne	22	5	3	14	38
Wrecclesham	22	5	5	12	37
Grayshott	22	1	11	10	21

1985

I'Anson Cup

	P	W	D	L	Pts
Rowledge	22	16	5	1	108
Grayshott	22	14	4	4	90
Tilford	22	11	6	5	88
Frensham	22	12	6	4	85
The Bourne	22	9	5	8	64
Thursley	22	5	6	11	39
Wrecclesham	22	5	6	11	37
Lindford	22	4	9	9	36
Churt	22	3	12	7	35
Whitehill	22	4	8	10	33
Headley	22	4	6	12	32
Elstead	22	3	10	9	31

Miller Cup

	P	W	D	L	Pts
Churt	22	15	5	2	100
Kingsley	22	9	5	8	65
Headley	22	8	5	8	63
Frensham	22	8	8	6	60
Grayshott	22	8	6	7	57
Whitehill	22	8	6	8	57
The Bourne	22	7	9	6	53
Elstead	22	8	4	10	53
Thursley	22	8	7	7	53
Tilford	22	6	8	8	47
Wrecclesham	22	5	6	11	41
Rowledge	22	5	5	12	37

Tie: Headley v Grayshott

1986

I'Anson Cup

	P	W	D	L	Pts
Frensham	22	13	6	3	108
Churt	22	14	6	3	100
Tilford	22	14	5	3	93
The Bourne	22	11	8	3	90
Grayshott	22	7	10	5	58
Lindford	22	6	7	9	53
Thursley	22	6	8	8	48
Headley	22	5	7	10	41
Wrecclesham	22	5	6	11	39
Elstead	22	3	9	10	33
Kingsley	22	3	6	13	32
Whitehill	22	3	6	13	27

Miller Cup

	P	W	D	L	Pts
Tilford	22	15	5	2	109
Churt	22	9	7	6	87
Grayshott	22	11	10	1	86
Whitehill	22	10	6	6	80
The Bourne	22	11	9	2	77
Elstead	22	9	6	7	70
Frensham	22	5	10	7	50
Lindford	22	7	6	9	50
Wrecclesham	22	5	6	11	40
Kingsley	22	4	5	13	39
Thursley	22	3	8	11	32
Headley	22	1	6	15	14

1987

I'Anson Cup

	P	W	D	L	Pts
Frensham	22	16	5	1	113
Tilford	22	15	6	1	106
Grayshott	22	12	7	3	95
Churt	22	8	8	6	70
The Bourne	22	6	10	6	58
Headley	22	8	4	10	56
*Whitehill	22	8	3	11	53
Elstead	22	6	8	8	52
Lindford	22	5	6	11	46
Wrecclesham	22	6	6	10	46
+Thursley	22	3	7	12	35
Kingsley	22	1	6	15	19

**6pts deducted (ineligible player)*
+ 6pts awarded

Miller Cup

	P	W	D	L	Pts
Tilford	22	17	4	1	124
Churt	22	15	5	1	114
Frensham	22	12	5	5	95
The Bourne	22	14	4	4	92
Grayshott	22	10	5	7	79
Lindford	22	10	6	6	78
Elstead	22	9	4	9	62
Whitehill	22	5	5	12	41
Headley	22	5	1	16	35
Wrecclesham	22	3	5	14	31
Kingsley	22	3	3	16	23
Thursley	22	2	6	14	18

1988

I'Anson Cup

	P	W	D	L	Pts
Grayshott	22	15	5	1	110
Frensham	22	12	6	4	96
Tilford	22	12	7	3	93
Churt	22	10	6	6	72
The Bourne	22	10	6	6	66
Whitehill	22	8	4	9	61
Headley	22	8	4	10	56
Elstead	22	5	8	9	48
Thursley	22	6	5	11	47
Wrecclesham	22	5	6	11	40
Kingsley	22	5	1	15	34
Lindford	22	4	2	15	34

Ties: Grayshott v Lindford, Whitehill v Kingsley

Miller Cup

	P	W	D	L	Pts
Frensham	22	15	5	2	109
Whitehill	22	13	5	4	97
Churt	22	13	6	3	96
Tilford	22	14	2	6	88
Grayshott	22	10	7	5	79
The Bourne	22	10	5	7	75
Elstead	22	9	4	9	60
Lindford	22	8	2	12	50
Wrecclesham	22	7	2	13	46
Thursley	22	5	2	15	32
Kingsley	22	3	5	14	25
Headley	22	1	3	18	13

1989

I'Anson Cup

	P	W	D	L	Pts
Frensham	22	16	5	1	115
Grayshott	22	13	7	2	97
Tilford	22	11	6	5	82
The Bourne	22	9	9	4	71
Churt	22	9	5	8	61
Whitehill	22	8	7	7	61
Elstead	22	6	7	9	47
Thursley	22	4	8	10	42
Wrecclesham	22	5	6	11	38
Lindford	22	5	4	13	34
Headley	22	4	5	13	33
Kingsley	22	1	13	8	27

Miller Cup

	P	W	D	L	Pts
Frensham	22	16	4	2	124
Whitehill	22	14	2	6	100
The Bourne	22	13	4	5	88
Tilford	22	12	2	7	81
Churt	22	10	7	5	75
Elstead	22	10	2	10	68
Lindford	22	8	6	7	65
Grayshott	22	8	4	10	56
Wrecclesham	22	6	5	11	40
Thursley	22	5	3	14	35
Headley	22	5	2	15	34
Kingsley	22	2	3	17	15

Tie: Tilford v Lindford

1990

I'Anson Cup

	P	W	D	L	Pts
Frensham	22	16	5	1	115
Tilford	22	17	4	1	108
Whitehill	22	12	7	3	87
Churt	22	11	7	4	77
Grayshott	22	7	11	4	73
The Bourne	22	7	8	7	56
Elstead	22	6	8	8	52
Lindford	22	7	3	12	45
Headley	22	6	4	12	44
Thursley	22	4	5	13	33
Wrecclesham	22	5	2	15	32
Kingsley	22	0	4	18	10

Miller Cup

	P	W	D	L	Pts
Frensham	22	16	3	3	121
Tilford	22	18	2	2	116
Churt	22	15	3	4	97
Whitehill	22	12	4	6	84
Grayshott	22	11	3	8	69
The Bourne	22	9	8	5	68
Lindford	22	7	4	11	56
Kingsley	22	7	2	13	46
Wrecclesham	22	4	3	15	35
Elstead	22	4	4	14	34
Headley	22	3	4	15	26
Thursley	22	4	4	14	26

1991

Division 1 (I'Anson Cup)

	P	W	D	L	Pts
Churt	16	8	7	1	58
Tilford	16	8	4	4	57
Frensham	16	8	3	5	52
Grayshott	16	6	6	4	51
The Bourne	16	7	3	6	49
Elstead	16	7	4	5	47
Headley	16	5	2	9	38
Whitehill	16	3	6	7	30
Lindford	16	0	5	11	10

Division 2 (Herald Shield)

	P	W	D	L	Pts
Thursley	16	11	3	2	75
Wrecclesham	16	12	2	2	71
Ald W Indians	16	9	3	4	59
Farncombe W	16	8	3	5	54
Tongham	16	8	2	6	52
Kingsley	16	7	2	7	45
D'mersfield II	16	6	1	9	40
Rowledge III	16	3	0	13	19
Badshot Lea	16	0	0	16	1

Miller Cup

	P	W	D	L	Pts
The Bourne	22	13	5	4	92
Tilford	22	12	5	5	88
Grayshott	22	10	8	3	86
Churt	22	13	6	3	85
Frensham	22	12	6	4	85
Whitehill	22	8	6	8	61
Lindford	22	7	5	10	51
Thursley	22	7	1	14	50
Kingsley	22	6	2	14	48
Headley	22	5	5	11	42
Elstead	22	5	4	13	40
Wrecclesham	22	5	3	14	36

Tie: Grayshott v Headley

1992

Division 1

	P	W	D	L	Pts
Tilford	18	9	8	1	68
Frensham	18	11	5	2	67
Headley	18	9	5	4	64
Grayshott	18	6	8	3	58
The Bourne	18	6	6	6	49
Churt	18	6	6	6	46
Thursley	18	5	7	6	45
Elstead	18	4	4	10	39
Whitehill	18	4	4	9	35
Wrecclesham	18	1	3	14	14

Tie: Whitehill v Grayshott

Hamish Macdonald, the captain, raised the I'Anson Cup in 1992 when Tilford won the trophy for the 11th time. They clinched the top spot in Division One in a desperately close finish at Headley, whose skipper, Dick Holden, can be seen over Macdonald's right shoulder.

Division 2

	P	W	D	L	Pts
Lindford	18	17	1	0	102
Ald W Indians	18	14	2	2	86
Farncombe W	18	11	1	6	66
Tilford II	18	11	0	7	61
Tongham	18	5	5	8	47
D'mersfield II	18	5	5	8	40
Badshot Lea	18	5	2	11	34
Rowledge III	18	4	1	13	26
The Bourne II	18	2	8	8	26
Kingsley	18	3	3	12	24

Division 3 (Miller Cup)

	P	W	D	L	Pts
Headley II	18	13	4	1	85
Churt II	18	11	3	4	73
*Frensham II	18	11	5	2	65
Lindford II	18	9	6	3	64
Grayshott II	18	9	4	5	63
Thursley II	18	8	5	5	62
Wrec'sham II	18	4	3	11	28
Whitehill II	18	3	3	12	23
Elstead II	18	3	1	14	19
Kingsley II	18	1	2	15	12

** 10pts deducted (ineligible player)*

Lindford, winners of Division Two in 1992. Skipper Mark Hoban received the Herald Shield from Norman Disney.

1993

Division 1

	P	W	D	L	Pts
Frensham	20	12	8	0	87
The Bourne	20	11	8	1	77
Headley	20	9	9	2	73
Grayshott	20	7	10	3	5
Tilford	20	6	7	7	54
Thursley	20	6	9	5	53
Elstead	20	7	4	9	51
Ald W Indians	20	3	9	8	40
Farncombe W	20	5	2	13	35
Lindford	20	2	9	9	29
Wrecclesham	20	3	3	14	26

Division 2

	P	W	D	L	Pts
Dogmersfield	22	16	3	3	101
Frimchett	22	13	6	3	88
Witley	22	13	5	4	87
Kingsley	22	10	5	7	69
Frensham II	22	10	4	8	66
Badshot Lea	22	8	6	8	62
Tilford II	22	9	3	10	58
The Bourne II	22	9	2	11	58
Headley II	22	7	4	11	53
Rowledge III	22	5	5	12	41
Tongham	22	2	7	13	28
Lindford II	22	2	6	14	26

Division 3

	P	W	D	L	Pts
Grayshott II	20	15	5	0	100
Crown Tavs II	20	12	5	3	85
Dogm'field II	20	10	6	4	70
Kingsley II	20	9	4	7	62
Witley II	20	8	4	8	57
Thursley II	20	5	7	8	44
Ald W Ind II	20	6	1	13	40
Frensham III	20	6	3	11	37
Wrec'sham II	20	4	2	14	30
Elstead II	20	1	4	15	17

1994

Division 1

	P	W	D	L	BP	Pts
The Bourne	22	7	15	0	14	93
Frensham	22	8	13	1	6	89
Grayshott	22	6	14	2	15	89
Dogmersfield	22	6	12	4	10	76
Headley	22	4	15	3	13	69
Ald W Indians	22	5	10	7	9	69
Tilford	22	4	15	3	3	64
*Lindford	22	6	13	3	2	57
Frimchett	22	5	11	6	4	57
Elstead	22	4	12	6	0	52
Farncombe W	22	1	9	12	3	45
Thursley	22	0	13	9	0	25

**10pts deducted (ineligible player)*

Division 2

	P	W	D	L	BP	Pts
Witley	22	11	10	1	12	108
Badshot Lea	22	12	7	3	9	100
Headley II	22	9	8	5	13	89
Frensham II	22	6	9	7	12	79
Kingsley	22	8	8	6	6	78
Tongham	22	6	10	6	7	67
Grayshott II	22	6	11	5	1	62
Wrecclesham	22	5	10	7	4	62
The Bourne II	22	6	8	8	4	57
Crown Tavs II	22	5	10	7	4	56
Tilford II	22	3	10	9	3	45
Rowledge III	22	1	8	13	3	33

Division 3

	P	W	D	L	BP	Pts
Witley II	22	12	10	0	8	108
Lindford II	22	9	11	2	17	100
Dogm'field II	22	10	9	3	14	97
Frimchett II	22	9	8	5	9	85
G&G RFC	22	7	11	4	10	83
DERA	22	7	13	2	9	82
Kingsley II	22	8	5	9	14	75
Ald W Ind II	22	6	7	9	7	62
Frensham III	22	4	13	5	10	61
Thursley II	22	4	11	7	3	52
Tongham II	22	4	9	9	2	49
Wrec'sham II	22	4	8	10	3	47
Elstead II	22	4	7	11	0	43
Bourne III	22	1	8	13	0	24

1995

Division 1

	P	W	D	L	BP	Pts
Frensham	22	15	6	1	6	112
Tilford	22	13	5	4	7	98
Dogmersfield	22	10	9	3	7	86
Grayshott	22	11	4	7	5	81
Frimchett	22	6	10	6	12	78
Badshot Lea	22	8	9	5	11	76
Witley	22	6	11	5	7	66
Headley	22	4	10	8	11	63
The Bourne	22	4	9	9	6	51
Lindford	22	3	11	8	4	44
Elstead	22	3	9	10	2	39
Ald W Indians	22	1	3	18	3	13

Division 2

	P	W	D	L	BP	Pts
Frensham II	22	14	7	1	18	119
Kingsley	22	11	10	1	8	100
Thursley	22	11	7	4	15	100
Witley II	22	10	8	4	14	96
Wrecclesham	22	9	5	8	13	82
Headley II	22	6	8	8	10	65
Lindford II	22	8	4	10	0	56
Tongham	22	5	8	9	4	55
The Bourne II	22	6	6	10	2	51
Farncombe W	22	5	6	11	3	51
Grayshott II	22	5	5	12	0	41
Crown Tavs II	22	2	6	14	2	24

Division 3

	P	W	D	L	BP	Pts
Milford	22	11	8	1	13	103
Tilford II	22	9	7	4	7	74
DERA	22	9	6	5	6	73
Frimchett II	22	9	5	6	8	73
G&G RFC	22	5	8	7	12	64
Dogm'field II	22	5	9	6	5	56
Frensham III	22	6	5	9	4	47
Kingsley II	22	4	5	11	0	32
Rowledge III	22	3	4	13	2	30

Division 4 (Bob Burchett Shield)

	P	W	D	L	BP	Pts
Chiddingfold	22	16	5	0	29	140
Thursley II	22	12	5	4	21	106
Badshot Lea II	22	9	5	7	8	75
Milford II	22	9	3	9	5	66
Tongham II	22	7	4	10	14	62
Elstead II	22	5	4	12	8	46
Wrec'sham II	22	6	3	12	0	45
Bourne III	22	4	3	14	0	31

1996

Division 1

	P	W	D	L	BP	Pts
Frensham	22	11	9	2	12	103
Grayshott	22	10	8	4	10	90
Badshot Lea	22	10	7	5	10	89
Lindford	22	9	7	6	11	82
Tilford	22	8	5	9	12	81
The Bourne	22	5	13	4	9	69
Headley	22	5	13	4	9	65
Witley	22	4	13	5	8	65
Dogmersfield	22	6	8	8	4	58
Frimchett	22	6	7	9	3	54
Kingsley	22	2	8	12	0	26
Thursley	22	2	7	13	4	25

Division 2

	P	W	D	L	BP	Pts
Elstead	22	12	7	3	9	112
Milford	22	12	6	4	10	96
Tongham	22	11	5	6	11	88
*Frensham II	22	7	11	4	20	85
Tilford II	22	9	6	8	4	71
Witley II	22	8	5	9	4	67
Wrecclesham	22	7	4	11	11	63
Farncombe W	22	5	10	7	4	54
The Bourne II	22	5	11	6	3	52
DERA	22	5	11	6	4	49
Lindford II	22	5	5	12	5	46
Headley II	22	4	4	14	1	33

**10pts deducted (ineligible player)*
Ties: The Bourne II v Tilford; Farncombe W v Witley II

Division 3

	P	W	D	L	BP	Pts
Chiddingfold	22	11	11	0	15	110
Wood Street	22	10	11	1	16	109
Hindhead	22	8	11	3	8	79
Dogm'field II	22	9	8	5	10	78
Frensham III	22	6	9	7	11	68
Grayshott II	22	6	9	7	6	67
G&G RFC	22	5	9	8	7	58
Thursley II	22	5	9	8	8	55
Kingsley II	22	6	6	10	4	50
Badshot Lea II	22	4	8	10	4	46
Frimchett II	22	4	10	8	1	43
*Crown Tvs II	22	4	7	11	8	40

**10pts deducted (ineligible player)*

Division 4

	P	W	D	L	BP	Pts
Milford II	18	13	3	2	18	106
Chidd'fold II	18	13	2	3	15	99
Wrec'sham II	18	11	4	3	13	89
Peper Harow	18	7	4	7	12	64
Tongham II	18	7	3	8	8	59
Elstead II	18	8	2	8	4	56
Rowledge III	18	7	0	11	6	48
Wood Street II	18	7	1	10	2	47
Bourne III	18	4	3	11	4	37
DERA II	22	1	2	15	2	12

Ties: Wrecclesham II v Peper Harow; Tongham II v Chiddingfold II

1997

Division 1

	P	W	D	L	BP	Pts
Frensham	22	8	13	1	14	97
Grayshott	22	11	8	3	11	95
Witley	22	8	9	5	16	89
Lindford	22	9	10	3	12	88
Tilford	22	9	9	4	6	77
The Bourne	22	5	8	9	10	60
Milford	22	6	8	8	5	59
Headley	22	5	10	7	7	59
Frimchett	22	3	11	8	7	52
Badshot Lea	22	4	11	7	8	51
Dogmersfield	22	3	11	8	2	47
Elstead	22	4	6	12	4	36

Division 2

	P	W	D	L	BP	Pts
Tongham	22	13	6	3	13	109
Chiddingfold	22	12	7	3	12	105
Wood Street	22	10	7	5	15	94
Kingsley	22	10	8	3	8	91
Frensham II	22	8	7	7	14	79
Tilford II	22	10	4	8	2	72
DERA	22	6	6	10	7	59
Thursley	22	4	13	5	8	53
The Bourne II	22	4	8	9	4	47
Farncombe W	22	3	9	10	4	43
Witley II	22	4	7	11	3	42
Wrecclesham	22	4	4	14	5	39

Tie: Kingsley v The Bourne II

Division 3

	P	W	D	L	BP	Pts
Hindhead	22	15	5	2	13	112
Thursley II	22	13	3	6	6	91
Dogm'field II	22	9	8	4	6	81
Lindford II	22	9	3	10	16	77
Badshot Lea II	22	8	7	7	7	74
Headley II	22	6	10	6	8	72
Grayshott II	22	7	7	8	4	65
Kingsley II	22	7	9	6	3	64
Chidd'fold II	22	6	8	8	4	60
G&G RFC	22	5	6	11	10	59
Frensham III	22	5	10	7	4	52
Milford II	22	0	7	14	2	22

Tie: Dogmersfield II v Milford II

Division 4

	P	W	D	L	BP	Pts
Fernhurst	20	14	5	1	14	113
Crown Tavs II	20	10	5	5	10	85
Frimchett II	20	10	4	6	7	79
Grayswood	20	9	4	7	14	78
Peper Harow	20	8	5	7	14	77
Rowledge III	20	7	4	9	11	63
Tongham II	20	8	7	5	4	61
Wrecc'sham II	20	6	4	10	7	53
Bourne III	20	8	0	12	4	52
Wood Street II	20	5	4	11	2	40
Elstead II	20	1	6	13	1	19

1998

Division 1

	P	W	D	L	BP	Pts
Tilford	22	11	10	1	9	123
Frensham	22	7	12	3	13	105
Chiddingfold	22	8	11	3	12	104
Witley	22	9	9	4	4	98
The Bourne	22	8	11	3	3	95
Grayshott	22	5	9	7	6	77
Tongham	22	4	14	4	7	73
Milford	22	6	9	7	3	72
Lindford	22	4	12	5	3	68
Headley	22	4	11	7	3	65
Frimchett	22	3	8	11	7	49
Badshot Lea	22	1	6	15	0	20

Tie: Grayshott v Lindford

Division 2

	P	W	D	L	BP	Pts
Frensham II	22	12	6	4	7	121
Dogmersfield	22	10	9	3	11	117
Wood Street	22	10	8	4	8	112
Farncombe W	22	10	5	7	6	96
Tilford II	22	8	7	7	11	95
Kingsley	22	8	9	5	3	91
Thursley	22	6	13	3	6	86
Elstead	22	3	13	6	7	72
Hindhead	22	4	13	5	4	66
Lindford II	22	4	9	9	1	53
The Bourne II	22	1	9	12	0	26
DERA	22	1	9	12	0	26

Division 3

	P	W	D	L	BP	Pts
Cranleigh SA	22	16	6	0	17	159
Fernhurst	22	12	9	1	6	124
Wrecclesham	22	9	8	5	6	98
Dogm'field II	22	7	10	5	11	95
Witley II	22	7	12	3	5	91
Crown Tavs II	22	7	11	4	5	91
Grayshott II	22	5	10	7	9	77
Kingsley II	22	5	9	8	4	62
Chidd'fold II	22	2	13	7	4	52
Headley II	22	3	8	11	2	46
Badshot Lea II	22	2	9	11	1	37
Thursley II	22	0	9	13	3	27

Division 4

	P	W	D	L	BP	Pts
Frensham III	22	12	8	2	21	145
Grayswood	22	12	9	1	14	136
Peper Harow	22	8	9	5	15	107
Pirbright	22	10	9	3	3	105
Rowledge III	22	6	10	6	17	99
Milford II	22	6	11	5	14	94
Elstead II	22	7	9	6	5	81
Frimchett II	22	4	13	5	8	70
Wood Street II	22	5	10	7	4	64
Tongham II	22	5	8	9	5	63
Wrecc'sham II	22	5	7	10	4	62
Bourne III	22	4	8	10	3	55
Hindhead II	22	4	5	12	6	53
*Cran SA II	22	3	8	10	6	47

** 8pts deducted (ineligible player)*
Tie: Hindhead II v Cranleigh SA II

1999

Division 1

	P	W	D	L	BP	Pts
Chiddingfold	22	15	6	1	19	157
Frensham	22	13	5	3	19	144
Witley	22	9	7	6	16	112
Tongham	22	8	6	7	18	103
Tilford	22	9	6	7	9	97
The Bourne	22	6	9	7	7	82
Lindford	22	6	9	7	6	82
Headley	22	5	12	5	6	76
Grayshott	22	6	7	9	4	70
Dogmersfield	22	5	8	9	2	64
Milford	22	4	5	13	5	51
Frimchett	22	1	8	13	1	27

Tie: Frensham v Tongham

Division 2

	P	W	D	L	BP	Pts
Fernhurst	22	11	9	1	8	131
Cranleigh SA	22	10	11	1	12	122
Kingsley	22	9	10	3	10	111
Frensham II	22	7	9	6	12	96
Elstead	22	7	5	9	9	88
Wood Street	22	7	7	8	6	82
Thursley	22	7	9	6	2	80
Badshot Lea	22	5	12	5	5	77
Farncombe W	22	6	7	9	11	76
Hindhead	22	6	6	10	6	66
Tilford II	22	3	11	8	5	58
Lindford II	22	2	6	14	0	30

Tie: Elstead v Fernhurst

Division 3

	P	W	D	L	BP	Pts
Puttenham	22	14	7	1	17	157
Crown Tavs II	22	11	8	3	11	123
The Bourne II	22	6	12	4	15	101
Wrecclesham	22	9	5	7	5	98
Dogm'field II	22	8	7	7	4	82
Frensham III	22	7	5	10	12	82
Chidd'fold II	22	6	10	6	10	82
Grayswood	22	5	8	8	8	79
Grayshott II	22	8	3	11	8	78
Witley II	22	6	9	7	6	76
DERA	22	6	8	8	3	73
Kingsley II	22	1	6	15	0	20

Tie: Wrecclesham v Grayswood

Division 4

	P	W	D	L	BP	Pts
Peper Harow	21	12	5	4	16	130
Pirbright	21	12	8	1	15	129
Badshot Lea II	21	11	5	5	10	112
Rowledge III	21	9	8	4	14	104
Headley II	21	7	9	5	6	92
Elstead II	21	6	3	12	2	56
Thursley II	21	5	1	15	8	50
Milford II	21	1	3	17	1	17

Division 5 (Norman Disney Shield)

	P	W	D	L	BP	Pts
Bourne III	18	13	3	2	9	123
Puttenham II	18	12	3	3	15	119
Wrecc'sham II	18	12	3	3	10	116
Hindhead II	18	6	7	5	11	83
Cran SA II	18	6	3	9	8	66
Rowledge IV	18	6	4	8	4	64
Wood Street II	18	5	5	8	4	56
Tongham II	18	4	5	9	7	53
Frimchett II	18	3	6	9	6	46
P Harow II	18	1	5	12	2	20

Puttenham captain Tony Champneys receives the Miller Cup from Cyril Crawte in 1999 after a runaway victory in Division Three. The remainder of the team were already en route to their last game of the season.

2000

Division 1

	P	W	D	L	BP	Pts
Frensham	22	12	8	2	15	137
Grayshott	22	10	9	3	14	124
Tilford	22	10	6	6	5	98
Headley	22	8	7	7	5	91
Fernhurst	22	8	8	6	2	86
Chiddingfold	22	6	10	6	11	85
The Bourne	22	5	12	5	6	78
Lindford	22	7	6	9	5	75
Witley	22	6	8	8	2	70
Dogmersfield	22	7	3	12	5	69
Tongham	22	4	6	12	9	59
Cranleigh SA	22	3	9	10	7	57

Division 2

	P	W	D	L	BP	Pts
Puttenham	22	13	5	3	19	144
Elstead	22	8	11	1	14	124
Hindhead	22	11	9	2	9	123
Milford	22	11	8	3	14	122
Wood Street	22	8	9	4	6	101
Badshot Lea	22	8	7	7	12	94
Kingsley	22	8	6	8	7	85
Frensham II	22	6	7	9	9	73
Crown Tavs II	22	4	6	12	3	49
Frimchett	22	4	4	14	7	49
Thursley	22	4	6	12	4	48
Farncombe W	22	3	6	13	3	41

Ties: Elstead v Wood Street; Elstead v Puttenham

Division 3

	P	W	D	L	BP	Pts
Grayswood	22	12	8	1	17	148
Tilford II	22	12	8	2	16	136
Grayshott II	22	9	9	4	5	99
Wrecclesham	22	8	9	5	8	98
Dogm'field II	22	7	9	6	5	85
The Bourne II	22	6	8	8	10	82
Peper Harow	22	6	9	6	7	80
Pirbright	22	5	9	8	5	71
Lindford II	22	6	3	12	6	65
Witley II	22	4	8	9	8	65
Frensham III	22	4	10	8	5	59
Chidd'fold II	22	2	8	12	6	42

Ties: Peper Harow v Witley II; Lindford II v Grayswood

Division 4

	P	W	D	L	BP	Pts
DERA	18	15	1	2	11	135
Bourne III	18	6	8	4	14	84
Headley II	18	8	5	5	7	83
Rowledge III	18	7	5	6	12	82
Badshot Lea II	18	7	4	7	6	78
Wrecc'sham II	18	7	4	7	5	71
Puttenham II	18	5	5	8	9	65
Kingsley II	18	5	8	5	3	64
Elstead II	18	5	5	7	4	59
Thursley II	18	0	3	14	1	14

Tie: Thursley II v Elstead II

Division 5

	P	W	D	L	BP	Pts
Fernhurst II	18	13	3	2	7	119
Milford II	18	9	6	3	6	94
Cran SA II	18	9	4	5	4	86
Hindhead II	18	8	5	5	5	85
Wood Street II	18	8	3	7	2	72
Rowledge IV	18	5	6	7	13	71
Frimchett II	18	6	5	7	8	70
Frensham IV	18	4	7	7	10	64
Tongham II	18	2	5	11	2	28
P Harow II	18	1	6	11	0	20

2001

Division 1

	P	W	D	L	BP	Pts
Frensham	22	8	12	2	18	122
Puttenham	22	9	11	2	13	117
Tilford	22	10	10	2	5	111
The Bourne	22	9	9	4	16	110
Grayshott	22	9	9	4	13	109
Fernhurst	22	5	11	6	4	72
Headley	22	4	13	5	7	71
Witley	22	5	11	6	4	70
Dogmersfield	22	3	9	10	3	48
Lindford	22	2	12	8	3	47
Elstead	22	2	10	10	3	42
Chiddingfold	22	2	11	9	0	40

Division 2

	P	W	D	L	BP	Pts
Thursley	22	11	10	1	5	119
Kingsley	22	10	9	3	15	119
Wood Street	22	8	11	3	9	101
Badshot Lea	22	7	9	6	6	86
Grayswood	22	7	8	7	7	83
Tongham	22	5	10	7	12	80
Cranleigh SA	22	5	13	4	6	77
Frensham II	22	5	11	6	4	72
Hindhead	22	4	11	7	8	70
Tilford II	22	4	11	7	7	63
Milford	22	5	6	11	4	56
Frimchett	22	3	7	12	2	40

Division 3

	P	W	D	L	BP	Pts
Wrecclesham	22	10	10	2	10	118
Grayshott II	22	7	12	3	9	101
Headley II	22	8	10	4	8	96
Pirbright	22	8	10	4	4	91
Cody (DERA)	22	7	10	5	1	81
Farncombe W	22	5	12	5	5	78
The Bourne II	22	6	9	7	5	75
Peper Harow	22	5	9	8	5	71
Witley II	22	4	12	6	5	69
Dogm'field II	22	3	12	7	2	58
Frensham III	22	3	12	7	5	55
Lindford II	22	3	8	11	4	44

Division 4

	P	W	D	L	BP	Pts
Fernhurst II	18	10	8	0	10	112
Badshot Lea II	18	12	4	2	4	110
*Wrec'sham II	18	10	5	3	8	94
Elstead II	18	6	7	5	2	64
Kingsley II	18	6	5	7	4	62
Cran SA II	18	5	5	8	9	61
Chidd'fold II	18	3	7	8	6	52
Puttenham II	18	3	8	7	5	51
Bourne III	18	4	3	11	4	44
*Milford II	18	4	2	12	2	30

**8pts deducted (ineligible player)*

Division 5

	P	W	D	L	BP	Pts
Frensham IV	16	8	5	3	18	96
Wood Street II	16	8	5	3	11	87
Thursley II	16	8	3	5	4	74
Frimchett II	16	7	3	6	10	72
P Harow II	16	6	3	7	7	63
Tongham II	16	6	4	6	6	62
Hindhead II	16	5	3	8	7	55
Grayshott III	16	4	5	7	4	46
Rowledge IV	16	2	5	9	1	29

Subscribers

John Allen
Michael Allen
Clive Andrews
Will Archer-Burton
Geoff Baker
Michael H. Barnes
Michael F. Barnes
Rod Berkeley
Ken Bone
Colin Blunden
Tony Cheeseman
Stan Clarke
Connie Collyer
John Commerford
Dave Cooper
Cyril Crawte
Stuart Croucher
Tony Dakeyne
Les Davis
Steve Davis
Brian Dean
Robin Dibdin
Norman Disney
Gary Dobson
Colin Dodge
Bob and Sue Doran
Michael Eddleston
Brian Francis
Robin Frommholz
Andrew Fry
John Gray
Peter Golding

Jeremy ('Jingles') Hall
Pat Hastings
David Havenhand
Gordon Haytree
Graham Heath
Stuart Henderson
Mark Hoban
Gray Howard
George Iliffe
Bryan Karn
John Knight
Martin and Terry Knott
Bob Laker
Dave Lambert
Charles LeClercq
Trevor Lee
Sir Donald Limon KCB
Frank Lunt
Audrey Mattock
Gavin May
David Maycock
Anthony Mayson
David Mayson
Keith Mayson
Ron Miles
John Moore
Dick Morant
Bev Moulds
Pat Murphy
Ron Neil
Doug Newell
Carl Obert

Eirwen Parry
Mike Pike
Mike Poulter
Martin Pryce
Mervyn Redman
Paul Roberts
Charles Rose
Graham Sampson
Don Saunders
Gareth Saunders
Owain Saunders
Peter Slinger
Rod Smithers
Antony Staden
Alan Staves
Mike Stoker
Doug Tanner
Clive Tester
John Thayer
Kevin and Claire Tidey
Neil Topliss
Geoff Tribe
Brian Turner
Mark Turpin
Rosemary Walker
Karston Waller
Ian Webster
Kenneth R. C. White
Ken Williams
George Wilson
Barry Woodger
Wood Street Cricket Club